Annual Editions: Education, 44/e

Sheron Fraser-Burgess

McGraw-Hill create®

Copyright 2020 by McGraw-Hill Education. All rights reserved.

Printed in the United States of America. Except as permitted under the United States Copyright Act of 1976, no part of this publication may be reproduced or distributed in any form or by any means, or stored in a database or retrieval system, without prior written permission of the publisher.

This McGraw-Hill Create text may include materials submitted to McGraw-Hill for publication by the instructor of this course. The instructor is solely responsible for the editorial content of such materials. Instructors retain copyright of these additional materials.

ISBN-13: 9781259922831

ISBN-10: 1259922839

Contents

Detailed Table Of Contents vii

Preface xi

UNIT 1	SCHOOL REFORM IN THE TWENTY-FIRST CENTURY 1
	INTRODUCTION 1
ARTICLE	IS TEST-BASED ACCOUNTABILITY DEAD? BY MORGAN S. POLIKOFF ET AL. 3
ARTICLE	HOLDING TEACHERS ACCOUNTABLE WITHOUT ADEQUATE TEACHER PREP PROGRAMS IS A SET-UP BY ZACHARY WRIGHT 10
ARTICLE	CHARTER SCHOOL REFORM: DOUBLETHINK AND THE ASSAULT ON THE VULNERABLE BY MORGAN ANDERSON 12
ARTICLE	PEDAGOGY AGAINST THE DEAD ZONES OF THE IMAGINATION BY HENRY A. GIROUX 21
ARTICLE	THE MYTH OF ACCOUNTABILITY: HOW DATA (MIS)USE IS REINFORCING THE PROBLEMS OF PUBLIC EDUCATION BY CLAIRE FONTAINE 24
ARTICLE	A NATION AT RISK: THE IMPERATIVE FOR EDUCATIONAL REFORM BY THE NATIONAL COMMISSION ON EXCELLENCE IN EDUCATION 31
UNIT 2	EDUCATIONAL EQUITY 38
	INTRODUCTION 38
ARTICLE	THE RADICAL MIDDLE: THE LIMITS AND ADVANTAGES OF TEACHING GRIT IN SCHOOLS BY VICKA BELL-ROBINSON 39
ARTICLE	...AND A CHILD SHALL LEAD THEM... BY EURYDICE STANLEY 44
ARTICLE	STRONG TEAMS, STRONG RESULTS: FORMATIVE ASSESSMENT HELPS TEACHER TEAMS STRENGTHEN EQUITY BY NANCY LOVE AND MICHELLE CROWELL 50

ARTICLE	OVERCOMING THE CHALLENGES OF POVERTY BY JULIE LANDSMAN 55	
ARTICLE	CREATING A CLIMATE FOR ACHIEVEMENT BY DEBORAH D. BRENNAN 60	
ARTICLE	BROWN V. BOARD OF EDUCATION OF TOPEKA, KANSAS BY U.S. SUPREME COURT 64	

UNIT 3 — LITERACY IS THE CORNERSTONE OF PARTICIPATORY DEMOCRACY 67

INTRODUCTION 67

ARTICLE	THE CHALLENGES OF GAMING FOR DEMOCRATIC EDUCATION: THE CASE OF ICIVICS BY JEREMY STODDARD ET AL. 68
ARTICLE	THE COMMON CORE AND DEMOCRATIC EDUCATION BY BENJAMIN J. BINDEWALD ET AL. 80
ARTICLE	DIGITAL LITERACY: THE QUEST OF AN INCLUSIVE DEFINITION BY JAMES K. NJENGA 92

UNIT 4 — TEACHING ENGLISH LANGUAGE LEARNERS 101

INTRODUCTION 101

ARTICLE	BECOMING SOCIOCULTURAL MEDIATORS: WHAT ALL EDUCATORS CAN LEARN FROM BILINGUAL AND ESL TEACHERS BY SONIA NIETO 103
ARTICLE	ESL AND CLASSROOM TEACHERS TEAM UP TO TEACH COMMON CORE BY LESLI A. MAXWELL 110
ARTICLE	A BETTER CHANCE TO LEARN: BILINGUAL BICULTURAL EDUCATION BY UNITED STATES COMMISSION ON CIVIL RIGHTS 113

UNIT 5 — TWENTY-FIRST CENTURY LEARNING TECHNOLOGY AND INTEGRATION 117

INTRODUCTION 117

ARTICLE	STANDARDS-BASED TECHNOLOGY INTEGRATION FOR EMERGENT BILINGUALS BY BRIANA RONAN 119

ARTICLE	UTILIZING TECHNOLOGY IN PHYSICAL EDUCATION: ADDRESSING THE OBSTACLES OF INTEGRATION BY BETH PYLE AND KERI ESSLINGER 125
ARTICLE	IMPLICATIONS OF SHIFTING TECHNOLOGY IN EDUCATION BY JANET HOLLAND AND JOHN HOLLAND 129
ARTICLE	ASSISTIVE TECH FOR EVERYONE? BY MICHELLE R. DAVIS 138
UNIT 6	**SPECIAL & EXCEPTIONAL EDUCATION 141**
	INTRODUCTION 141
ARTICLE	INCLUSIVE EDUCATION: LESSONS FROM HISTORY BY BARBARA BOROSON 142
ARTICLE	TEXT-TO-SPEECH: NOT JUST FOR SPECIAL EDUCATION STUDENTS! BY KRISTINE NAPPER 147
ARTICLE	MOBILE APPS THE EDUCATIONAL SOLUTION FOR AUTISTIC STUDENTS IN SECONDARY EDUCATION BY AGATHI STATHOPOULOU ET AL. 149
ARTICLE	5 STRATEGIES FOR INCLUSIVITY IN SPECIAL EDUCATION BY KAREN ACHTMAN 157
ARTICLE	EDUCATION OF ALL HANDICAPPED CHILDREN ACT BY U.S. CONGRESS 159
UNIT 7	**ETHICS & COMMUNITY ENGAGEMENT 163**
	INTRODUCTION 163
ARTICLE	THE NEXT "EVOLUTION" OF CIVIC LEARNING BY TANIA D. MITCHELL 164
ARTICLE	DEMOCRACY IN EDUCATION BY JOHN DEWEY 166
UNIT 8	**IDENTITY & INTERSECTIONALITY IN EDUCATION 171**
	INTRODUCTION 171
ARTICLE	BUILDING LGBTQ AWARENESS AND ALLIES IN OUR TEACHER EDUCATION COMMUNITY AND BEYOND BY LAURA-LEE KEARNS ET AL. 172
ARTICLE	HERE'S WHAT I WISH WHITE TEACHERS KNEW WHEN TEACHING MY BLACK CHILDREN BY AFRIKA AFENI MILLS 176

UNIT 9	**STEM 178**	
	INTRODUCTION 178	
ARTICLE	ELEMENTS OF MAKING: A FRAMEWORK TO SUPPORT MAKING IN THE SCIENCE CLASSROOM BY SHELLY RODRIGUEZ ET AL. 179	
ARTICLE	DON'T ASK ME WHY BY ANNA ÖQVIST AND PER HÖGSTRÖM 185	
ARTICLE	THE U.S. IS FALLING WAY BEHIND IN STEM BUT KENTUCKY'S POWERING THE COMEBACK BY GARRIS LANDON STROUD 194	

Detailed Table of Contents

UNIT 1: School Reform in the Twenty-First Century

Is Test-Based Accountability Dead? Morgan S. Polikoff, Jay P. Greene, and Kevin Huffman, *Education Next*, 2017
Experts weigh in the prospects for standards-based education under a regime of high-stakes testing.

Holding Teachers Accountable Without Adequate Teacher Prep Programs Is a Set-Up, Zachary Wright, *Education Post*, 2019
A proponent of value-added student growth metrics, Zachary Wright argues that holding teachers accountable on this basis is a reasonable expectation. He argues that teacher preparation should be modified to include one-on-one video-based coaching that equips teacher candidates with the requisite skills.

Charter School Reform: Doublethink and the Assault on the Vulnerable, Morgan Anderson, *Journal of Thought*, 2016
Anderson discusses the relationship between the erosion of public schools and the genealogy of charter schools. Their proliferation poses the greatest threat to the children of families who are already on the societal margins.

Pedagogy against the Dead Zones of the Imagination, Henry A. Giroux, *Transformations*, 2016
Giroux proposes that the ultimate aim of neo-liberal school reform is to eradicate public schools as a democratic institution. In so doing, a primary source of developing basic civic virtues in our children will have been silenced.

The Myth of Accountability: How Data (Mis)Use Is Reinforcing the Problems of Public Education, Claire Fontaine, *Data & Society*, 2016
The history of standardized testing and data collection in American education has placed disproportionate emphasis on quantification and statistical analysis to measure learning. Accountability fails to address the sources of the achievement gap that has a basis in the different kinds of education available according to socioeconomic status.

A Nation at Risk: The Imperative for Educational Reform, The National Commission on Excellence in Education, 1983
This report provided an argument for the view that American education was in crisis. Ponting to diminishing American global influence and superiority, the authors of the report advocated radical reform in education in order to hold schools accountable for student performance on the academic areas that provided basic skills.

UNIT 2: Educational Equity

The Radical Middle: The Limits and Advantages of Teaching Grit in Schools, Vicka Bell-Robinson, *The Journal of School & Society*, 2016
Bell-Robinson highlights the benefits of the growth mindset for students facing academic challenges but offers cautions about the unconditional embrace of grit as its motivation. Where there is systemic inequality, school reforms ought to support the individual student in breaking down these barriers.

…And a Child Shall Lead Them…, Eurydice Stanley, *Journal of Language and Literacy*, 2018
Stanley urges her audience to revisit the contentious school desegregation issue after the Brown vs. Board of Education of Topeka (1954) ruling. Together, with Elizabeth Stanley, who was one of the Little Rock Nine, she underscores that qualities of respect and tenacity that were essential then are also necessary in the present day.

Strong Teams, Strong Results: Formative Assessment Helps Teacher Teams Strengthen Equity, Nancy Love and Michelle Crowell, *The Learning Professional*, 2018
Actions involved in formative assessment can be pivotal in advancing educational equity. The data provided is a sound basis for ongoing monitoring of whether instructional strategies are effective in building on students' prior knowledge.

Overcoming the Challenges of Poverty, Julie Landsman, *Educational Leadership*, 2014
Landsman states that we may have forgotten our duty to provide basic needs and an education for all children in the United States. She reminds us of the conditions with which many children live on a daily basis and provides a list of ways we can cultivate a more nurturing classroom environment for all students.

Creating a Climate for Achievement, Deborah D. Brennan, *Educational Leadership*, 2015
In an effort to turn around a failing school population, the teachers in one school decided to create a climate for achievement. They began by strengthening their academics with goal setting and sharing, tracking learning, and intervening early. They also strengthen social-emotional learning by building relationships, grading for hope, and using proactive discipline.

Brown v. Board of Education of Topeka, Kansas, U.S. Supreme Court, 1954
This landmark decision ended school desegregation across the nation. The plaintiff argued that education was a property right that was being denied to black students who were forced to attend subpar schools farther away than the white schools that were closer. The plaintiffs argued that school segregation failed to extend to minority children equal protection under the law that the Fourteenth Amendment guaranteed. The ruling, which was unanimous, made school segregation unconstitutional.

UNIT 3: Literacy Is the Cornerstone of Participatory Democracy

The Challenges of Gaming for Democratic Education: The Case of iCivics, Jeremy Stoddard et al., *Democracy and Education*, 2016
The authors evaluate a game platform delivery format for civics education.

The Common Core and Democratic Education: Examining Potential Costs and Benefits to Public and Private Autonomy, Benjamin J. Bindewald, Rory P. Tannebaum, Patrick Womac, *Democracy and Education*, 2016
The Common Core is national curriculum that claims to represent all of the approved knowledge that is required for literacy. The authors argue that imposing these standards hampers the autonomy of local schools.

Digital Literacy: The Quest of an Inclusive Definition, James K. Njenga, *Reading & Writing*, 2018
This article evaluates the universal and transcultural meaning of digital learning. The paper proposes an alternate conception that accommodates the economic realities of developing countries.

UNIT 4: Teaching English Language Learners

Becoming Sociocultural Mediators: What All Educators Can Learn from Bilingual and ESL Teachers, Sonia Nieto, *Issues in Teacher Education*, 2017
The best ESL teachers serve as bridges between the child's home culture and that of the school. Non-specialists can learn from the solidarity that this instruction involves.

ESL and Classroom Teachers Team Up to Teach Common Core, Lesli A. Maxwell, *Education Week*, 2013
Diversity in an inclusive school presents challenges. In this article, two teachers explain what led them to become co-teachers to meet the needs of English language learners. Other teachers explain their strategies for meeting the needs of students, professional learning communities, and the "push-in" model.

A Better Chance to Learn: Bilingual Bicultural Education, United States Commission on Civil Rights, 1975
According to the 1964 Civil Rights Act Title VI, schools should accommodate English Language Learners. This report discusses permutations of various pedagogical arrangements to advance this goal. These include a discussion of students' rights to learn in their first language and the effectiveness of bicultural-bilingual education where students are pulled out of regular classrooms for instruction.

UNIT 5: Twenty-First Century Learning Technology and Integration

Standards-based Technology Integration for Emergent Bilinguals, Briana Ronan, *Multicultural Education*, 2018
In a standards-driven K-12 environment, teachers of emergent bilinguals face the ongoing challenge of complying with standards in multiple domains. Using the Technological, Pedagogical, and Content Knowledge (TPACK) model, the article discusses ways in which bilingual curriculum can advance literacy through technology integration.

Utilizing Technology in Physical Education: Addressing the Obstacles of Integration, Beth Pyle and Keri Esslinger, *Delta Kappa Gamma Bulletin*, 2014
Perhaps you have wondered why teachers in physical education, the arts, and other activity-centered classes need to be concerned with technology standards? This article explains why technology is important in physical education and obstacle to technology integration.

Implications of Shifting Technology in Education, Janet Holland and John Holland, *TechTrends*, 2014
Recently many of us feel that every day brings newer, bigger, and better technology devices. This explosion of technology choices comes with increased quality of the tools and more research to practice articles for integrating technology. How are teachers to implement meaningful integration of new technologies while aligning research to practice?

Assistive Tech for Everyone? Michelle R. Davis, *Education Week*, 2014
What were once technology tools designed for and used by persons with disabilities are moving into the mainstream and being used by students who do not have an identified disability. A primary reason is the adoption of Universal Design for Learning methods and materials for all students.

UNIT 6: Special & Exceptional Education

Inclusive Education: Lessons from History, Barbara. Boroson, *Educational Leadership*, 2017
Boroson aligns advocacy for inclusive placements for students with disabilities with the advocacy of persons from previous civil rights efforts that were anti-desegregation.

Text-to-Speech: Not Just for Special Education Students! Kristine Napper, *McGraw-Hill*, 2019
The benefits of text-to-speech for students who are blind or vision-impaired are well known. However, all students can benefit from the independence and confidences that it fosters.

Mobile Apps the Educational Solution for Autistic Students in Secondary Education, Agathi Stathopoulou, et al., *International Journal of Interactive Mobile Technologies*, 2019
This article explores the extent to which autistic children can be served by mobile apps that compensate for their gap and comfort level with social skills. These apps allow for self-guided instruction and have a structured approach that is compatible with the way that autistic students learn.

5 Strategies for Inclusivity in Special Education, Karen Achtman, *McGraw-Hill*, 2018
Instructional strategies to promote inclusivity offer a broad pedagogical umbrella that increases the likelihood that every child in the classroom overcomes hurdles to learning. Fostering an inclusive classroom environment requires the teacher to have a high level of awareness of the needs of all children in her classroom.

Education of All Handicapped Children Act, U.S. Congress, Public Law 94-142, 1975
This legislation established the nomenclature and policy basis for extending equal rights to children with disabilities in their education. It mandated that individualized education plans (IEP) be standard for all identified special education students as part of a comprehensive plan that was designed to meet their educational needs.

UNIT 7: Ethics & Community Engagement

The Next "Evolution" of Civic Learning, Tania D. Mitchell, *Peer Review: Emerging Trends and Key Debates in Undergraduate Education*, 2017
Community-engaged learning is a new buzz term in higher education; Mitchell reflects on whether there is true reciprocity of commitment between university and the community and whether sufficient efforts are being made to foster community leadership.

Democracy in Education, John Dewey, *The Elementary School Teacher*, 1903
This excerpt from John Dewey's tome still stands as the most in-depth and thorough theorization of democracy and the role of schools within it. The work centers the consistently of democratic ends with groups who are seeking to be stable and sustainable.

UNIT 8: Identity & Intersectionality in Education

Building LGBTQ Awareness and Allies in Our Teacher Education Community and Beyond, Laura-Lee Kearns, Jennifer Mitton Kukner, and Joanne Tompkins, *Collected Essays on Learning and Teaching*, 2014
The authors discuss how they work to build awareness and allies within the higher-education context. They developed a curriculum to use in their pre-service teacher education program with the purpose of creating a pedagogy that embraces, celebrates, and honors all learners.

Here's What I Wish White Teachers Knew When Teaching My Black Children, Afrika Afeni Mills, *Education Post*, 2019
Afrika Afeni Mills challenges predominantly white teachers in K-12 schools to broaden their cultural competence of America history in the context of the experience of minoritized persons. Only by disrupting their predominant cultural lens can they be effective teachers of all students.

UNIT 9: STEM

Elements of Making: A Framework to Support Making in the Science Classroom, Shelly Rodriguez et al., *Science Teacher*, 2018
Making is a curricular innovation that fosters a do-it-yourself mindset in problem-solving from design to production. The authors offer a matrix for lesson development and implementation.

Don't Ask Me Why: Preschool Teachers' Knowledge in Technology as a Determinant of Leadership Behavior, Anna Öqvist and Per Högström, *Journal of Technology Education*, 2018
This research study examines the correlation between the attitudes that preschool teachers have toward the underlying elements of implementing technology in the classroom and their confidence in guiding their students' learning.

The U.S. Is Falling Way Behind in STEM But Kentucky's Powering the Comeback, Garris Landon Stroud, *Education Post*, 2018
Reliable strategies for expansion of rigorous STEM education are well documented but not broadly implemented in the United States. Through making schools accountable for science education, providing cutting edge computer science classes and partnering with community and business stakeholders, Kentucky K-12 schools are bucking the downward national trend.

Preface

The significance of public education for a participatory democracy is self-evident. A society whose system of government relies upon an informed public has an unquestionable investment in protecting as sacrosanct the political values of liberty and justice for all. Such a system requires a strong tradition of inclusive education for the long-term sustainability of democracy as a way of life. Reconciling the public purposes of education with the other defining sectors of society is the ongoing task of each successive generation and prompts thorough exploration of schools' role in a society that values pluralism. How to reconcile this value with the competing interests of industry, geo-political demands, and ecological constraints are a few of the salient considerations.

Technological innovation has characterized the coming of age of this generation. The rapidly evolving technology of our times that has provided smart phones, technology platforms of social media, and Web 2.0 interactive software of Google Docs has revolutionized labor and society. Rapid demographic change in which the percentage of Anglo-American majority is decreasing steadily is motivating forms of social unrest particularly where political differences also enflame the social divide. Significant gaps between the wealthy and economically disadvantaged also are a societal marker and economic segregation means that our social networks are increasingly more homogenous that recent times in American history. There is also growing concern about the ability of American public education to continue to provide spaces where children from diverse backgrounds can find common ground. This year's articles curate research, first person's narratives, and opinions pieces that feature the convergence of democratic values and social issues as they bear on education. Specific topics include educational reform, teaching English language learners, issues raised by accommodating special and exceptional learners in education, educational ethics in a community setting and considering schools in the context of identity, its meaning for society, and forms of intersectionality. Interwoven throughout these topics are reoccurring themes of integrating technology and the ethics, practice and policy of accommodating differences among learners. A presupposition of this assembled work collectively is the imperative of making educational advancement a robust possibility for all children.

These multiplicities of technological, social, and political factors that are converging on every of aspect public education at this moment are evident in the discourse of school reform and its ramifications for every facet of K–12 education as it has been delivered traditionally. Beginning with President Regan's Nation at Risk (1983) report and Bill Clinton's "Goals 2000" education reform and gaining increasing momentum with of No Child Left Behind (2002), the standards-based movement has exercised increasing influence and control over K–12 curriculum. Since the implementation of No Child Left Behind (NCLB), public schools have faced an accountability regime that has transformed dramatically the face of public education. Persisting through two terms of a Republican and then a Democratic President, it is evident that this policy will characterize education for the foreseeable future. Distinctive of NCLB and its successor, Every Student Succeeds Act (2016) is the reductive definition of student achievement as performance on standardized tests. As a result, the performative approach to learning and assessment has become a prominent feature of public education. With the rapid growth of school vouchers, which allow the transfer of public funds to charter schools, private and, in some case, parochial schools, the means of delivering K–12 education has undergone significant change. As additional factors, the proliferation of for-profit institutions and alternative teacher education programs are just a few of the myriad of ways through which private corporations are influencing the economy of the funding for public schools and supporting elements.

The current movements to reform schools revisit the long-standing questions of democratic education. What is educational equality? How can we ensure the best quality education for all children? What are the educational implications of cultural, ethnic and other differences among learners? How are we to address societal inequities along the lines of race, social class, and gender identity and the ways in which schools are a microcosm of society? What kind of preparation should teacher candidates have in order for them to become competent educators? The pursuit of the acceptable responses around which we can all agree persists. The quest challenges persons who care about education to foreground the ethical and professional standards that should frame education practice and theory and teaching.

Interpreting educational equity today involves recognizing the systemic sources of inequality and its institutional manifestations. This process can call into question long-standing lenses through which researchers theorize the sources of intergenerational poverty and pathways to social mobility. Viewing students' families in terms of their strengths is one approach that also relates to acknowledging the role of resilience in holding limitless possibilities for mitigating the effects of poverty. The capacity for children to persevere through difficult times does not absolve other education stakeholders and the larger society from the obligation to dismantle the unjust policies that underwrite them. Making equity possible ultimately involves strategic practice that is informed by evidence-based interventions.

Teaching English language learners (ELL) and accommodating exceptional learners center critical aspects of fulfilling the role of public schools. There is the argument that instructional strategies that benefit emergent bilingual learners are models for academic instruction that bridge the classroom and students' home culture. K–12 education and the higher education faculty who prepare future practitioners have been challenged to integrate technology into the classrooms at a pace that keeps up with innovation.

Can classrooms adequately leverage learning technology to positively impact learning while cultivating the qualities that promote human connection and empathy? It is a development imperative while integrating technology in positive and constructive ways. One of these areas relate to not encouraging sedentary and passive use of tools such as the iPad and laptop computers. Research about fostering community connection and empowerment suggests that these experiences can be embedded in classroom learning. Most aspirational, incorporating a community component to school outreach has the potential to advance positive social change.

In compiling the articles for this edition, much effort was devoted to bringing forward important conversations for the present and future implementation of K–12 education. Nevertheless, such a substantive but varied exploration of educational research, scholarship and articles promises to be accessible. It is hoped that regardless of the vantage point from which one approaches these articles, their curation will instigate a greater awareness of the extent to which every person in a participatory democracy has some stakes in the delivery and persistence of public education.

Editor

Dr. Sheron Fraser-Burgess is professor of social foundations of education and multicultural education at Ball State University in Muncie, Indiana. A presupposition of her teaching, research and service is that schools are nested within society and therefore can reflect the broader societal patterns and relationships. In teaching courses in the social, historical, and philosophical foundations of education, Dr. Fraser-Burgess seeks to raise responsible social justice advocates for democratic education.

Academic Advisory Board Members

Members of the Academic Advisory Board are instrumental in the final selection of articles of *Annual Editions* books. Their review of the articles for content, level, and appropriateness provides critical direction to the editor(s) and staff. We think that you will find their careful consideration reflected here.

Christopher Boe
Pfeiffer University

Perry Castelli
Florida Southern College

Saran Donahoo
Southern Illinois University

La Vonne Fedynich
Texas A&M University, Kingsville

Kathleen E. Fite
Texas State University, San Marcos

Barbara Hanes
Neumann University

Laura Heitritter
Northwestern College

Jason Helfer
Knox College

John Janowiak
Appalachian State University

Tammy Ladwig
University of Wisconsin

Doris Metz
University of Maine, Fort Kent

Eliana Mukherjee
Palm Beach State College

Leigh Neier
University of Missouri

Patrick O'Connor
Worcester State University

Gary Padgett
University of North Alabama

Jessie Panko
Saint Xavier University

Rusty Powlas
Maple Woods Community College

Stephen T. Schroth
Knox College

John R. Shoup
California Baptist University

Mark Sidelnick
University of North Carolina

Amy Slater
Metropolitan Community College, Blue River

Susan Studer
California Baptist University

Thomas Walsh
Kean University

Barry Witten
Western Illinois University

UNIT

Prepared by: Sheron Fraser-Burgess, *Ball State University*

School Reform in the Twenty-First Century

We are a democratic society, committed to the free education of all our children, but are we accomplishing that goal? There has been a deep divide about this question which has resulted in much discussion of school reform and several attempts to find the perfect reform solution for our schools.

In an attempt to give direction to the reform movement, the Clinton administration established Goals 2000 under the *Educate America Act*. One of these goals continues to be important to the discussion of what constitutes a well-educated citizen.

Goal 2 states that "The high school graduation rate will increase to at least 90%" (U.S. Department of Education, n.d.). To date, data indicate that we have not reached this goal and are far from achieving it. Educators have acknowledged that high school graduates get more satisfactory jobs, are happier in their job choices, and earn higher salaries than non-graduates. Heckman and LaFontaine (2010) note the decline in high school graduation since 1970 (for cohorts born after 1950) has flattened growth in the skill level of the U.S. workforce. We must confront the drop-out problem to increase the skill levels of the future workforce. We must also consider how high schools that respond only to higher education demands may be ignoring the needs of the nation at-large for a skilled workforce that can compete in a global market. Bridgeland, DiIulio, and Morrison (2006) found in a survey of dropouts that 47 percent reported a major reason why they left school was the classes were not interesting and did not prepare them for their adulthood goals and the life they wished. We should consider that by simply preparing students to attend traditional four-year institutions, we may be ignoring their interests and desires, thus alienating them.

Next we had the No Child Left Behind legislation which placed emphasis on the specific student subgroups—requiring schools to be accountable for the progress of minority students and students with disabilities and quantifying achievement gaps. The fundamental philosophy underlying the legislation is that all children can learn and schools must demonstrate that their students have made progress. Schools are issued annual report cards based on standardized assessments and must demonstrate *adequate yearly progress* (AYP). In their latest report, the Center on Educational Policy (2012) stated.

An estimated 48% of the nation's public schools failed to make adequate yearly progress based on 2010–11 test results. This marks the highest national percentage of schools ever to fall short and an increase of 9 percentage points from the previous year (p. 9).

In 2009, the Secretary of Education issued a call to action by stating that education is the civil rights issue of this generation and the fight for education is about much more than just education; it is about social justice (Duncan, 2009). In 2009, President Obama's *Race to the Top* was passed and established new goals for schools, teachers, and students. However, is it realistic to expect that schools will make greater strides now than in the past? Boyle and Burns ask an important question: "Why do we ask citizens rather than education professionals to govern public schools?" Their concerns are centered on the responsibility of schools to socialize children into society. We transmit our collective knowledge and shared values via the public schools. Therefore, we must have public debate about the purpose of public education. Part of that debate may well include discussion of trust and accountability. Do we, as a nation, trust our teachers to do what they should or must we regulate every topic in the curriculum and hold them accountable via standardized assessments? This is a primary question that has political parties, teachers and their associations, and parents taking sides for and against Common Core and high-stakes standardized testing.

As we consider the educational system of the United States, we must engage in an intensively reflective and analytical effort. Further, we must give considerable contemplation and forethought to the consequences, because our actions will shape not only the students' futures, but also the future of our country in the global community. Prospective teachers are encouraged to question their own individual educational experiences as they read the articles presented in this section. All of us must acknowledge that our values affect both our ideas about curriculum and what we believe is the purpose of educating others. The economic and demographic changes in the last decade and those that will occur in the future necessitate a fundamental reconceptualization of how schools ought to respond to the social and economic environments in which they are located. There are additional articles in the next unit on poverty that, with the articles in this unit, will offer practical ideas to help answer the following question. How can schools reflect the needs of, and respond to, the diverse group of students they serve while meeting the needs of our democratic society?

References

Bridgeland, J. M., DiIulio, J. J., & Morrison, K. B. 2006. "The Silent Epidemic: Perspectives of High School Dropouts." Bill & Melinda Gates Foundation. Retrieved on 28 May 2008 from www.gatesfoundation.org/Pages/home.aspx.

Article

Prepared by: Sheron Fraser-Burgess, *Ball State University*

Is Test-Based Accountability Dead?

MORGAN S. POLIKOFF, JAY P. GREENE, AND KEVIN HUFFMAN

Learning Outcomes

After reading this article, you will be able to:

- Articulate the relationship between standardized tests and accountability.
- Characterize the role and significance of No Child Left Behind (NCLB, 2002) & Every Student Succeeds Act (ESSA, 2016) Education policy in influencing the current climate towards accountability.
- Describe the impact of the accountability regime on students' performance on the National Assessment of Education Progress (NAEP).

Since the 2001 passage of the No Child Left Behind Act, test-based accountability has been an organizing principle—perhaps *the* organizing principle—of efforts to improve American schools. But lately, accountability has been under fire from many critics, including Common Core opponents and those calling for more multifaceted measures of teacher and school performance. And yet the Every Student Succeeds Act, NCLB's successor law, still mandates standardized testing of students and requires states to have accountability systems. So: is accountability on the wane, or is it here to stay? If accountability is indeed dying, would its loss be good or bad for students?

In this issue's forum, we present three different viewpoints on those questions from Morgan S. Polikoff, associate professor of education at the University of Southern California's Rossier School of Education; Jay P. Greene, professor of education at the University of Arkansas; and Kevin Huff-man, former Tennessee commissioner of education.

Why Accountability Matters, and Why It Must Evolve

By Morgan S. Polikoff

Try to think of an education policy that 1) has been shown, in dozens of studies across multiple decades, to positively affect student outcomes; 2) has the overwhelming support of parents and voters; 3) reinforces many other policies and facilitates quality research; and 4) has been used widely at the district, state, and national levels for decades or more.

You might be thinking that such a policy doesn't exist, and if it did, we'd surely want to keep it around. But the truth is precisely the opposite. Such a policy does exist—it's called school accountability—yet the powers that be seem increasingly ready to throw it out and leave education to the whims of the all-but-unregulated free market.

School accountability, specifically test-based accountability, has been a staple of K–12 education policy since the 1990s (and even before that, in some states and districts). Over that time, we've learned quite a lot about it.

First, we've learned that it can work. We've seen this in studies of individual districts, individual states, and the nation as a whole: David Figlio and Susanna Loeb's 2011 review of research summarizes this literature comprehensively. The effects observed in many studies are substantial, especially given that they typically occur schoolwide. The effect of No Child Left Behind (NCLB) on students' mathematics achievement documented by Thomas Dee and Brian Jacob and confirmed by Manyee Wong and colleagues is equivalent to the gain from spending three or four years in an average urban charter school, according to the latest data from Stanford University's Center for Research on Education Outcomes. Accountability doesn't seem to do a great job at closing achievement gaps (though it certainly shines a light on underperformance), but there's considerable evidence that it can raise student achievement.

Second, we've learned that parents and voters feel strongly that accountability is essential. Polls show overwhelming bipartisan support for the common-sense idea that schools receiving public dollars to educate children should be accountable for providing a good education. *Education Next's* 2016 poll reported at least two-thirds support for annual testing among both Republicans and Democrats. In the 2016 PACE/USC Rossier poll of Californians that I led, we asked what schools should be held accountable for; voters rated standardized test results last among the options presented, but 69 percent of them still believed accountability for test results was important. We also know that parents prioritize student achievement when selecting a school for their children. In our increasingly resource-constrained and globally competitive world, this desire for outcomes will only intensify.

Third, we've seen that accountability mutually reinforces other policies and provides essential data to support education research and improvement. For instance, there is suggestive evidence that charter schools perform better in contexts where accountability is high (that is, where strong authorizing laws shut down poorly performing schools) than where it is weak or nonexistent. Accountability was intended to provide weight to state standards and encourage teachers to implement them, and evidence suggests it does focus teachers' attention on the content that state policymakers want teachers to emphasize. Not to mention that the data emerging from the same tests used for school accountability have powered a revolution in education research that has allowed scholars to dramatically improve the relevance and rigor of their work.

Finally, we've learned a lot about how to design accountability policy to better target the schools that most need improvement. It is now generally understood that the simplest performance measures—those that defined test-based accountability under NCLB—mainly tell you who's enrolling in a school, not how well the school is educating those students. We know that performance indexes and growth measures are much fairer and more accurate ways to classify school performance. There's also a growing consensus that in the next generation of accountability policies, we must broaden the criteria beyond test scores, and the new federal education law, the Every Student Succeeds Act (ESSA), encourages this kind of creative rethinking.

We've also learned that the design of accountability policies can affect the way teachers respond to them. For instance, policies that focus attention on raising the achievement of low-performing students may be more effective than those that offer rewards for high student performance in general. And teachers do seem to respond rationally to accountability policies by focusing more on the grades and subjects that are tested. As for concerns about NCLB's negative impact on teacher working conditions, Jason Grissom and his colleagues have shown that the law's implementation did not diminish teachers' job satisfaction or increase their levels of stress. While the unintended consequences of accountability can be pernicious, they can also be addressed, at least in part, through policy design.

Countering the Opposition

Despite this track record of modest success, many parties seem poised to throw the policy overboard and use the guise of "parental choice" or "local control" to return us to a time when we had little idea which schools were educating children well and which were not. The opposition to accountability in education is largely political; my 2016 analysis of California poll data, for instance, found that disapproval of President Obama was among the strongest predictors of Common Core opposition, and *Education Next* and others have routinely found that voters support "common standards" or "common assessments" when they are not tied to the Common Core name.

There are of course more principled concerns with accountability, and it is worth taking a moment to address them. One issue is that accountability in general, and test-based accountability in particular, can have negative effects on instruction, such as a dumbed-down, narrowed curriculum. This problem can be addressed in large part by improving content standards and the assessments used to gauge student performance. Recent work I co-led with Nancy Doorey indeed finds that the two state-assessment consortia have made considerable improvements over even the best NCLB-era tests. This issue can also be addressed by broadening the set of indicators against which schools are evaluated, which many states are poised to do under the new federal accountability law.

Another concern is that the tests used for accountability do not predict important life outcomes, and thus that we might be focusing on the wrong things. To be sure, studies do not show a perfect one-to-one relationship between impacts on test scores and impacts on later life outcomes—no one expects they would. But several studies do show longer-term effects of accountability policies; we have strong evidence from Raj Chetty and colleagues that impacts on test scores do predict impacts on other important life outcomes; and, again, many states appear poised to broaden accountability measures beyond just test scores.

What Comes Next?

There is no doubt that the coalition that once supported accountability policy has frayed. The Republican leaders in the executive and legislative branches, which once championed accountability, have turned to school choice as the primary strategy to produce reform (even as public opinion on choice, especially more extreme forms such as vouchers, has begun to sour). But choice without accountability is unlikely to work.

Without test results, for instance, we would not know that online and virtual charters appear to be demonstrably harmful to students, as are many Louisiana private schools attended by students using vouchers. Nor would we know that Boston's well-regulated charter high schools produce truly stunning positive effects on students' test scores and early college decisions. Choice programs that do not contain accountability provisions offer us zero assurances that educational dollars are being well spent.

Where should we go from here? We must continue to recognize that the design of accountability policy matters, and we must refine our policies over time. ESSA allows states to do this. It allows states to include better test-based measures of school performance, and they should. It allows them to incorporate measures of school climate, student attendance and discipline, and progress toward college and career readiness, and states should adopt and experiment with these measures. It allows them to target consequences on a smaller subset of low-performing schools and move away from NCLB-era interventions that were largely ineffective, and states appear to be focusing their efforts on more promising interventions that target growth and effective practices. Will the next round of state accountability policies be perfect? They will not. Will they be better than what they replaced? They almost certainly will.

Over the last several decades, we have made real, if incremental, progress in education. Test scores on the National Assessment of Educational Progress are up for every student subgroup (even accounting for the downward blip in 2015), and graduation rates are, too. Accountability systems have worked well with other reforms—such as effective choice policies, the expansion of early-childhood-education and other school-readiness programs, and efforts to improve the teaching force through evaluation and tenure reform—to improve education for children around the country. There is simply no reason to think that abandoning accountability at this point would be an effective strategy. The coming years will see new and creative uses of accountability in states and districts. We must encourage and study this innovation if we are to continue improving America's public schools.

Futile Accountability Systems Should Be Abandoned

By Jay P. Greene

Is Test-Based Accountability "on the wane"? The question is based on a fallacy. For something to be on the wane, it has to exist, and test-based accountability has never truly existed in the United States. Holding people accountable requires that they face significant consequences as a result of their actions. Despite years of "high stakes" student testing, very few of the nation's 3.14 million public-school teachers have ever lost a job, had their pay reduced, or otherwise faced meaningful consequences because of these test results.

It's true that under the No Child Left Behind (NCLB) accountability regime, schools have been given labels, such as "in need of improvement." Some have even been threatened with reorganization or closure. But these threats have only rarely been carried out, and the educators in these schools have typically just been reshuffled to other locations or new management. This enterprise does not constitute true accountability. It's more akin to "double secret probation," the toothless threat imposed on the party-mad frat boys of the 1978 film *Animal House*.

The real question we should address here is whether the hollow threats of this double-secret probation are on the wane. I think they are, and I say good riddance. While testing has failed to produce meaningful accountability, it has distorted the operation of schools to the detriment of educational quality—and it has proven politically unviable.

Educational Harm

Test-based accountability is essentially a central-planning exercise similar to that used by officials in the Soviet Union in attempting to manage the country's economy. In both cases, a distant official selected a particular goal for production, focused on a limited set of metrics to assess whether goals were met, and then threatened to impose rewards or sanctions based on whether those metrics showed desired results. Central planning failed in the Soviet Union, and it is failing here in public education—and for similar reasons.

First, education goals established by distant officials cannot possibly capture the diverse spectrum of local priorities in our nation. Officials have focused on improving math and reading ability, but emphasizing those subjects has come at the expense of other goals. Several studies, including a recent paper by the University of Virginia's Daphna Bassok and colleagues, as well as widespread reports from educators, show that schools have shortchanged history, science, physical education, art, music, and civics. They've also cut back on culturally enriching field trips. Even within math and reading, schools tend to focus narrowly on tested items, which often exclude poetry, literature, and more abstract math.

Providing students with math and reading skills that are useful in the workplace is a worthy goal of education, but so is helping students become good citizens—cultured, tolerant, self-disciplined, and creative. With test-based accountability, distant officials have imposed their preferences on the rest of us. In addition, studies such as the ongoing research of David Grissmer and colleagues indicate that long-term achievement in math and reading depends on a broader education that includes the type of general knowledge conveyed by history, science, art, and music. Paradoxically, a narrow focus on math and reading may undermine later success in math and reading.

Second, the limited metrics used to assess math and reading achievement are easily gamed and further distort the educational process. If success is defined by the percentage of students who exceed a threshold for proficiency, officials will be tempted to lower the bar for what constitutes "proficient." Schools will also be tempted to focus on students whose performance is below but close to the proficiency threshold, neglecting both high achievers and students who are unlikely to pass even with a reasonable amount of extra attention. School administrators and teachers will be tempted to cheat, as in the recent scandal in Atlanta, or to narrow their instruction, as mentioned earlier. And given that test-based accountability systems are almost entirely built around proficiency levels rather than growth, schools can *appear* more successful if they can avoid serving too many students who are difficult to educate.

Third, schools are gradually figuring out that few real consequences will befall them if they fail to meet the imposed metrics. School leaders' bluffs about mass firings could only be sustained for so long. As a result, scores on the National Assessment of Educational Progress rose in the early years of test-based accountability, but more recently, those gains have stalled.

Furthermore, test-based accountability is built on the assumption that test results are reliable proxies for success later in life, but research has called that assumption into question. It's true that test scores are correlated with some measures of later life success, but for test-based accountability to work we would need to see that *changes* in test scores caused by schools are associated with *changes* in later life success for students. Test-based accountability proponents can point to research by Raj Chetty and colleagues that shows a connection between improvements in test scores and improved outcomes in adulthood, but their work examines testing from the 1980s, prior to the high-stakes era, and therefore does not capture how the threat of consequences might distort the relationship between test-score changes and later life outcomes.

Furthermore, findings such as theirs are more the exception than the rule. A growing number of studies show a disconnect between short-term progress on test scores and long-term success. That is, even when we measure the extent to which schools contribute to student test-score growth—something that test-based accountability systems rarely do—we cannot consistently predict which programs or schools will help students be more successful later. We cannot centrally plan success if we cannot reliably predict success.

Political Weakness

The educational failures of test-based accountability, as detrimental as they are, will not spell its demise. Rather, accountability that centers on testing is doomed because it has many political adversaries but no enduring political constituency. Parents have never rallied to demand that their children be tested more, that tests be used to retain students or prevent them from graduating, or that tests be used to determine teacher pay or employment. Educators revile test-based accountability even more. Test-based accountability was initiated by policy elites frustrated over rising education costs and subpar results. But elites cannot sustain such a policy in the face of opposition from educators and families. American politics is shaped by the activity of organized interests, not poll results. Other countries may be able to impose meaningful systems of test-based accountability, but the decentralized nature of American education and politics gives far more power to organized groups of upper-middle-class families and educators than to the technocratic elite.

The political weakness of test-based accountability helps explain why there are no meaningful consequences attached to it. Opponents have not been able to repeal testing, since there is broad support for *information* on student achievement—even partial and distorted information—but these adversaries have effectively neutered the consequences of accountability. So, the Every Student Succeeds Act continues to require testing, but the accountability piece is even more anemic than it was under NCLB.

The collapse of the Common Core State Standards illustrates the political folly of test-based accountability. Common Core attempted to transform largely symbolic accountability systems into something tougher, which is precisely why it failed. The standards were an effort to better articulate the proper goals of education. The federally subsidized tests aligned to Common Core and developed by the SBAC and PARCC consortia were intended as the rigorous metrics for this stronger accountability regime (see "The Politics of the Common Core Assessments," *features,* Fall 2016). And centralized teacher-evaluation systems being pioneered by the Gates Foundation in their Measures of Effective Teaching effort were supposed to impose meaningful consequences for failure to perform well on those metrics.

Even these baby steps toward a real accountability system produced a fierce political backlash, led largely by suburban middle- and upper-middle-class families. Such families are accustomed to having significant autonomy with respect to what and how their children are taught, either by choosing the public or private schools their children attend or by influencing locally elected and appointed school officials. By its nature, test-based accountability shifts control away from these parents. Suburban families see Common Core as an infringement on their autonomy, and they have the savvy to fight back. As they do, we are seeing fewer than half of the states sticking to one of the Common Core testing consortia. Soon Common Core will become the same type of nonentity it was meant to replace.

What might constitute real accountability in K–12 education? The power of middle- and upper-middle-class families to exercise control over how and what their children are taught is one example. Suburban schools that stray from parental preferences may lose students and revenue or have to answer to angry parents. Test-based systems are politically doomed because middle- and upper-middle-class families tend to prevail in education politics. This phony accountability harms education and undermines schools' direct accountability to parents. Rather than doubling down on such futile efforts, education reformers should seek to expand true accountability by increasing school choice for more families. The solution to rising costs and subpar results is not central planning but greater control over education on the part of all families, rich and poor.

If Parents Push for it, Accountability Can Work

By Kevin Huffman

The Greatest Trick the devil ever pulled in education is convincing the American public that we have had test-based accountability. The media and politicians adopted the rhetoric of "high stakes" tests without bothering to ask the question: what, exactly, *are* the stakes? For most adults in education, there were none. Shockingly few public-school educators have lost salary or received a raise or a promotion because of their students' test results. By the same token, very few teachers have been counseled onto a different career track or been required to complete targeted professional development. Outside of a handful of states and cities, true test-based accountability has never been implemented.

This is a problem, because the stakes *are* extremely high for students. Parents and teachers complained—with some legitimacy—that the No Child Left Behind (NCLB) era set loose an avalanche of weak fill-in-the-bubble tests to assess student mastery of watered-down state academic standards.

Yet even these substandard assessments were predictive of future life outcomes. As Tennessee's commissioner of education, I could look at the results on the state's old tests and make a highly accurate prediction how any particular 8th grader would eventually score on the ACT, which, itself, is highly predictive of completing a two- or four-year postsecondary degree. Correlation doesn't equal causation, but the test results—with all of their inherent weaknesses—gave a strong indication of how students were faring in our system.

While we spent recent years pretending that a teacher might lose his or her job because of an 8th grader's poor test results, we gave short shrift to the reality facing the 8th grader: a lifetime of truncated opportunities dictated by weak performance at an incredibly young age.

Today, we face two questions. First, will the pseudo-accountability of the last 15 years dial back, stay the same, or be transformed into something real? And second, should we care?

On the first question, my guess is that our attempts at accountability will stay much the same but the rhetoric will dial back. Under the Every Student Succeeds Act (ESSA), states will give annual tests; the results will be published and released; schools will receive some form of rating, based largely on those results; and the very lowest-performing schools will be subject to some form of intervention.

For the average school and school district, the real impact will be public scrutiny and potential embarrassment as a result of receiving a lower "grade" or being placed on a watch list—in most cases, with little formal consequence.

With states now appropriately crafting accountability frameworks that focus not just on test scores but on multiple measures, we also will hear less heated rhetoric about the consequences of poor results. The draft state ESSA plans that I have seen cite measures such as technical assistance for districts and "continuous improvement feedback cycles." Toning down the rhetoric of accountability—particularly when the realities didn't match the heated language—makes sense, as long as we don't lose our resolve to use student results as a barometer of whether educators are succeeding.

Accountability Works

Because, while teachers and parents may have grown tired of accountability, here's the rub: test-based accountability, even executed poorly, works. From 1999 to 2011, during the heyday of NCLB and its state-level predecessors, overall student scores improved on the National Assessment of Educational Progress (NAEP) in both reading and math (see Figure 1). Furthermore, scores rose faster for African American and Hispanic students, narrowing achievement gaps. State bubble tests may have been weak, the over-fixation on tests in some schools may have been real, but it is a flat-out fact that kids—particularly low-income and minority kids—got a better education.

And while the pace of progress on NAEP has slowed over the past six years, some states and districts continued to make major gains. Tennessee and Washington, D.C., showed the most growth of any state and city in the country, with major improvements in reading and math (and, in Tennessee, also in science). These two places happened to be the leaders in applying test-based accountability to teachers, putting teacher tenure on the line (in Tennessee) and teachers' jobs and salary on the line (in D.C.). While no studies prove what was responsible for the test-score improvements, these results would seem to imply that actually holding adults responsible for student progress can have a positive impact on outcomes.

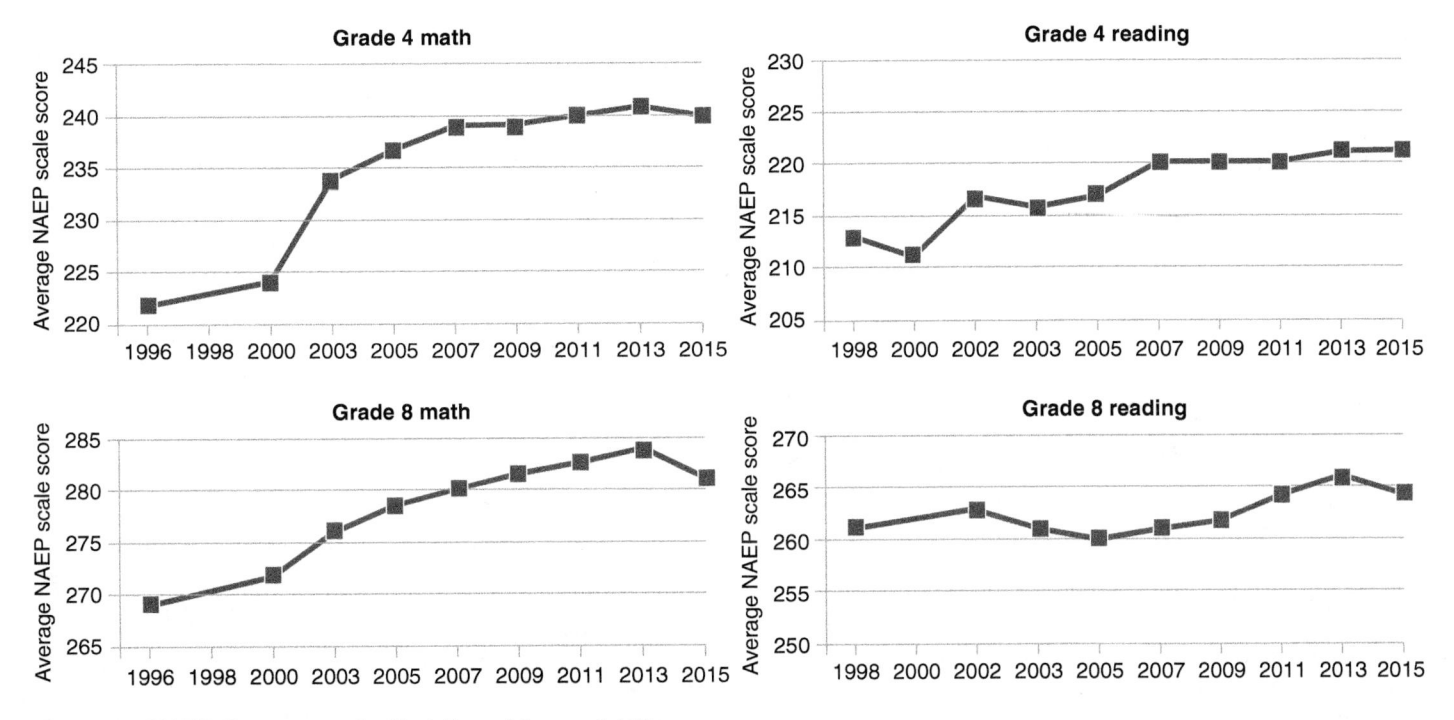

Figure 1 NAEP Progress under Test-Based Accountability
From 1999 to 2011, during the heyday of No Child Left Behind and its state-level predecessors, overall scores of public school students improved significantly on the National Assessment of Educational Progress in both reading and math.
Source: U.S. Department of Education, National Center for Education Statistics

Federalists will often make the case that we should let a thousand flowers bloom, sit back, and wait for the cross-pollination to occur: if states, districts, or schools apply test-based accountability and it works, then others will willingly adopt those best practices.

Reality shows that this is a pipe dream. The national response to improved results in Tennessee and D.C. has been a deafening silence. There have been some laudatory news articles, but precious little cross-pollination. We haven't seen states and districts beating a path to Nashville and D.C. to learn how they improved results. Nor have we seen an increase in states evaluating teachers using student achievement growth and making decisions based on the results. Few if any districts are upending the tenure track and paying teachers different salaries based on student outcomes.

And herein lies the conundrum of accountability and the question of its viability in the coming decade: if test-based accountability works to improve student results but is unpopular with people who make their living in schools, can we reasonably expect it to find a foothold?

Unfortunately, public school educators are far from the only ones pushing back against hardcore accountability. The fundamental reality is that test-based accountability commands precious little political will all around. While some portray this lack of support as a repudiation of the NCLB era, it actually stems more from the populist policymaking of modern America. Visit any state legislature and you will generally find Democrats spouting union-fed lines about over-testing and demoralized teachers. You will find Republicans repeating talk-radio tropes about the Common Core and its associated tests. And you will find partisans on both sides—given the growing political homogeneity of large cities and rural counties—spouting the merits of local control. That attitude is likely to be reinforced by the new Trump administration and a Republican-controlled Congress.

Right–left fissures in the reform community have reduced the chance of rebuilding a strong bipartisan coalition for accountability. Additionally, the broader education-reform community—the foundations, nonprofits, and think tanks that historically pushed school systems to adapt and change—increasingly have given test-based accountability the cold shoulder. Charter schools have become fetishized at the expense of reforming the traditional public-school system. That's a shame, given that the vast majority of low-income kids today, tomorrow, and 20 years from now are and will be served by traditional school systems.

Do We Care?

We know beyond a shadow of a doubt that some schools, districts, and states are doing better work than their peers. Some are getting better results, and some are driving faster improvements. How do we know this? Because of tests. Because we can see actual evidence that kids have learned things and that schools have improved. Even in the absence of true consequences for low performance, we at least have the ability to identify and learn from the places that are succeeding—if we can spur the necessary actions.

ESSA ensures that annual tests are here to stay, but it also formalizes a reality that has been true for a while: states decide what accountability for results looks like. Their choices will be shaped by public will. The future of accountability—and of using test scores to improve our schools—will depend on one thing: does the public care enough to advocate for the "eat-your-vegetables," common-sense annual tests and the associated accountability?

Most parents favor such tests. But if the loudest and most active (read: white upper-middle-class suburban) parents think standardized tests are just an annual annoyance, if these parents and other activist voters choose to disbelieve the results in the fact-free era of modern political discourse, then accountability will be diluted down to the posting of test results and the annual finger wagging of the local news media.

This is where leadership must come into play. It is imperative that governors, state chiefs of education, and other local leaders vocally advocate for the potent change shaper of accountability and convince the public of that power. I am optimistic that state education leaders are availing themselves of the chance to draft stronger, multifaceted measurement systems under ESSA. If voters and parents get behind these systems, and we implement them with fidelity, we will be able to use test results—and other measures—to dramatically improve our public schools.

Critical Thinking

1. Why should teachers be held responsible for students' performance on standardized tests?
2. Differentiate between the response of white upper-middle-class suburban parents and that of the parents of black and brown children?
3. What kinds of changes would be recommended to present practice in order to best implement the best models of accountability?

Internet References

Accountability
https://educationpost.org/conversation/blog/accountability/

National Assessment of Education Progress
https://nces.ed.gov/nationsreportcard/

Using Student Assessments for Educational Accountability
https://www.nap.edu/read/5143/chapter/10

Polikoff, Morgan S., Jay P. Greene and Kevin Huffman. "Is Test-Based Accountability Dead?" EducationNext, Summer 2017, Vol 17, No 3. Used by permission of Harvard Kennedy School.

Holding Teachers Accountable Without Adequate Teacher Prep Programs Is a Set-Up

ZACHARY WRIGHT

Learning Outcomes

After reading this article, you will be able to:

- Articulate the arguments for teacher evaluation.
- Distinguish value-added growth from versus performance on proficiency tests as a basis of teacher evaluation.

One of my resolutions for this new year is to think outside of silos and to start connecting the dots between the wide, disparate, and interwoven factors within education, among them teacher accountability, teacher preparation and teacher support.

Even after 10 years in the classroom, I'm frequently accused of being anti-teacher. I'm not surprised, though. When you write about the need for teacher accountability, people tend to retreat to their bastions of pre-formulated opinion.

Despite this, my beliefs haven't changed. I believe that teachers who are effective ought to be rewarded and that teachers who are not ought to be supported, coached and, if need be, removed.

Accountability is non-negotiable. We need to measure student learning and teacher effectiveness if we truly say we prioritize student achievement.

But I should be clear, I also believe accountability needs to work in tandem with other practices that ensure teachers are empowered with the training and feedback they need to succeed.

Specifically, I think the keys to implementing meaningful accountability for teachers depends on strong teacher prep programs, value-added student growth metrics, and video-based coaching that can help all teachers develop, hone their craft and become master educators.

Strong Prep Is Key

I'll just come out and say it: A lot of our teacher prep just stinks.

A perfect case study for the failure of these programs can be found in a recent startling report from American Public Media's Emily Hanford: Most teachers have not been taught how children learn to read.

One teacher spoke a truth that likely resonates with teachers all across the country. "I can say I was totally unprepared to teach reading, especially to struggling readers that I had at the beginning of my career."

How can we hold teachers accountable for student learning when their preparation doesn't include something as basic as reading instruction? How can we hold teachers accountable for student learning when their preparation doesn't include something as basic as reading instruction?

Of course, teachers still need a strong foundation in the theoretical aspects of education—Piaget, Bloom, Skinner, Vygotsky and Montessori.

But the practical aspects are just as important—those everyday teacher moves that too many teachers have to learn on the fly. How to stand and deliver instructions, how to set and reinforce expectations, how to use public and individual redirections, how to circulate the classroom and collect data, how to introduce new material and make lessons stick.

Bottom line: It all starts with good teacher prep.

Value-Added Is Your Friend

I know that test scores can be the third rail in talking about teacher evaluation. But here's my take.

Test scores are an essential measure of student learning, but they are only useful in gauging teaching effectiveness when viewed through the lens of student growth.

That means using value-added metrics, not simply proficiency rates.

At its most basic level, it means that rather than holding teachers accountable for all students earning at least a 75 percent on a standardized test for example, we hold teachers accountable for students showing significant growth on these assessments. Moving that 35 percent to 50 percent, or that 55 percent to 75 percent—or even that 75 percent up to an 85 percent.

The emphasis must be on student growth, not passing a test. After all, teachers often are charged with educating students who arrive in their classrooms significantly below grade level.

Indeed, I started every year in my Philadelphia classroom responsible for entire classrooms of students reading significantly below grade level.

It is not fair, one could even say nearly impossible, for a teacher to raise an entire classroom of 30 students, more than half of whom are below grade level, up past proficient on a standardized assessment. But by analyzing these assessments with a value-added paradigm, we were able to zero in on individualized student growth. For me, that meant test scores weren't the bogeyman. They were honest measures of where my students were and also a reflection of all the work I was doing to help them down the path to proficiency.

Video Doesn't Lie

When I was teaching, one of my coaches insisted I film my lesson so we could reflect on it together. I was resistant. Actually, I was defiant. There is nothing more unsettling than teaching with a camera in the background.

Why?

Because video doesn't lie.

I was going to have to see the truth of my teaching practice, whether I liked it or not. I was going to have to see the truth of my teaching practice, whether I liked it or not.

As it turns out, I was not alone.

In a recent piece in Edsurge, teachers recounted their experiences filming themselves while teaching. One teacher reflected that "the recordings provided an objective and accurate peek into [her] classroom's goings on. It can be easy to dismiss the results of live observations as a reflection of the observer's bias. It's harder to dismiss them when video evidence is staring you in the face."

Much like how value-added framing can de-claw the impact of using test scores to measure student learning and teacher effectiveness, filming lessons can help insert objectivity and trust into the class observation process.

Both teachers and principals can feel empowered and comforted by the fact that filming the lesson helps take away the possibility of subjective disagreements about what went down in an observed lesson.

In addition, my coach filmed our observation debriefings. This was huge because it made accountability a two-way street. Not only was I accountable to my teaching practice, my coach was accountable for providing clear and practical feedback that would take my teaching to the next level. Our work felt less evaluative and more collaborative. I became a better teacher, and my coach become a better guide.

Putting It All Together

All of these pieces are needed.

I had to be held accountable for my student learning. I, after all, was given the charge of educating other people's children and there is nothing holier and more sacred than that.

But holding teachers accountable without adequate teacher prep programs is a set up. Accountability aligned solely alongside proficiency-based assessments is a set up. Accountability without filmed observations and coaching debriefings is a set up.

We need to connect the dots in our educational discourse, get out of our limited entrenchments, and do what's best for kids.

Critical Thinking

1. What is the importance of teacher accountability and what forms does it take?
2. How important is teacher preparation to good K–12 educational outcomes?
3. Why are proficiency levels poor indicators of a teacher's impact on student learning?

Internet References

School Growth Explanation: School Value-Added Growth
http://dese.ade.arkansas.gov/public/userfiles/ESEA/Documents_to_Share/School%20Growth%20Explanation%20for%20ES%20and%20DC%20111017.pdf

Accountability
https://www.edweek.org/ew/issues/accountability/index.html

ZACHARY WRIGHT, a national finalist for the U.S. Department of Education's School Ambassador Fellowship, is an assistant professor of practice at the Relay Graduate School of Education serving Philadelphia and Camden. Prior to that, he was the 12th-grade world literature and AP literature teacher at Mastery Charter School Shoemaker Campus for the last eight years, teaching the school's first eight graduating classes.

Wright, Zachary. "Holding Teachers Accountable Without Adequate Teacher Prep Programs Is a Set-Up." https://educationpost.org/holding-teachers-accountable-without-adequate-teacher-prep-programs-is-a-set-up/. Used by permission of the author.

Charter School Reform
Doublethink and the Assault on the Vulnerable

MORGAN ANDERSON

Learning Outcomes

After reading this article, you will be able to:

- Explain the contours of the "doublethink" that is the relationship between seeking equity in education while promoting market-based reforms.
- Identify the traits of an educational system that is oriented towards the public good.
- Draw conclusions about the kind of threat that charter schools can pose for equitable public education.

The landscape of American society is rapidly changing. The ongoing financial crises following the "Great Recession" of 2008 continue to destabilize faith in bedrock institutions as Americans grow increasingly disillusioned by growing wealth inequality, stagnant wages, unemployment, and "failing schools." Discourse touting the "free market" as the panacea for public ills has seemingly won the day. As Michael Apple has argued, "[t]he attacks on the very idea that something 'public' might actually be valuable have intensified."[1] Additionally, Michael Fabricant and Michelle Fine have shown, "[w]e are witnessing a strategic redefinition of democracy in which the free marketplace of goods and services is not merely a necessary prerequisite, but represented as the highest form of democracy."[2] Because, as William Watkins aptly illustrated, "[p]ublic education exists within, not outside, this context,"[3] public schools are one of the many institutions being questioned by our shifting social order.

The growing intensity of the charter school movement in the United States is reflective of this ideological shift in the American ethos. Supported by a national discourse that public schools are "failing" and "in crisis,"[4] advocates of charter school reform are able to capitalize on common conceptions of public schools by advancing charters as the best viable solution. Referred to openly by charter reformers as "creative destruction" or "churn," "the goal of the corporate school movement is not to improve public education; rather, is to replace public education with a privatized national system of schools competing for scarce dollars, regularly going out of business and allowing profit-seekers to try their hand at making a dollar."[5]

Despite its beginnings as a democratically minded campaign, where charter schools would *support* traditional public schools by creating and sharing "innovative" educational practices[6] the charter school movement has since been co-opted to serve the neoliberal agenda of consumer logic and "school choice." Emphatically embraced by both sides of the political aisle—as demonstrated by the policies of both the Bush and Obama administrations—the dominant logic of the charter school movement relies on the theory that introducing competition into the educational "marketplace" will increase the value of the "product." Recasting parents and students as consumers, so the logic goes, will force charter and traditional public schools alike to compete for customers in their attempts at producing the best possible product (i.e. test scores).

At the outset, however, it is important to address a prevailing tension in the broader critique of charter schools—namely, the problematic dichotomy that is assumed when we divide the landscape into two discrete sectors where "public" is assumed to be necessarily superior to the semi-private sphere that charter schools often exist in.[7] This blurring between the "public" and "private" sectors further complicates the landscape of educational reform. Democratically elected officials, for example, are often involved in the diversion of schools out of public control and into the hands of charter groups or other semi-private organizations. The proposed Opportunity School District in Georgia, which will be put to a vote in the upcoming November 2016 election, is a key example of the ways in which the "public/private" dichotomy—on which so many critiques of charter

Plyler v. Doe (1982)

In the case of *Plyler v. Doe* (1982) the Supreme Court debated the constitutionality of a Texas law that sought to "deny undocumented school-aged children the free public education that the state provided to children who were citizens of the United States or legally admitted aliens."[27] The ruling additionally blocked the Tyler Independent School District from attempting to charge undocumented students a $1,000 fee in order to offset the financial burden of enrolling such students. This case is of particular interest because the ruling extended the Equal Protection Clause under the Fourteenth Amendment to account for undocumented students in our K-12 schools.[28] The court ruled, "[w]hatever savings might be achieved by denying these children an education, they are wholly insubstantial in light of the costs involved to these children, the State, and the Nation."[29] Furthermore, "denying enrollment in public schools to children not legally admitted to the country imposes a lifetime hardship on a discrete class of children not accountable for the disabling status."[30] The court argued that such discrimination "can hardly be considered rational unless it furthers some *substantial goal of the State*."[31] Additionally Justice Brennan added, "[b]y denying these children a basic education, we deny them the ability to live within the structure of our civic institutions, and foreclose any realistic possibility that they will contribute in even the smallest way to the progress of our Nation."[32]

Ultimately, the rationale behind the *Plyler* ruling is less progressive than it may initially appear. The argument put forth by the majority was essentially an economic one; the cost of educating undocumented students is outweighed by the gain in that they go on to "contribute" to society. As Petronicolos and New have argued, the ruling in *Plyler* was largely motivated by the societal goals of "fiscal health and public order."[33] However lamentable it may be that undocumented students' right to a public education was defended on economic rather than ethical or moral grounds, the proceedings clearly illustrated the belief that education as an institution is tied to the collective public interest, and the interests of the State and other civic institutions. Echoing *Brown*, *Plyler* reaffirmed the important role education must play in advancing the public good in a democratic society.

Brown v. Board of Education of Topeka, *Lau v. Nichols*, and *Plyler v. Doe* all serve as touchstone examples of our conception of the role of education in a democratic society. Each ruling upheld the notion that education plays a valuable role as a public good (irrespective of how problematically the public good is sometimes conceived) by expanding access to and enhancing the quality and equality of public education.

While it is clear that there is a longstanding precedent for understanding education as a collective-based public good, recent debates surrounding charter school reform indicate that we are in the midst of shifting social tides. Corporate intrusion into public schools is shifting our understanding of education as a collective-based public good to an individual-based commodity. As Black has argued, "The public's concept of a good education is seemingly devolving toward education as a service or commodity, indistinct from any other service or commodity that the government or private industry might provide."[34] Supported by a powerful discourse that claims school are "failing" and "in crisis," and backed to the tune of millions of dollars through the rise of venture philanthropy,[35] privatized solutions in the form of charter schools are gaining traction. As Watkins has noted, "[t]he triumph of techno-global neoliberalism finds corporations and corporate wealth interjecting themselves into the policymaking process as never before... corporate forces now possess extensive, near monopolistic powers in re-imagining, reforming, and restricting public education."[36] In what follows, I argue that these contradictions are a modern example of doublethink as such corporate solutions continue to alter our conception of the role of education in society while claiming to serve the interests of the public.

Shifting Tides: Doublethink in Educational Policy

I believe that the doublethink which permeates contemporary educational reform is best captured by the conflicting—if not mutually incompatible—ideologies behind the Common Core State Standards and Race to the Top. The CCSS are the most recent iteration of a series of standards-based reforms, which scholars generally agree dates back to the release of *A Nation at Risk*.[37] Reform initiatives such as Goals 2000 and No Child Left Behind have been generally regarded as "piecemeal" and underwhelming in their "effectiveness" at raising results (i.e. test scores). A 1991 article in the *Yearbook of the Politics of Education Association* called instead for a "systems approach that aligned curricular materials, assessments, and professional development to a set of goals (later called standards) that spelled out the knowledge and skills that all students should learn."[38] This shift in thinking, coupled with an ever-increasing concern that Americans consistently trail behind our global competitors, laid the groundwork for what would eventually become the Common Core State Standards.

The CCSS garnered increasing support as the public discourse regarding our "failing schools" and the ever-widening "achievement gap" between poor students of color and their more affluent, White peers gathered momentum.[39] Despite a history of conflicting views regarding government overreach in educational matters, by 2010, the majority of states had adopted the standards.[40] Many scholars attributed the widespread embrace of the national standards to the significant amount of Race to the Top—a $4.35 billion grant—funds that would be available through competitive bids if states agreed to work toward the implementation of the core standards. Race to the Top was designed as a competitive grant, rewarding and "incentivizing" states for successfully "supporting the transition toward implementing the standards."[41] Perhaps more importantly, states were rewarded more Race to the Top funds if they agreed to lift their caps on the number of charters that could operate in their state.[42] However ill-conceived and motivated by corporate ideology (e.g. school success and failure can be measured by test scores; students are not succeeding due to a lack of standardized expectations instead of a lack of equitable resources; the function of school is to prepared students to compete in the global economy, etc.), the CCSS were designed in spirit to promote the collective public good. While I reject whole-heartedly the notion that schools should serve our national economic interests, I do not doubt the sincerity of the crafters and advocates of CCSS when they claim to have *all* students' interests in mind.

What is of interest, however, is the linking of the implementation of CCSS to RTT, which greatly expands possibilities for charter schools and market-based reforms. Predicated on the notion that free-market competition between schools will enhance the quality of education through a system of parent choice, charter school reform embraces a privatized, consumer logic. In a system of free-market competition where schools are left to compete for consumers and enhance quality of their "product," there *necessarily* will be "winners" and "losers." As Black highlights "unequal choices are what allow individuals to identify quality education."[43] In other words, a system of school choice only "works" because parents can (albeit through questionable metrics) identify which schools are "better" and "worse." Differences *are built into* the concept of a school choice model, which directly undercuts the spirit of the Common Core, which purports to create a system of equitable schooling for all students. Here, I believe our doublethink is revealed: We desire a system of equity for all children, while endorsing school choice, which necessarily creates difference. We might also say that we've shifted from a *collective-based* understanding of the public good to an *individualistic*, consumeristic understanding of the public good. As Black illustrates, "[c]ollective-based education is motivated by the fact that educational successes and failures pose serious societal losses and gains, whereas an individual-based education treats those society effects as ancillary to the individual effects."[44] Furthermore, "[a]n individual-based education system conceptualizes education and its role in society far differently. Under the individual concept, education is a commodity—albeit an extremely valuable one—to be consumed by individuals."[45]

The Cost of Cost-cutting: Vulnerable Populations in the Charter Model

It does not take much imagination to consider the potentially hazardous consequences of treating other public services as consumer goods. We would likely scoff at the thought of having to shop for the best firefighters to rescue us from danger, or at the idea that sanitation workers offer communities the "product" of public cleanliness. One might easily anticipate the grizzly effects of a society where firefighters attempted to cut costs and vie for customers. However, despite mounting evidence that charter schools are no more successful than traditional public schools,[46] scholars have observed that Americans increasingly support corporate logic in public schools. According to a 2010 Gallup Poll:

> Americans increasingly embrace public charter schools. Sixty-eight percent of Americans have a favorable opinion of charter schools, and almost two out of three Americans would support a new public charter school in their communities. Sixty percent of Americans say they would support a large increase in the number of public charter schools operating in the United States.[47]

Unfortunately, one doesn't need an imagination to observe the devastating consequences that massive charter takeovers in the name of serving the public good have had on public schools and communities. For example, Kristen Buras has extensively documented the ways in which the "Recovery" School District (RSD) in Louisiana has wreaked havoc on schools and communities, having particularly devastating consequences for African Americans.[48] This is especially alarming as the proposed Opportunity School District in Georgia is explicitly aimed at modeling the "success" of the RSD in Louisiana.[49] Note that what little "success" the RSD has been able to boast has been the result of outright manipulation of both test scores and cut-offs for which schools count as "failing" in order to justify chartering them—which should raise grave suspicion regarding the intentions of similar takeovers.[50]

This ideological shift from understanding education as a collective-based public good toward an individual-based educational system that treats education as a commodity, rather than a public service, has had an array of consequences. While the prevailing logic of market-based schools reforms is to improve the quality of the "product," mounting evidence suggests quite the contrary. As the paradigm of education shifts to a business model, quality is forsaken as the goal becomes to cut costs and attract consumers. As Saltman has argued:

> Such cost-cutting has historically included displacing and underpaying local experienced teachers; hiring

inexperienced teachers and burning them out while their salaries are low; using inexpensive, inexperienced, Teach for America teachers and uncertified teachers, and relying on alternative certification; union-busting; manipulating test scores; importing cheap teachers from overseas; counseling or pushing out special-needs students and English Language Learners to raise test scores; and contracting the running of schools to for-profit management companies.[51]

While the goal of a public institution is to utilize public monies to advance the interests of the public good, the goal of a business is to maximize profit. When schools are conceived of as businesses, what were once institutions aimed at promoting the lives of individuals in a democratic society—ideals reflected in some of the most monumental Supreme Court rulings of the past century—become a means for generating revenue for an elite few. Populations of students, who have been historically viewed as more "difficult" to educate, are viewed as more "costly" in the charter model. Cultural and linguistic minorities, special education students, and low-income students are all a threat to profit when the aim of education is to attract more "consumers" by bolstering a valuable "product." Research has confirmed that the effects of school choice have negatively impacted these groups. Additionally, these results actively contradict many of the precedents set by cases such as *Brown v. Board*, *Lau v. Nichols*, and *Plyler v. Doe*.

While some charters exist to capitalize off of resource-starved communities in the urban cores, and others serve as havens of "White flight," studies have shown that school choice has resulted in increased racial segregation. Frankenberg and Lee have found that:

> 70% of all black charter school students attend intensely segregated minority schools compared with 34% of black public school students. In almost every state studied, the average black charter school student attends school with a higher percentage of black students and a lower percentage of white students.[52]

Furthermore:

> Because of the disproportionately high enrollment of minority students in charter schools, white charter school students go to school, on average, with more nonwhite students than whites in non-charter public schools. However, there are pockets of white segregation where white charter school students are as isolated as black charter school students.[53]

In Kristen Buras' study of the impacts of charter schools in New Orleans she concluded that, "[r]ather than universally respecting students' right to learn, charter schools focus on cost containment in special education and may fail to adequately serve or exclude students based on such concerns."[54] The *Guide* published by the Recovery School District (RSD) encourages other cities that wish to adopt the RSD model to consider some of the following when implementing special education programs:

1. Allow charters to develop specialized programs for certain disabilities so that parents have choices that include programs tailored to their children's needs, and so that economies of scale can be captured in program delivery; and
2. Create risk pools that individual schools can participate in to cover the potential costs of serving students with high needs.[55]

As Buras aptly points out, "terminology such as 'economies of scale' and 'risk pools' does not sit well with special education advocates, those who respect federal law, or those who are concerned that inclusion will be supplanted in favor of some form of segregation of children with disabilities."[56] Additionally, the language above indicates that students with disabilities are being viewed opportunistically as *markets*. By encouraging charter schools to tailor specialized programs that can reach economies of scale, we run the risk of students being marketed to based on their disabilities, and consequently, violating the mandate for the least restrictive environment.

Lastly, there is ample evidence that suggests English Language Learners are being negatively influenced by school choice. As Buckley and Bajaj have found in their study of New York City schools, ELL students are less likely to attend charter schools. Their research reveals that even in the areas of the city most densely populated by ELL students—Harlem and the South Bronx—these students are far less likely to be represented in charter schools when compared to local public schools.[57] This is unsurprising when we consider the barriers that recently-arrived students and their families must face if they hope to navigate a complex system of school choice. The barriers created by the challenge of navigating school choice in English contributes to undermining advances made via the *Lau v. Nichols* ruling—which legislated that students for whom English is a second language receive a fair and appropriate public education—is characteristic of the charter school movement. Navigating a system of school choice necessarily creates a barrier for ELL students and their families. Furthermore, it is likely that charter schools will elect to selectively advertise as to avoid attracting populations such as ELLs. As Monica de Sousa has pointed out, Texas is the only state with a statute that demands that charter schools advertise to the public at all.[58] This lends itself to enrollment patterns that are highly self-selected as charter information is passed along through word of mouth, potentially through elite parent networks. As research has reflected, treating schools like businesses not only undermines the public school as an institution dedicated to advancing the interests of the public good, but systematically oppresses our most vulnerable children.

Buyer Beware

The charter school model continues to destabilize one of our most sacred public institutions. Battles that have long since been fought and won are now resurfacing in our era of doublethink. Cast as the next social justice frontier, charter schools have undermined many of the actual gains in equality and civil rights over the last century. Despite outcry from some parents and scholars, charter schools continue to appear all over the country. Atlanta's plans for the Opportunity School District, which will go to the ballot in November of 2016, modeled off the RSD in New Orleans, despite damning evidence of its failure.[59]

The stakes are high and the outlook is bleak. Despite lip-service paid to democratic ideals of equity and societal advancement, the charter school movement is contributing to heightened rates of racial re-segregation, and casting ELLs and special education students aside in attempts to maximize profit and cut costs. All of our children are under siege as for-profit charters seek to capitalize on the educational "market." We must turn the mirror back on ourselves and reexamine our public values if we are to create a society truly committed to an education system that advances the interests of all of its citizens. If not, I'm afraid we will get the schools we deserve.

Notes

1. Michael W. Apple, *Educating the "Right" Way: Markets, Standards, God, and Inequality* (New York: Routledge, 2006), xiv.
2. Michael Fabricant and Michelle Fine, *Charter Schools and the Corporate Makeover of Public Education: What's at Stake?* (New York: Teachers College Press, 2012), ix.
3. William H. Watkins Ed., *The Assault on Public Education: Confronting the Politics of Corporate School Reform* (New York: Teachers College Press, 2004), 2.
4. This rhetoric has especially gained momentum since the publication of *A Nation at Risk*. See *A Nation at Risk: The Imperative for Educational Reform, National Commission on Excellence in Education* (April 1983).
5. Kenneth J. Saltman, *The Failure of Corporate School Reform* (Boulder, CO: Paradigm Publishers, 2012), 10.
6. See, for example, the discussion regarding Albert Shanker and the AFT in Janelle T. Scott and Catherine C. DiMartino, "Hybridized, Franchised, Duplicated, and Replicated: Charter Schools and Management Organizations," in Christopher A. Lubienksi and Peter C. Weitzel Eds., *The Charter School Experiment: Expectations, Evidence, and Implications* (Cambridge, MA: Harvard University Press, 2010), 175.
7. I too must continually reflect on the ways that my critique of charter takeovers relies on a false dichotomy between "public" and "private." I do, however, believe that these terms are still useful for painting a broader picture of the trends in educational reform, but it is important to continue to underscore the ways that this distinction can be misleading.
8. See "Georgia's Proposed Opportunity School District—Overview," The Office of the Governor https://gov.georgia.gov/sites/gov.georgia.gov/files/related_files/site_page/GA%20OSD%20Overview%20051816.pdf
9. Ty Tagami, "Georgia PTA Slams State Over New Wording for Constitutional Amendment," *Atlanta Journal Constitution*, August 26, 2016 http://www.myajc.com/news/news/local-education/georgia-pta-slams-state-over-new-wording-for-const/nsMj6/.
10. Jurgen Habermas took this distinction even further, for example, by claiming that "the public," as a site of political discourse over the conception of the public good as conceptually distinct from "the state," both of which are distinct from market relations. See Jurgen Habermas, *The Structural Transformation of the Public Sphere: An Inquiry into a Category of Bourgeois Society*, trans. Thomas Burger and Frederick Lawrence (Cambridge, MIT Press, 1989). Nancy Fraser reminds us that "the public sphere" has been a contested concept among feminist philosophers as some have understood "the public" as anything that takes place outside the home or familial sphere. See Nancy Fraser, "Rethinking the Public Sphere: A Contribution to the Critique of Actually Existing Democracy" in *Justice Interruptus: Critical Reflections on the 'Postsocialist' Condition* (New York: Routledge, 1997), 69-98.
11. Thomas Pedroni uses this phrase to explain alliances between working-class African Americans and elite policy networks in support of voucher programs. See Thomas Pedroni, *Market Movements: African American Involvement in School Voucher Reform* (New York: Routledge, 2007).
12. See Michael Apple, *Educating the Right Way: Markets, Standards, God, and Inequality*, 2nd. Ed. (New York: Routledge, 2006), 29-49.
13. See Margaret E. Raymond, "To No Avail: A Critical Look at the Charter School Debate," *The Phi Delta Kappan*, vol. 95, no. 5 (February 2014), 9.
14. "Common Core State Standards Initiative: Preparing America's Students for College and Career." The Council of Chief State School Officers. 2014. http://www.corestandards.org/about-the-standards/ accessed 6/14/15, my emphasis added.
15. George Orwell, *1984* (London, UK: Martin Secker & Warburg Ltd, 1949).
16. Milton Friedman, *Capitalism and Freedom* (Chicago, IL: University of Chicago Press, 1962), 89-91.

17. See, for example, Sonya Douglass Horsford, *Learning in a Burning House: Educational Inequality, Ideology, and (Dis)Integration* (New York: Teachers College Press, 2011). Horsford carefully illustrates the ways in which Brown was harmful to the Black communities and the Black working class.
18. See Gloria Ladson-Billings, "From the Achievement Gap to the Education Debt: Understanding Achievement in U.S. Schools, "*Educational Researcher,* vol. 35, no. 7 (October 2006): 3-12 for her treatment of the "educational debt" as opposed to the "achievement gap."
19. Horsford, 23.
20. Martha Minow, "After Brown: What Would Martin Luther King Say?" *Lewis & Clark Law Review,* vol. 12, no. 1 (2008), 604.
21. Derek W. Black, "Charter Schools, Vouchers, and the Public Good," *Wake Forest Law Review,* vol. 48, no. 1 (April 2013), 456.
22. L. Ling-Chi Wang, "Lau v. Nichols: History of Struggle for Equal and Quality Education," *Asian American Bilingual Newsletter,* vol. 1, no. 1 (October 1975), 3.
23. Ibid., 2.
24. Ibid.
25. Ibid., 6.
26. Ibid., 7.
27. Loucas Petronicolos and William S. New, "Anti-Immigration Legislation, Social Justice, and the Right to Equal Educational Opportunity," *American Educational Research Journal,* vol. 36, no. 3 (Autumn 1999), 379.
28. Ibid.
29. Ibid, 380.
30. Ibid.
31. Ibid., 381, emphasis added.
32. Ibid.
33. Ibid.
34. Black, 446.
35. See, for example, Kenneth Saltman, "The Rise of Venture Philanthropy and the Ongoing Neoliberal Assault on Public Education: The Eli and Edythe Broad Foundation," in William H. Watkins Ed., *The Assault on Public Education: Confronting the Politics of Corporate School Reform* (New York: Teachers College Press, 2004): 55-78.
36. William H. Watkins, "The New Social Order: An Educator Looks at Economics, Politics, and Race" in William H. Watkins Ed., *The Assault on Public Education: Confronting the Politics of Corporate School Reform* (New York: Teachers College Press, 2004), 25.
37. For more historical context on the standards movement and other policies which are regarded as part of standards project (Goals 2000, No Child Left Behind) see Mark Lavenia, Lora Cohen-Vogel, and Laura B. Lang, "The Common Core State Standards Initiative: An Event History Analysis of State Adoption," *American Journal of Education,* vol. 121, no. 2 (February 2015): 145-182.
38. Ibid., 146.
39. See Gloria Ladson-Billings, "From the Achievement Gap to the Education Debt: Understanding Achievement in U.S. Schools," *Educational Researcher,* vol. 35, no. 7 (October 2006): 3-12 for her notion of the "educational debt" as opposed to the "achievement gap."
40. Ibid., 149.
41. Ibid., 150.
42. Fabricant and Fine, 10.
43. Black, 462.
44. Derek W. Black, "Charter Schools, Vouchers, and the Public Good," *Wake Forest Law Review,* vol. 48, no. 1 (April 2013), 452.
45. Ibid.
46. Kenneth Saltman, *The Failure of Corporate School Reform,* 8.
47. Fine and Fabricant, 3.
48. See Kristen L. Buras, *Charter Schools, Race, and Urban Space: Where the Market Meets Grassroots Resistance* (New York: Routledge, 2015).
49. See "Georgia's Proposed Opportunity School District – Overview," The Office of the Governor https://gov.georgia.gov/sites/gov.georgia.gov/files/related_files/site_page/GA%20OSD%20Overview%20051816.pdf
50. See Buras' discussion of Act 35, passed in the Louisiana General Assembly in November 2005 in Kristen Buras, "It's All About the Dollars: Charter Schools, Educational Policy, and the Racial Market in New Orleans" in William H. Watkins Ed., *The Assault on Public Education: Confronting the Politics of Corporate School Reform* (New York: Teachers College Press, 2004), 160-188.
51. Kenneth Saltman, *The Failure of Corporate School Reform,* 7.
52. Erica Frankenberg and Chungmei Lee, "Charter Schools and Race: A Lost Opportunity for Integrated Education," *Education Policy Analysis Archives,* vol. 11, no. 32 (July 2003), 7.
53. Ibid.
54. Kristen L. Buras, *Charter Schools, Race, and Urban Space: Where the Market Meets Grassroots Resistance* (New York: Routledge, 2015), 175.
55. Ibid., 179.
56. Ibid., 180.
57. Jack Buckley and Carolyn Sattin-Bajaj, "Are ELL Students Underrepresented in Charter Schools? Demographic Trends in New York City, 2006-2008," *Journal of School Choice,* vol. 5 (January 2011): 40-65.
58. Monica Teixeira de Sousa, "Compelling Honesty: Amending Charter School Enrollment Laws to Aid Society's Most Vulnerable," *American Bar Association, Fall Council Meeting and Educational Law Symposium* (October 2012), 8.

59. See, for example, Kristen L. Buras, *Charter Schools, Race, and Urban Space: Where the Market Meets Grassroots Resistance* (New York: Routledge, 2015). Additionally, a recent article in the *Atlanta Journal Constitution* entitled "Ga. Challenge: Make Charter Schools Work" listed 18 failing charter schools. Despite such mass failure, Georgia policymakers remain confident that they can make the charter model successful.

Critical Thinking

1. What are some ways in which charter schools have failed to live up to their original intent?
2. Compare the three Supreme Court cases that the article discusses in terms of their distinct contribution to establishing societal norms related to educational equality.
3. In what ways are charter schools that are established by market-based reforms capable of promoting an individualistic approach that treats education like a commodity?

Internet References

About Charter Schools
https://www.publiccharters.org/about-charter-schools

The Costs of Misusing Test-Based Accountability in Schools
https://www.brookings.edu/blog/brown-center-chalkboard/2017/10/10/the-costs-of-misusing-test-based-accountability-in-schools/

The False Markets of Market-Based School Reform
https://www.washingtonpost.com/news/answer-sheet/wp/2014/03/05/the-false-markets-of-market-based-school-reform/?noredirect=on&utm_term=.d047ca125d5d

Anderson, Morgan. "Charter School Reform: Doublethink and the Assault on the Vulnerable." Journal of Thought 50, no. 3–4 (2016): 33–48. Used by permission of Caddo Gap Press.

Article

Prepared by: Sheron Fraser-Burgess, *Ball State University*

Pedagogy against the Dead Zones of the Imagination

Henry A. Giroux

Learning Outcomes

After reading this article, you will be able to:

- Summarize the pedagogical ideals inherent in the goals of democratic education.
- Relate critical pedagogy to developing students' critical literacy and being civic-minded.
- Ponder the reasons that democracy, in this political moment, may be on the ropes and in need of rescuing.

The reach of pedagogy extends from schools to diverse cultural apparatuses such as the mainstream media, alternative screen cultures, and the Internet. Far more than a teaching method, pedagogy is a moral and political practice actively involved not only in the production of knowledge, skills, and values but also in the construction of identities, modes of identification, and forms of individual and social agency. Accordingly, pedagogy is at the heart of any understanding of politics. Across the globe, the forces of free-market fundamentalism are waging an assault on higher education by substituting the culture of democratic schooling with the culture of business. This assault is part of a larger attack that includes dismantling historically guaranteed social provisions provided by the welfare state, public schools, unions, women's reproductive rights, and civil liberties, among others, all the while undercutting public faith in the defining institutions of democracy.[1] Recognizing that this conflict is not only about reworking the commanding structures of the economy but is also intellectual and pedagogical in nature, the apostles of neoliberalism are using schools, think tanks, foundations, and the mainstream media to produce subjectivities, identities, and values that mimic market-driven values and social relations.

As market mentalities and moralities tighten their grip on all aspects of society, democratic institutions and public spheres are being downsized, if not altogether disappearing. As these institutions vanish—from public schools to healthcare centers—the discourses of community, justice, equality, public values, and the common good are being seriously eroded. One consequence is the emergence of what the late Tony Judt called an "eviscerated society"—"one that is stripped of the thick mesh of mutual obligations and social responsibilities to be found in" any viable democracy (qtd. in Eagleton 78). This grim reality has been called a "failed sociality"—a failure in the power of the civic imagination, political will, and open democracy (Honneth 188). It is also part of a politics that strips the social relations of any democratic ideals and undermines any understanding of education as a public good and pedagogy as an *empowering* practice, a practice that acts directly upon conditions that bear down on our lives in order to change them when necessary.

One challenge facing the current generation of educators and students is the need to reclaim the role that education has historically played in developing critical literacies and civic capacities. We must address education's role in encouraging students to be critically engaged agents, attentive to addressing important social issues and being alert to the responsibility of deepening and expanding the meaning and practices of a vibrant democracy. At the heart of such a challenge is the question, "What should education accomplish in a democracy?" What work do educators have to do to create the economic, political,

---

[1] See, for example, Harvey, *New Imperialism* and *A Brief History*; Brown; Giroux, *Against the Terror*; and Steger and Roy.

and ethical conditions necessary to endow young people with the capacities to think, question, doubt, imagine the unimaginable, and defend education as essential for inspiring and energizing the citizens necessary for a robust democracy? In a world in which egalitarian and democratic impulses are increasingly abandoned, what will it take to educate young people to challenge authority and hold power accountable? What role might education and critical pedagogy have in a society in which the social has been individualized, emotional life collapses into the therapeutic, and education is reduced to either a private affair or a kind of algorithmic mode of regulation in which everything is reduced to a desired outcome (Morozov)? In a culture drowning in a relentless love affair with instrumental rationality, that which is not measurable—compassion, vision, the imagination, care for the other, and a passion for justice—withers.

We should develop forms of critical pedagogy that not only inspire and energize but also challenge the growing number of antidemocratic practices and policies under the tyranny of casino capitalism. They must resurrect a radical democratic project that provides the basis for imagining a life beyond a social order that is immersed in inequality, assaults the environment, and elevates war and militarization to national ideals. Critical pedagogy rejects the notion that higher education is simply a site for training students for the workforce and that the culture of higher education is synonymous with the culture of business. Educators must recognize the power of education to create the formative cultures necessary to both challenge the various threats being mobilized against the ideas of justice and democracy. Educators must also fight for alternative modes of identity, thinking, social relations, and a politics that deepens and expands democratic ideals and practices.

As *Transformations* has been making clear for twenty-five years, pedagogy is a moral and political practice that is always implicated in power relations because it offers particular versions and visions of civic life, community, the future. It asks how we might construct representations of ourselves, others, and our physical and social environments. Any discussion of pedagogy must begin with a discussion of educational practice as a particular way in which a sense of identity, place, worth, and, above all, value is informed by practices that organize knowledge and meaning and further contribute to expanding formative culture capable of sustaining a vibrant democracy (Giroux, *Education* 10). Critical pedagogy emphasizes critical reflection and bridges the gap between learning and everyday life. It understands the connection between power and difficult knowledge, and extends democratic rights by using the resources of history and theory. Critical pedagogy takes place not only in schools but is also part of what I have elsewhere called diverse forms of public pedagogy. To analyze and engage public pedagogy we must ask fundamental questions about the educative nature of the culture, what it means to engage common sense as a way to shape and influence popular opinion, and how diverse educational practices in multiple sites can challenge the vocabularies, practices, and values of the oppressive forces that are at work under neoliberal power structures.

Pedagogy is central to politics itself because it is about changing the way people see things and recognizes that politics is educative. As the late Pierre Bourdieu reminded us, "the most important forms of domination are not only economic but also intellectual and pedagogical, and lie on the side of belief and persuasion" (Bordieu and Grass 2). Pedagogies that are largely disciplinary and have little regard for contexts, history, making knowledge meaningful, or expanding what it means for students to be critically engaged agents all too easily become a form of symbolic and intellectual violence that assaults rather than educates. One can see this in forms of high-stakes testing and empirically driven teaching, which numb the mind and produce what might be called "dead zones of the imagination." This is also evident in a celebrity culture, which, in the age of Trump, drives the mainstream media.

Early in the twenty-first century, notions of the social and the public are being reconstructed while public forums for serious debate, including public education, are being eroded. Reduced either to a crude instrumentalism, business culture, or defined as a purely private right rather than a public good, teaching and learning are removed from the discourses of democracy and civic culture. Under the influence of powerful financial interests, we have witnessed the takeover of public education, and increasingly of higher education by corporate logic and pedagogy that promotes winning at all costs and teaches students how to be good consumers. Consequently students do not learn how to question authority, how to be thoughtful, critical, or attentive to the power relations that shape everyday life and the larger world.

What role might educators play as public intellectuals in light of poisonous assaults waged on public schools by the forces of neoliberalism? We can bring all of our intellectual and collective resources together to critique and dismantle the imposition of high-stakes testing and other commercially driven modes of accountability on schools. We can speak out against modes of governance that have reduced faculty to the status of part-time Walmart employees, and we can take back the governing of universities from administrators that now outnumber faculty, at least in the United States. We can mobilize young people and others to defend education as a public good by advocating for policies that invest in schools rather than in the military-industrial complex and its massive and expensive weapons of death.

One of the most serious challenges facing teachers, artists, journalists, writers, and other cultural workers is the task of developing a discourse of both critique and possibility. This means developing pedagogical practices that connect reading the word with reading the world, and doing so in ways that enhance the capacities of young people as critical agents and engaged citizens. In taking up this project, educators and others should attempt to create the conditions that allow students to become critical and engaged citizens who have the knowledge and courage to struggle in order to make desolation and cynicism unconvincing and hope practical.

Democracy should be a way of thinking about education, one that thrives on connecting equity to excellence, learning to ethics, and agency to the imperatives of social responsibility and the public good. The question regarding what role education should play in democracy becomes all the more urgent at a time when the forces of authoritarianism are on the march in the United States. As public values, trust, solidarities, and modes of education are under siege, the discourses of hate, racism, rabid self-interest, and greed are exercising a poisonous influence in American society, most evident in the discourse of the right-wing extremists vying for the US presidency.

Democracy is on life support, but rather than this being a rationale for cynicism, this situation should create moral and political outrage, a new understanding of politics, and the educational and social formations needed to allow American democracy to breathe once again. *Transformations* has taken a leading role in this project and offers a model of scholarship that inspires, energizes, and offers hope for producing a new era of civic imagination, a renewed sense of social agency, and an impassioned political will.

References

Bourdieu, Pierre, and Gunter Grass. "The 'Progressive' Restoration: A Franco-German Dialogue." *New Left Review* 14 (2002): 62–77. Print.

Brown, Wendy. *Edgework*. Princeton: Princeton UP, 2005. Print.

Eagleton, Terry. "Reappraisals: What Is the Worth of Social Democracy?" *Harper's Magazine* (2010): 78. Print.

Giroux, Henry A. *Against the Terror of Neoliberalism*. Boulder: Paradigm, 2008. Print. ———. *Education and the Crisis of Public Values*. 2nd ed. New York: Peter Lang, 2015. Print.

Harvey, David. *A Brief History of Neoliberalism*. Oxford: Oxford UP, 2005. Print. ———. *The New Imperialism*. New York: Oxford UP, 2003. Print.

Honneth, Alex. *Pathologies of Reason*. New York: Columbia UP, 2009. Print.

Morozov, Evgeny. "The Rise of Data and the Death of Politics." *The Guardian*. 20 July 2014. Web.

Olson, Gary, and Lynn Worsham. "Staging the Politics of Difference: Homi Bhabha's Critical Literacy." *Journal of Advanced Composition* 18 (1998): 361–391. Print.

Steger, Manfred B., and Ravi K. Roy. *Neoliberalism: A Very Short Introduction*. Oxford: Oxford UP, 2010. Print.

Critical Thinking

1. What does it mean to be critical literate in education today?
2. From what conditions does the author believe that schools need rescuing?

Internet References

Resisting Trump's Gilded Age: Making the Political More Pedagogical
https://wildculture.com/article/resisting-trumps-gilded-age-making-political-more-pedagogical/1607

Vision Song—the Children Ask, "Are We Worth Saving?
https://medium.com/@suzannecloud/vision-song-the-children-ask-are-we-worth-saving-3364c21b6b7e

---

Henry A. Giroux currently holds the McMaster University Chair for Scholarship in the Public Interest in the English and Cultural Studies Department and a Distinguished Visiting Professorship at Ryerson University. His most recent books are *The Violence of Organized Forgetting* (City Lights, 2014), *Dangerous Thinking in the Age of the New Authoritarianism* (Routledge, 2015), and, coauthored with Brad Evans, *Disposable Futures: The Seduction of Violence in the Age of Spectacle* (City Lights, 2015). His newest book is *America at War with Itself* (City Lights, 2016). His website is www.henryagiroux.com.

Giroux, Henry A., "Pedagogy against the Dead Zones of the Imagination." Transformations: The Journal of Inclusive Scholarship and Pedagogy, vol. 26 no 1, 2016, pp 26-30. Project MUSE. Used by permission.

Article

Prepared by: Sheron Fraser-Burgess, *Ball State University*

The Myth of Accountability: How Data (Mis)Use Is Reinforcing the Problems of Public Education

CLAIRE FONTAINE

Learning Outcomes

After reading this article, you will be able to:

- Relate the accountability movement in education to free market economics.
- Link data collection to the focus on standards in the accountability movement.

Introduction

There is an ongoing tension in the American public education system between the values of excellence, equity, and efficiency. Accountability has emerged as a framework in education reform that promises to promote and balance all three values. Yet this frame is often contested due to disagreements over the role of incentives and penalties in achieving desirable change, and concerns that the proposed mechanisms will have significant unintended consequences that outweigh potential benefits. More fundamentally, there is widespread disagreement over how to quantify excellence and equity, if it is even possible to do so. Accountability rhetoric echoes a broader turn toward data-driven decision-making and resource allocation across sectors. As a tool of power, accountability processes shift authority and control to policymakers, bureaucrats, and test makers over professional educators.

Today, measurements of school performance have become so commonplace that they are an assumed part of education debates. As new forms of data are easier to collect and analyze, drawing on and interacting with information to measure the impact of programs and to inform decision-making and policy has emerged as a key strategy to foster improvement in public schools (Coburn and Turner 2012). But when did our national obsession with educational data start? What are the historic precursors to accountability as we now know it? What set of political, economic, cultural, and social conditions led to test scores becoming the main measure of a school's success? How do current data-driven practices compare to historical data-driven practices and how have the terms shifted over time? Who does accountability serve? What are the incentive structures, and how is accountability gamed and resisted? In short, accountability of what, to whom, for what ends, at what cost?

The accountability movement reflects the application of free market economics to public education, a legacy of the Chicago School of Economics in the post-World War II era (Spring 2015). As a set of policies, accountability was instantiated in the Elementary and Secondary Education Act (ESEA) of 1965, reauthorized as the No Child Left Behind Act (NCLB) of 2002, and reinforced by the Every Student Succeeds Act (ESSA) of 2015. ESSA gives more autonomy and flexibility to states than they had under NCLB through competency-based assessments, which could drive the development of personalized learning technologies. ESSA's accountability processes also require new types of data collection and disaggregation, including of non-academic indicators of school quality. Significantly, ESSA mandates the collection and reporting of per pupil expenditure data at the school level. Teaching and learning are increasingly being measured and quantified to enable analysis of the relationship between inputs (e.g., funding) and outputs (e.g., student performance) with the goal of maximizing economic growth and productivity and increasing human capital.

The accountability movement is built on a long history of standardized testing and data collection that privileges quantification and statistical analysis as ways of knowing. An underlying assumption is that learning can be measured and is an effect of instruction. This is an empiricist perspective descended from John Locke and the doctrine that knowledge derives primarily from experience. Accountability in education also holds that schools are fundamentally responsible for student performance, as opposed to families, neighborhoods, communities, or society at large. This premise lacks a solid evidentiary basis, as research shows that student performance is more closely linked to socioeconomic status (Coleman 1966; Sirin 2005). Finally, efforts to achieve accountability presume that market-based solutions can effectively protect the interests of society's most vulnerable.

As has been true in other sectors when data-driven surveillance and assessment practices are introduced, outcomes may not be as expected. It is unclear whether this data push will promote equality of opportunity, merely document inequality, or perhaps even increase racial and socioeconomic segregation, as Pauline Lipman (2011) has argued in her work on neoliberal educational reform in Chicago. Furthermore, little is understood about the costs of increased assessment on the health and success of students and teachers, externalities that are rarely measured or considered in the march to accountability. States will need to generate stakeholder buy-in and think carefully about the metrics they include in their accountability formulas in order to balance mandates for accountability, the benefits that accrue to students from preserving teacher autonomy and professionalism, the social good of equal opportunity, and public calls for transparency and innovation.

In order to ground conversations about the use of data analytics in education, this paper examines what accountability allows us to see and what it obscures from our vision. As accountability has become a mainstay of public education, we must also consider how accountability instruments and related education reform platforms are themselves assessed and held accountable. Education reform and the battles over accountability are increasingly intersecting with new technologies, which are imagined to create new forms of accountability with little consideration for the longstanding history of current trends. Taking a step back is necessary to successfully move forward.

Excellence, Equity, and Efficiency

Schools are an institution where political agendas play out and power struggles unfold. In the public and political imagination, schools matter because they produce the citizens, leaders, and workers of the future. As both the population basis and the economic organization of our society change, so too do the requirements for productive citizenry, and schools are on the front lines of adapting to these challenges (Kliebard 2004, Tyack 1974). In the early days of the republic, United States schools were embedded in communities and were responsive to the particular needs of these communities. Schools aimed to solidify the social order and were seen as instruments of "deliberate social purpose" (Bailyn 1960, 22). As Alexis de Tocqueville noted in 1835, "in the United States politics are the end and aim of education," in contrast with Europe where "its principal object is to fit men for private life" (1945). As a representative democracy, the United States needed educational institutions to equip citizens with the intellectual tools and civic knowledge necessary for self-governance.

By the beginning of the nineteenth century, population expansion caused by immigration created new demands on schools to assimilate recent arrivals into American society and, in effect, white Anglo-Saxon culture. Comprehensive systems of public education were needed, and Boston created the first one in 1789 (Schultz 1973). Wealthy members of the merchant class in many urban centers built monitorial schools in which advanced students, known as monitors, taught less advanced ones. With up to five hundred poor and immigrant students assigned to each teacher, these schools were an early embodiment of the principle of efficiency, and were optimized for visual surveillance, rote learning, the management of bodies, and social control (Upton 1996). The organization of space, with tight seating arrangements and tables organized to face the teacher, reflected notions of the ideal docile citizen, a theory of knowledge as structured, orderly and fact-driven, and a scalable transmission theory of learning and pedagogy.

The efficiency mandate intensified as immigration continued to increase through the late nineteenth and early twentieth century alongside the rise of industrial capitalism, and compulsory education and anti-child labor laws effectively legislated state school systems into existence (Kessner 1977). Control over schools became more centralized and principles of scientific management were adopted from the industrial sector (Brumberg 1986). Comprehensive schools were built, a largely female teaching force was hired, schools of teacher education were founded, and managerial systems were devised to handle the broadened scope of work now under schools' purview (Rousmaniere 1997). Many populations were systematically excluded from public education in this era, either through legal or de facto segregation, including the disabled, African Americans, Chinese Americans, and Mexican Americans, while other groups, notably Native Americans, were forcibly removed from their communities and educated in boarding schools.

By the mid-twentieth cetnry, the priorities of equity, fairness, and nondiscrimination had become more salient, exemplified by the 1954 Supreme Court decision in *Brown v. Board of Education*, which famously declared state laws establishing separate schools for black and white students unconstitutional. The Civil Rights Act of 1964 further encouraged the desegregation of schools to prevent race-based discrimination and school systems increasingly came under community control (Podair 2002). In 1965, the Elementary and Secondary Education Act (ESEA) was passed as part of Johnson's War on Poverty, granting states federal funds for compensatory education to close achievement gaps. Title I, which distributes funds to schools and school districts with a high percentage of students from low-income families, is one provision of ESEA. ESEA placed an evaluation requirement on local agencies to report on the progress of their federally funded programs, but there was no explicit threat of funding removal if program goals were not met. Evaluation is concerned with effectiveness, while accountability is concerned with effectiveness and efficiency and depends on the existence of rewards and punishments (Richburg 1971). Without such a "stick," ESEA's evaluation requirement was not an accountability measure but rather an accounting procedure (Dyer 1971), and yet it foreshadowed the accountability movement by establishing precedent for an expanded federal role in education.

Meanwhile, rising anxieties about global competitiveness in the Cold War era led to the re-emergence of excellence as a central value. Notions of human capital had become embedded in educational research as economic thinking emanated from the Chicago School of Economics, and public schools were framed as a means of increasing the productivity of the individual and the nation-state (Spring 2015). Internationally comparative tests seemed to indicate that American students were falling behind their counterparts abroad. Published in 1983, the watershed report *A Nation at Risk* ominously predicted that "The educational foundations of our society are presently being eroded by a rising tide of mediocrity that threatens our very future as a Nation and a people." The perceived threat of a loss of global competitiveness justified an education reform project of standards-based assessment aimed at improving student performance.

The accountability movement brilliantly tapped into the tension between equity and excellence and seemed capable of addressing both goals at once. Leon Lessinger, future U.S. Associate Commissioner for Elementary and Secondary Education, argued that schools in a democratic society should be responsive to the public but that decision-making power should rest with professionally trained experts (Spring 2014). He believed that community control should give way to expert control, and he proposed the establishment of a national education accounting firm empowered to measure school performance through achievement tests and to report the results to the public (Lessinger 1970). *A Nation at Risk* put education on the federal agenda, but the reforms themselves were undertaken voluntarily and by states. George H. W. Bush and Clinton assembled teams of governors to work on these issues throughout the 1980s and 1990s, building buy-in and creating infrastructure within states dedicated to measuring and enhancing student performance (Ravitch 2010).

The 2000s saw significant education reform rooted in evaluation, standards, and a dramatically expanded federal role. No Child Left Behind (NCLB), a key piece of legislation passed during the first term of the George W. Bush presidency, moved the standards movement onto the national stage and fundamentally altered the relationship between states and the federal government. It passed Congress with broad bipartisan support in 2001 and was signed into law in January 2002. NCLB mandated regular standardized testing of students and funding reductions for schools whose students failed to meet established goals. It required schools to demonstrate adequate yearly progress (AYP) or face financial consequences, state takeover, or even school closure. In particular, schools were required to show improvement across various demographic groups, particularly among historically underperforming groups.

Many of the drawbacks of high stakes testing emerged in the wake of NCLB, highlighting the unintended consequences of heavy reliance on student test scores. The pressures of testing culture led to cheating by states, school leaders, and teachers. States could engineer higher passing rates by lowering the passing mark or making the test content easier (Kamenetz 2015). Principals of small schools and charter schools in school choice markets could game the system by restricting the admission of low-performing students, by requiring an interview with parents of applicants or limiting acceptance rates of English language learners (ELLs). But the most common and widespread strategy for gaming the system remains test-prep pedagogy. When schools, particularly low-performing schools, concentrate attention on the subjects and grade levels with high stakes tests, less time remains for the arts, citizenship, and critical thinking, which may lead to teacher burnout and student boredom.

Testing experts agree that tests have their limitations, and even testing companies like Harcourt Brace and Riverside Press have publicly stated that important decisions shouldn't be made solely on the basis of a single test score (FairTest 2007). Tests may contain embedded bias and may create disproportionate pressures for members of minority groups (Santelices and Wilson 2010). Furthermore, high stakes tests are more extrinsically than intrinsically motivating, which may negatively impact students' experience of school, as intrinsic motivation is predictive of healthy development and general well being (La Guardia 2009). Broad frustration with high stakes testing, the Common Core, and the expanded federal role in education exemplified by No Child Left Behind (NCLB) led to a policy correction in the form of the Every Student Succeeds Act (ESSA), which replaced NCLB in December 2015. ESSA scales back the federal role in elementary and secondary education and calls on states to incorporate factors other than standardized test scores into their accountability systems.

Deconstructing Accountability

Accountability is wrapped up in a set of values, commitments, theories, and power stakes that are worth unpacking. Doing so can help us better understand the cultural work of accountability, and how and why the education reform project of which it is a part may increase inequality while purporting to address it. Accountability reflects a longstanding cultural bias toward quantification. It imagines learning as measurable and as an instructional outcome. It asserts that schools are principally responsible for student performance and that school-based interventions can effectively remedy deep social inequalities. It thus obscures broader political economic and social forces that impact upon students' educational experiences and trajectories. Lastly, accountability figures data distribution and the market as viable means of equalizing opportunity.

Accountability has been able to take such firm root in part because standardized testing and data collection have an extensive history in American public education. For example, as far back as 1845, the Boston School Committee administered written standardized achievement tests as part of school improvement efforts. The committee published the results in their annual report to the public in an implicit assertion that school effectiveness should be public knowledge. In the years following World War I, intelligence tests initially designed to sort army recruits were adapted for schools, where they were used to assign students to instructional tracks. Intelligence testing found support among diverse groups, from progressive educators who saw it as a child-centered practice; to schools of teacher education who sought to use tests to elevate the field from a craft to a science and minimize oversight by non-educators; to adminstrators and educational bureaucrats who regarded it as more objective than teachers' assesssments and as an efficient means of allocating resources; to eugenicists, whose racist claims of European genetic superiority benefited from the veneer of science the tests offered (Jensen 1969; Reddy 2008).

Other well-established testing programs include the National Assessment of Educational Progress (NAEP), first administered in 1969, and international assessments like the Trends in International Math and Science Study (TIMSS), implemented in 1995. Federal-level data collection began in 1867 with the establishment of the U.S. Department of Education. Early federal data collection focused on enrollment figures, attendance rates, teacher salaries, expenditures, and numbers of high school graduates. This function has been fulfilled by the National Center for Educational Statistics (NCES) since 1974. NCES now collects data on early childhood through postsecondary education, domestically and internationally, and compiles and disseminates data on state level educational reform activities. It laid the groundwork for the success of the accountability movement in establishing the quantitative as a valid way of knowing about education and in creating an infrastructure for the collection and recording of quantitative data.

Furthermore, accountability presumes an instrumental view of learning and considers student learning to be the product of an instructional process. It takes student learning as an output, and assumes a meaningful causal relationship between that output and educational inputs like funding, pedagogy, and curriculum.

Whereas in Platonic epistemology, learning is understood as an intrinsic, naturally emerging phenomenon, and knowledge acquired is a recollection of something already known, learning under an accountability paradigm borrows from the empiricist perspective of John Locke, with the individual born as a blank slate and learning achieved through exposure and experience. In this materialistic view, that which is measurable is valued, while intangibles like insight, presence, social attunement, and political commitment, more circuitiously developed and more difficult to quantify, are devalued.

Third, the construct of accountability presumes that if students fail to perform, it is the responsibility of the school or the home environment. To be sure, school conditions and family support matter, but not enough to counteract the pernicious effects of poverty, structural racism, and mass disinvestment in public welfare. This fact was firmly established in 1966 by the Equality of Educational Opportunity study, commonly referred to as the Coleman report. Commissioned by the United States Department of Health, Education, and Welfare in response to provisions of the Civil Rights Act, the study surveyed a national sample of schools to assess the availability of equal educational opportunities for members of minority groups in comparison to white students. Assessing inputs like curriculum, school facilities, and academic practices in relation to the output of student performance, the Coleman report found that the success of low-income students is tied to whether they attend schools with wealthier students, whose advantages benefit all.

Recent research has reinforced the correlation between socioeconomic status and educational performance, demonstrating that poorer students bring a range of challenges with them when they come to school, including worse health and environmental stressors, which significantly impact their readiness to learn (Orfield and Lee 2005). Accountability programs draw on discourses like the achievement gap and a culture of low expectations, suggesting that the socio-emotional, cognitive, and health impacts of the material conditions of poverty can be disentangled from student performance. In so doing, these programs outsource responsibility for deep social problems to schools, teachers, families, and students. However, it becomes politically difficult to speak out against these discourses because accountability, like the ideology of meritocracy, is deeply rooted in American optimism and egalitarianism. As a country, we are still unwilling to face our colonial past and the ways that the legacy of slavery continues to differentially structure opportunities, making student performance disparities more an education debt than an achievement gap (Ladson-Billings 2006).

Finally, accountability as a lever for equity presumes that market-based solutions serve the best interest of all students, including the less advantaged. Combined with school choice policies, it positions parents and students as consumers in an educational marketplace and autonomous free agents responsible for maximizing their own opportunities. Schools are likewise figured as service providers who must navigate a competitive choice marketplace as they vie for students/customers. They do so by distinguishing their market niche and by using data to demonstrate their effectiveness. Educational marketplaces disproportionately advantage those with the time, social capital, and institutional knowledge to navigate the system. They benefit the relatively privileged within all racial and social class groups and function to keep middle and upper middle class families invested in public schools in gentrifying areas (Ball, Bowe and Gewirtz 1995). As a result, accountability programs may backfire and have the unintended consequence of reinforcing school segregation as parents eschew neighborhood schools in favor of higher performing schools elsewhere. One such example can be found in the New York City public school system, which is among the most segregated in the nation due to a combination of school choice, zone line systems, and complicated enrollment policies (Kucsera and Orfield 2014).

Perhaps the most fundamental problem with the framework of accountability as a lever for change is that it imagines information as leading to better outcomes, without interrogating how the provision of information may differentially advantage some individuals and groups over others. It is unclear whether accountability is likely to promote the cause of equity, as its proponents hope, or whether it is more likely to reinforce the unequal distribution of educational opportunities by race and class.

The Promises and Hazards of Digitization

The Every Student Succeeds Act (ESSA) of 2015 is the latest effort to implement measures towards accountability. ESSA gives states more autonomy and flexibility than they had under No Child Left Behind and includes a provision for competency-based assessments, which can be systematized by technology in a way that appeals to those invested in personalized and adaptive learning tools. We are likely to see a move toward automated assessment and digital data collection on student learning. We will also see new types of data collection and disaggregation on school conditions, including of non-academic indicators of school quality to be determined by states. States can select any indicator that "allows for meaningful differentiation in school performance," which is "valid, reliable, comparable, and statewide" and can be disaggregated by school to show how it affects students in different subpopulations. Possible indicators might include data on student engagement, educator engagement, graduation rates, dropout rates, disciplinary statistics, data from social-emotional surveys, number of students in advanced classes, access to and completion of advanced coursework, postsecondary readiness, and school climate and safety (Figlio and Loeb 2011). Requiring states to collect, analyze, and report per pupil expenditure data on a school-by-school basis, ESSA seeks to further clarify the relationship between funding and student performance.

As has been true in other sectors when data-driven surveillance and assessment practices are introduced, outcomes are not always as expected (Mateescu, Rosenblat, and boyd 2015). Data is, after all, socially produced, and reflects existing social biases. Data mining, for example, is often seen as a neutral algorithmic technique that can insulate decision-making from human prejudices. However, the resulting decisions can disparately impact historically disadvantaged groups and lead to discrimination, reproducing race, gender, and class-based systems of inequality in matters of hiring and employment (Barocas and Selbst 2015), risk assessment in criminal sentencing (Angwin, Mattu, Larson and Kirchner 2016), and other domains. Therefore it is critical to treat data with a healthy skepticism and remember its non-neutrality when considering its use in making consequential decisions.

Under ESSA, evermore aspects of teaching and learning will be measured and quantified, continuing the trend of shifting power, authority, and influence from teachers and administrators to lawmakers, educational bureaucrats, and policymakers. Teachers will likely continue to experience these power shifts in various, complex and sometimes contradictory ways depending on local conditions and school culture, as well as their own sense of identity and agency (Sloan 2006). Novice teachers working in under-resourced environments may find that accountability systems support their efforts to deliver higher quality and more equitable instruction despite their inexperience (Scheurich, Skrla and Johnson 2004). More seasoned teachers may find that such measures strip them of professional autonomy, de-professionalize their work, and lead to greater workplace surveillance (Jones et al. 1999; McNeil 2000; Lipman 2009; Apple 2009; Gilliom 2009).

In all likelihood, educational data and accountability systems that present as mechanisms for promoting student learning will impact teachers' work environments in unanticipated ways. More specifically, data on students may be used to monitor teachers. To date, most privacy scholarship is based on a *dyadic* model in which information is collected on a given subject (e.g., a student) and used to monitor that subject. In a *refractive* model, surveillance over one party (e.g., a student) can give rise to a new control relationship over another party (e.g., a teacher) (Levy and Barocas 2016). Applying such an ecological model of refractive surveillance in the education space may help explain the multiple and overlapping effects of accountability policies for various actors—students, teachers, parents, and administrators. In other sectors, workplace monitoring technologies and practices are applied (e.g. closed circuit cameras in the retail and food service sectors, and email and browser monitoring in white-collar work environments)

Article

Prepared by: Sheron Fraser-Burgess, *Ball State University*

A Nation at Risk: The Imperative for Educational Reform

THE NATIONAL COMMISSION ON EXCELLENCE IN EDUCATION

Learning Outcomes

After reading this article, you will be able to:

- Refer to one of the defining phrases from *A Nation at Risk*: "a rising tide of mediocrity."
- Describe the concept of "excellence" that served to define the Excellence Movement of the 1980s.
- Identify the themes for the five recommendations that were to strengthen the American public education system.

"Our Nation is at risk. . . . the educational foundations of our society are presently being eroded by a rising tide of mediocrity that threatens our very future as a Nation and a people. What was unimaginable a generation ago has begun to occur—others are matching and surpassing our educational attainments." (p. 5) With the release of this presidential blue-ribbon commission report on April 26, 1983, public education changed forever. Taking a commonsense approach to schooling and maintaining a simple-mindedness towards teaching and learning, politicians saw themselves as leaders to save our failing schools. As the economic purpose of education proceeded to define most discourse, a business-oriented perspective became the source of inspiration for educational reform. Clarity and organization became defining values. Education was blamed for America's economic and technological decline, and business leaders were convinced that school reform could restore the country's global superiority with a better-quality workforce. *A Nation at Risk* introduced a "fear rhetoric" that caused educational policy to become front-page news. Placing education firmly as a form of national security and using terms such as "unilateral educational disarmament," the report stated that "if an unfriendly foreign power had attempted to impose on America the mediocre educational performance that exists today, we might well have viewed it as an act of war. As it stands, we have allowed this to happen to ourselves." (p. 5)

A Nation at Risk seemingly blamed professional educators for this state of affairs and fostered "systemic reform" as a way to solve educational problems. The rudiments of this type of change included state and federal omnibus reform bills and policies defined by benchmarks and definable outcomes. The word "excellence" became a unique professional concept, and educational expectations were standardized in an effort to obtain "quality education." The selected excerpt depicts *A Nation at Risk*'s "Recommendations" that have set the stage for our contemporary high-stakes testing, economic goals-based, No Child Left Behind educational system.

. . .

Our Nation is at risk. Our once unchallenged preeminence in commerce, industry, science, and technological innovation is being overtaken by competitors throughout the world. This report is concerned with only one of the many causes and dimensions of the problem, but it is the one that undergirds American prosperity, security, and civility. We report to the American people that while we can take justifiable pride in what our schools and colleges have historically accomplished and contributed to the United States and the well-being of its people, the educational foundations of our society are presently being eroded by a rising tide of mediocrity that threatens our very future as a Nation and a people. What was unimaginable a generation ago has begun to occur—others are matching and surpassing our educational attainments.

If an unfriendly foreign power had attempted to impose on America the mediocre educational performance that exists today, we might well have viewed it as an act of war. As it stands, we have allowed this to happen to ourselves. We have even squandered the gains in student achievement made in the wake of the Sputnik challenge. Moreover, we have dismantled essential support systems which helped make those gains possible. We have, in effect, been committing an act of unthinking, unilateral educational disarmament.

Our society and its educational institutions seem to have lost sight of the basic purposes of schooling, and of the high expectations and disciplined effort needed to attain them. This report, the result of 18 months of study, seeks to generate reform of our educational system in fundamental ways and to renew the Nation's commitment to schools and colleges of high quality throughout the length and breadth of our land.

That we have compromised this commitment is, upon reflection, hardly surprising, given the multitude of often conflicting demands we have placed on our Nation's schools and colleges. They are routinely called on to provide solutions to personal, social, and political problems that the home and other institutions either will not or cannot resolve. We must understand that these demands on our schools and colleges often exact an educational cost as well as a financial one.

On the occasion of the Commission's first meeting, President Reagan noted the central importance of education in American life when he said: "Certainly there are few areas of American life as important to our society, to our people, and to our families as our schools and colleges." This report, therefore, is as much an open letter to the American people as it is a report to the Secretary of Education. We are confident that the American people, properly informed, will do what is right for their children and for the generations to come.

Excellence in Education

We define "excellence" to mean several related things. At the level of the *individual learner*, it means performing on the boundary of individual ability in ways that test and push back personal limits, in school and in the workplace. Excellence characterizes a *school or college* that sets high expectations and goals for all learners, then tries in every way possible to help students reach them. Excellence characterizes a *society* that has adopted these policies, for it will then be prepared through the education and skill of its people to respond to the challenges of a rapidly changing world. Our Nation's people and its schools and colleges must be committed to achieving excellence in all these senses.

We do not believe that a public commitment to excellence and educational reform must be made at the expense of a strong public commitment to the equitable treatment of our diverse population. The twin goals of equity and high-quality schooling have profound and practical meaning for our economy and society, and we cannot permit one to yield to the other either in principle or in practice. To do so would deny young people their chance to learn and live according to their aspirations and abilities. It also would lead to a generalized accommodation to mediocrity in our society on the one hand or the creation of an undemocratic elitism on the other.

Our goal must be to develop the talents of all to their fullest. Attaining that goal requires that we expect and assist all students to work to the limits of their capabilities. We should expect schools to have genuinely high standards rather than minimum ones, and parents to support and encourage their children to make the most of their talents and abilities.

The search for solutions to our educational problems must also include a commitment to life-long learning. The task of rebuilding our system of learning is enormous and must be properly understood and taken seriously: Although a million and a half new workers enter the economy each year from our schools and colleges, the adults working today will still make up about 75 percent of the workforce in the year 2000. These workers, and new entrants into the workforce, will need further education and retraining if they—and we as a Nation—are to thrive and prosper. . . .

Recommendations

In light of the urgent need for improvement, both immediate and long term, this Commission has agreed on a set of recommendations that the American people can begin to act on now, that can be implemented over the next several years, and that promise lasting reform. The topics are familiar; there is little mystery about what we believe must be done. Many schools, districts, and States are already giving serious and constructive attention to these matters, even though their plans may differ from our recommendations in some details.

We wish to note that we refer to public, private, and parochial schools and colleges alike. All are valuable national resources. Examples of actions similar to those recommended below can be found in each of them.

We must emphasize that the variety of student aspirations, abilities, and preparation requires that appropriate content be available to satisfy diverse needs. Attention must be directed to both the nature of the content available and to the needs of particular learners. The most gifted students, for example, may need a curriculum enriched and accelerated beyond even the needs of other students of high ability. Similarly, educationally disadvantaged students may require special curriculum materials, smaller classes, or individual tutoring to help them master the material presented. Nevertheless, there remains a common expectation: We must demand the best effort and performance from all students, whether they are gifted or less able, affluent or disadvantaged, whether destined for college, the farm, or industry.

Our recommendations are based on the beliefs that everyone can learn, that everyone is born with an *urge* to learn which can be nurtured, that a solid high school education is within the reach of virtually all, and that life-long learning will equip people with the skills required for new careers and for citizenship.

Recommendation A: Content

We recommend *that State and local high school graduation requirements be strengthened and that,* at a minimum, all *students seeking a diploma be required to lay the foundations in the Five New Basics by taking the following curriculum during their 4 years of high school: (a) 4 years of English; (b) 3 years of mathematics; (c) 3 years of science; (d) 3 years of social studies; and (e) one-half year of computer science. For the college-bound, 2 years of foreign language in high school are strongly recommended in addition to those taken earlier.*

Whatever the student's educational or work objectives, knowledge of the New Basics is the foundation of success for the after-school years and, therefore, forms the core of the modern curriculum. A high level of shared education in these Basics, together with work in the fine and performing arts and foreign languages, constitutes the mind and spirit of our culture. The following Implementing Recommendations are intended as illustrative descriptions. They are included here to clarify what we mean by the essentials of a strong curriculum.

Implementing Recommendations

1. The teaching of *English* in high school should equip graduates to: (a) comprehend, interpret, evaluate, and use what they read; (b) write well-organized, effective papers; (c) listen effectively and discuss ideas intelligently; and (d) know our literary heritage and how it enhances imagination and ethical understanding, and how it relates to the customs, ideas, and values of today's life and culture.
2. The teaching of *mathematics* in high school should equip graduates to: (a) understand geometric and algebraic concepts; (b) understand elementary probability and statistics; (c) apply mathematics in everyday situations; and (d) estimate, approximate, measure, and test the accuracy of their calculations. In addition to the traditional sequence of studies available for college-bound students, new, equally demanding mathematics curricula need to be developed for those who do not plan to continue their formal education immediately.
3. The teaching of *science* in high school should provide graduates with an introduction to: (a) the concepts, laws, and processes of the physical and biological sciences; (b) the methods of scientific inquiry and reasoning; (c) the application of scientific knowledge to everyday life; and (d) the social and environmental implications of scientific and technological development. Science courses must be revised and updated for both the college-bound and those not intending to go to college. An example of such work is the American Chemical Society's "Chemistry in the Community" program.
4. The teaching of *social studies* in high school should be designed to: (a) enable students to fix their places and possibilities within the larger social and cultural structure; (b) understand the broad sweep of both ancient and contemporary ideas that have shaped our world; and (c) understand the fundamentals of how our economic system works and how our political system functions; and (d) grasp the difference between free and repressive societies. An understanding of each of these areas is requisite to the informed and committed exercise of citizenship in our free society.
5. The teaching of *computer science* in high school should equip graduates to: (a) understand the computer as an information, computation, and communication device; (b) use the computer in the study of the other Basics and for personal and work-related purposes; and (c) understand the world of computers, electronics, and related technologies.

In addition to the New Basics, other important curriculum matters must be addressed.

6. Achieving proficiency in a *foreign language* ordinarily requires from 4 to 6 years of study and should, therefore, be started in the elementary grades. We believe it is desirable that students achieve such proficiency because study of a foreign language introduces students to non-English-speaking cultures, heightens awareness and comprehension of one's native tongue, and serves the Nation's needs in commerce, diplomacy, defense, and education.
7. The high school curriculum should also provide students with programs requiring rigorous effort in subjects that advance students' personal, educational, and occupational goals, such as the fine and performing arts and vocational education. These areas complement the New Basics, and they should demand the same level of performance as the Basics.

8. The curriculum in the crucial eight grades leading to the high school years should be specifically designed to provide a sound base for study in those and later years in such areas as English language development and writing, computational and problem solving skills, science, social studies, foreign language, and the arts. These years should foster an enthusiasm for learning and the development of the individual's gifts and talents.
9. We encourage the continuation of efforts by groups such as the American Chemical Society, the American Association for the Advancement of Science, the Modern Language Association, and the National Councils of Teachers of English and Teachers of Mathematics, to revise, update, improve, and make available new and more diverse curricular materials. We applaud the consortia of educators and scientific, industrial, and scholarly societies that cooperate to improve the school curriculum.

Recommendation B: Standards and Expectations

We recommend *that schools, colleges, and universities adopt more rigorous and measurable standards, and higher expectations, for academic performance and student conduct, and that 4-year colleges and universities raise their requirements for admission. This will help students do their best educationally with challenging materials in an environment that supports learning and authentic accomplishment.*

Implementing Recommendations

1. Grades should be indicators of academic achievement so they can be relied on as evidence of a student's readiness for further study.
2. Four-year colleges and universities should raise their admissions requirements and advise all potential applicants of the standards for admission in terms of specific courses required, performance in these areas, and levels of achievement on standardized achievement tests in each of the five Basics and, where applicable, foreign languages.
3. Standardized tests of achievement (not to be confused with aptitude tests) should be administered at major transition points from one level of schooling to another and particularly from high school to college or work. The purpose of these tests would be to: (a) certify the student's credentials; (b) identify the need for remedial intervention; and (c) identify the opportunity for advanced or accelerated work. The tests should be administered as part of a nationwide (but not Federal) system of State and local standardized tests. This system should include other diagnostic procedures that assist teachers and students to evaluate student progress.
4. Textbooks and other tools of learning and teaching should be upgraded and updated to assure more rigorous content. We call upon university scientists, scholars, and members of professional societies, in collaboration with master teachers, to help in this task, as they did in the post-Sputnik era. They should assist willing publishers in developing the products or publish their own alternatives where there are persistent inadequacies.
5. In considering textbooks for adoption, States and school districts should: (a) evaluate texts and other materials on their ability to present rigorous and challenging material clearly; and (b) require publishers to furnish evaluation data on the material's effectiveness.
6. Because no textbook in any subject can be geared to the needs of all students, funds should be made available to support text development in "thin-market" areas, such as those for disadvantaged students, the learning disabled, and the gifted and talented.
7. To assure quality, all publishers should furnish evidence of the quality and appropriateness of textbooks, based on results from field trials and credible evaluations. In view of the enormous numbers and varieties of texts available, more widespread consumer information services for purchasers are badly needed.
8. New instructional materials should reflect the most current applications of technology in appropriate curriculum areas, the best scholarship in each discipline, and research in learning and teaching.

Recommendation C: Time

We recommend *that significantly more time be devoted to learning the New Basics. This will require more effective use of the existing school day, a longer school day, or a lengthened school year.*

Implementing Recommendations

1. Students in high schools should be assigned far more homework than is now the case.
2. Instruction in effective study and work skills, which are essential if school and independent time is to be used efficiently, should be introduced in the early grades and continued throughout the student's schooling.

3. School districts and State legislatures should strongly consider 7-hour school days, as well as a 200- to 220-day school year.
4. The time available for learning should be expanded through better classroom management and organization of the school day. If necessary, additional time should be found to meet the special needs of slow learners, the gifted, and others who need more instructional diversity than can be accommodated during a conventional school day or school year.
5. The burden on teachers for maintaining discipline should be reduced through the development of firm and fair codes of student conduct that are enforced consistently, and by considering alternative classrooms, programs, and schools to meet the needs of continually disruptive students.
6. Attendance policies with clear incentives and sanctions should be used to reduce the amount of time lost through student absenteeism and tardiness.
7. Administrative burdens on the teacher and related intrusions into the school day should be reduced to add time for teaching and learning.
8. Placement and grouping of students, as well as promotion and graduation policies, should be guided by the academic progress of students and their instructional needs, rather than by rigid adherence to age.

Recommendation D: Teaching

This recommendation *consists of seven parts. Each is intended to improve the preparation of teachers or to make teaching a more rewarding and respected profession. Each of the seven stands on its own and should not be considered solely as an implementing recommendation.*

1. Persons preparing to teach should be required to meet high educational standards, to demonstrate an aptitude for teaching, and to demonstrate competence in an academic discipline. Colleges and universities offering teacher preparation programs should be judged by how well their graduates meet these criteria.
2. Salaries for the teaching profession should be increased and should be professionally competitive, market-sensitive, and performance-based. Salary, promotion, tenure, and retention decisions should be tied to an effective evaluation system that includes peer review so that superior teachers can be rewarded, average ones encouraged, and poor ones either improved or terminated.
3. School boards should adopt an 11-month contract for teachers. This would ensure time for curriculum and professional development, programs for students with special needs, and a more adequate level of teacher compensation.
4. School boards, administrators, and teachers should cooperate to develop career ladders for teachers that distinguish among the beginning instructor, the experienced teacher, and the master teacher.
5. Substantial nonschool personnel resources should be employed to help solve the immediate problem of the shortage of mathematics and science teachers. Qualified individuals including recent graduates with mathematics and science degrees, graduate students, and industrial and retired scientists could, with appropriate preparation, immediately begin teaching in these fields. A number of our leading science centers have the capacity to begin educating and retraining teachers immediately. Other areas of critical teacher need, such as English, must also be addressed.
6. Incentives, such as grants and loans, should be made available to attract outstanding students to the teaching profession, particularly in those areas of critical shortage.
7. Master teachers should be involved in designing teacher preparation programs and in supervising teachers during their probationary years.

Recommendation E: Leadership and Fiscal Support

We recommend *that citizens across the Nation hold educators and elected officials responsible for providing the leadership necessary to achieve these reforms, and that citizens provide the fiscal support and stability required to bring about the reforms we propose.*

Implementing Recommendations

1. Principals and superintendents must play a crucial leadership role in developing school and community support for the reforms we propose, and school boards must provide them with the professional development and other support required to carry out their leadership role effectively. The Commission stresses the distinction between leadership skills involving persuasion, setting goals and developing community consensus behind them, and managerial and supervisory skills. Although the

latter are necessary, we believe that school boards must consciously develop leadership skills at the school and district levels if the reforms we propose are to be achieved.
2. State and local officials, including school board members, governors, and legislators, have *the primary responsibility* for financing and governing the schools, and should incorporate the reforms we propose in their educational policies and fiscal planning.
3. The Federal Government, in cooperation with States and localities, should help meet the needs of key groups of students such as the gifted and talented, the socioeconomically disadvantaged, minority and language minority students, and the handicapped. In combination these groups include both national resources and the Nation's youth who are most at risk.
4. In addition, we believe the Federal Government's role includes several functions of national consequence that States and localities alone are unlikely to be able to meet: protecting constitutional and civil rights for students and school personnel; collecting data, statistics, and information about education generally; supporting curriculum improvement and research on teaching, learning, and the management of schools: supporting teacher training in areas of critical shortage or key national needs; and providing student financial assistance and research and graduate training. We believe the assistance of the Federal Government should be provided with a minimum of administrative burden and intrusiveness.
5. The Federal Government has *the primary responsibility* to identify the national interest in education. It should also help fund and support efforts to protect and promote that interest. It must provide the national leadership to ensure that the Nation's public and private resources are marshaled to address the issues discussed in this report.
6. This Commission calls upon educators, parents, and public officials at all levels to assist in bringing about the educational reform proposed in this report. We also call upon citizens to provide the financial support necessary to accomplish these purposes. Excellence costs. But in the long run mediocrity costs far more.

America Can Do It

Despite the obstacles and difficulties that inhabit the pursuit of superior educational attainment, we are confident, with history as our guide, that we can meet our goal. The American educational system has responded to previous challenges with remarkable success. In the 19th century our land-grant colleges and universities provided the research and training that developed our Nation's natural resources and the rich agricultural bounty of the American farm. From the late 1800s through mid-20th century, American schools provided the educated workforce needed to seal the success of the Industrial Revolution and to provide the margin of victory in two world wars. In the early part of this century and continuing to this very day, our schools have absorbed vast waves of immigrants and educated them and their children to productive citizenship. Similarly, the Nation's Black colleges have provided opportunity and undergraduate education to the vast majority of college-educated Black Americans.

More recently, our institutions of higher education have provided the scientists and skilled technicians who helped us transcend the boundaries of our planet. In the last 30 years, the schools have been a major vehicle for expanded social opportunity, and now graduate 75 percent of our young people from high school. Indeed, the proportion of Americans of college age enrolled in higher education is nearly twice that of Japan and far exceeds other nations such as France, West Germany, and the Soviet Union. Moreover, when international comparisons were last made a decade ago, the top 9 percent of American students compared favorably in achievement with their peers in other countries.

In addition, many large urban areas in recent years report that average student achievement in elementary schools is improving. More and more schools are also offering advanced placement programs and programs for gifted and talented students, and more and more students are enrolling in them.

We are the inheritors of a past that gives us every reason to believe that we will succeed. . . .

A Final Word

This is not the first or only commission on education, and some of our findings are surely not new, but old business that now at last must be done. For no one can doubt that the United States is under challenge from many quarters.

Children born today can expect to graduate from high school in the year 2000. We dedicate our report not only to these children, but also to those now in school and others to come. We firmly believe that a movement of America's schools in the direction called for by our recommendations will prepare these children for far more effective lives in a far stronger America.

Our final word, perhaps better characterized as a plea, is that all segments of our population give attention to the implementation of our recommendations. Our present plight did not appear overnight, and the responsibility for our current situation is widespread. Reform of our educational system will take time and unwavering commitment. It will require equally widespread, energetic, and dedicated action. For example, we call upon the National Academy of Sciences, National Academy of Engineering, Institute of Medicine, Science Service, National Science Foundation, Social Science Research Council, American Council of Learned Societies, National Endowment for the Humanities, National Endowment for the Arts, and other scholarly, scientific, and learned societies for their help in this effort. Help should come from students themselves; from parents, teachers, and school boards; from colleges and universities; from local, State, and Federal officials; from teachers' and administrators' organizations; from industrial and labor councils; and from other groups with interest in and responsibility for educational reform.

It is their America, and the America of all of us, that is at risk; it is to each of us that this imperative is addressed. It is by our willingness to take up the challenge, and our resolve to see it through, that America's place in the world will be either secured or forfeited. Americans have succeeded before and so we shall again.

Critical Thinking

1. What was the intent of a federally sponsored commission using such volatile and alarming rhetoric to describe the state of education in the United States?
2. Since today's college students' educational experiences were defined by *The Nation at Risk*'s recommendations, did the lengthening of the school day and school year positively influence student learning?
3. What recommendations from *The Nation at Risk* strengthened or diminished the educational experience of students?

Internet References

U.S. Department of Education
www2.ed.gov/rschstat/research/pubs/risk25.html

Education Week
www.edweek.org

From A Nation at Risk by The National Commission on Excellence in Education, 1983.

UNIT
Prepared by: Sheron Fraser-Burgess, *Ball State University*

Educational Equity

This unit features articles that juxtapose the historical sources of oppression with empowering paradigms through which to theorize fostering student agency. An abiding challenge for educational equity is the systemic sources of educational inequality. Structural forces reify socioeconomic status by limiting access to educational opportunities and can further exacerbate preexisting disparities This gap is evidenced in disparate outcomes along the lines of race or ethnicity and social class. Discourse about bridging these gaps can exhibit a deficit approach to the cultural background and lived experiences of minorities.

Two prevailing theories that reject the cultural deficit approach to the education and other social problems that plague vulnerable communities and those of color are predominant in the literature. Yosso (2005) draws on critical race theory (Bell 1987, 1997) and Bourdieu & Passeron (1977) to propose an alternate view of the lived experiences of black and Latino communities and the challenges that they can confront. Kretzmann and Mcknight (1993, 1996) appeal to a capabilities conception of Amartya Sen to offer alternate frameworks of community problem solving and development. Yosso (2005) proposed an interpretation of Bourdieu & Passeron's (1977) cultural capital theory that is mediated by Derrick Bell's critical race theory. Bourdieu and Passeron attribute the greatest social capital to social classes whose practices and beliefs correlate with social mobility. Yosso's notion of "community cultural wealth" turns on its head the idea that only forms of knowledge that the middle and upper socioeconomic classes can claim are inherently of high value in a socially stratified society. The concept "community cultural wealth" encompasses an array of knowledge, skills, abilities and contacts possessed and utilized by Communities of Color to survive and resist macro and micro-forms of oppression" (p. 77). Collectively the forms of community wealth counter the deficit-based view of communities of color that is an implication of Bourdieu and Passeron's theory. The sources of capital that Yosso posits are the following: aspirational, familial, social, navigational, resistant, linguistic, and cultural.

Each of these constructs expresses a set of assumptions that can position students to better negotiate a highly hierarchical society and to improve the chances of education producing social mobility. For example, aspirational capital refers to an enhanced capacity to exhibit resilient hope in the face of sustained adversity and struggle. Kretzmann and Mcknight (1993) developed the theory of Asset-Based Community Development (ABCD) that offered an alternative perspective from the traditional models of community intervention. The extant approaches relied upon the disadvantages that face individuals in struggling and under-served neighborhoods, which are categorized as such because of the host of social ills and economic obstacles that they confront (e.g. unemployment or underemployment; poor housing conditions; underperforming schools). Calling into question, this approach is the fact that these states of affairs can occur as a result of the convergence of structural factors that students and their families have little power to control. Additionally, this "power of needs" approach had unintended consequences that further entrenched communities in a cycle of poverty and helplessness and diluted the efforts of service providers.

The research articles and stories featured in this unit offer paradigms of empowerment that foster student agency in the face of overwhelming odds. Taking a critical/analytical approach, this section begins with the increasing presence of a grit mindset in the scholarship on poverty. It also includes both an excerpt from the Brown v. Board of Education (1954) ruling and a contemporary perspective of the remaining and ongoing fight against school segregation.

Additional readings usefully rehearse the nature of the challenge that intergenerational poverty poses and considers ways to integrate an equity-focus into pedagogy through assessment.

References

Bell, D. (1987). And we will not be saved: the elusive quest for racial justice (New York, Basic Books).

Bell, D. (2002). *Faces at the bottom of the well: The permanence of racism*. New York, NY: Basic Books.

Bourdieu, P., & Passeron, J. (1977). *Reproduction in education, society and culture (La reproduction, engl.) Transl by Richard Nice*.

Kretzmann, J., & Mcknight, J. P. (1996). Assets-based community development. *National Civic Review, 85*(4), 23–29. doi:10.1002/ncr.4100850405

Smyth, E., & Vanclay, F. (2017). The Social Framework for Projects: A conceptual but practical model to assist in assessing, planning and managing the social impacts of projects. *Impact Assessment and Project Appraisal, 35*(1), 65–80. doi:10.1080/14615517.2016.1271539

Yosso, T. J. (2005). Whose culture has capital? A critical race theory discussion of community cultural wealth. *Race Ethnicity and Education, 8*(1), 69–91. doi:10.1080/1361332052000341006

Article

Prepared by: Sheron Fraser-Burgess, *Ball State University*

The Radical Middle: The Limits and Advantages of Teaching Grit in Schools

VICKA BELL-ROBINSON

Learning Outcomes

After reading this article, you will be able to:

- Summarize the pedagogical ideals inherent in the goals of democratic education.
- Relate critical pedagogy to developing students' critical literacy and being civic-minded.
- Articulate the reasons that democracy, in this political moment, may be on the ropes and in need of rescuing.

We live at a time when we're constantly asked to pick a side: Public or Charter, Trump or Clinton, Black Lives Matter or All Lives Matter.

When thinking about the potential impact of teaching grit to students, it's easy to feel like one has to pick between teaching grit or sheltering students from the realities of adulthood. On the one hand, being able to demonstrate grit and resilience is an important component of adulthood. As such, it stands to reason that educators should spend time exposing students to opportunities for grit development. At the same time, it is important to recognize that grit is not always the best response when faced with a difficult undertaking. Quitting, dissenting, and seeking assistance may all be completely reasonable reactions to a challenging task.

The conversation about whether grit should be taught in schools does not have to result in an *either-or* response—there is a radical middle ground that exists. That space is between teaching that every challenge can be overcome with the right amount of grit and the recognition that the obstacles students face may be the result of conditions that they cannot control. Choosing the middle, seeing the validity of both sides of an argument is a relatively radical notion.

The goal of this piece is to encourage an embracing of the radical middle through a dialogue about the complexities of infusing character education, focused specifically on grit, into the curriculum.

The Goodness of Grit

Grit is not a new topic, but it has gotten new life in part by research conducted by Angela Duckworth[1] and others who posit that the difference between those who are able to achieve their goals and those who are not is the willingness to apply the appropriate amount of effort and time to see their quest through to the end.

In many ways, Duckworth's work builds upon that of Carol Dweck who posited in her 2006 book *Mindset: The New Psychology of Success*[2] that people who believe in their ability to learn, grow, and develop, are better off than those who believe they are endowed with natural talent or disposition but decline to work hard. Both psychologists implied that those who are not successful in accomplishing their desired goals have not applied the appropriate amount of continuous effort.

Dweck argued that individuals with a fixed mindset quit when they encounter challenges where they feel inept. Instead of believing that applying more effort will result in a successful outcome, they assume that they will never be successful, and, thus, continued effort is not worth their energy. Folks with a growth mindset believe that any difficulty they face is temporary and that, with the right amount of time and effort, they

---

[1]Duckworth, Angela. *Grit: The Power of Passion and Perseverance.* New York: Scribner, 2016.
[2]Dweck, Carol. *Mindset: The New Psychology of Success: How We Can Learn to Fulfill Our Potential.* New York: Ballantine, 2006.

will eventually be able to overcome whatever difficulty they are facing and successfully accomplish their goal.

As both an educator and a mother, I see the importance of not only exhibiting grit for my children and students, but also encouraging the development of grit among children in the wider society. Duckworth and Dweck are not incorrect. It is important for everyone, children and adults, to have the capacity to start a task and stick with it—even it if becomes difficult. Particularly true in education, the confidence that comes with learning new material can take both time and effort. Without grit or a growth mindset, individuals who are used to having the completion of tasks and the accomplishment of goals come to them easily, find themselves frustrated and disheartened about the difficulty associated with completing an especially challenging task. The difficulty can lead them to internalize their struggles and believe that they are fundamentally flawed.

Bandura[3] described *self-efficacy* as the belief that individuals have in their action to produce their desired results. Since our self-efficacy is connected to our ability to feel that our actions can help us achieve our desired outcomes, when we lack self-efficacy, or when we have low or no hope in our own abilities, we might not try as hard to be successful in our endeavors.

Hope is tied to grit, and grit is tied to self-efficacy. Like self-efficacy, people develop the capacity to hope through their owned lived experiences, hearing about the experiences of others, and by being encouraged by others. Parents and educators should encourage the development of grit among the young people over which they have influence. We must encourage grit, while simultaneously acknowledging that individual differences and life circumstances do impact the level of grit one must exhibit in order to achieve desired outcomes.

I was recently speaking with an individual who is quite used to having most things go her way. Her personality and natural talent contribute to her ability to succeed in just about everything she tries to do. A slight change in her job description forced her to learn a new skill, one that she needed to show students in her class. After a few weeks without any sustained success, she felt dejected and disempowered.

As we were talking about her plight, she said "I'm just not made for this." With the topic of grit and hope in the forefront of my mind, I gently, but firmly, corrected her assumption. I reminded her that she had repeatedly demonstrated her ability to be successful. I challenged her to dig deep, and work just a little bit harder to produce the results she desired. I also provided her with a few small ideas about how to enhance her skill development as well as her confidence. I told her that I believed that she could do it; she just needed to believe it too.

A few days later she called and told me that the efforts she had put forth produced the results she wanted. She thanked me for encouraging her and for challenging her to be better than she ever thought she could be. This story provides a wonderful example of why grit is important. Of how past success can actually lessen grit in certain situations, when we haven't yet learned how to "fail well". Of how we can influence each other to keep going even when we want to quit.

Grit in Schools

Elliott Eisner[4] famously argued that there were parts of the curriculum that were formal and obvious, like reading, writing, and math, as well as other topics that were more implicit or "hidden" such as rituals designed to produce competitiveness and compliant behavior. Indeed, there is a benefit to having schools socialize students into the behavioral expectations of society. Some level of conformity is helpful when it comes to order and safety.

There is also, however, a disadvantage associated with implicitly teaching "common" values and expectations via the compulsory school system. That disadvantage occurs because the values presented are not always an accurate representation of the human experience, nor are they always moral or just.

The historical foundations of the educational system ignored the pluralistic nature of the United States. The current system of education also aims to move individuals from the margins or fringe sections of society by ignoring the uniqueness of each person's experiences and forcing them to assimilate to the dominant culture. Teaching students to simply demonstrate more grit when faced with any type of difficulty leaves no room for them to critically reflect upon and respond to situations in which a different response might be required.

We cannot teach students to demonstrate more grit without also giving them an understanding of the civic and societal responsibility we have for one another. Stitzlein[5] explained how new requirements for teachers in the areas of reading and math resulted in a reduction of time focused on social studies. Historically, social studies, government, and other civic content were where students were explicitly educated about their roles and responsibilities as citizens.

The most disturbing part about less time being spent in civically-oriented classes is that some populations of students are more impacted by the reduced time than others. Stitzlein noted that students enrolled in underperforming schools—which typically face increased pressure to raise scores on standardized test—are disproportionately poor and of color. The

---

[3]Bandura, Albert. *Self-efficacy: The Exercise of Control.* New York: Freeman, 1997.
[4]Eisner, Elliott. *The Educational Imagination: On the Design and Evaluation of School Programs (3rd ed.).* New Jersey: Prentice Hall, 1994.
[5]Stitzlein, Sarah. *Teaching for Dissent: Citizenship Education and Political Activism* (Colorado: Paradigm Publishers, 2014), 168.

lack of intentional transmission of knowledge about the power and promises of citizenship disenfranchises these already marginalized students and limits their ability to "access the skills and knowledge they need to secure their own justice and equality".[5] Anderson[6] shared a similar sentiment when he articulated that "another generation will lack societal analysis that would provide them with the tools to defend democracy and work to ensure that our society is living out an authentic allegiance to its cherished ideals". Teaching children with marginalized identities that the key to success is to demonstrate grit ignores the social realities in which many of them exist. In doing this we encourage students to believe that they and others are always personally and solely responsible for whatever negative occurrences they face. Without any context or ability to discern what situations need grit and what situations need a different response, student may find themselves trying to overcome scenarios of systematic inequality that they were assigned to or inherited.

When we consider teaching grit in schools, we assume that everyone is responsible for their own behavior and outcomes. This aligns with the flawed belief in a just world, which basically presumes that we live in a world where people get what they deserve. The just world belief rewards people for the good things that happen to them and punishes people for the bad things that happen to them.

The most quoted words from the Declaration of Independence are "all men are created equal." followed quickly by "life, liberty, and the pursuit of happiness." Many people in the United States, regardless of their political persuasion, love to recount both of these line, and conveniently forget that each of these statements, when written, spoke of a very specific and narrow group: white men. Author TaNehisi Coates[7] reminded readers that at the very time the country's founding fathers were promoting liberty, they were enslaving an entire race of people:

> Slavery is this same woman born in a world that loudly proclaims its love of freedom and inscribes its love on essential text, a world in which the same professors hold this woman a slave, hold her mother a slave, her father a slave, her daughter a slave, and when this women peers back into the generations all she sees is the enslaved.

Like the founding of the United States, the educational system made assumptions about who would be participating in schooling. Although the makeup of who attends school has changed, many of the assumptions and practices have not. It is no wonder that certain populations' tendencies align more closely with the expectations and experiences of schooling. Despite the flaws in the original design, the actions and behaviors of students from marginalized populations are frequently used as rationale for why the gap between them and white students persists. In education, we treat all students as if they have equal opportunity to be successful, and that is simply not true.

Marginalization excludes entire populations from access and opportunities specifically because of their membership in a social group. Young Black and Latino men have difficulty finding employment because of the stereotyping associated with their social identity[8]. The ability to marginalize a group of people is not restricted to negatively impacting their ability to access material possessions, as individuals can also be marginalized by restricting their ability to participate in social gatherings or other human experiences, which may require them to exhibit grit more frequently than their majority counterparts.

Not that long ago, I was engaged in a conversation with a Black colleague who was experiencing some difficulty in his workplace. He began telling me a story about how some basic interactions with his supervisor had gone poorly. He kept having interactions that seemed to be inconsistent with the treatment that his fellow team members were receiving, including being disciplined for everyday actions like asking questions and sharing his opinion.

When he spoke with his supervisor about his concerns, the supervisor explained that she had found his general demeanor aggressive and that he seemed angry all of the time. This feedback alarmed my colleague. He feared that his supervisor was making racial assumptions about his motivations and demeanor. I explained to my friend that his experience sounded like this could be related to harassment and discrimination and that he might want to consult with people in his organization's equal opportunity office.

Situations involving harassment and discrimination cannot be redressed by having the harassed person try harder not to be harassed. It would have placed an undue burden for my colleague to try to tolerate unequal treatment on the basis of race from his supervisor. As we look to using the educational system to create a better present and a more prosperous future, we cannot promote the idea of infusing the educational system with grit development without acknowledging that sometimes the answer to a problem is not more grit—sometimes the answer is a much needed adjustment to inequitable practices.

The appropriate place to demonstrate grit is in a specific task, where the obstacle is more internal than external. Internal obstacles are barriers people put in place for themselves, like lack of motivation. External obstacles exist when systems

---

[6]Anderson, Gary. *Advocacy Leadership: Toward a Post Reform Agenda in Education* (New York: Routledge, 2009), 47.
[7]Coates, Ta-Nehisi. *Between the World and Me* (New York: Spiegel and Grau, 2015), 70.
[8]Young, Marion. *Justice and the Politics of Difference.* New Jersey: Princeton University Press, 1990.

and procedures give an advantage to certain populations, while disadvantaging another population, like discrimination.

In those situations, the disadvantaged population should not be just expected to demonstrate grit in order to get over the injustice. The inequities of the system must be addressed through making an adjustment to practices or allocating additional resources. A student who has the intellectual capacity and access to appropriate resources but is performing poorly because of a refusal to complete the appropriate assignments has created his own internal barrier to success. That student needs to exhibit grit in order to succeed.

Simultaneously, a student who has the intellectual capacity, but does not have access to appropriate resources, and, thus, is limited in her ability to complete the appropriate assignments faces an obstacle to success that is external to her control. In that instance, she should receive assistance to address her lack of resources, and not be further disadvantaged because of something that is beyond her control. It is of the utmost importance that educators and policy makers be able to determine the difference.

Education as a Solution for Societal Problems

Our belief in the ability of the compulsory educational system to address and/or solve many of the problems we face in our society is the best demonstration of both grit and hope. We are hopeful for educational experiences that enhance the present and the future of the citizenry, and we demonstrate grit through our willingness to repeatedly address the flaws we identify in education.

It is much easier to ask the question about what we should be teaching children in school and much harder to figure out the answer. Currently, we find ourselves dissatisfied at the latest approach of standardized testing. Despite all of the scare tactics, closed schools, and threats, the performance gap between white students and students of color has not been significantly altered.[9] Faced with our continued disappointment, we return to a space where we once again began to think about what children should learn in school. As a nation, we stake the future of our civilization on how well our children learn what they are supposed to learn in school. When the results are not up to our satisfaction, we panic and change course.

Whether we're talking about infusing grit, increasing standardized testing, or teaching cultural literacy, educational reform will never successfully accomplish goals associated with equality and inclusion simply by changing the curriculum. This is because our educational system exists in a society that regularly advantages some people while it disadvantages others.

The reality is that conversations about educational reform are a constant game of trying to design circumstances where some students, generally those who are socioeconomically disadvantaged and/or racially underrepresented, catch up with the rest of the group without fundamentally altering the system. It is likely that students will benefit from the inclusion of character education, specifically focused on developing grit, into the curriculum. This addition must occur simultaneously with an understanding that the life many students have to navigate outside of school requires a constant demonstration of grit.

Early exposure to violence, poverty, and injustice forces some people with underrepresented social identities to create grit in order to successfully operate in the world. The recent publicity on the shooting of unarmed Black men has had an effect on others holding a similar social identity regardless of their proximity to the victims and/or the location where the shooting occurred. When we refuse to acknowledge the different lived experience students have due to a variety of factors that are beyond their control and insist that they need more grit, we do them a tremendous disservice while perpetuating systems that are innately unjust.

Final Thoughts

Educational leaders and policymakers do not have to decide between teaching grit in schools and fixing a broken educational system. As leaders reflect on the role that character education specifically surrounding grit has in the curriculum, they should keep a few things in mind.

First, educational reform, regardless of approach, cannot totally rectify the injustices that exist in our society. Attempts to address injustices must occur beyond the population of the citizenry that are ages 5-18.

Second, there is goodness in grit. Exhibiting effort to accomplish a task, even in the midst of that task being difficult, is a good thing to do. People are not always able to complete tasks in an easy manner—sometimes they need to persist through to the end, even when it is hard.

Third, it is important for individuals to be able to determine the difference between situations in which more effort needs to be applied and scenarios that are designed in an inherently unjust way. Educators and policymakers have to commit to not allowing grit to be used as an excuse to ignore the inequities that exist in our society and educational systems.

There is a closely connected relationship between individuals and the society in which they live. People are responsible for the society that is produced and systematic environmental design makes society responsible for the people that are

---

[9] Ravitch, Diane. *The Death and Life of the Great American School System: How Testing and Choice are Undermining Education.* New York: Basic Books, 2010.

nurtured within that society. The nature of our school system does not give us the appropriate amount of time or access to know the unique circumstances for each individual student and adapt our expectations of them appropriately.

In lieu of being able to identify which students are not achieving academically because of internal barriers, from those students who are not achieving academically because of external barriers, we must create schools and systems that are designed with the goal of removing all barriers to academic success, while instilling in students the value of hard work and grit. We must embrace the radical middle.

Critical Thinking

1. What does it mean to be critical literate in education today?
2. From what conditions does the author believe that schools need rescuing?

Internet References

Angela Duckworth
https://angeladuckworth.com/qa/

Decades of Scientific Research that Started a Growth Mindset Revolution
https://www.mindsetworks.com/science/

The Truth about Grit
https://www.psychologytoday.com/us/blog/media-spotlight/201606/the-truth-about-grit

---

VICKA BELL-ROBINSON, PhD, is an associate director of Residence Life at Miami University in Oxford, Ohio. Her research interests include dissent, self-efficacy, diversity, and inclusion in educational settings, and organizational development. She is the mother of a three school-aged children.

Bell-Robinson, Vicka. "The Radical Middle: The Limits and Advantages of Teaching Grit in Schools." The Journal of School & Society, 3(2) 11–17. Used by permission of The John Dewey Society.

Article

Prepared by: Sheron Fraser-Burgess, *Ball State University*

...And a Child Shall Lead Them...

EURYDICE STANLEY

Learning Outcomes

After reading this article, you will be able to:

- Connect the groundbreaking 1957 experiences of Elizabeth Eckford and the Little Rock Nine in Arkansas to the current anti-bullying efforts.
- Explore the meaning of oppression as a broad category within which to place current movements such as the anti-gun violence activities of the Marjory Stoneman Douglas students in Florida and efforts to end the school-to-prison pipeline that resist the political and corporate powers that perpetuate these conditions.
- Amass a range of instructional strategies with which to disrupt the social reproduction of oppressive treatment of forms of difference.

As a diversity facilitator of more than 30 years, I was so impressed by the 2018 Journal of Language and Literacy Education conference and Dr. Peter Smagorinsky's introspective essay that I jumped at the opportunity to communicate with the next generation of educators and administrators, whom I'll address as you in this essay. As the mother of two, I can't thank the educators who participated in this priceless forum enough for continually seeking new strategies to reach students in divergent populations.

What you are doing matters because it shows that you care. As we shared in our presentation, Reframing Anti-Bullying Education: Leveraging History and Prose to Increase Student Awareness and Resilience kindness and empathy literally saved Elizabeth Eckford's life while she[1] endured the trauma of desegregating Central High School in Little Rock, Arkansas. Our presentation of Elizabeth's experiences was part of an ongoing effort to convey the difference educators can make in a student's world by creating inclusive learning environments and intervening instead of turning a blind eye when bullying behavior is observed.

I can honestly say that I began mentally drafting a message to JoLLE educators while still at the conference, addressing a myriad of training concepts that have proven most effective over the years, such as understanding one's personal socialization process and identifying microaggressions. I felt compelled to write, because I was awe-struck by the intriguing training topics and high level of participant interaction observed in the JoLLE sessions. The energy was contagious. Honestly, there is simply no better way to inadvertently honor a civil rights icon like Elizabeth, who suffered great personal loss to implement the Supreme Court's 1954 Brown v. Board of Education decision to desegregate schools, than to continue your inclusive conversations for the betterment of all students. Elizabeth was truly touched by your efforts.

These are historic times. September 25, 2017, marked the 60th anniversary of the desegregation of Central High. The city of Little Rock held week-long events to honor the sacrifices of nine courageous students who endured a year of torture at the hand of segregationists. On March 26, 2018, we lost Linda Brown, the child who became known as the lead plaintiff in the Brown vs. Board case; and April 4th marks the 50th anniversary of the senseless assassination of Dr. Martin Luther King. Today, we focus on his dream, but his message broadened at the end of his life as he vehemently opposed the Vietnam War and spoke out for the poor and disenfranchised. Elizabeth is very cognizant of the passage of time and often notes her own mortality. It is never a conversation that I want to have, none of us do, but it emphasizes her point none of us have time to waste. We must determine how to coexist on this planet. As Dr. King said, "We must learn to live together as brothers or perish together as fools."

---

[1] I acknowledge that there is a gender spectrum and that myriad pronouns exist that I can use when referring to individuals in my writing. Throughout this article I use pronouns to refer to individuals that correspond with the pronouns that they use to refer to themselves.

The initial focus of my article sought to address the issues that led to our current level of racial division. However, the horrific school shooting that took the lives of 17 students and faculty on February 14th at Marjory Stoneman Douglas High School in Parkland, Florida, changed my emphasis. Watching Parkland families convey their sorrow due to the pointless slaying of their loved ones was heartbreaking. It was a textbook example of a *victim versus system* focus. In the days following the shooting, it was invigorating to watch the students unabashedly leverage their privilege and platform to address the issue of gun violence with notable success, much to the chagrin of gun advocates. The subsequent treatment both parents and students received as they disavowed the use of assault weapons, including the fabrication that they were crisis actors rather than students traumatized by the Parkland shooting was infuriating.

A new era of youth leading the charge for justice is being introduced across the country as massive marches and movements take place demanding student safety and gun reform. You can learn more about their platform at marchforourlives.com. I believe Dr. King would be proud; Elizabeth certainly is. While it is beautiful to watch, it was also frustrating on many accounts to see students be demeaned and maligned for views that differ from many in power. History seems to continually repeat itself as Parkland students receive hateful smears and even death threats. Like the Little Rock Nine, Elizabeth's classmates who desegregated Central High in 1957, the Parkland students' tenacity will benefit the greater good. It is in the country's best interest to march with them *now*, rather than honor their efforts years later, as experienced by the Little Rock Nine.

Outrage due to the Parkland shooting has been significant on both ends of the political spectrum. Unlike the Little Rock Nine, who were threatened with expulsion if they responded in kind to the physical and mental abuse they experienced daily, Parkland survivors have used every form of media available to convey their disdain for the slow response to their requests for increased safety in American schools. As evidenced by the March 24th march, citizens worldwide stand united with the students as they seek gun reform. Those supporters include Central High students, who walked out in honor of the stand taken by the Little Rock Nine 60 years ago with the blessing of their Principal, Nancy Rousseau. Rousseau told NPR, "The Little Rock Nine stood up for what they thought was the right thing for their education and their futures, and that is what the children did today."

As the principal of one of the most famous high schools at the country—a landmark of civil rights education—Rousseau understands the value of civil unrest. She suspended classes for 17 minutes to ensure student participation. Conversely, schools and counties more interested in control than compassion penalized students who walked out of class with everything from detention to suspension. Educators, as you become influencers in your respective institutions of education, choose to be one who inspires rather than intimidates. Regardless of whether or not the proposal for arming teachers comes to fruition, know that educators serve on the frontline of defense for students in numerous ways. Personally, I prefer leaving the issue of physical safety to school resource officers. Instead, we should arm teachers with the knowledge necessary to understand the impact of the invisible wounds left by school bullies.

In our presentation, Elizabeth noted, "None of us have permanent physical scars, but all of us have been deeply hurt. Life goes on." Elizabeth is truly a survivor. She is reaching back to encourage those who have been deeply pained by life's scars. For them, life does not go on if they choose the option of suicide, a rising phenomenon that we want to see end. In our book, written completely in verse, we wrote:

> Know that bullies are influenced by what they were taught and their own personal insecurities.
>
> When they lash out against your uniqueness, they expose their own self-doubts in a distorted way.
>
> I know what it is to endure the endless taunts of tormenters and persons filled with hate,
>
> But hurting myself or suicide due to someone else's shortcomings was never an option – give tomorrow one more day! (p. 113)

The Worst First Day addresses a myriad of issues that reflect the collective pain of our day. For example, in Little Rock, there were two attempts to remove Elizabeth from being hounded by the crowd, but they were from men, one a fellow Little Rock Nine teen, Terrence Roberts. These acts were something Elizabeth knew her mother, whom she refers to as "The Queen of No," would never approve.

In an essay included in *The Worst First Day*, my 15-year-old daughter Grace addresses the issue of human trafficking and the dehumanizing way African American women have been raped, kidnapped, and abused since enslavement by tormentors seeking what they perceived would be an "exotic" sexual encounter. That truth has been overlooked for years in the news. Shaun King addressed the issue in an exposé about girls stolen from Washington, DC, and 11-year-old Naomi Wadler gave a moving account during the March for Our Lives by speaking for black girls who have been victimized and whose stories are not told. Now, their stories are being told, and after 60 years, Elizabeth is telling her own story as well.

In *The Worst First Day*, we attempt to bring history to life and make the story applicable to today's reader, particularly young people who like graphic novels. The focus throughout the book is not solely race. It is difference. Elizabeth and the Little Rock Nine were abused due to her difference. That same difference continues to hold students captive in schools across the country.

In the collective experience of the writing team, acts of kindness received during times of trial have had monumental impact. So much so, in fact, that Elizabeth credits two students, Ann (Williams) Wedaman and Ken Reinhardt, with literally saving her life.

I recently had the opportunity to speak with and thank Ann for her courage. When I shared Elizabeth's comments, Ann was touched that Elizabeth continued to speak so highly of her. I asked Ann what prompted her to speak to Elizabeth every day during their last period of school when her other white classmates ignored, shunned, attacked, or berated the members of the Little Rock Nine. Ann simply and humbly responded, "That is the way I was raised." Ken shared the same sentiment. They saw Elizabeth's humanity, which clearly was not the case for the segregationists who threatened her life.

In the scale of prejudice developed by psychologist Gordon Allport (1958), racial prejudice begins with antilocution (hate speech) and continues through four additional levels: *avoidance*, *discrimination*, *physical attack*, and *extermination*. The Little Rock Nine experienced each of those levels except actual extermination, but it wasn't without trying. Countless weapons were routinely confiscated from the segregationist mobs who tried to prevent Elizabeth and the rest of the Little Rock Nine from attending Central High. Those who could not prevent Elizabeth's attendance at Central High sought to kill her spirit. For years, they succeeded. But now, every time Elizabeth speaks and shares her story, she releases more of the pain that held her captive in past years.

Our greatest hope is that readers will learn from Elizabeth's story and understand the impact of their own socialization. By becoming a student of the socialization process, you can better understand the experiential learning that shaped your own development and craft methodologies that will be impactful in the classroom. By remaining cognizant of the ways students learn and are influenced as you develop your lesson plans, you can better connect with, uplift, and encourage them. I know it is a tall order, but I have had the privilege of conducting this type of training for the Department of Defense. There is nothing like seeing that "lightbulb" turn on in the mind of a student who couldn't grasp concepts they had not previously experienced. Once you have that experience, positively changing lives can become addictive.

Becoming aware of one's socialization can also reduce stereotypes. It will allow you to better see each student for themselves, not the stereotype they represent. If left unchecked, said stereotypes can become validation for personal prejudices. For example, if a teacher believes that African Americans are violent, they could perceive danger in interactions they would normally consider benign with other groups. This misperception has caused a significant pattern to emerge in-school arrests. Children engaging in childish misbehavior are being perceived as aggressive, arrested and fall victim to the school-to-prison pipeline, which creates felons before students can reach graduation. In my hometown of Pensacola, Florida, during the 2014-2015 Escambia County, Florida, school year, black students comprised only 35% of the population, yet they represented 77% of student arrests according to a report from the Southern Poverty Law Center (SPLC). The report was reflected data from the Florida Department of Juvenile Justice.

I have witnessed reactions change toward my own son Christian, now 12. I have watched him transition from "cute kid" to potential "trouble" as he navigates his way through his first year of middle school, and it is horrifying. It has been quite a wake-up call, one that may prove grounds for a family move in the near future to a school environment where he will be perceived as what he is, a child of *promise*, rather than a potential *problem*. Perception can become reality.

Although Escambia County is a national leader in the school-to-prison pipeline, its national standing seems to be a best-kept community secret. When I shared my concerns with one of my son's teachers, he remarked, "That doesn't happen here." He was partially correct. More than likely, it wouldn't happen … to him or his children. Our discussion represents yet another frustrating barrier between parents and educators, particularly teachers who do not, as Covey (2013) says, "seek first to understand." As with most things, one is aware of issues that affect them. Seek to understand issues outside of your normal purview or comfort zone. You'll be amazed at the world outside the walls of your daily experience.

Dylan Klebold and Eric Harris killed 13 and injured 21 in the first high-profile school massacre in Columbine, Colorado, April 20, 1990. This year, on the 19th year of their horrific assault, there will be another student protest at 10 AM. You can learn more at #NationalSchoolWalkout. Klebold and Harris were bullied in school and committed suicide at the scene. It is interesting to note that our current school "zero-tolerance" rules which disproportionately affect students of color were enacted after their case. In *The New Jim Crow*, Michelle Alexander describes such occurrences as part of a racial caste system where "a stigmatized racial group is locked into an inferior position by law and custom" (p. 12).

Invariably, whenever I conduct training regarding the school-to-prison pipeline with adults, the discussion almost always turns to the inevitability of African Americans going to jail due to the programming they receive from their music and their culture. However, when I speak with students, the discussion focuses on how to break perceptual barriers and stereotypes. I prefer interacting with students. They give me hope for the future.

Unfortunately, students trapped within the prison pipeline are essentially the victims of overt efforts to reinstitute segregation, resulting in students of color serving as filler for privatized prisons before they even have had an opportunity to live their lives and contribute to society. Until we recognize such occurrences and the discriminatory motivations behind them, the cycle will continue. Efforts to segregate through prison are not new. In *Slavery by Another Name*, Douglas Blackmon (2008) exposes the practice of involuntary servitude that continued after the Civil War through World War II. We must be cognizant of the legacy of racism if we are to have any hope of ending its inheritance.

To move forward together as a people, we must demand a level playing field *for all*. On April 26, 2018, the Equal Justice Initiative (EJI) was founded by Bryan Stevenson, a crusader for justice. Stevenson is expanding his courtroom battles by showing the *conditions* that led to false arrests and senseless lynchings to the world. The EJI will open the Legacy Museum & National Memorial for Peace and Justice in Montgomery, Alabama. Counts' iconic photograph of Elizabeth will be featured in the museum as yet another reflection of racism in America and the necessity of justice for all. In *Just Mercy*, Stevenson (2015) shares his experiences representing "... the poor, the incarcerated and the condemned" (p. 17). He shares powerful lessons observed in our judicial system, particularly the unfair prosecutions and convictions of abused and neglected children trapped in the school-to-prison pipeline, who were "... prosecuted as adults and suffered more abuse and mistreatment after being placed in adult facilities" (p. 17).

We need to end the mindset that would so easily condone the criminalization of our future. Hopefully, Stevenson's effort will start much-needed conversations that have not taken place in the United States. It did in South Africa through the Truth and Reconciliation Commission. I had the opportunity to conduct human relations training for the South African National Defense Force in 2000 after Transformation. I was incredulous when training participants shared the admissions heard through the commission in the hope of achieving racial reconciliation. In exchange for full admissions, assailants were not held accountable for their offenses. Mr. Dullar Omar, former South African Minister of Justice, noted, "... a commission is a necessary exercise to enable South Africans to come to terms with their past on a morally acceptable basis and to advance the cause of reconciliation." The admissions gave family members the opportunity to know what happened to their loved ones.

The Equal Justice Initiative museum features numerous images of American lynchings and documents the names of 4,400 lynchings America has as of yet to admit to the sin and the legacy of once socially accepted practices condoned a very short time ago. Those who do not understand the significance of the Charlottesville white nationalist weekend rally may gain a deeper understanding by visiting the national memorial. The ultimate goal is peace, redemption and reconciliation, which does not come without truth. In *The Worst First Day*, Elizabeth notes, "If we have honestly acknowledged our painful but shared past, then we can have reconciliation" (p. 102).

As I have attempted to share with recent examples, prejudice did not end in 1957 after the 101st Airborne secured the safe passage of the Little Rock Nine into Central High. Now, overt policies have become covert, and even seemingly benign issues such as zero-tolerance school policies are inadvertently affecting students who were not the policy's intended target. *The Worst First Day* seeks to help readers see the impact that bias, racism, and discrimination can have through Elizabeth's teen eyes. The autobiography was written by a diverse team that focused on illuminating different perspectives of Elizabeth's first-person experiences. Grace ensured that the writing retained the interest of youth. For this reason, the book is written completely in verse. As a retired Army officer, I focused on the military operation side of Elizabeth's days at Central High by including executive and military documentation from what was known as "Operation Arkansas." Combined, *The Worst First Day* provides a historical backdrop and civics lesson that most readers aren't privy to in an autobiography. Beyond the writing, the book is complemented by essays to include Principal Rousseau, Robin White, the Superintendent of the Little Rock Central High National Park Site, and the compelling photography of Kirk Jordan and Pulitzer Prize-nominated photographer Will Counts.

The photo that Counts captured of Elizabeth being surrounded by hostile segregationists became one of the most iconic images of the 20th century. Since photographs weren't available to depict incidents in school, we recreated Elizabeth's memories through the compelling graphic artwork of Harding University senior Rachel Gibson. We wanted readers to understand the utter pandemonium and bitter violence Elizabeth and the Little Rock Nine experienced every single day while simply attempting to obtain an education.

Through the book, we hope to inspire expectations of excellence and denounce stereotypes that can become self-fulfilling prophecies. The Brown v. Board of Education case was won with compelling testimony elicited by Thurgood Marshall and his legal team from Drs. Kenneth and Mamie Clark. The researchers placed two dolls, black and white, in front of African American children and asked them to point out the "good" doll. By and large, the white doll was chosen without hesitation, because that was all the students saw in a world dominated by segregation. Their internalization of such a self-pathologizing perception was among the most compelling testimony against segregated schools.

The Brown decision was supposed to end segregation and prevent the pervasiveness of policies that led to such widespread, self-depreciative beliefs among African Americans, but it took years to actually implement. Students continue to be impacted today. One of the most effective ways to break the stronghold of influences such as the media and peers begins at home and is greatly influenced by perceptive, caring educators. Please remain aware and question policies and procedures that disproportionately have a negative effect on one particular group, whether the group is discriminated against by race, sex, sexual orientation, or another demographic feature. Remain vigilant and serve as an advocate for students who are not empowered to speak for themselves, as Anne and Ken did on behalf of Elizabeth. Look at the impact, not only the intent of school discipline. Do not allow your students to fall victim to the graveyard of broken spirit through socially accepted injustice approved by school leadership. Be vocal about practices that marginalize. Their influence can last a lifetime.

In countless training sessions I have conducted over the years, it has not been unusual to see audiences wide-eyed at the day's conclusion. When I served as an Instructor at the Defense Equal Opportunity Management Institute, we provided 16 weeks of intense training identifying personal biases and societal discrimination. Our students had the challenging responsibility of helping commanders address contentious issues such as racism and discrimination within their commands. After their training, many participants felt overwhelmed by the discriminatory behavior that they simply had not been able to see prior to their immersion. The greatest benefit that I see to JoLLE's educational work is the invaluable exposure to issues that may not have been part of one's awareness without this venue. Maximize the opportunity by not only reading the articles, but also interacting within the JoLLE community. Visionaries flourish with the support of like-minded spirits. Rise together.

Without fail, after training I am usually asked the $100,000 question, "What can I do?" It is easy to feel overwhelmed by institutional discrimination, especially when one considers its enormity. I am as taken aback by some of the images in *The Worst First Day*—to include citizens holding signs saying "Race Mixing is Communism" or the Little Rock Nine being escorted by the 101st Airborne—as I am by listening to the gun lobbyists make disparaging remarks about Parkland students. Although it can be overwhelming, we must begin where we can: with ourselves, by expanding our personal knowledge base and becoming aware of our personal biases. It is only when we challenge our own stereotypes that we can ascertain the source of our beliefs and change behaviors that do not coincide with professed values. Introspection can uncover hidden biases that originated from a grandparent, rather than reflecting your current beliefs. Invariably, we are creatures of habit. We do what is familiar until we recognize something different. If you want to expand your worldview, expand your circle of influence. If everyone you know looks and thinks the way you do, it can create tunnel vision. Expand your personal influences. It will expand your mind. Angela Davis said, "I am no longer accepting the things I cannot change. I am changing the things I cannot accept." Educators, please follow the lead of the Little Rock Nine and the students who spoke out for the voiceless during the March For Our Lives. They were not willing to accept the bullying and bias that they have been subjected to since the school massacre. One of the most resonant voices, Parkland student David Hogg, noted that African American students who survived the Parkland massacre have been silenced. Similar comparisons have been made to students who spoke out against the shootings of unarmed African Americans, especially protestors associated with social justice groups such as #BlackLivesMatter. Hogg's comments give me great hope because he is not only cognizant of his privilege, but he makes every attempt possible to share it whenever possible until there is a level playing field for all. As more voices are heard and opinions understood, more walls come down.

Parkland students are leading the way by standing up and fighting organizational apathy with action and engagement. As you continue your careers as educators known for creating inclusive environments, don't limit your view by seeking out blatant acts of overt racism. Instead, adjust your personal lens to look below the surface to be able to identify the countless layers of institutional discrimination that would impact your students without your intervention. As Ann and Ken proved, your effort can be as simple as treating students with kindness and respect, but it can have a life-long impact.

Bullying excludes, awareness informs, and empathy unites. We salute you because we know that you have one of the most challenging jobs in America. Although you are most likely under-resourced and under-funded, please always remember why you sought to become an educator. Elizabeth Eckford and the Little Rock Nine endured unimaginable cruelty and unabashed hatred by maintaining their vision of desegregating Central High and securing the best education possible.

We thank JoLLE Conference co-chairs S. R. Tolliver and T. Hunter Strickland for the invitation to present in Athens and Principal Editor Heidi Hadley and the entire JoLLE editorial team for being such wonderful hosts. Most importantly, many thanks to each conference participant for your heartfelt response. This was our first conference since publishing our book, and JoLLE will always have a warm place in our hearts. We envision with delighted expectation the classrooms you will positively influence in the future and the educational culture you will transform, one student at a time. The example you set will make discrimination what it should be: taboo and obsolete.

Always remember that what you do makes a difference. Elizabeth often remarks that much progress has been made since her traumatic year at Central High, but she felt compelled to share her experiences in *The Worst First Day* because there is still much work yet to be done. This book is so timely, and will be a powerful means of teaching students civics lessons by utilizing compelling stories from American history.

We hope readers will remember Central High and remain cognizant of their interactions with others as well as their own behaviors while dealing with those who are different. Educators, never forget the difference you can make by serving as an advocate for your students. Positively influence them and please, don't turn your head in apathy to their distress. A kind word from you can make all the difference in the world, and it could be one of the few they ever receive. Who knows? Years from now, you may have students walk up to you and thank you for saving their lives ... just like Elizabeth.

References

Alexander, M. (2010). *The New Jim Crow: Mass incarceration in the age of colorblindness.* New York, NY: The New Press.

Allport, G. (1958). *The nature of prejudice.* New York, NY: Anchor Books.

Blackmon, D. (2008). *Slavery by another name.* New York, NY: Anchor Books.

Covey, S. R. (2013). *The 7 habits of highly effective people: Powerful lessons in personal change.* New York, NY: RosettaBooks.

Eckford, E., Stanley, E., & Stanley, G. (2018). *The worst first day: Bullied while desegregating Central High.* Pensacola, FL: Lamp Press.

Stevenson, B. (2015). *Just mercy: A story of justice and redemption.* New York, NY: Spiegel & Grau.

Critical Thinking

1. What patterns are evident in the examples of activism presented?
2. Surmise the role that difference is playing in persons who are identified as the objects of marginalization and oppression in society.
3. What conclusions can be drawn from the article about the qualities of actions that bring about positive social change?

Internet References

Brown v. Board of Education (1954)
https://www.ourdocuments.gov/doc.php?flash=true&doc=87

In Her Own Words: Elizabeth Eckford
https://www.facinghistory.org/resource-library/her-own-words-elizabeth-eckford

Parkland: A Year After the School Shooting That Was Supposed to Change Everything
https://www.nytimes.com/2019/02/13/us/parkland-anniversary-marjory-stoneman-douglas.html

---

EURYDICE STANLEY (www.dreurydice.com) is an international motivational speaker, United States Army veteran, mommy and co-author of *The Worst First Day: Bullied While Desegregating Central High*, available on Amazon or at bit.ly/WorstFD. She specializes in leadership, human relations and inclusion topics. Follow her on Twitter @ dreurydice or on her Facebook pages, Dr. Eurydice, Family CEO First or Stand United Against Racism.

Stanley, Eurydice. "...And a Child Shall Lead Them..." Journal of Language and Literacy Education, v14 no 1 Spr 2018. Used by permission of the author.

Article

Prepared by: Sheron Fraser-Burgess, *Ball State University*

Strong Teams, Strong Results
Formative Assessment Helps Teacher Teams Strengthen Equity

NANCY LOVE AND MICHELLE CROWELL

Learning Outcomes

After reading this article, you will be able to:

- Describe the qualities of effective teacher team work.
- Interpret the constitutive steps to team-based formative assessment cycle in terms of their efficacy for student learning.
- Surmise the attributes of classrooms and schools that exemplify educational equity.

At a diverse elementary school, a grade-level planning team is meeting about an upcoming lesson and creating an exit ticket, a brief formative assessment tool to check for students' understanding. School administrators have recently asked special educators and language development specialists to become part of the collaborative team.

As the group begins working on the exit ticket, one special education teacher expresses concern: "My students couldn't do that. It's too hard for them. They will get discouraged."

Her teammate pushes back gently, "I think with modifications this assessment can work for all our kids. Let's see if we can modify the task to make it more accessible to your students. We want all our students to hit the standard."

Another teacher chimes in, "The modifications might work better for our English language learners, too."

The team creates two versions of the assessment, and teachers choose which version to give to their own students. The following week, they analyze the results together and plan for reteaching and extension based on the results.

The special education teachers are elated to discover how well their students performed. "We just weren't expecting enough of them," one teacher reflected. "Our special education students are excited, too. They know they're doing the same work as their classmates."

Role of Teacher Teams

Sitting in our schools right now is one of the most powerful levers we have for deepening equity: teacher teams focused on developing collective expertise in high-leverage, equity-promoting practices.

One conversation at a time, teams like the one in the vignette above, a composite of teams we have observed over time, chip away at low expectations, racism, and cultural biases that have marginalized special education students, English language learners, students of color, and others who have not traditionally been served well by schools.

While many schools have a general orientation toward equity and "all students achieving," those values come to life when team members confront specific limiting beliefs about individual students in the context of their work together on formative assessment. Working together in this way, teams can strengthen courage, conviction, and cultural proficiency to make progress toward equity, one team meeting at a time.

This was the approach of the Madeline English School, a culturally and linguistically diverse K-8 school with 825 students in Everett, Massachusetts. For years, standardized test results at the school showed below-average growth. In particular, special education students' and English language learners' achievement was flat. Teachers examined assessment data, but it was often too little too late, occurring after the students who took the tests had moved on.

Then, in spring 2017, the school launched a partnership with Research for Better Teaching to implement data coaching, a yearlong professional learning program sponsored by the Five District Partnership. The partnership is a network of urban districts in greater Boston, funded by the Massachusetts Network Initiative grant from New Venture Fund.

Over the course of a year, the school became committed to an equity-based approach to formative assessment and data-driven instruction.

Common planning time team meetings transformed from unproductive conversations to focused analysis of common exit tickets, careful planning for immediate next steps for reteaching and extension, and shared accountability for taking action in the classroom. The divide between special and general educators dissolved as teachers became collaborators in holding all students to high standards.

Special educators and language development specialists became regular contributors at team meetings, sharing strategies for reteaching, modifying standards-based exit tickets aligned with general education assessments, and analyzing student formative assessment results with their colleagues.

Mindsets shifted as teachers challenged each other and changed practices, and the school began to see positive impacts on students. On the most recent diagnostic assessments, Grade 7 special education students' growth spurted, exceeding the targeted growth expectations by an average of 160% in reading and 44% in mathematics from the middle to the end of the academic year. Grade 4 special education students and English language learners exceeded targets by 21% in reading and 13% in mathematics.

The school's Five District Partnership Benchmark Assessments showed improvements in all grades for all students, with grade 7 making the greatest gains of almost 20 percentage points.

"The special education students are really benefitting from our team work," special educator Christine Downing said. "Before, they had this perception that they were dumb. Now they know that we are going to push them and that they can push themselves."

What alchemy made this change happen? Four key ingredients were:

1. Professional learning for team leaders and administrators that is based in a practical framework with protocols for team learning and equity;
2. Thoughtful rollout;
3. A regular structure and schedule for team meetings; and
4. Consistent follow-through by school leaders.

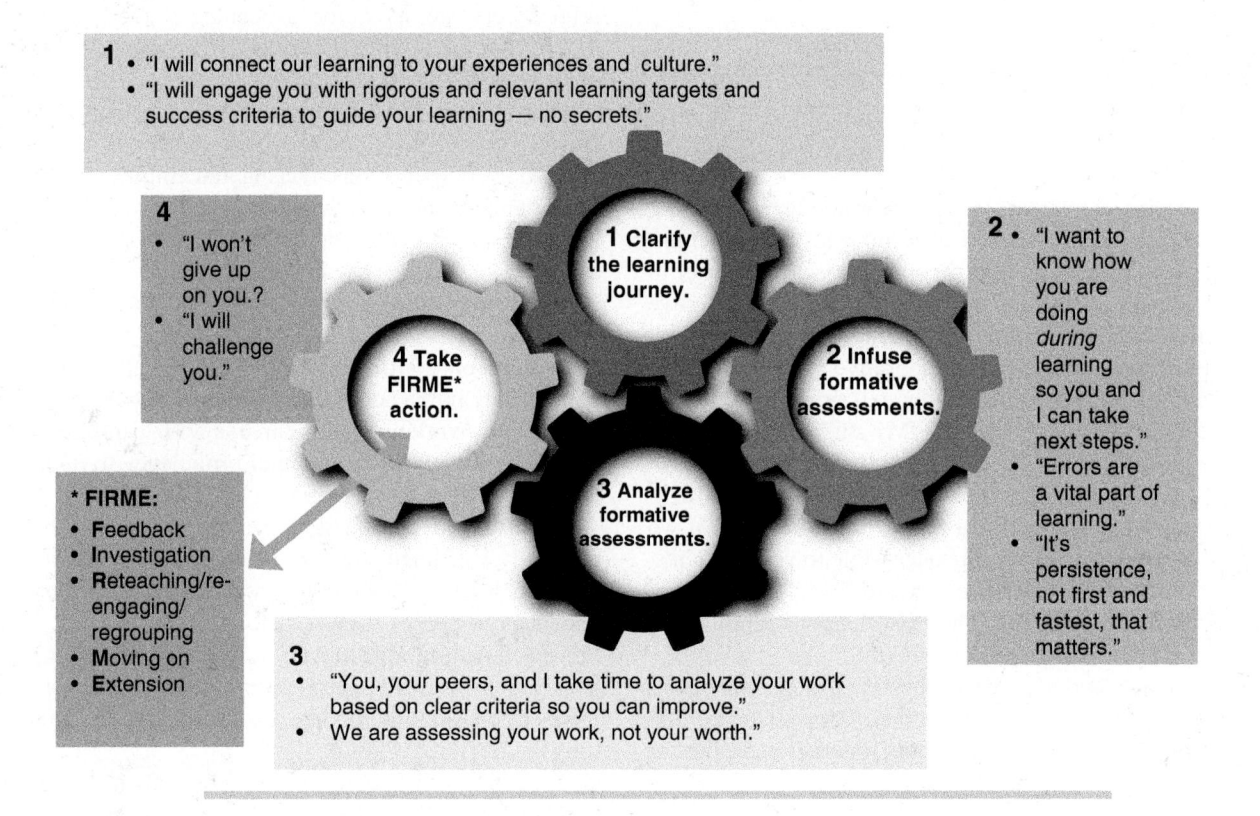

The Formative Assessment for Results Cycle with High-expectations Messages

A Professional Learning Framework for Equity

Data coaching is a team-based approach to helping schools use formative assessment data to drive short cycles of improvement. It is grounded in the knowledge that strengthening cultural proficiency is essential for making this process work.

"We have learned through our experience in the Using Data Process that issues of race/ethnicity, class, culture, gender, and other differences ... cannot and ... should not be avoided when examining data and engaging in collaborative inquiry. Our responses and reactions to these differences deeply affect how we interpret data and have a profound effect on student learning," say the authors of *The Data Coach's Guide to Improving Learning for All Students* (Love, Stiles, Mundry, & DiRanna, 2008, p. 92.)

The focus of professional learning in data coaching is on the Formative Assessment for Results Cycle (see diagram above), a framework to guide teacher teams in developing collective expertise in classroom formative assessment and the equity-promoting practices and messages that support its effective use.

The cycle includes four steps. Embedded in each are high-expectation messages that teachers continually communicate to students both through their words and their actions so that students can internalize the growth mindset and their teacher's belief that they can succeed.

When teachers and students regularly experience this cycle and these messages, they chip away at limiting beliefs such as "mistakes are a sign of weakness," "speed counts," and "only the few bright can achieve at high levels" (Saphier, Haley-Speca, & Gower, 2018, p. 410).

Each step of the cycle requires that teachers are curious about and continually deepening their understanding of each of their students' cultures, experiences, and thinking while monitoring their own biases and assumptions.

The steps are:

1. Clarify the learning journey.
In this step, teachers focus and motivate learning by communicating specific success criteria to their students. Success criteria level the playing field by making explicit what success looks like through checklists, rubrics, and exemplars, so students don't have to guess what's on the teacher's mind—a phenomenon that tends to privilege students whose backgrounds are similar to teachers'. According to John Hattie's (2017) research, this kind of teacher clarity has a .75 effect size on

Taking Firme Action

Action in response to formative assessment	What it is	Why it matters for equity
FEEDBACK	Provide objective, descriptive information about students' performance relative to standards and success criteria.	Teams focused on equity learn about both effective practice and "wise feedback." "Wise feedback" (Cohen & Steele, 2002) helps combat stereotypes of intellectual inferiority among students of color by combining honest, direct feedback linked to standards alongside assurances that the student is capable and can improve performance.
INVESTIGATION	Examine student thinking in daily diagnostic questions and discussions.	In the words of math teacher Jessica Salem, "Now we ask our students to explain their thinking. Then I get to understand their thought process. They always have a reason. Once we understand, we can help them correct errors."
RETEACHING, RE-ENGAGING, REGROUPING	Use different approaches for students who need another opportunity to master a learning target.	Students with different learning needs and backgrounds do not all learn in the same way. Teams committed to equity collaborate to expand their teaching and grouping repertoires and make the best match for individual students.
MOVING ON	A legitimate step after the previous step when most, even if not all, students have achieved proficiency.	Equity means ensuring all students have access to a rigorous curriculum so the curriculum does not to grind to a halt for one or two students. However, if some students have not mastered a concept or skill, it is important to have a plan for how they will do so.
EXTENSION	Provide additional challenges to students who master learning targets before others.	Extension ensures that all students are continually learning and stretching. "Now our students who reach a standard before others know they are going to be challenged," said reading coach Mary Beth Benedetto.

student outcomes. (For comparison, .4 represents a typical year of student growth.)

Also in this step, teachers gather information about students and their backgrounds through surveys, interviews, and one-on-one relationships with individual students so they can identify culturally relevant examples and metaphors and connect them to the content being taught.

2. Infuse formative assessments.

In this step, teachers weave formative assessments throughout instruction, using carefully crafted diagnostic questions that align with learning targets, assess success criteria, and surface gaps or errors in student thinking.

When teachers and students use assessments to make timely adjustments in teaching and learning tactics, they can effectively double the speed of learning (Black & Wiliam, 2009). These assessments can take the form of quick quizzes, exit tickets, responses to writing prompts, or entries in science or math journals.

In grade-level teams, teachers work together to craft common diagnostic questions, road-test them with students, and bank those that worked well for future use. In vertical teams, assessments are not common but align with learning progressions within and between grades and thus are relevant for all teachers on the team.

In this step, teachers are mindful of creating diagnostic questions that are as free from racial, cultural, and socioeconomic biases (Popham, 2017) as possible.

3. Analyze formative assessments.

This step is about analyzing results frequently (ideally, daily or weekly). Individually, teachers might do this on the fly, quickly sorting student work to determine who's got it and who doesn't, and regrouping or reteaching accordingly. In a team, teachers use protocols to take a deeper dive into student work to determine whether the success criteria are met or not and plan for next instructional steps.

Understanding students' cultures comes into play in making accurate interpretations of the meaning of the data.

For example, one teacher team analyzed results of a mathematics assessment where students were asked to estimate the answer. The team was surprised to discover that, when disaggregating data by race, Asian students performed worse than other racial groups.

As they dug deeper, they discovered that these students had estimation skills, but they also had a cultural bias against estimating and favored computing accurately. Without honoring and addressing these students' assumptions, teachers were not likely to help them improve.

4. Take FIRME action.

FIRME stands for five actions teachers can take in response to formative assessment results to improve instruction in ways that meet students' needs. (See above table for more information.)

Together, the four steps of the Formative Assessment for Results Cycle and their embedded high-expectations messages achieve what John Hattie (2012) refers to as "visible learning" or "students' assessment capabilities" (p. 141), where students are clear about goals and success criteria, self-assess their progress, and take next steps in their learning, thus moving from dependent to independent, self-directed learners.

While important for all students, these practices are a vital for marginalized learners, who, Zaretta Hammond argues, need an ally to help "dependent learners begin and stay on the arduous path toward independent learners" (Hammond, 2015, p. 89).

Structures and Support for Success

At Madeline English School, this work is supported by three additional key elements: thoughtful rollout, structures and schedules, and leadership team follow-through.

Thoughtful rollout. After engaging in learning about the Formative Assessment for Results Cycle, the school team needed to contextualize the professional learning to the school and, as one member said, focus on "what works for our building." They prioritized workshop content they would deliver to the whole staff.

The math and reading coaches and assistant principal then developed presentations in four chosen topic areas and delivered them starting in October during each grade-level common planning time meeting. This was so successful that, by January, teachers at all grade levels confidently facilitated common planning time meetings themselves and followed data coaching protocols, with guidance and expertise provided by the reading and mathematics coaches.

Structures and schedules. For these efforts to work, teachers need dedicated and regular meeting times. Teachers meet by grade level once (grades K-2) or twice (grades 3-8) in an eight-day cycle and are joined by special educators, language development specialists, interventionists, and coaches. In grades 7-8, teachers meet in vertical teams by content area.

Leadership team follow-through. The leadership team went beyond creating structure and meeting schedules. They followed through with regular attendance at team meetings, classroom observations, and review of team documentation.

For example, math coach Howard Tuttman, reading coach Mary Beth Benedetto, and assistant principal Michelle Crowell visited classrooms daily to follow up on topics discussed during common planning time and celebrate successes of individual teachers and students.

In addition, all teacher teams shared formative assessments and results with Crowell and coaches through Google Classroom and Google Forms. This helped the leadership team track progress and teachers stay accountable to each other. Teachers appreciated the structure, schedule, and follow-up. As Tiffany Boakye, 4th-grade teacher, said, "Our administrators are the backbone that has made this successful. ... Because they are so passionate about it, they made us passionate about it."

A Climate of High Achievement

At Madeline English School, passion and persistence resulted in a climate of high achievement for all that permeates the school and is accompanied by encouraging test results, especially for special education students and English language learners.

With the right combination of professional learning on formative assessment practices and the structures and follow-through to support those practices, teacher teams are showing it is possible to create equity breakthroughs in as little as one year.

As reading coach Mary Beth Benedetto puts it, "The impact of our collaboration on equity has been huge. It used to be special education teachers and students felt isolated. Now all the teachers are thinking about all of our kids."

References

Black, P. & Wiliam, D. (2009). Developing the theory of formative assessment. *Educational Assessment, Evaluation, and Accountability, 21*(1), 5–31.

Cohen, G.L. & Steele, C.M. (2002). A barrier of mistrust: How stereotypes affect cross-race mentoring. In J. Aronson (Ed.). *Improving academic achievement: Impact of psychological factors on education* (pp. 305–327). Oxford, England: Academic Press.

Hammond, Z. (2015). *Culturally responsive teaching & the brain: Promoting authentic engagement and rigor among culturally and linguistically diverse students.* Thousand Oaks, CA: Corwin Press.

Hattie, J. (2017, December). *250+ influences on student achievement.* Available at www.visiblelearningplus.com.

Hattie, J. (2012). *Visible learning for teachers: Maximizing the impact on learning.* New York, NY: Routledge.

Love, N., Stiles, K.E., Mundry, S., & DiRanna, K. (2008). *The data coach's guide to improving learning for all students.* Thousand Oaks, CA: Corwin Press.

Popham, J. (2017). *Classroom assessment: What teachers need to know* (8th ed.). Boston, MA: Pearson.

Saphier, J., Haley-Speca, M., & Gower, R. (2018). *The skillful teacher: The comprehensive resource for improving teaching and learning* (7th ed., p. 410). Acton, MA: Research for Better Teaching.

Critical Thinking

1. What underlying messages do collaborative teamwork assessment send to students about the potential for educational achievement and success?

2. Support the link that the article makes for each of the steps of formative assessment to advancing equity.

3. How might working in these teams be advantageous for teachers?

Internet References

Benefits of Collaboration
http://neatoday.org/new-educators/benefits-of-collaboration/

For Effective Schools, Teamwork is Not Optional
https://www.edutopia.org/blog/effective-schools-teamwork-not-optional-sean-glaze

---

NANCY LOVE is a senior consultant at Research for Better Teaching. Michelle Crowell (mcrowell@everett.k12.ma.us) is the principal of Parlin School in Everett, Massachusetts.

Love, Nancy and Michelle Crowell. "Strong Teams, Strong Results: Formative Assessment Helps Teacher Teams Strengthen Equity." The Learning Professional, Vol 39, No 5, October 2018. Used by permission of Learning Forward.

Article

Prepared by: Sheron Fraser-Burgess, *Ball State University*

Overcoming the Challenges of Poverty

Here are 15 things educators can do to make our schools and classrooms places where students thrive.

JULIE LANDSMAN

Learning Outcomes

After reading this article, you will be able to:

- Summarize actions educators can take to help students thrive.
- Critique the practice of teaching in different ways to students of different economic circumstances.

Last year, when I was leading a staff development session with teachers at a high-poverty elementary school, a teacher described how one of her kindergarten students had drifted off to sleep at his seat—at 8:00 A.M. She had knelt down next to the child and began talking loudly in his ear, urging him to wake up. As if to ascertain that she'd done what was best for this boy, she turned to the rest of us and said, "We are a 'no excuses' school, right?"

A fellow teacher who also lived in the part of Minneapolis where this school was located and knew the students well, asked, "Did you know Samuel has been homeless for a while now? Last night, there was a party at the place where he stays. He couldn't go to bed until four in the morning."

I couldn't help but think that if the "no excuses" philosophy a school follows interferes with basic human compassion for high-needs kids, the staff needs to rethink how they are doing things. Maybe they could set up a couple of cots for homeless students in the office to give them an hour or two of sleep; this would yield more participation than shouting at children as they struggle to stay awake.

This isn't the first time I've heard of adults viewing low-income children as "the problem" rather than trying to understand their lives. In a radio interview I heard, a teenage girl in New Orleans after Hurricane Katrina told her interviewer that she thought many people viewed poor families like hers as criminals. Crying, she described how it felt when city officials blamed her family for the lack of food and shelter they experienced after the hurricane.

A Forgotten Duty?

Sometimes it seems that we do not believe it's our duty to provide basic needs and an education for all children in the United States, no matter where they grow up. For instance, in some schools I know of, when a student cannot pay for a reduced-price meal, the lunch is dumped into the trash in front of the entire school, humiliating that child.

The attitudes of policymakers also reflect a shift toward teaching students in differing ways depending on their economic status. Teachers often hear that poor kids come from violent, chaotic homes and that only regimented curriculums will allow them to succeed. Although wealthier children are taught through a variety of approaches that emphasize developing the whole child, the emphasis for low-income children is often on developing obedience.

At the same time, many rural, urban, and suburban schools serving low-income students challenge such prescriptive teaching. They quietly provide, intellectually and materially, for high-poverty students. For instance, they create programs that arrange transportation for students to theaters, concerts, and museums. Because Saturday and Sunday are two days of the week many poor children go hungry, some schools send kids home for the weekend with backpacks of food. They create a welcoming environment where even the poorest parents feel comfortable.

Teachers and administrators at these schools offer challenging instruction while simultaneously addressing basic needs. This is a tricky balancing act that requires dedication, self-reflection, and reexamining what works—or doesn't. Here, gathered from schools that succeed with students living in poverty, are suggestions for how to manage that balancing act.

What Teachers Can Do
Make Time for Extras
Can you create times for students to make up schoolwork, work on a project for history class, or just enjoy music and art? It doesn't have to be every day. Teachers in a building might coordinate to set times before and after classes during which a child with an unstable home life can use a computer or read in silence—and when teachers can give guidance and build trust.

In one middle school where I worked, we let students spend their lunch hours with us, providing chess and checkers. It's amazing how much information young men and women will share over a game board, from tasks they're having trouble accomplishing to worries about food over the weekend. What we learned from these times helped us create programs that met students' greatest needs.

Tell Students to Ask for Help
Spell out that you expect learners to come talk with you about a low test score, a comment on a paper, or their needs for resources. Some students simply don't know the expectations regarding behavior, work, and interaction with their teacher. One teacher in a suburban high school assumed her students had access to the Internet and assigned work on the basis of that assumption. When she found out that many students had no Internet at home, she organized time after classes for students to work on school computers—and transportation home—giving careful instructions about what she wanted from their time online.

Cut deals with students who don't have essential supplies by providing those supplies while, at the same time, pushing these kids to work hard on their assignments. A homeless girl may have lost a pencil in the trudge around the city finding a place for the night or left her homework in the office of a shelter. A boy may not be able to get his work done by the due date because he has no quiet place to concentrate. By keeping a supply of pencils, paper, and notebooks handy and adjusting due dates for individual students, you can make sure students know you're willing to modify conditions but you expect work to be done.

Use Visuals to Help Organize Assignments
Students whose lives are chaotic need to be reminded of exactly what work is due and when. Calendars and charts are visual cues that help kids organize time and tasks together, especially if you refer to them often. Write different tasks and events connected to each assignment—outline due date, media center day, or first draft due—on the calendar squares. A calendar both reminds students of the day of the week and creates a visual map to future tasks.

Imagine Their Obstacles— and See Their Strengths
If you grew up with economic security, remind yourself that you might not understand the things adults and children in families with barely enough for the basics have to do just to survive—and the obstacles they face. Some schools expect parents to get to parent conferences in the evening, which can involve a bus ride, babysitting expense, or taking time off from the late shift. To illuminate what such expectations involve, one school's social worker surveyed parents and teachers to see how many owned cars. Every teacher and teacher's aide owned a car, but only 40 parents—in a school with 500 students—did.

Find ways to accommodate such realities. For instance, I worked as a visiting poet in a school where one-third of the students were homeless. We made sure each kid had two copies of the poems they wrote, one to leave at school and one to take to their parents, to keep their writing from getting lost in transit.

When high-poverty schools hire people from the surrounding neighborhood who are acquainted with the poverty there, these people can be experts regarding students' situations. Connect with these staff members; ask their advice on how to affirm and provide for particular children. Jared, a young adult hall monitor at a school where I taught writing, brought into my class a poetry book by rapper Tupac Shakur. I read some of those poems with my students. Soon Jared was visiting my poetry sessions during breaks from his work, helping students with their writing and homework.

Understanding students' obstacles should help you give them credit for their amazing resilience and delight in learning. Low-income children are often described in terms of what they *don't* have or *cannot* do. Reframe your thinking to recognize the strength it takes for a child who had to find a couch to sleep on last night to simply make it in the school door.

Listen

In our rush to create silent classrooms and push test preparation, we lose sight of the complexity of children's lives, and we lose our delight in knowing how they feel, reason, joke, or concoct ideas. In just 10 minutes, you can encourage students to write from a prompt like "I am from _____" or "I used to_____, but now I _____." Read their pieces to a small group or to the entire class. Elementary teachers often have a daily circle time and even in secondary school, you can pull the chairs into a circle at the end of class and ask students about their plans for the rest of the day or a neighborhood event.

This listening is an important part of your job. Listening means slowing down or stopping, even for a minute as a student lingers by your desk. It means having music playing as you work in your classroom in the morning and nodding to a student who comes in early. If you let that student relax there most mornings, he might make it a habit to talk with you before each day begins.

Don't Tolerate Teasing

By establishing clear classroom guidelines, including no teasing about clothes or possessions and talking with students about what these guidelines mean, you'll establish a climate of safety. Effective guidelines state positive behaviors, such as, Be Physically Considerate, Be Verbally Considerate, or Try New Things. Talk about what concepts like *consideration* mean; for instance, showing verbal consideration includes not taunting or hurting anyone's feelings. When you spend time up front working on behaviors, you save time the rest of the year. Classes become communities, and discipline problems diminish.

Connect Curriculum to Students' Interests

When possible, connect the content you're teaching to things students are fascinated with, like a song or video they keep talking about or the pollution in their neighborhood. By tapping into learners' concerns, you can develop bridges to literature, science, or math. You might engage students in projects connected to community issues or problems, like cleaning up a playground or advocating for a bus for summer programs. Students can write letters to the editor, ask scientists to come in and talk about pollution, or find journalists who will talk to the class about issues in their city. Such actions give low-income students a sense of agency and possibility. You might also infuse their families' traditions and talents into classwork. Financially poor students often come from families rich in culture.

Speak Out

Advocate for impoverished children by speaking up about which students are tracked into general courses versus gifted programs or advanced classes. Insist on the giftedness of some of your poorer students. Some schools have programs that parallel advanced classes yet don't require applicants to demonstrate academic skills that they may not have going in—but could develop. These demanding courses both challenge and support low-income students.

Other schools have opened up advanced placement or International Baccalaureate classes to anyone who wants to try them. Suggest similar programs and push for changes like providing bilingual conferences for parents who don't speak English. You may get push back from those who want no deviation from the status quo. Be willing to be unpopular for your advocacy.

Find Allies

It's hard to do this work in isolation. Forge a supportive network that keeps you going as you strive to make a difference for students and push for academic equity—through a book group, inquiry team, or lunchtime discussion on issues related to education and poverty. You'll have someone to call when you're trying to anticipate how your suggestions will go over at the next faculty meeting—and someone to talk with about how it went. There are more teachers willing to advocate for kids than is often apparent.

What Administrators Can Do

Principals and superintendents can do much to support both struggling students and committed teachers. Think in terms of getting resources to the neediest schools and students.

Develop a Trusting Relationship with Teachers

Can teachers talk with you about an idea or solution they have for addressing the needs of poorer students? One of the most successful urban principals I ever worked with asked teachers to come to him often with a problem combined with a suggested solution.

Standing up for overworked teachers builds trust. When the district tries to mandate more requirements or protocols in March or to add a new test, voice your concern for the load this might put on teachers, many of whom may be already providing for students materially. When you have a devoted staff, make sure they know you'll challenge those who would add more burdens.

Spend Time in Classrooms

Observe not to evaluate, but to see how teachers do what they do successfully. Administrators, counselors, social workers, and even superintendents can be remarkable supporters for teachers by coming to classrooms—to work with students on a project, play piano for them, or just talk to them. When done in cooperation with teachers, such encounters add a great deal to a school's collaborative climate.

Give Teachers a Picture of Students' Realities

Through tapping the insights of social workers and district demographic services, and through family surveys, find out what household income and resources are like in your area and what resources students probably do or don't have at home. Share with your faculty facts like the income ranges of your families or the absence of grocery stores or libraries in their neighborhoods—details that clarify what it means to be poor.[1]

This information will help teachers avoid assumptions about what students have in their homes and appreciate the resilience of youth from high-poverty families who get to school each day filled with hope and energy.

Advocate for High-Quality Classes

Be aware of how tracking works in your school or district. Are poor students getting slotted into classes for low-skilled students early in their lives? Advocate for low-income kids to receive gifted education services.

Get more teachers into the neediest classrooms. A principal who states publicly that having five classes each containing 45 students is unacceptable—and that he or she will work to change these conditions—wins teachers' trust.

Offer After-school Programs and Services

Work with teachers to find groups like the YMCA to provide volunteers for your school, so students have supervision and stimulation—including physical activities, art, and academic activities—more hours in the day. Local groups, businesses, and cultural venues will often contribute if approached by the principal or superintendent (see "Sources of Grants for Projects and Materials"). Consider providing wraparound services for your low-income students, such as access to medical and mental health professionals.

Communicate Commitment

Make clear that as an administrator, you're in this for the long haul and will work on long-term solutions to inequity for children in your district. It is important that your entire staff knows you will persist in getting the services and programs your building needs.

Toward Vibrant Classrooms

These are just a few ways educators can ensure students aren't marginalized by poverty—without making students feel they are a "problem." Each school district will need to explore what might work in its unique situation. But my hope is that no school ever becomes a place where sleepy children are yelled at or where teachers lose our human compassion. Let's create vibrant classrooms that tap into the brilliance of each child.

Sources of Grants for Projects and Materials

RGK Foundation awards grants for projects in K–12 education (math, science, reading, and teacher development) and after-school enrichment programs. The foundation is interested in programs that attract female and minority students into STEM.

National Geographic Education Foundation provides professional development and education materials connected to geography education.

American Honda Foundation supports youth and scientific education projects, including those that offer unique approaches to teaching youth in minority and underserved communities.

Dollar General Literacy Foundation funds programs for youth and adult literacy, school library relief, and preparation for the GED. Dollar General Grant Programs support nonprofits in U.S. states in which company stores are located.

The ING Foundation awards grants to nonprofits working in education, particularly physical education and for programs addressing child obesity.

Teaching Tolerance makes grants of $500 to $2,500 for projects designed to reduce prejudice, improve intergroup relations in schools, and support professional development in these areas.

Note

1. Many documentaries and public television programs (such as *A Place at the Table, Viva la Causa,* and *Why Poverty*) show what life is like for families living in poverty—for example, the realities of doubling up with relatives or taking two bus rides to get groceries.

Critical Thinking

1. Ask a teacher in a high poverty school what works for them. Compare with the list in this article. Reflect on similarities and differences and infer the reasons for differences.
2. Select one of the suggestions and develop a plan or activity to implement the suggestion.
3. Select one of the sources for grants and submit a grant for your school or a school you know.

Internet References

National Center for Children in Poverty
http://www.nccp.org

Southern Education Foundation
http://www.southerneducation.org

The National Association for the Education of Homeless Children and Youth
http://www.naehcy.org

JULIE LANDSMAN is a consultant on equitable education. She is the author of many books on education, including *A White Teacher Talks About Race* (R & L Education, 2005), and is the coeditor with Paul Gorski of *The Poverty and Education Reader* (Stylus, 2014).

Landsman, Julie, "Overcoming the Challenges of Poverty", *Educational Leadership,* June 2014, pp. 16–21. Copyright ©2014 by Association for Supervision & Curriculum Development. Used with permission.

Creating a Climate for Achievement

To turn around achievement at this Title I school, teachers collaborated to enhance both academic and social-emotional learning.

DEBORAH D. BRENNAN

Learning Outcomes

After reading this article, you will be able to:

- Explain how the three tiered Response to Invention helped turn around a Title I school.
- Use practical suggestions for improving a school's climate.

Four years ago, I was the first principal of a new Title 1 school in Round Rock, Texas. My excitement at this opportunity was tempered when I studied the assessment results for the incoming students. Nearly 300 of the approximately 850 students entering Robert P. Hernandez Middle School had failed the state assessment in reading. Even more had failed in math.

Clearly, the reality for our student population didn't resemble that of the traditional Response to Intervention pyramid, in which 75–85 percent of a school's students flourish with Tier 1 instruction (the instruction and preventive strategies all students receive). We needed to immediately strengthen our Tier 1 instruction while providing Tier 2 help—academic intervention and supports—for a large group, a tall order in itself.

I realized, however, that it wasn't only academic support Hernandez students needed to thrive; they also needed social-emotional skills that would enable them to learn. Many students who'd been forced to transfer to Hernandez were upset at the loss of friends. Our first year, behavior problems threatened to derail plans for improved instruction. Fights in the girls' bathroom broke toilets and sinks, graffiti tagged the school, and groups wore certain colors to show allegiance with gangs. Student divisions often appeared to be based on race.

The first order of the day for tackling both academic and behavioral challenges was to collaborate to strengthen our instruction and relationships within the school.

Strengthening Our Academics

Staff development was a big part of innovating instruction in the first two years of the school. Our staff studied Robert Marzano's *Art and Science of Teaching* (ASCD, 2007) and John Hattie's *Visible Learning* (Routledge, 2008) and chose to try these high-yield strategies: clearly articulated learning goals aligned with our state's standards, formative assessment, tracking of student learning, and targeted interventions on the basis of student data. I broke down the research into three steps toward improving academics.

1. *Setting—and Sharing—Learning Goals*

    We needed to set learning goals together, to help our instruction match the thinking level the standards required. So our school schedule maximized planning time for course-alike teachers. Teachers met weekly as subject-matter departments (grades 6–8) and daily as content-alike teams during one of their planning periods.

    In these meetings, teachers discussed the kind of student work they'd accept as evidence of mastery. They planned units to ensure that instruction included all standards, was aligned across grades, and would lead to mastery of each standard at the right level of rigor. An instructional coach attended planning meetings and guided this work.

Teachers designed graphic organizers of unit standards to create a map of the intended learning. Each classroom teacher posted these organizers (plus daily learning targets) and referred to them during instruction. They discussed with students how classroom learning activities supported each goal, emphasizing the relevance and real-world connection of the learning.

2. *Creating Assessments and Tracking Learning*

As part of creating common summative assessments, teachers discussed how to assess each standard in a way that would yield reliable data about learning. They asked questions like, Is there sufficient evidence that a standard has been mastered? Does the test question match the rigor of the standard?[1] Schoolwide, we talked about formative assessment. I provided resources for such assessment, like clickers, and teachers began checking for understanding often to catch students before they failed a unit test.

After each teacher-created summative assessment and district-created benchmark test, we disaggregated assessment results by student sub-populations and by the standard assessed. Doing this after teacher-created tests was especially powerful. Teachers together analyzed results, reflected on their instruction, and improved it on the basis of what assessment data showed.

We also helped students track their own progress. As more departments adopted the graphic unit organizer, teachers had students use them to track their individual formative and summative assessment results. In science classes, students tracked their own progress in mastering standards by tracking scores on each assessment in their class notebook.

3. *Intervening Early*

Hernandez students weren't allowed to fail. We committed to filling students' learning gaps rather than moving through the curriculum and leaving students behind. Although teachers weren't required to reteach and retest content or standards that a group of learners had missed, doing so became the norm. Reteaching happened through before- and after-school tutorials, with all our dedicated teachers pitching in. Tutorials focused on particular standards. Students who hadn't demonstrated mastery on that standard were strongly urged to attend.

Our science teachers were more intentional. They set up a series of Saturday sessions focused on standards many students missed. Although these were open to all students, low-scoring students were specifically invited. As word spread about the effectiveness of this intervention, social studies and math teachers adopted the practice.

Results—and Looking for Reasons

By the end of our third year using these practices, Hernandez students showed small gains in their passing rates on state assessments in most subjects. They showed passing rates of 82 percent (with 12 percent scoring as advanced) in science and 68 percent (with 11 percent scoring as advanced) in social studies.

Because all staff had attended the same trainings and collaborated in these processes, we explored what accounted for the greater success in science and social studies. These teachers had set their students up for achievement by not only planning collaboratively, but also intentionally creating routines to implement research-based practices. For instance, science teachers dedicated one wall in their classrooms to a graphic organizer illustrating what students would study the entire semester, with each standard broken down into key concepts and vocabulary. As each new unit was introduced, teachers would unveil a portion of the graphic organizer.

The science and social studies departments also used their planning time in a highly productive way. Each teacher shared benchmark and other assessment data among the department's teachers at all grade levels. For example, 8th grade United States history teachers shared with all their social studies colleagues the fact that their students showed a lack of understanding on standards related to the U.S. Constitution and Bill of Rights. The 7th grade Texas history teachers promised to build a foundation of vocabulary and background information about major government documents during lessons on the Texas constitution.

Strengthening Social-Emotional Learning

At the end of year two, I came to a realization: The students who were failing classes and state assessments were the same ones who were visiting the office for discipline, were suspended, or were often absent.

Although as a staff we had talked about relationships, classroom management, and discipline matrices, we'd left the implementation up to each teacher rather than setting up a schoolwide system for forging relationships and positive discipline. I didn't understand at first how intentional we needed to be. Emotional connections with students had always been a part of my teaching experience, and I thought every teacher naturally made connections with students that transcended the classroom. I soon saw that we needed to become intentional in our approach to the social-emotional side of education, to work as hard on that aspect of learning as we worked on academics.

Creating a strong social-emotional school culture begins with the people who have the most direct contact with students: teachers. In year three, we focused on creating a sense of a team with a shared purpose among our faculty. We looked for small gains in our data and had the teachers behind those wins share their insights and practices. Each faculty meeting began with staff members thanking one another for small acts of kindness or sharing good news. Several teachers began to form a greeting line to shake hands with people as they entered faculty meetings. Our mission and vision statements were painted on the walls and discussed at meetings. We started to refer to ourselves as the "Bulldog Nation." Staff members developed pride in their school and one another.

During the summer before our third year, we used grant funds to train teachers in the Capturing Kids' Hearts[2] approach and brought expert Eric Jensen in to discuss the effects of poverty on children. We created teacher-led committees to build systems that would support a strong campus culture and empower teachers to solve problems collaboratively.

We revamped our interventions for students who were struggling with behavior and strengthened our classroom procedures, just as we had done on the academic side of the Response to Intervention pyramid.

Building Relationships

The first step was guiding teachers to be intentional in relationship building. Most teachers care about students; it's why they teach. Unfortunately, many students, especially struggling or diverse students, don't perceive that message from their teachers. Each teacher was required to be in the halls between periods and encouraged to interact positively with students—to comment on activities or just greet a student. Each class created a social contract about how they would treat one another. Besides starting each day with the pledge, "Today, tomorrow, and always, I will treat others with kindness and respect," many classes adopted the faculty's practice of sharing "good things."

Our training with Eric Jensen helped teachers understand students' need for social learning and active engagement. We trained teachers in how to teach students behaviors that support productive group interaction and encouraged teachers to arrange students' seating in groups.

We began celebrating students who showed positive behavior and attributes. The teacher committee charged with celebrations created not only staff events, but also reward rallies, attendance celebrations, and other gatherings for students. We turned our student of the month recognition into a dog tag celebration, featuring dog tags in different colors for each behavior attribute (principled, caring, and so on). At a morning reception for parents and students, teachers presented each honored student with a dog tag in the color matching the attribute that student exemplified.

I instituted a Principal's Advisory Committee. Advisory teachers identified about 20 students in each grade level whom other students tended to follow—for good or bad. I met with these students, talked about school pride and the behaviors we expected from all students, and empowered them to together choose activities the school should offer as options for all students. These students led their advisory classes toward meeting high behavior expectations.

Grading for Hope

Hernandez teachers wanted to ensure that grades supported student learning. Our belief was that all students must learn—and that some might take more time than others. So one of our committees guided creation of a campuswide grading policy. This policy allowed students to retest and even turn in work late without penalty. For the most part, zeros weren't assigned. Homework was referred to as "home practice" and often wasn't given a grade that would go in the grade-book. When teachers called parents to alert them to their child's impending low grade, they told parents about extended opportunities for students to learn the material.

Using Proactive Discipline

Discipline was probably the most challenging area to change. Too many of our minority students, especially black boys, had discipline referrals. Our training with Eric Jensen gave teachers some insight, and Capturing Kids' Hearts gave us practices to try. I knew we had to get in front of the discipline issue, however, so we started tracking which students had problems in which classes.

We focused on 6th graders so we could change the history of discipline problems that came with many of them from elementary school. Each school counselor worked on positive peer interactions with a group of 6th graders about whom they had discipline concerns. In partnership with a community group, we began to hold leadership classes, and adults from this group mentored students who struggled behaviorally.

Our discipline committee created our Friday Academy. Teachers handled day-to-day classroom discipline, contacted parents, and supervised teacher detentions; if these measures didn't work, they recommended a student for Friday Academy. With parent permission, these students stayed after school for two hours on Friday and performed community service, supervised by volunteer teachers who built relationships with each student during the activities. Only a handful of students who experienced this intervention were repeat offenders.

Results—and Hope

The school's test scores remain high—higher than those of schools in our district that have lower percentages of students living in poverty. By implementing practices that address the behavioral side of the Response to Intervention pyramid as well as the academic one, we hope to break the correlation between high poverty and low student achievement at Robert Hernandez Middle School.

Notes

1. We trained teachers on "cut scores" so they could differentiate among a student response that was at mastery level, above mastery level, or not quite at the required level for mastery.
2. Capturing Kids' Hearts (www.flippengroup.com/education/ckh.html) is a program that helps educators build positive, trusting relationships among themselves and with students.

Critical Thinking

1. If you could only implement two of the six steps for creating a climate for achievement, which would they be? Defend your answers.
2. Using what you know about educational psychology and child development, explain why the six steps used in this school were successful.
3. Allowing students to retake failed assessments and hand in required assignments late has some critics. What do you think about these policies? Be sure to look at both the student and teacher side. Also, think about long term consequences.

Internet References

Capturing Kids' Hearts
http://www.flippengroup.com/education/ckh.html
National School Climate Center
http://www.schoolclimate.org/
What Kids Can Do
http://www.whatkidscando.org/

DEBORAH D. BRENNAN is the former principal of PFC Robert P. Hernandez Middle School in Round Rock, Texas.

Brennan, Deborah D., "Creating a Climate for Achievement", Educational Leadership, February 2015, pp. 56–59. Copyright ©2015 by Association for Supervision & Curriculum Development. Used with permission.

Article

Prepared by: Sheron Fraser-Burgess, *Ball State University*

Brown v. Board of Education of Topeka, Kansas

U. S. SUPREME COURT

Learning Outcomes

After reading this article, you will be able to:

- Paraphrase the most well-known passage from the ruling: "We conclude that in the field of public education the doctoring of 'separate but equal' has no place. Separate educational facilities are inherently unequal."

- Identify the amendment of the Constitution of the United States that provided the "equal protection of the laws" clause that permitted the overturning of the "separate but equal" principle of schooling.

- Identify the 1896 court ruling that originally justified segregated, "separate but equal" practices.

Brown v. Board of Education of Topeka, Kansas (347 U.S. 483), from which the following selection is taken, is composed of several NAACP-sponsored court appeals. This May 17, 1954 U. S. Supreme Court decision overturned the 1896, *Plessy v. Ferguson* decision where the Supreme Court had ruled that railroad companies could maintain separate cars for blacks and whites as long as the facilities were of equal condition.

Brown v. Board of Education was filed in Kansas and listed first among several related court cases since it was thought that a civil rights case from a Midwestern state may not be viewed as incendiary to the general public. Other cases included *Briggs v. Elliott* from South Carolina (1952), *Davis v. County School Board of Prince Edward County* from Virginia (1952), *Belton v. Gebhart* and *Bulah v. Gebhart* from Delaware (1952), and *Bolling v. Sharpe* from the District of Columbia (1954). The United States Supreme Court's 1954 interpretation of the meaning of the Equal Protection Clause of the Fourteenth Amendment to the Constitution of the United States led to its ruling that "in the field of public education the doctrine of 'separate but equal' has no place. Separate educational facilities are inherently unequal." Prior to this ruling, states had invoked the "separate but equal" principle from *Plessy v. Ferguson* to justify segregation of students of differing races in the public schools. The *Brown* decision declared such segregation unconstitutional with lawyers drawing upon social science research to demonstrate the psychological harm of segregation and its effects on African American children. Further, the court addressed the decision as a "class action" ruling, thereby providing the "equal protection of the laws" clause to all segregated persons.

Unfortunately, the 1954 *Brown* decision did not specify the means to achieve racial desegregation in schools and, in 1955, the Supreme Court considered a plan for implementation—arguments and methods to end discrimination in public education in what is often called *Brown II*. A ruling was made to delegate to district courts the responsibility to determine the means to integrate schools "with all deliberate speed." This ambiguous phrase permitted many states to delay and avoid school desegregation for many years after the historic 1954 ruling. Current discussion of the *Brown* decisions often adds the distinction that the ruling sought to end segregation and to desegregate public education. Desegregated schools, however, are not necessarily integrated schools.

. . .

Mr. Chief Justice Warren delivered the opinion of the Court.

These cases come to us from the States of Kansas, South Carolina, Virginia, and Delaware. They are premised on different facts and different local conditions, but a common legal question justifies their consideration together in this consolidated opinion.

In each of the cases, minors of the Negro race, through their legal representatives, seek the aid of the courts in obtaining admission to the public schools of their community on a nonsegregated basis. In each instance, they had been denied admission to schools attended by white children under laws requiring or permitting segregation according to race. This segregation was alleged to deprive the plaintiffs of the equal protection of the laws under the Fourteenth Amendment. In each of the cases other than the Delaware case, a three-judge federal district court denied relief to the plaintiffs on the so-called "separate but equal" doctrine announced by this Court in *Plessy* v. *Ferguson.* . . . Under that doctrine, equality of treatment is accorded when the races are provided substantially equal facilities even though these facilities be separate. In the Delaware case, the Supreme Court of Delaware adhered to that doctrine, but ordered that the plaintiffs be admitted to the white schools because of their superiority to the Negro schools.

The plaintiffs contend that segregated public schools are not "equal" and cannot be made "equal," and that hence they are deprived of the equal protection of the laws. Because of the obvious importance of the question presented, the Court took jurisdiction. Argument was heard in the 1952 Term, and reargument was heard this Term on certain questions propounded by the Court.

Reargument was largely devoted to the circumstances surrounding the adoption of the Fourteenth Amendment in 1868. It covered exhaustively consideration of the Amendment in Congress, ratification by the states, then existing practices in racial segregation, and the views of proponents and opponents of the Amendment. This discussion and our own investigation convince us that, although these sources cast some light, it is not enough to resolve the problem with which we are faced. At best, they are inconclusive. The most avid proponents of the post–War Amendments undoubtedly intended them to remove all legal distinctions among "all persons born or naturalized in the United States." Their opponents, just as certainly were antagonistic to both the letter and the spirit of the Amendments and wished them to have the most limited effect. What others in Congress and the state legislatures had in mind cannot be determined with any degree of certainty.

An additional reason for the inconclusive nature of the Amendment's history, with respect to segregated schools, is the status of public education at that time. In the South, the movement toward free common schools, supported by general taxation, had not yet taken hold. Education of white children was largely in the hands of private groups. Education of Negroes was almost nonexistent, and practically all of the race were illiterate. In fact, any education of Negroes was forbidden by law in some states. Today, in contrast, many Negroes have achieved outstanding success in the arts and sciences as well as in the business and professional world. It is true that public education had already advanced further in the North, but the effect of the Amendment on Northern States was generally ignored in the congressional debates. Even in the North, the conditions of public education did not approximate those existing today. The curriculum was usually rudimentary; ungraded schools were common in rural areas; the school term was but three months a year in many states; and compulsory school attendance was virtually unknown. As a consequence, it is not surprising that there should be so little in the history of the Fourteenth Amendment relating to its intended effect on public education.

In the first cases in this Court construing the Fourteenth Amendment, decided shortly after its adoption, the Court interpreted it as proscribing all state-imposed discriminations against the Negro race. The doctrine of "separate but equal" did not make its appearance in this court until 1896 in the case of *Plessy* v. *Ferguson, supra,* involving not education but transportation. American courts have since labored with the doctrine for over half a century. In this Court, there have been six cases involving the "separate but equal" doctrine in the field of public education. In *Cumming* v. *County Board of Education* . . . and *Gong Lum* v. *Rice* . . ., the validity of the doctrine itself was not challenged. In more recent cases, all on the graduate school level, inequality was found in that specific benefits enjoyed by white students were denied to Negro students of the same educational qualifications. *Missouri* ex rel. *Gaines* v. *Canada; Sipuel* v. *Oklahoma; Sweatt* v. *Painter; McLaurin* v. *Oklahoma State Regents*. In none of these cases was it necessary to reexamine the doctrine to grant relief to the Negro plaintiff. And in *Sweatt* v. *Painter, supra,* the Court expressly reserved decision on the question whether *Plessy* v. *Ferguson* should be held inapplicable to public education.

In the instant cases, that question is directly presented. Here, unlike *Sweatt* v. *Painter,* there are findings below that the Negro and white schools involved have been equalized, or are being equalized, with respect to buildings, curricula, qualifications and salaries of teachers, and other "tangible" factors. Our decision, therefore, cannot turn on merely a comparison of these tangible factors in the Negro and white schools involved in each of the cases. We must look instead to the effect of segregation itself on public education.

In approaching this problem, we cannot turn the clock back to 1868 when the Amendment was adopted, or even to 1896 when *Plessy* v. *Ferguson* was written. We must consider public education in the light of its full development and its present place in American life throughout the Nation. Only in this way can it be determined if segregation in public schools deprives these plaintiffs of the equal protection of the laws.

Today, education is perhaps the most important function of state and local governments. Compulsory school attendance laws and the great expenditures for education both demonstrate our recognition of the importance of education to our democratic society. It is required in the performance of our most basic public responsibilities, even service in the armed forces. It is the very foundation of good citizenship. Today it is a principal instrument in awakening the child to cultural values, in preparing him for later professional training, and in helping him to adjust normally to his environment. In these days, it is doubtful that any child may reasonably be expected to succeed in life if he is denied the opportunity of an education. Such an opportunity, where the state has undertaken to provide it, is a right which must be made available to all on equal terms.

We come then to the question presented: Does segregation of children in public schools solely on the basis of race, even though the physical facilities and other "tangible" factors may be equal, deprive the children of the minority group of equal educational opportunities? We believe that it does.

In *Sweatt* v. *Painter, supra,* in finding that a segregated law school for Negroes could not provide them equal educational opportunities, this Court relied in large part on "those qualities which are incapable of objective measurement but which make for greatness in a law school." In *McLaurin* v. *Oklahoma State Regents, supra,* the Court, in requiring that a Negro admitted to a white graduate school be treated like all other students, again resorted to intangible considerations: ". . . his ability to study, to engage in discussions and exchange views with other students, and, in general, to learn his profession." Such considerations apply with added force to children in grade and high schools. To separate them from others of similar age and qualifications solely because of their race generates a feeling of inferiority as to their status in the community that may affect their hearts and minds in a way unlikely ever to be undone. The effect of this separation on their educational opportunities was well stated by a finding in the Kansas case by a court which nevertheless felt compelled to rule against the Negro plaintiffs:

> Segregation of white and colored children in public schools has a detrimental effect upon the colored children. The impact is greater when it has the sanction of the law; for the policy of separating the races is usually interpreted as denoting the inferiority of the Negro group. A sense of inferiority affects the motivation of a child to learn. Segregation with the sanction of law, therefore, has a tendency to retard the educational and mental development of Negro children and to deprive them of some of the benefits they would receive in a racially integrated school system.

Whatever may have been the extent of psychological knowledge at the time of *Plessy* v. *Ferguson,* this finding is amply supported by modern authority. Any language in *Plessy* v. *Ferguson* contrary to this finding is rejected.

We conclude that in the field of public education the doctrine of "separate but equal" has no place. Separate educational facilities are inherently unequal. Therefore, we hold that the plaintiffs and others similarly situated for whom the actions have been brought are, by reason of the segregation complained of, deprived of the equal protection of the laws guaranteed by the Fourteenth Amendment. This disposition makes unnecessary any discussion whether such segregation also violates the Due Process Clause of the Fourteenth Amendment.

Because these are class actions, because of the wide applicability of this decision, and because of the great variety of local conditions, the formulation of decrees in these cases presents problems of considerable complexity. On reargument, the consideration of appropriate relief was necessarily subordinated to the primary question—the constitutionality of segregation in a public education. We have now announced that such segregation is a denial of the equal protection of the laws. In order that we may have the full assistance of the parties in formulating decrees, the cases will be restored to the docket, and the parties are requested to present further argument.

Critical Thinking

1. What was the constitutional meaning of the Supreme Court's decision in *Brown*?
2. How have other cultural minorities and women benefited from the constitutional principles set down in *Brown*?
3. What is the difference between a desegregated school and a racially integrated school?

Internet References

The National Parks Service
www.nps.gov/nr/travel/civilrights/ka1.htm

***Teaching Tolerance,* a publication of the Southern Poverty Law Center**
www.tolerance.org

From Brown vs. Board of Education of Topeka, Kansas by U.S. Supreme Court, 1954.

UNIT

Prepared by: Sheron Fraser-Burgess, *Ball State University*

Literacy Is the Cornerstone of Participatory Democracy

In this unit of Annual Editions, there is an argument for going beyond the basic skills of literacy viewed as merely reading and writing towards actively fostering a critical engagement with texts broadly. The meaning of literacy has changed dramatically as American society has evolved. While reading skills are essential for being literate, they are necessary and not sufficient for participatory democracy in contemporary society. Once meaning the ability to decipher letters on a page, it has come to mean an ability to triangulate among the multifarious sources of knowledge in order to acquire an accurate picture of reality. Former debates about cultural literacy (Hirsch, 1988) sought to dictate American identity through establishing the cultural norms and literary canon. On this reading of the American story, the triumphal picture prevails over the complicated and brutal history of manifest destiny, chattel slavery, and the genocide of native peoples. Literacy in its critical form equips persons, for example, to recognize propaganda, place current events in historical context, and detect as ideology, systems of beliefs that are impervious to reasoned challenge. By this method, literacy goes against merely transmissive instructional strategies (Mason, 2000). Mason maintained that classrooms are spaces where teachers mediate the curriculum through being *sociocultural critics*. As Mason states

> The task of the art critic does not lie in the trivial sense of the term, to *criticise* the weaknesses of the work. It is to make the work *more accessible* to the viewer, in all its nuances and subtleties, in what it says and in its silences, in its history and context and in what it presages, in its complexities of meaning and import, in the questions it raises and their consequences. In like manner, teachers as socio-cultural critics are responsible for making the culture, worldview, social arrangements, and everyday practices of their society more accessible to their students. This would mean raising a lot of what they assume as normal or natural to the level of conscious critical analysis and assessment—by asking questions about how they view the world, about those arrangements and practices that they take for granted.

Paolo Freire (1988) referenced a similar idea in the concept of *critical consciousness* as the ideal mindset of the learner with respect to the knowledge being presented in the classroom. Students are aware of themselves as agents who have the capacity to not only decode the words about appreciate their meaning and implications within the social, political and historical context.

The reading in this section focusses on civics and knowledge of democratic governance as desirable bodies of knowledge and skills in order to acquire critical literacy. In addition, one research article explores the digital equivalence of literacy and its relationship to the economic well-being of developing countries.

References

Freire, P (1988). *Pedagogy of the Oppressed* New York, NY: Continuum.
Hirsch, E.D. (1988). *Cultural literacy: What every American needs to know.* New York, NY: Houghton Mifflin Company.
Mason, M. (2000). Teachers as critical mediators of knowledge. *Journal of Philosophy of Education.* 34 (2), p. 343–352.

Article   Prepared by: Sheron Fraser-Burgess, *Ball State University*

The Challenges of Gaming for Democratic Education: The Case of iCivics

JEREMY STODDARD, ET AL.

Learning Outcomes

After reading this article, you will be able to:

- Analyze the claims to the general pedagogical value of gaming.
- Relate the technological innovation of gaming to democratic ideals for education.
- Infer the criteria for distinguishing effective civics education from the ineffective one.

WHILE PLAYING THE iCivics game *Immigration Nation*, which asks young players to identify which potential immigrants we should allow into the United States and for what reasons, we received the following feedback from the Statue of Liberty, the in-game feedback agent:

> You know what we do with boat thieves in these parts ... ?
> That's right: WE DON'T LET THEM INTO THE COUNTRY!
> Get rid of this jerk! Oh, and call the police.

This kind of feedback may seem jarring, but it is one of many examples of responses designed to clearly give young players feedback that their decision was incorrect based on the rules in the game, rules that are based on commonly taught U.S. immigration laws as they are presented in textbooks or state academic standards.

It is also intended to be funny and thus motivate the player to continue to play, win, and master the content. I include this example of what a player experiences in *Immigration Nation* as it is indicative of many of the iCivics games and seems to represent the primary objective of the game design: to engage young people in civics content in a way that leads them to a clear and defined correct answer that is also intended to be more entertaining than the usual civics lesson. It is also hoped that students play these games outside of the school or that they can be used as an introductory activity for one of the more traditional lessons available to teachers on the iCivics website (http://www.icivics.org).

However, the attempt to be entertaining here also includes language (i.e., *jerk*) and sentiments not often promoted in democratic education, and especially in an activity intended for elementary students. As the game designers build these cases (the content) and the rules of the game, they shape the possible narrative arcs players may construct, and thus the "ideological world" (Squire, 2006) of the game. In the case starting this article, the rule about criminals not being allowed to immigrate is greatly oversimplified. While being a criminal is a major hurdle to being allowed to immigrate, it is not a hard "rule" as presented in the game because someone labeled as a criminal in one country may count as an asylum seeker in the United States.

These designed experiences also shape how young players will view the world and their roles as democratic citizens. It is important to consider if these games will help students connect the individual actions in the game to larger, sometimes controversial, ethical and political issues in society (Raphael, Bachen, Lynn, Baldwin-Philippi, and McKee, 2010). For example, the issue of immigration in the game represents the textbook version of who gets to immigrate and is set at a place, Ellis Island, and via a mode of transportation, a boat, that have little relevance to the issue of U.S. immigration today. Further, the example of a boat thief is not as clear-cut when we consider the example of political refugees from Cuba who took boats to seek asylum in Florida in the late 1970s. In this study we examine how four iCivics games are designed to engage young people as learners and as citizens-in-training and attempt to answer the following question: What are the affordances and constraints of iCivics games for democratic education?

iCivics

iCivics is a national civic education nonprofit organization founded by former U.S. Supreme Court Justice Sandra Day O'Connor in order to provide "students with the tools they need for active participation and democratic action" (www.icivics.org/our-story). It has developed over fifteen games for use in and out of school and accompanying curriculum and resources for teachers to use in their classes and has provided numerous regional professional development opportunities for teachers. The games are intended to be a gateway to the curriculum provided on the site and focus on topics such as constitutional rights, the roles of the different branches of the government, and specific issues such as immigration and fiscal policy. iCivics was designed to be as approachable and accessible as possible—the goal is to get its games, and civic education, into classrooms and living rooms. To this end, the organization has been quite successful, as it claims that over 70,000 teachers have registered for the site and that the games have been played more than 10 million times (www.icivics.org/our-story). We selected iCivics for our study as it has been so successful at developing games and reaching out to such a broad audience of teachers and students.

Games and Gaming to Learn

The use of video games in education is far from a new phenomenon. The past decade has seen an increased interest in the learning potential for games and gaming beyond just motivation, including: the development of literacies through gaming (Gee, 2003); gaming and simulations that model professional or disciplinary models for teaching STEM disciplines and civic education (e.g., Shaffer, 2004; Shaffer & Gee, 2006; Poole, Berson, & Levine, 2008); and the use of commercial games to teach subjects such as history and geography (e.g., Squire, 2005; Squire, DeVane, & Durga, 2008). Studies on student engagement in immersive virtual worlds designed for inquiry learning have shown particular promise within the STEM fields, especially when grounded in problem-based learning (Barab et al., 2009; Barab, Sadler, Heiselt, Hickey, & Zuiker, 2010) or when used as a medium to learn about student scientific reasoning (Dawley & Dede, 2014).

Games have been similarly promoted for use in the social studies classroom (Watson, 2010), but little empirical research has been done to show the effectiveness of these proposed practices. The majority of the scholarship on games and civic education is conceptual in nature, including frameworks for using games in class, anecdotal examples from classroom practice, and critical analyses of games and simulations promoted for classroom use (e.g., Bers, 2010; Curry, 2010; Marino & Hayes, 2012). Raphael et al. (2010) presented a framework for research and design of games for civic education and raised several central issues, including the importance of aligning games with civic content and citizenship-related skills. They argued that games that successfully integrate "civic content and game play will be more effective at fostering civic learning than games that do not" (p. 206). They also promoted the use of games to engage students in contemporary public issues and to inspire action that can be applied outside of the game, noting that "games that set rules, goals, and roles that require players to act and reflect on public matters will be more effective for civic learning" (p. 208). Unlike the STEM games and learning research that utilize purposefully built games such as *Quest Atlantis*—the virtual immersive world built by Barab and his colleagues to engage students in STEM problem-based inquiry—the work in social studies relies more often on commercial games or more simplistic single player games.

Research into the iCivics games specifically is extremely limited despite their popularity and has come most often in the form of evaluation studies. A study by Kawashima-Ginsberg (2012) found that the iCivics online writing tool Drafting Board, designed to help young people develop skills in constructing argumentative essays related to issues such as the electoral college and community service, had a significant positive effect on participants specific to explicit skill development around argumentative writing. Other studies of the impact of iCivics games on student learning focus narrowly on gains in civic knowledge measured with selected response standardized test-like items. For example, a series of studies conducted by Baylor University researchers found positive effects in middle school participants in both basic civic knowledge and in areas such as motivation as a result of playing selected games (Blevins, LeCompte, Wells, Moore, & Rodgers, 2012; LeCompte, Moore, & Blevins, 2011). These studies focused on explicit outcomes of iCivics: skill development in evidence and argumentative essays, acquisition of factual knowledge, dispositions, and motivation. They are not able to measure the kinds of inquiry, deliberation, or conceptual-level understanding that researchers in the STEM fields have focused on. Nor have they been able to measure students' thinking in ways that Squire and his colleagues (2008) did using the more open ended *Civilization* games in world history classes.

Does this mean that games are not effective mediums for democratic education? There are historical reasons to be skeptical of games being promoted for democratic education, as there have been many technologies that preceded games also viewed as an educational panacea (Cuban, 1986) or as solutions for the digital divide and educational inequity (Cuban, 2001; Margolis, 2008). In addition, there are serious concerns raised about the narratives players may construct in the ideological worlds of the games (Squire, 2006). Historically, one of the most widely used games in social studies classes, *The Oregon Trail*, is viewed as including misleading and stereotypical representations of American Indians and the experiences of settlers moving west in the late 1800s (e.g., Bigelow, 1997). Further, games viewed as educational and easily accessible, such as *The Oregon Trail* and the iCivics games, often result in teachers and parents encouraging young people to play these educational games as an alternative to other media forms without any kind of reflection on what they are learning from the games (Caftori & Paprzycki, 1997). Raphael et al. (2010) noted the importance of having students reflect on how the design and production of the game reflect particular views. This research suggests that games often used as a reward or outside of a structured activity have the potential to produce naïve understandings among students.

Democratic Education Framework

Our primary focus is to understand how these games may be a medium for democratic education. There is some disagreement about the goals of democratic education, which encompasses civic or citizenship education. Most state standards and textbooks for government and civics courses focus on the structures and processes of government (e.g., branches of government, how a bill becomes a law). These curricula emphasize the characteristics of what Westheimer and Kahne (2004) described as a personally responsible citizen: law abiding, informed, but staying within the system. Other scholars in democratic education focus on deliberative democracy, which emphasizes student discussion and deliberation of controversial issues as a way to prepare them to engage as active and informed citizens (Hess, 2009; Parker, 2003). Still others advocate for a more action or justice-oriented democratic citizenship that emphasizes advocacy and political action for the common good (Levinson, 2012; Westheimer & Kahne, 2004). *The Guardian of Democracy: Civic Mission of Schools* (Gould, 2011) report, which is intended to inform state and national policy related to civic education, emphasizes a combination of teaching deliberative democracy, sharing knowledge of the structures of government, and to a lesser degree, equipping students for direct civic action. It also promotes the use of simulations and role-playing to help students understand the structures and processes of government.

In this study we focus on how well the iCivics games provide students the opportunities to engage in these different aspects of democratic education. We know that certain types of thinking are particularly important for democratic citizenship: being able to inquire about problems or questions for which there are multiple competing answers, being able to take a position and use evidence to warrant that position, and being able to discuss and deliberate controversial issues (Hess, 2009; Parker, 2003). We also know that many young people are engaged politically and civically on their own using social and other online media (Banaji, Buckingham, Van Zoonen, & Hirzalla, 2009; Cohen & Kahne, 2012) and that some have argued that civic education should be designed to help young people engage in a more mediated and participatory global culture (Kahne, Hodgin, & Eidman-Aadahl, 2016). Therefore, we examine the accuracy and level of complexity of the content in the games; whether or not the games engage players in open or closed issues or questions (Hess, 2009); whether or not issues related to policies present the "best case, fair hearing of competing points of view" (Kelly, 1986); and how the roles students assume in the games are designed to develop skills to prepare them to act as citizens in a mediated world.

Raphael et al. (2010) also raised the issue of the impact of a more or less structured game narrative. They noted that having a game that is efficient in getting players to the "right" answer does not necessarily promote the kinds of thinking aligned with civic engagement. The analysis of the nature of issues presented as being open or closed, and the inclusion or exclusion of competing perspectives, helps to provide us with a sense of the ideological worlds constructed through the designed experience of the iCivics games (Squire, 2006).

Analysis of iCivics

Our research team utilized eight participant-researchers, law students, and upper-class undergraduate government majors, all with expertise in the content areas of the games to generate data through play and provide initial analyses. We selected four games designed for upper-elementary and middle school audiences that reflect prominent contemporary issues in American politics and society that also align tightly with common state standards for middle school civics classes: *Do I Have a Right?* (constitutional rights, including free speech); *Executive Command* (executive power, policymaking); *Immigration Nation* (immigration policy, routes to citizenship); and *People's Pie* (fiscal policy, debt).

Do I Have a Right? is set in a law firm with the player in the role of the managing partner whose job it is to select lawyers and to partner each potential client with a lawyer who has the correct "specialty" in a particular amendment. The goal of the game is for the player to learn and apply various constitutional rights (e.g., First Amendment, Fourth Amendment) in order to attempt to improve the firm's "prestige" score.

Immigration Nation is designed for the youngest players and, therefore, is the least sophisticated and the quickest to play. The player takes the role of an immigration officer in New York Harbor whose job it is to decide who should be allowed to enter the country, to which "harbor" successful petitioners should be sent, and who should be denied entry altogether. The harbors represent the various routes to citizenship or legal entry, including the Born in the USA harbor for those who can claim citizenship by birthright and the Permission to Work harbor for those who qualify for legal residency.

Executive Command focuses on the powers and responsibilities of the executive branch. The player assumes the role of the president and manages the many tasks of the executive, including giving speeches to Congress, playing the role of commander in chief, and taking diplomatic missions aboard Air Force One. The player wins by maintaining the president's public approval score.

In *People's Pie*, the player is asked to make decisions regarding federal revenue generation and spending, such as setting the tax rate and the retirement age for social security. The player then makes decisions about funding specific programs, such as Financial Services and Agriculture. Inevitably, the player overspends during the first round of budget decisions and must borrow money to balance the budget while attempting to maintain "citizen satisfaction" by funding programs that gain high public approval.

Methods

In order to analyze both the content and structure of the game as a designed experience, we generated data through gameplay that helped illustrate the content, game rules and structures, and the overall narratives related to citizenship, nation, and the core issues of each specific game. Using a data generation method previously established for gaining insights into students' thinking and experiences in game-based learning (Wideman et al., 2007), we assigned the student research assistants to play two assigned games in pairs. The government majors played *Executive Command* and *People's Pie* while the law students played *Do I Have a Right?* and *Immigration Nation*. The computers were equipped with Screenflow, a program that allowed us to record the gameplay, the reactions of, and the conversations between the two research assistants in each pair.

The research assistants were instructed to follow a "think-aloud" protocol, explaining their actions, decisions, and reactions to game feedback. Think-aloud protocols have been found to be effective in providing evidence related to the experiences and thinking of students in a situated learning context that is difficult to capture in a self-report measure or follow-up interview (Cotton & Gresty, 2006; Wideman, et al., 2007). These recordings provide evidence related to the participants' affective reaction to the game as well as create a record of their thinking and the overall narrative they create through their gameplay related to democratic education. The research assistants then transcribed these conversations along with the game actions and feedback recorded from the screen into a transcript from their hour of play to use for coding.

This data was coded line by line, with each line representing a particular scenario posed, a decision made by the player, or a feedback or response in the game. In addition to coding each portion of the transcripts (e.g., *decision*, *feedback*), we also coded the nature of tasks, questions, or problems posed (e.g., *open/closed*) and whether or not we identified any content that was either inaccurate or simplified to the point of being trivial. For example, a scenario from *Immigration Nation* in which the player is asked to accept or reject a character who says, "Help! I was born in Minnesota, but I went for a long walk and wound up in Canada by accident. Can you let me back in?" would be coded as a closed scenario as there is a correct answer expected by the game. Additional codes were generated as they emerged in the data that built from our framework of democratic education. These initial codes were used to develop conceptual memos first for each gameplay episode (i.e., each research assistant session) and then compared to other gameplay episodes from the same game to look for similar and contrasting themes. Finally, these themes were compared across games to identify major themes about what the iCivics games pose as affordances and constraints for democratic education.

Our analysis as presented here is limited to the context in which the data was collected and based on the interactions between our research assistants and the games, as well as our analysis as researchers. Put differently, we likely did not play out every possible scenario or narrative that could be constructed from the games; nor do the views and actions of our research assistants match those of the 10-to-13-year-olds who are the games' target audience. Even given these limitations, our study adds a layer of analysis when compared to other curriculum studies that focus only on a critical or deconstructionist analysis of content or gameplay, especially within a dynamic and affective gaming environment.

Results

Four themes emerged from our analysis of the four iCivics games. The first of these themes illustrates the particular affordances for democratic education, such as the explicit design of the games for use in schools, scaffolding, and ties to standards and civic concepts. The three additional themes illustrate tensions in the game design and experience of players that act as constraints of the games. These include a lack of emphasis on a more dynamic "nontextbook" civic content, no clear applications to real civic action for players, and few opportunities for players to engage in decision making that presents best case, fair hearings of competing points of view or evidence in the iCivics games. In particular, we focused on the nature of the intellectual work in the games as it relates to democratic education and, as part of our analysis of the ideological world of the games, on whether the issues presented as open actually push the player to a "correct" answer. These findings also reflect a tension in iCivics' attempt to be both as accessible as possible to all teachers and students and to attempt to prepare students for their stated goal of "active participation and democratic action."

Affordances of iCivics Games

iCivics is explicit and intentional about making their games and resources as accessible as possible for teachers and students. Unlike many projects within educational gaming that restrict access to their games to research projects, the goal of iCivics is to be in every school in the United States. This desire for accessibility also includes students and teachers who may not be as familiar with playing video games, as well as students who may need a little extra scaffolding to learn how to move through the game world successfully. Three characteristics of the games reflect their affordances toward this goal of accessibility that also align with aspects of democratic education, in terms of learning about structures and concepts related to government, and are presented here.

Designed for the Classroom

iCivics games are notable for small bobblehead characters, upbeat soundtracks, and designs that emphasize active participation with heavily scaffolded gaming models. The games are designed to be used within the limits of the 50-minute class period or outside of the classroom with little additional support needed to learn the basic gameplay. When entering a game for the first time, pop-up windows explain the components of the game and basic actions to get the player started (see Figure 1). This kind of explicit "hard" scaffolding introduces the player to both the features of the game world and the basic steps for playing, and allows the player to quickly learn how to engage with the core tasks in the game.

In addition to the scaffolding windows that help players acclimate to the structure of the game, each game also has multiple forms of feedback. The feedback agents provide positive feedback when the players make the "correct" choices and provide helpful guiding feedback when they make the "wrong" choices. In the example we use in the introduction from *Immigration Nation*, the feedback agent is the Statue of Liberty. Lady Liberty tells the players whether or not they have allowed the correct immigrants in and whether or not they have sent them to the right harbors (i.e., allowed them in under the correct rules). In *Executive Command*, a journalist helps narrate the overall story of the game and transition between the four-year-long terms in the game, and a chief of staff tells the players what tasks need to be completed or reminds them if they forget to do something. These feedback agents help players to learn the rules and provide feedback to correct any mistakes.

Concept Based

The iCivics games' designs are tightly tied to the concepts that are the "content" to be learned from playing each game and are designed to get the players to learn the concept and apply them. These concepts are aligned with state academic standards. For example, in *People's Pie*, the focus is on introducing concepts from economics, particularly the array of departments that the federal government funds. In *Immigration Nation*, players are engaged in learning and applying the five major criteria, or "rules," that can be used to gain entry to the United States as a citizen or legal immigrant: U.S.-born citizen, child of U.S. citizens, marriage to a U.S. citizen, political refugee, or someone allowed entry for work. *Do I Have a Right?* focuses on the acquisition of a conceptual understanding of the constitutional rights of individuals, such as the right to free speech or to protection from unreasonable search and seizure. The players are introduced to these concepts through the partners that they select for the firm, such as Chuck Freepress (First Amendment) or Sally Fourth (Fourth Amendment). The players are then asked to apply this knowledge by determining whether or not potential clients have rights based on their complaints and whether there is a partner who is skilled in each particular conceptual area. The feedback the players receive pushes players toward the correct answers that will help them to pass each level or successfully complete each task, indicating a mastery of the concept/content being presented. This structural aspect to the games makes the games accessible to a broad audience and also means that the games will align with state standards for civics in many states. As we will note, this affordance for reaching a broad audience through aligning with textbook- and standards-based civic knowledge can also be a constraint when compared with the goals of action civics or deliberative democratic education. However, if young players are able to transfer their knowledge of rights of citizens under the U.S.

Constitution from the games to their engagement as citizens, this is essential knowledge for democratic education.

Designed Affective Response

One of the strongest themes in our analysis is the powerful affective reaction our participant-researchers had while playing the games. Those who played *Executive Command* were noticeably stressed by trying to juggle all of the demands of their avatar president. Midway through her game, one student exclaimed, "I am getting really stressed out playing this game!" and started yelling, "Walk faster," to her computer avatar as she attempted to finish tasks. Her partner in the session later summed up what he saw as this affective aspect of the designed experience in *Executive Command*.

> *You get a sense of the stress of the job . . . The way that this is designed, what are you seeing? There are certain things that you take to certain places to get them done, and you have a lot to do, and it is hard to do it all at once, and it is hard to keep everybody pleased . . . Basically, there is so much happening . . . and then at the end they say, "Oh, wow," and, "Time flew," and goodbye. The exhaustion aspect is implicit.*

Similarly, those who played *People's Pie* talked about their frustration with having to borrow money and how much they empathized with the frustration felt by legislators related to budget issues. These affective elements are an affordance that also aligns with the goal of simulating civic-related roles identified in the *Civic Mission of Schools* report and likely acts as a motivational force to learn the game content (Gould, 2011). However, as we explore, these affective responses also shape the narratives players may construct as part of the designed experience of the game narratives that emphasize particular ideological views about politics, policies, and the role of citizens.

Constraints of iCivics
Abstract and Expedient vs Relevant and Complex

There is no doubt that the games are designed to both engage players and align with traditional civic content. In the case of *Immigration Nation*, the game is designed for young audiences and focuses on explicit policies, such as the example in the article opening illustrates: Criminals will not be allowed citizenship. This attempt to break down immigration policy into a set of clear rules, with five "criteria" for being legally allowed into the United States, illustrates the desire of game designers, much like textbook authors, to effectively transfer this knowledge to the player. This is the type of expediency in game design that Raphael et al. (2010) identified as a major issue in designing games for civic education.

Creating clear rules, and engaging the player in learning and applying these rules, makes for an efficient and effective instructional design. Of course, the real world cannot always be represented with clear rules, which is hinted at in some of the language used in feedback. For example, when a player allows in someone who was born in Kentucky, the Statue of Liberty responds that "just about anyone born in the United States is automatically a citizen," though the game declines to address in what circumstances that general rule would not apply.

Further, the examples of immigrants who should be admitted include characters who possess strong positive traits, such as desirable work expertise or courage in the face of an oppressive regime in their home country, whereas those who are denied entry offer obviously ridiculous reasons for their desire to enter, such as asking to "travel around the country to make fun of Americans" or wanting to come to the United States because they are "REALLY LOUD" and want to be in the United States "SO EVERYTHING WILL BE AS LOUD AS ME." These kinds of very unrealistic and even silly examples likely are used to entertain or motivate players in the games, but they also may distract from the goals of the game and diminish the likelihood that players can connect concepts from the game to the world outside of the game. In this way, an affordance may also be a constraint.

Other less realistic immigrant examples may be even more problematic as they simplify the issue of immigration in the game. For example, a player may assume something about the potential immigrant who claims, "In my country, I have been a strong opponent of my government's policies. The government has now decided to throw my whole political party in jail because of it." The player may think that person would automatically be admitted as a refugee seeking asylum. The United States does grant refugee status to more people than any other country, but this does not mean that this process is automatic, nor is the number of refugees who qualify for asylum unlimited, as there are ceilings for refugees and limits on resettlement programs. Further, had the boat thief in this article's opening example been a Cuban refugee, as we postulated, this rule in the game becomes even more blurred. Can someone who might be considered a criminal in some ways also qualify for asylum? Further, although the language in the opening example is meant to be engaging, is calling the "boat thief" a "jerk" the type of modeling that we want for citizens?

The other games face similar abstraction issues. In *Do I Have a Right?* current issues such as free speech, gun rights, and voting rights are trivialized by using examples such as the client Sam Colt, who says, "Last week Congress banned all guns except for water guns. I like hunting, but I can't hunt with a water gun. Do I have a right to a gun I can hunt with?" On the issue of suffrage, the character Taylor Townsend says, "My state has purposely made it much harder for Asian people to vote for governor, because my current governor says that Asian people don't know enough about voting. I'm Asian—do I have a right to vote?" This could be made into a relevant discussion of an issue and application of the 15th Amendment, but with only the information provided here, the player could be left with a trivial understanding of the amendment and the current issues where it applies today.

In *Executive Command*, every scenario our research assistants played involved a war being fought against an imaginary country (Neverland or Wonderland), but this war is not a conflict like any the United States has seen since World War II. This is a traditional war, formally declared and conventionally fought. Does such a scenario help players understand the nature of military conflict since the War Powers Act? Or the nature of the current conflicts that the United States is involved in? The goal in the game is that the players understand the roles of the executive branch, Congress, and the military (e.g., Air Force, Army), as outlined in the Constitution. Similar to the previous examples, however, certain scenarios in the game trivialize this important knowledge by using examples that avoid complexity and do not apply in the current geopolitical context (e.g., war on terror).

Goals in the Games vs Goals of Democratic Education

Two of the games, *Do I Have a Right?* and *Immigration Nation*, include issues that were almost entirely coded as being closed. These games are designed to help students learn the "correct" answer related to concepts surrounding constitutional rights and immigration law, respectively. However, as previously noted, using simplistic criteria for concepts and abstract examples is great for expediency but not for engaging young players in the types of messy problems that promote active citizenship. We are not arguing that the content and rules in the games are inaccurate, only that they are oversimplified and irrelevant to the contemporary political context. Since the goal of the games is to teach players to apply explicit rules that align with the textbook version of content included in most state standards, the game experience is not much different from that of many classrooms, where this content is also simplified and taught out of the contemporary context.

The other two games, *Executive Command* and *People's Pie*, had many tasks that were coded as being open, as they asked the players to make decisions between two or more potential options. In *Executive Command*, seemingly open tasks appear from the beginning: A player starts by setting a primary agenda issue for the presidency, with options including deficit reduction, education, and security. The player also gets to make decisions on signing or vetoing legislation, make executive decisions on diplomacy, and fulfill the role as commander in chief for military matters. In *People's Pie*, the players set the levels of income tax, payroll tax, and corporate tax, as well as the retirement age for Social Security and Medicare. They then make decisions on which programs to fund within departments such as Agriculture, Financial Services, and Homeland Security, and whether or not to borrow money to help pay for any debt when they outspend revenue. For both of these games, winning is measured by the amount of citizen support or satisfaction that the players' decisions create. The goals of the games are to help students to recognize the various roles of the executive branch and the tensions involved in making federal budget decisions.

In both of these games, however, a different tension emerges. Both games include tasks that appear to be open and could potentially involve the types of decisions that ask players to weigh the "best case, fair hearing of competing points of view" that Kelly (1986) recommended for democratic education. However, despite these seemingly deliberative scenarios, the open decisions are actually designed with "correct" answers in mind that are reinforced by the feedback and the criteria for winning designed into each game.

The tension that emerges is the one between the goal of the game (winning through accumulating points or maintaining citizen satisfaction) and the goal of democratic education. The seemingly arbitrary reward system for "winning" in these games does not seem to be tied to the specific concepts or issues. Instead, it promotes attempts by the player to discover the patterns that will likely result in "winning" based on adherence to the rules. For example, we found that you can easily win *Executive Command* by approving all laws where the public will benefit and by quickly ending the war; in *People's Pie*, which is a complex game, you simply need to lower taxes, raise the retirement age, and fund small-budget projects to keep the citizens satisfied.

In addition to this pitfall, elements from both games also suffer from the fact that individual choices that seem open-ended up having a "more correct" answer. For example, if you select Security as an administrative priority in *Executive Command* and give a speech to a joint session of Congress to promote the issue, you are given two choices at each stage of your "speech" to try to get a high approval rating. The options you get, however, are not diplomacy versus using the threat of military force, or taking an isolationist versus an interventionist stance toward a nation that asks us to intervene. Instead, one legitimate perspective on the issue is paired with a rather ridiculous answer intended to be "wrong." In the case in Figure 2, the options are "I will work day and night to make sure that no terrorists attack this country" or "We should shut down all police stations and fire stations, so all police and firefighters can go on vacation." Similar to the earlier "closed" task games, here there is an obvious correct choice that is juxtaposed to an obviously incorrect one. These options do not engage the player in weighing legitimate competing options but instead push a player toward a particular ideologically driven view on foreign policy and domestic security.

The legislative decisions in *Executive Command* offer more choice and more realistic examples, although none that would cause the player to weigh an issue from two different sides, especially as the bills that are sent for the president's signature are judged only by how popular they are with the public and have no ramifications in terms of the budget. In one scenario, a player was sent a bill titled "Preventing Climate Change" with three provisions: "Develop new technologies to help limit climate change"; "Research ways to control and reduce greenhouse gas emissions to limit climate change"; and "Encourage people to pollute a lot and then research what's happening." Instead of taking the intended path, which was to veto the bill because of the third provision and then wait for the bill to come back amended, our player approved all three clauses by signing the bill as is. She was awarded 25 points for each of the first items and deducted 40 for approving the third. This presentation of obvious right and wrong decisions, reinforced by the awarding or deducting of points, does not encourage the player to weigh political views in making any sort of thoughtful decision.

In *People's Pie*, the player has even more opportunity to make seemingly open selections, with feedback coming in the form of a rise or fall in "citizen satisfaction." This game provides more realistic choices in projects to fund, but, as in *Executive Command*, seemingly valid funding programs are coupled with ridiculous ones. For example, programs under Homeland Security include the serious Disaster Insurance Program and the absurd Sniffing Cats program to "train cats to help customs officers." This is problematic because these games reflect real contemporary issues and are structured around content based on "textbook" concepts, similar to the two other games, but also include a mix of both trivial examples (e.g., sniffing cats) and political content with clear views (e.g., climate change) that can potentially influence the players' understanding of government and their views on particular relevant issues.

Further, the rules that warrant success in the game, such as gaining points or congressional or citizen approval, do not match the rules of society. The fictional worlds of the games lead to simplification of the issues and place the focus for players, even our undergraduate and law student researchers, on figuring out how to win the game rather than on the ramifications for cutting spending on entitlements (*People's Pie*) or for advocating a stricter foreign policy role (*Executive Command*). The game design thus focuses on intellectual work more in tune with behaviorism and the transfer of knowledge rather than constructivism and the active construction of knowledge and working to follow a path based on democratic deliberation. These games neither engage students in authentic deliberative activities nor engage them in realistic scenarios or data as they are designed based on apolitical textbook content instead of cases of political or civic engagement argued for by democratic educators (e.g., Hess, 2009; Parker, 2003).

Designed Experience, Affect, and Ideological Complications

In addition to looking at the affordances of design and the nature of intellectual work in the game, we also considered the overall experiences of players: a combination of their affective responses, the narratives that they constructed, and ideologies that may be reflected in their experiences. It is easy, given the interactive nature and design of these games, to see them as fun, engaging, and neutral. However, it is important to be aware that there are people behind the designs of the games with political views, values, goals, and objectives of their own (Raphael et al., 2010; Squire, 2006).

What are the overall stories that players construct through engaging with these games? That people coming through immigration include only "worthy" and "good" people such as those with technical skills, like computer programmers? That running a law firm means only defending people you know are on the side of right and that those people will always prevail? *Immigration Nation* and *Do I Have a Right?* may lead to some beliefs about their content that is simplified or naïve, and those beliefs will give students little understanding of the issues in today's context of immigration reform or the battle over gun rights. These ideological messages are not clearly conveyed, but are instead built into game rules and content that are designed in many ways to mimic the neutral tone of a textbook.

For the policy-oriented games, the stories that are constructed reflect larger political views, but they don't allow the players to construct their own views based on weighing real differences on issues. This was apparent in the example of the agendas selected by the president in *Executive Command* and their relationship to the larger message that the game sends about how to be a successful president. For example, one player selected Deficit Reduction as the primary issue agenda. As described, the players are given a series of choices between one serious statement and one absurd statement as they give their speech. These selections form a larger view on deficit reduction that players do not really have a choice about. In our example, the speech included:

- I am concerned about the high level of debt this country has . . .
- Reducing the deficit must be a national priority . . .

- We cannot leave this huge debt for our children and other future generations . . .
- Reducing the debt will take sacrifice and courage from all of us . . .

Although there likely are a lot of politicians on both sides of the aisle who may believe in these statements, they reflect views about the economy and fiscal policy from a particular perspective. There are many economists and politicians who believe running a deficit and accruing debt is sometimes necessary in order to use funds to stimulate the economy. This is not a closed issue but an open one with legitimate competing points of view. The players of *Executive Command*, however, are not engaged in weighing these decisions.

Similarly, they have no diplomatic option to avoid war but must engage as a way to learn that the navy is used to fight battles at sea and the army is the force to stop Neverland's invasion of Maine. One player remarked that it was

> stressful . . . They want you to get that there is a lot more going on than making appearances and that when a crisis happens, like a war, that Congress doesn't sleep while you handle the war . . . that you still have your education bills and all of these things that need to get to where they need to go.

In *People's Pie*, our research assistant players would often rack up large debts in the first round of play as they were hesitant to deny funding to popular and important programs aimed at providing those in need with vital assistance or at investing in and improving the national infrastructure, in part because of the way it impacted their citizens' satisfaction. One player remarked upon completion, "Wow, that was hard . . . Looking at the way I played the game . . . it is a good metaphor for the snowball effect that can occur [with government spending] that you fund one thing and then another, and pretty soon it is out of control." The players empathized with members of Congress and the executive branch as a result of the challenges represented in the games. When you combine these affective reactions with the policy messages in these games—both in content and in the game design—a larger game narrative is formed, that narrative in this game's case being that it is bad to accrue debt to fund even worthy programs. This is not the only message that may be taken from the game, but it is the one that is most likely to be experienced based on our repeated play of the game.

In terms of democratic education, these games introduce players to key concepts and knowledge, as well as major issues, but fall short of engaging them in the skills of developing, weighing, supporting, or acting on a given position—which is the stated goal of iCivics. For the most part, the player is not faced with decisions based on a fair hearing of competing points of view. Instead, there appears to be a "right" answer the game is designed to push the player toward.

Discussion and Implications

Our analysis illustrates the great potential of games such as iCivics to engage young people in learning civic concepts and assuming the roles of civic agents to develop empathy through an affective and designed experience. These concepts are also viewed as being one important characteristic of high-quality democratic education (Gould, 2011). This analysis also, however, describes the constraints of these games and how these tensions between game design and democratic education reflect larger tensions in the field. It also reflects the tension for organizations such as iCivics that want to both reach a broad audience, and therefore feel the need to align closely with state standards and textbook content, and hope to work toward ambitious democratic education goals for producing active democratic citizens. It is important to note that this tension goes well beyond iCivics; it is present in almost any civic education curriculum or civic-based game.

The iCivics games we studied have the potential to meet some of the goals of democratic education. Specifically, the iCivics games place the player in a simulation environment related to government officials, which is promoted by Gould (2011), and the alignment with civic skills and roles in the framework presented by Raphael et al. (2010). However, two other key recommendations from this work are not reflected. The games do not fully guide players in the kinds of deliberation of controversial issues and engagement with different perspectives necessary for deliberative democratic education (Hess, 2009; McAvoy & Hess, 2013). The player is rarely if ever asked to weigh multiple positions and evidence on the same issue in a way that would promote the kind of "best case, fair hearing, of competing points of view" identified by Kelly (1986). Further, although the games align closely with middle-grades civic content, they do not align as well with civic skills nor do they actively ask players to apply what they have learned in the game to situations outside of the game—in terms of taking the kind of civic action indicative of strong democracy (Raphael et al., 2010).

These issues reflect larger issues in the field of civic education. These tensions exist in large part because there is no consensus about what the goals of citizenship education should be (e.g., content vs skills) nor what a "good" citizen looks like (Westheimer & Kahne, 2004). Therefore, the content to which the game is aligned, and which is present in most civic textbooks and curriculum, is written to appear apolitical and is not designed to engage young people in contemporary issues for fear of the perception that teachers are attempting to indoctrinate students toward particular political views (McAvoy & Hess, 2013; Hess & McAvoy, 2014). What iCivics games have the potential to do, however, is to at least engage students outside of the classroom in civic-related content and roles that may help them to understand the roles of government and important contemporary issues, even if not in the most authentic context or with the most accurate information. Given the limited access to democratic education in many areas of the United States, these games provide access to informal education that contributes to some key aspects of democratic education through an engaging medium.

Given the virtual and abstract nature of these games, however, what will young players take away from playing these games? The games represent major contemporary issues but are not designed to engage players in the issues in a way that represents the contemporary context. Will a young person think that taking on debt at the federal level is a bad but necessary evil? That the law is as simple as identifying cases where a client has a right and therefore will automatically win their case? That immigration officers identify good people who get to enter the country and bad ones who do not? That a good president is one who does things to keep constituents happy and the wars short regardless of cost in dollars or lives? They also do not prepare young people to engage in civic action in today's media driven political environment (Kahne, Hodgin, Eidman-Aadahl, 2016).

These narratives that players construct are the result of context, the players' knowledge and experiences, and the designed experience created by game producers, experiences that often reflect the ideologies and realities of the time and place where the game was produced as well as the views of those who made it (Squire, 2006). For example, the designed affective response to *People's Pie* we described—that taking on debt to fund programs was a necessary evil of sorts—represents a particular ideological view promoted often by conservative groups who favor austerity. Similarly, the examples of potential immigrants in *Immigration Nation* makes the issue of immigration seem as if it is a good/bad distinction in many ways and does not include the poor working-class immigrant attempting to access the United States in order to make money to support his or her family back home.

How can we ensure that the goal that Raphael et al. (2010) and others identified as essential when games are used in democratic education—of having young players apply the concepts and content from games to the world outside of the diegesis of the game—is met? Put differently, how can teachers take advantage of the affordances of iCivics and limit the constraints? Without the application of gameplay and concepts to contemporary issues, as well as a recognition that the games represent particular views on these issues, iCivics players may believe that Homeland Security really is trying to train sniffing cats or that there is only one sensible policy that a president can follow when it comes to defense. Game designers and educators need to collaborate with each other to find the best way to align gameplay with the types of specific skills necessary for democratic citizenship and outcomes where winning represents the goals of citizenship in a game that is still found to be fun and engaging. It may be that the kind of gamification of civic and governmental roles in the iCivics games may not be the best medium for preparing democratic citizens; simulations such as *The Redistricting Game* (http://www.redistrictinggame.org/) that represent more authentic contexts and data may be more useful for young people to develop the key concepts and skills for democratic engagement.

The most direct solution for the constraints of the games, and the one that the iCivics developers are counting on, is thoughtful teachers who will help players debrief their game experiences and apply their new knowledge to relevant real-world issues. However, as we know from many previous studies (e.g., Cuban, 1986, 2001), this assumption that teachers will seamlessly integrate new technologies and media into high-quality practice is not grounded in evidence. Although iCivics includes many quality lesson plans and resources on its site, these are more traditional lessons that extend from the content in the games but do not promote models or specific strategies for engaging students in playing and directly applying this content from the games.

The role of the teacher (or facilitator, mentor, or parent) in game-based pedagogy and curriculum is a major issue yet to be seriously addressed in much of the game-focused research. This is in part because the vast majority of this research is being done outside of classroom settings or by researchers in fields such as the learning sciences, whose focus is on constructing students' learning environments with the games and not on large-scale implementation in schools. In order for iCivics to overcome the constraints described previously, the teacher needs to be central, and the resources that accompany iCivics online need to include more built-in scaffolding for teachers in the same way they do for players. For example, the iCivics site could provide prompts for students to think about while playing and questions or activities to help them debrief and reflect on their play.

In addition to helping teachers think about strategies for engaging their students in the games and questions to ask and ideas for debriefing the games, iCivics could use new media tools to help players tie the abstract issues to real-time data. This aligns with the ways in which many young people become informed of social and political issues and could be combined with developing skills in critically reading and understanding news and political sources. After playing *People's Pie*, students could be sent automatically to links to polls looking at what the public really views are priorities in spending or views on the retirement age or to graphs showing the real impact of decisions in these areas to be compared with what the player did in the game. There are limits on what can be done in a game designed to be easy to access and use, but one of the goals of using a game with the affordances of the iCivics games should be taking advantage of more dynamic and contemporary issues and data. It is likely that more recent iCivics games are working toward these goals. These types of engagements could more powerfully model the skills and knowledge of young democratic citizens engaging in the types of participatory politics using online and social media documented by Banaji et al. (2009) and Cohen and Kahne (2012).

In this way, the games are a first step to young people developing the concepts that can be used to participate in or take civic action. Even this, however, will likely require a role for a teacher or parent to help them reflect upon, and apply, the concepts that they learn in the games to those helpful for democratic participation. It is with these goals in mind that game designers, democratic educators, and researchers should work together to take advantage of the many affordances evident in the iCivics games to more strongly work toward the goals of democratic education.

References

Banaji, S., Buckingham, D., Van Zoonen, L., & Hirzalla, F. (2009). Synthesis of CivicWeb results and policy outcomes. Centre for the Study of Children, Youth and Media, Institute of Education, London, UK. Retrieved from http://eprints.lse.ac.uk/27602/

Barab, S., Gresalfi, M., Ingram- Noble, E., Hickey, D., Akram, S., & Kizer, S. (2009). Transformational play and virtual worlds: Worked examples from the Quest Atlantis project. International Journal of Learning and Media, 1(2). Retrieved from http://ijlm.net/knowinganddoing/10.1162/ijlm.2009.0023

Barab, S. A., Sadler, T. D., Heiselt, C., Hickey, D., & Zuiker, S. (2010). Erratum to: Relating narrative, inquiry, and inscriptions: Supporting consequential play. Journal of Science Education and Technology, 19(4), 387–407.

Bers, M. (2010). Let the games begin: Civic playing on high-tech consoles. Review of General Psychology, 14(2), 147–153.

Bigelow, B. (1997). On the road to cultural bias: A critique of The Oregon Trail CD-ROM. Language Arts, 74(2), 84–93.

Blevins, B., LeCompte, K., Wells, S., Moore, B., & Rodgers, J. (2012). Citizenship education goes digital: A three dimensional analysis of iCivics. Paper presented at the annual meeting of the College and University Faculty Assembly of the National Council for the Social Studies, Seattle, WA.

Caftori, N., & Paprzycki, M. (1997). The design, evaluation and usage of educational software. In J. Willis, J. Price, S. McNeil, B. Robin, & D. Willis (Eds.), Proceedings of Society for Information Technology & Teacher Education International Conference (pp. 23–27). Chesapeake, VA: Association for the Advancement of Computing in Education (AACE).

Cohen, K, and Kahne, J. (2012). Participatory politics: New media and youth political action. Chicago, IL: MacArthur Foundation.

Cotton, D., & Gresty, K. (2006). Reflecting on the think-aloud method for evaluating e-learning. British Journal of Educational Technology, 37(1), 45–54.

Cuban, L. (1986). Teachers and machines: The classroom use of technology since 1920. New York, NY: Teachers College Press.

Cuban, L. (2001). Oversold and underused: Computers in the classroom. Cambridge, MA: Harvard University Press.

Curry, K. (2010). Warcraft and civic education: MMORPGs as participatory cultures and how teachers can use them to improve civic education. The Social Studies, 101, 250–253.

Dawley, L., & Dede, C. (2014). Situated learning in virtual worlds and immersive simulations. In J. M. Spector (Ed.), Handbook of research on educational communications and technology (pp. 723–734). New York, NY: Springer.

Gee, J. (2003). What video games have to teach us about learning and literacy. New York, NY: Palgrave Macmillan.

Gould, J. (2011). Guardian of democracy: The civic mission of schools. Philadelphia: University of Pennsylvania, Annenberg Public Policy Center.

Hess, D. (2009). Controversy in the classroom: The democratic power of discussion. New York, NY: Routledge.

Hess, D., & McAvoy, P. (2014). The political classroom: Evidence and ethics in democratic education. New York, NY: Routledge.

Kahne, J., Hodgin, E., & Eidman-Aadahl, E. (2016). Redesigning civic education for the digital age: in pursuit of equitable and impactful democratic engagement. Theory and Research in Social Education, 44(1), 1–35.

Kawashima-Ginsberg, K. (2012). Summary of findings from the evaluation of iCivics' Drafting Board Intervention (Working Paper No. 76). Retrieved from The Center for Information & Research on Civic Learning and Engagement http://www.civicyouth.org/wp-content/uploads/2012/12/WP_76_KawashimaGinsberg.pdf

Kelly, T. E. (1986). Discussing controversial issues: Four perspectives on the teacher's role. Theory and Research in Social Education 19, 113–138.

LeCompte, K., Moore, B., & Blevins, B. (2011). The impact of iCivics on students' core civic knowledge. Research in the Schools, 18(2), 58–74.

Levinson, M. (2012). No citizen left behind. Cambridge, MA: Harvard University Press.

Margolis, J. (2008). Stuck in the shallow end: Education, race, and computing. Cambridge, MA: MIT Press.

Marino, M., & Hayes, M. (2012). Promoting inclusive education, civic scientific literacy, and global citizenship with videogames. Cultural Studies of Science Education, 7(4), 945–954.

McAvoy, P., & Hess, D. (2013). Classroom deliberation in an era of political polarization. Curriculum Inquiry, 43(1), 14–47.

Norton, D., Stone, A., Folwarski, J., & Novick, J. iCivics [video games]. Madison, WI: Filament Games.

Parker, W. (2003). Teaching democracy: Unity and diversity in public life. New York, NY: Teachers College Press.

Poole, K., Berson, M., & Levine, P. (2010). On becoming a legislative aide: enhancing civic engagement through a digital simulation. Action in Teacher Education, 32(4), 70–82.

Raphael, C., Bachen, C., Lynn, K. M., Baldwin-Philippi, J., & McKee, K. A. (2010). Games for civic learning: A conceptual framework and agenda for research and design. Games and Culture, 5(2), 199–235.

Shaffer, D. W. (2004). Pedagogical praxis: The professions as models for post-industrial education. Teachers College Record, 10(1), 1401–1421.

Shaffer, D. W., & Gee, J. P. (2006). Before every child is left behind. How epistemic games can solve the coming crisis in education [Electronic version]. Retrieved from http://www.academiccolab.org/resources/documents/learning_crisis.pdf

Squire, K. (2005). Changing the game: What happens when video games enter the classroom. Innovate: Journal of Online Education, 1(6), Article 5. Retrieved from Available at: http://nsuworks.nova.edu/innovate/vol1/iss6/5

Squire, K. (2006). From content to context: Videogames as designed experience. Educational Researcher, 35(8), 19–29.

Squire, K. D., DeVane, B., & Durga, S. (2008). Designing centers of expertise for academic learning through video games. Theory into Practice, 47(3), 240–251.

Watson, W. R. (2010). Games for social studies education. In A. Hirumi (Ed.), Playing games in school: Video games and simulations for primary and secondary education (pp. 173–202). Washington, DC: International Society for Technology in Education.

Westheimer, J., & Kahne, J. (2004). What kind of citizen? The politics of educating for democracy. American Educational Research Journal, 41(2), 237–269.

Wideman, R., Owston, R., Brown, C., Kushniruk, A., Ho, F., & Pitts, K. (2007). Unpacking the potential of educational gaming: A new tool for gaming research. Simulation & Games: An International Journal, 38(1), 10–30.

Critical Thinking

1. What is the significance of civics education being dictated by current education policy but not funded in President Trump's budget?
2. What arguments does the article offer to convince a civics education skeptic of its importance for students and society?
3. Why is conforming to the democratic education of such importance?

Internet References

Gaming to Learn
https://www.apa.org/monitor/2015/04/gaming

The Hidden Value of Gaming in Education
https://www.sagu.edu/thoughthub/the-hidden-value-of-gaming-in-education

How Video Games Can Be an Educational Tool
https://www.washingtonpost.com/opinions/an-education-in-gaming/2015/05/28/b6920cbe-edcc-11e4-8666-a1d756d0218e_story.html?utm_term=d5ef4c41544e

---

JEREMY STODDARD is an associate professor in the School of Education at the College of William & Mary and associated faculty member in the Film and Media Studies Program.

ANGELA BANKS is a professor of law in the School of Law at the College of William & Mary.

CHRISTINE NEMACHECK is an associate professor of government at the College of William & Mary and serves as the college's pre-law adviser.

ELIZABETH WENSKA is a recent graduate of the School of Education at the College of William & Mary and reporter at *WYDaily*.

Stoddard, J., Banks A.M., Nemacheck, C., Wenska, E. (2016). "The Challenges of Gaming for Democratic Education: The Case of iCivics." Democracy and Education, 24 (2), Article 2. Used by permission of Democracy and Education.

Article

Prepared by: Sheron Fraser-Burgess, *Ball State University*

The Common Core and Democratic Education
Examining Potential Costs and Benefits to Public and Private Autonomy

BENJAMIN J. BINDEWALD, RORY P. TANNEBAUM, AND PATRICK WOMAC

Learning Outcomes

After reading this article, you will be able to:

- Identify the distinguishing curricular focus of the Common Core State Standards (CCSS).
- Analyze the arguments against CCSS.
- Foreground the public emphasis of democratic education as distinct from individual autonomy as an underlying premise of classroom knowledge.

By October 2013, forty-five states, the District of Columbia, four territories, and the Department of Defense Education Activity had adopted the Common Core State Standards (CCSS). Some states, such as Indiana, South Carolina, and Oklahoma, however, have since backed away from their earlier decisions to adopt the standards. Strong resistance to the Common Core continues and is likely to intensify as the 2016 U.S. presidential race progresses, as the standards have already emerged as one of GOP nominee, Donald Trump's targets. Anticipating a renewed national focus on the subject, our primary objectives in this article are to assess the merits of prevalent critiques of the Common Core and determine whether the standards are likely to support or undermine key democratic aims of education.

Consideration of the standards' likely effect on two key components of democratic education—*public autonomy* (defined, for our purposes, as a community's opportunity and capacity to influence public life and shape public policy) and *private autonomy* (defined, for our purposes, as one's opportunity and capacity to think for oneself, to set one's own goals, and to pursue those goals free from excessive outside influence)—provides a framework through which to assess prevalent critiques of the standards and analyze the standards ourselves. Our analysis shows that while adoption of the standards presents some potential limitations to local control over schools (a factor relating to public autonomy), many critiques of the Common Core are either overstated or misguided and may be mitigated by the standards' likely contribution to overall gains in both public and private autonomy. Additionally, we discuss how the standards might be improved to better reflect key aims of democratic education.

Our study provides analysis and evaluation of the *Common Core State Standards for English Language Arts & Literacy in History/Social Studies, Science, and Technical Subjects* (Common Core Standards Initiative, 2013).[1] Therefore, when we use the labels *CCSS, Common Core,* or *the standards* in the analysis that follows, we are referring to these literacy standards. Our use of the final version of the standards produced by the National Governors Association Center for Best Practices and the Council of Chief State School Officers rather than a

---

[1] In this article, we do not consider the math standards. We recognize their potential contributions to the preparation of students for democratic citizenship, but we limited our analysis due to space constraints and our own expertise.

more comprehensive review of each state's slightly modified version of the standards may be a limitation of our analysis. However, as we focus on the skills and dispositions components of the standards, which are consistent from state to state, this limitation is not so severe as to undermine the legitimacy of our argument. Additionally, it is worth noting that our analysis is of the standards themselves, and not the lesson plans, curriculum materials, or assessment and accountability measures associated with Common Core, which vary from state to state.

We begin with an analysis of critiques of the Common Core related to public and private autonomy. We then examine the meaning of autonomy and argue that a democratic society has an obligation to both develop young citizens' capacities for autonomy and employ democratic procedures for adopting and implementing educational standards to accomplish this aim. Finally, we assess the Common Core in terms of its likely contributions to the enhancement of public and private autonomy for all citizens.

Critiques of the Common Core

We have defined *public autonomy* as a community's opportunity and capacity to influence public life and shape public policy. Most critiques of the CCSS focus on potential losses to local control over school policy and curricular decisions—conflating adoption and implementation processes with the standards themselves—and thereby deal only with the opportunity component of public autonomy. A second type of criticism, which is less common but which we find more compelling, deals with the actual standards as they relate to developing students' capacity for public autonomy. In this section, we discuss both types of criticism concerning the relation between the standards and public autonomy.

Though criticism of the Common Core comes from individuals and groups with varying political perspectives, some of the strongest critiques come from leaders and organizations on the political right. Of particular salience to the present discussion, many conservative critics claim that adoption of "national standards," which they perceive the Common Core to be, will lead to a significant loss of state and local influence and opportunities for deliberation over public school policy and curricula (Graebe, 2013; Kurtz, 2013; McCluskey, Evers, & Stotsky, 2013; Paul, 2013; Russo, 2013; Scott, 2013; Smith, 2013). This development, they have argued, would amount to a sacrifice of the interests of students, parents, and other members of school communities to those of distant special interest groups with influence at the federal policymaking level. Such arguments commonly reference the idea that the standards are yet another step in a series of efforts to bring about a federal monopoly over public education, which would inevitably lead to less opportunities for the exercise of public autonomy (or at least in relation to local control over public school policy and curriculum decisions), less competition, and poorer academic performance by American students.[2]

This type of argument is seen in the findings of an analysis of over 10,000 online survey responses to a March 2010 version of the CCSS, which found that a "significant number of respondents oppose all federal standards, which they perceive the CCSS to be" and that some "feel very strongly that any standard not perceived as local is problematic. Many of these respondents see this initiative as a first step toward a required national curriculum and loss of parental freedom." Similarly, in their analysis of over 14,000 tweets from the top 150 Twitter subscribers who posted messages about the Common Core from February to July of 2013, Goldsworthy and Sam (2015) categorized approximately two-thirds of those tweets as oppositional toward CCSS. Among the most prevalent themes that emerged from their analysis was a widespread concern that the standards represented a significant threat to the local control component of what we refer to as public autonomy, signifying "an annexation of local decision-making, or wresting of control from those who should be making decisions about local education" (p. 5).

Sentiments such as these, centered on the perception that the CCSS are "national standards" that will lead to a loss of autonomy, have become so widespread that Secretary of Education Arne Duncan (2013) delivered a speech to directly address them. Duncan sought to push back against misinformation about the standards, stating: "The Common Core has become a rallying cry for fringe groups that claim it is a scheme for the federal government to usurp state and local control of what students learn." He requested those in attendance—primarily newspaper editors—to ask their sources to "identify a single lesson plan that the federal government created . . . any textbook that the federal government created . . . [or] any element, a single word of the Common Core standards that was developed or required by the federal government." Though the federal government had no direct role in the creation of the CCSS, the belief that the standards represent a federal takeover of public education remains widespread.

A strong voice in libertarian politics, Republican U.S. Representative Ron Paul (2013) echoed the above-mentioned fears relating to the loss of public autonomy: "We must oppose further encroachment on the autonomy of local public schools and

---

[2]The new Every Student Succeeds Act allows states to adopt Common Core but does not require it. In fact, the act requires the federal Education Department to remain neutral toward the CCSS.

work to roll-back existing interference" (para. 7). Similarly, Marco Rubio, U.S. Senator from Florida and unsuccessful 2016 GOP presidential primary candidate, referred to the CCSS as a means for the Obama administration "to turn the Department of Education into what is effectively a national school board" (Smith, 2013, para. 4). Graebe (2013) claimed that the "CCS[S] removes any instructional flexibility despite the possibility that their curriculum may not be what works best for a particular class" (para. 8). In a similar vein, Scott (2013) noted that many see the CCSS as an unproven endeavor undermining state autonomy to "direct their own educational programs and that set aside the high quality standards and assessments some states have created in favor of lower quality standards and less academically demanding assessments" (p. 4). These politically conservative critics of the Common Core have predicted that, by encroaching on the autonomous practices of local communities, the "national standards" will limit their ability to differentiate curricula based on student needs and particularities and will cause the quality of instruction to suffer.

Others criticize the standards based on their limitations of classroom readings to mostly informational rather than literary texts and general focus on developing transferrable critical thinking/reading skills rather than more specific knowledge.[3] Bauerlein and Stotsky (2012) predicted that a heavier focus on informational texts will make students less college ready based on the belief that problems in college readiness stem from "an incoherent, less-challenging [student-centered, multicultural] literature curriculum from the 1960s onward" (p. 1). They warned that, because the Common Core focuses more on developing skills than specific canonical knowledge, widespread adoption of the standards presents an opportunity to those who would adopt less worthy contemporary texts over great works of English and American literature. Berry (2014) and Robbins (2013) sounded the alarm about the standards' potential to be used by the political left through mass-marketed, standards-aligned informational texts and to promote "a social engineering ideology" as a substitute for traditional religious and family values. Thus, these authors held, nationwide adoption of standards that place too few requirements on schools to adopt literary classics creates a situation that gives large publishing houses too much influence over public education and opens the door for leftist mischief.

Critiques of the Common Core, however, extend beyond those of conservative politicians and scholars. Ravitch (2013) noted that the CCSS were "developed by an organization called Achieve and the National Governors Association both of which were generously funded by the Gates Foundation [and that] there was minimal public engagement in the development of the Common Core. Their creation was neither grassroots nor did it emanate from the states" (para. 10). From another angle, Au (2013) argued that the CCSS will "inevitably lead to restrictive high-stakes, standardized testing similar to that associated with No Child Left Behind" (p. 1). Thus, Au suggested, high-stakes, standardized testing can play a significant role in undermining local influence over what goes on in schools by encouraging "teaching to the test."[4]

Though we were unable to locate many published scholarly critiques of the Common Core guided by explicitly communitarian or multiculturalist frameworks, we think such arguments ought to be taken up as part of this broader analysis. Particularly, concerns about cultural loss for local (and, especially, minority) communities should be considered, including the concern that a nationwide adoption of a single set of standards (though versions of the CCSS do, indeed, vary somewhat from state to state) would impose a monolithic vision upon all students and might drown out the voices of cultural and religious minorities, people of color, and other historically marginalized groups. For instance, in one of the few published critiques of this kind, Gangi and Benfer (2014) criticized the standards' list of 171 recommended texts for elementary children for only containing 18 works by authors of color and few that reflect the lives of children of color and the poor. They argued that acquisition of literacy skills and identity development requires students to be able to make meaningful connections with the people and stories in the texts they read. Consequently, the authors suggested, by recommending only a few works with which children of color are likely to relate, the standards do these students a significant injustice. Furthermore, they contended, stocking every classroom with literature that would allow children from the dominant, mainstream culture exposure to stories about others who look and live differently would likely yield social and democratic benefits. Further, some may see the standards' primary focus on college and career readiness to come at the cost of the democratic aim of promoting tolerance and respect for cultural diversity. These are serious concerns that merit additional scholarly attention.

Not everyone is concerned, however, that the CCSS will encroach upon state and local autonomy. Some of the research on the Common Core has emphasized the fact that the adoption of the standards is strictly voluntary and that the federal

---

[3] The standards require readings to consist of 70% informational texts and 30% literary texts across the high school curriculum, with a 50/50 split in high school English classes.
[4] Some scholars may be concerned about losses to teacher autonomy (as opposed to autonomy of the local community) due to adoption of the CCSS, but these concerns do not fit within our public–private autonomy framework and, thus, exceed the scope of this analysis.

government legally cannot mandate any state to adopt them (StudentsFirst, 2013). Along these lines, Pearson and Hiebert (2012) noted that the "CCSS provide a core set of expectations and intentionally leave much to districts, schools, and teachers to figure out for themselves—to, if you will, put a local signature on their implementation of the core" (p. 3). Scholars at the Aspen Institute (2012) similarly claimed that by focusing on the capacities of students, "the CCSS does not advocate one particular pedagogical approach over another" (p. 1). Further, the Aspen scholars emphasized that, in comparison to standards that focus on rote learning and content memorization, the Common Core standards afford local schools stronger autonomy as they implement the standards.

The above critiques focus primarily on issues relating to local control of school curricula—that is, on issues that only correspond to the opportunity component of public autonomy. Critiques of the actual content of the standards relating to their suitability for developing students' capacity for public autonomy, however, were far less commonplace. In one of the few such critiques, social studies scholar Singer (2013a and 2013b) claimed that the Common Core standards do not promote the broad aims of a democratic education. Singer noted, "In the entire document, there is no real discussion of life in a democratic society and the role of education in promoting democracy processes and democratic values" (2013b, para. 1). And this, to Singer, is problematic, given that the leading organization in the social studies, The National Council For the Social Studies (NCSS), explicitly has stated that "the goal of schooling . . . is not merely preparation for citizenship, but citizenship itself; to equip a citizenry with the knowledge, skills, and dispositions needed for active and engaged civic life" (National Council for the Social Studies, 2010, para. 1). Thus, by not directly focusing on issues relating to democratic participation, Singer implied that citizens miss out on opportunities to develop knowledge, skills, and commitments that enhance public autonomy.

We need some way of assessing this collection of claims, and the public–private autonomy framework is useful in that regard because it addresses fundamental dimensions of the most prevalent Common Core critiques and enables us to more comprehensively understand the complex nature of autonomy that is at stake. Our aim of providing a substantive assessment of the above critiques requires that we direct our attention to the standards themselves. It also compels us to provide a straightforward account of the set of assumptions that grounds our argument. Therefore, we will assess these critiques after analyzing the standards through our public–private autonomy framework, which we explain in greater detail in the following section.

Public and Private Autonomy

Various assumptions about the appropriate role and purposes of public education inform our analysis. In addition to preparing students for college and career (the stated primary goals of Common Core), we believe public schools have a duty to help young citizens develop knowledge, skills, and dispositions required for active participation in a pluralist, democratic society. Toward these efforts, democratic societies are obliged to develop capacities for and guarantee opportunities for the exercise of both private and public autonomy in their young citizens. Furthermore, major curricular decisions, such as the adoption of state standards, should be made in a manner that aligns with democratic values. These assumptions and the thesis they inform are grounded in liberal political theory and a conception of democratic education constructed upon the foundational works of Dewey (1916), Rawls (1971, 1993/1996, 2005), Gutmann (1987), and Habermas (1995, 1984) and supported by more recent works of scholars Reich (2002), Fletcher (2000), and Creppell (2012).

We consider both private and public autonomy to be central components of democratic life and the development of these capacities to be important aims of democratic education. Our understanding of private and public autonomy derives from an intellectual exchange between political philosophers Rawls (1971, 1993/1996, 2005) and Habermas (1995) over the process of political decision making.[5] In this debate, Rawls emphasized the importance of protecting individual liberty through universal, rationally justifiable, constitutional principles (relating to private autonomy). Habermas critiqued Rawls's position, arguing that it relied too heavily on abstract justification rather than on the actual consent of citizens. In other words, he said that Rawls's view imposed a top-down system of ready-made principles onto citizens, foregoing a participatory and deliberative democratic process (relating to public autonomy).

The capacities component of public autonomy, however, required a critical mass of citizens who were rational, critical thinkers with both the skills and the desire to deliberate with people from other cultural backgrounds—capacities that Rawls seemed to overlook, Habermas seemed to take for granted, and we think must be intentionally developed in young citizens. Public education, though not the only one, is an important setting through which democratic societies might develop

---

[5]Rawls responded to Habermas's critique (1995) of his work in Lecture 9 of the Expanded Edition of Political Liberalism, which was published in 2005.

young citizens' capacities for public autonomy. Furthermore, a community's capacity for public autonomy is severely undermined when its governing bodies fail to provide opportunities for its exercise. Thus, the opportunities component of public autonomy requires certain preconditions for its realization. There must be some significant degree of local control over and opportunities for democratic input into policy decisions. Because public autonomy requires a critical mass of individuals with the ability to deliberate effectively, the state has a responsibility to promote its citizens' development of the knowledge, skills, and dispositions required for life in a pluralist, democratic society.

The ability to think and read critically is an essential component of both private and public autonomy and, thus, a key aim of democratic education. In addition to helping students develop as individuals, critical thinking is essential for the healthy functioning of a democratic state, lest its citizens fall victim to groupthink, mass media manipulation, or the propaganda and brainwashing of authoritarian regimes. Significant threats to liberal democracies arise when societies fail to foster a critical spirit in their future citizens. If students are not encouraged to question tradition, cultural norms, and authority, and demand justice and equality under the law, democratic societies will be ill-prepared to face the challenges they will inevitably encounter. Thus, the development of critical thinking skills in young citizens provides both individual and social benefits.

Yet, as important as critical thinking is, there are other skills and virtues that are also essential components of good citizenship and a good education. One manner in which schools can help to develop future citizens is by educating individuals with the moral qualities needed for the functioning of a productive, deliberative democracy. Gutmann (1999) said that, "a democracy is deliberative to the extent that citizens and their accountable representatives offer one another morally defensible reasons for mutually binding laws in an ongoing process of mutual justification" (p. xii). She argued that public schools play a central role in developing the capacities for this type of deliberation in students:

> A primary aim of publicly mandated schooling is therefore to cultivate the skills and virtues of deliberation. . . . Deliberation is not a single skill or virtue. It calls upon skills of literacy, numeracy, and critical thinking, as well as contextual knowledge, understanding, and appreciation of other people's perspectives. The virtues that deliberation encompasses include veracity, nonviolence, practical judgment, civic integrity and magnanimity. By cultivating these and other deliberative skills and virtues, a democratic society helps secure both the basic opportunity of individuals and its collective capacity to pursue justice. (pp. xii–xiii)

The teaching of tolerance and respect is also an important component of democratic education. Students living in democratic societies ought to be made aware of their rights as well as the responsibilities that accompany them. One of the responsibilities of good citizenship is our obligation to respect the rights of others. Students can learn how to respect others' rights through classroom discourse, guided by their teachers, in which each student is required to accord all others with respect as persons and to recognize what Rawls (1971) called the "burdens of judgment." The burdens of judgment, which are basically factors that illustrate how reasonable people can disagree on matters of deep importance, call upon citizens of pluralist societies to recognize that none of us has a monopoly on truth and to exercise toleration toward one another.

In addition to teaching tolerance, public schools can provide meaningful opportunities for democratic deliberation among diverse students to cultivate a sense of trust and community in their classrooms. Along these lines, it is desirable to foster in future citizens a sense of *intersubjectivity* (Habermas, 1984) or *mutuality* (Creppell, 2008), initiated and sustained by a commitment to engage across differences in a shared political project. Mutuality, the term we prefer, asks citizens not to set differences aside (which is asking quite a lot) but only to commit to maintaining public relationships, in which individuals and groups engage in ongoing democratic deliberations across meaningful differences. Rather than focusing only on our own individual or group rights and identities, mutuality requires that we recognize others' rights and identities and seek to engage with others in a public discourse through which differences might be negotiated diplomatically. This is certainly a tall order for schools, which are already saddled with enormous responsibilities (many of which remain presently unfulfilled). Nevertheless, the benefits and obligations of citizenship are too important to remain underexplored, and as one of the greatest purposes of public schooling, democratic education ought not to remain marginalized in the curriculum.

Furthermore, because public autonomy requires a critical mass of free citizens who have the ability to articulate their individual and group interests and assess the competing claims of their interlocutors, it seems that public autonomy, to a significant degree, requires some number of individual citizens who have the capacity for private autonomy. This is not to say that private autonomy is not valuable in and of itself but to acknowledge that both capacities are core components of our conception of democratic education. Private autonomy is a necessary but not sufficient component of public autonomy, and, therefore, the two must come as a package deal as part of an adequate democratic education. Scholars from various theoretical backgrounds, however, have conceptualized private autonomy differently, so some further clarification of what we mean by the term is in order. While the following cursory discussion is far from a comprehensive review of the literature on autonomy, we think it will direct readers' attention to a few important concerns relating to the topic and provide a clearer picture of the conception of private autonomy we reference in our argument.

Fletcher's (2000) notion of *autonomy as authenticity* takes into account how our "immediate circumstances necessarily shape the capacity we have to create and pursue our life-plans" (p. 119). The conception of authenticity envisions communities and relationships as potential avenues for supporting the development of individual autonomy:

> When individuals draw on these local resources in ways that expand the range and possibility of their choices, increase the potential of their choices to meet their needs, and encourage the development of new interests and talents, then these relationships and communities support a capacity for autonomy that is generally not explained, and in some cases not supported, by universalist theories alone. (pp. 119–120)

This notion of autonomy as authenticity acknowledges the importance of recognition (Taylor, 1994) and takes into account how identity is formed not in total isolation from others but through

> both the inward experience of our deliberation over possible choices and life-plans, and the outward experience of recognition we feel through the understanding and support that others express for our choices. These two aspects, one experienced self-reflectively, the other in our relations with others, are key aspects of authenticity. (Fletcher, 2000, p. 120)

This notion of autonomy as authenticity is emancipatory in the sense that it draws our attention to pressures for mainstream cultural conformity and calls upon educators to avoid practices that constrain or silence students' expression of identities that lie outside of the mainstream or at the margins of society. Insights from Fletcher's autonomy as authenticity—including the positive role communities play in shaping identity and providing opportunities for expression of individual members' autonomy—inform our conception of private autonomy. Underemphasized, however, in this conception of autonomy is the tendency of some illiberal cultural groups to stifle individuality or dissent among members. Reich's (2002) conception of minimalist autonomy provides additional insights that take a more critical approach to the potentially limiting aspects of culture and offers some ideas for how schools might respond to such challenges.

Like Fletcher (2000), Reich (2002) acknowledged the importance of community and rejects egoistic and hyper-rational conceptions of autonomy. He argued that these "strong conceptions of autonomy" are "too exacting to encompass the forms of life most people actually live or would wish to live" (p. 99), and they sever "autonomy from emotion and worldly passions" and seem to negate "the possibility of acting autonomously if we choose to act out of loyalty or love rather than out of duty to the dictates of reason" (pp. 96–97). He rejects any account of autonomy that constructs an ideal of the radical individualist who cuts communal ties and group commitments, which most people consider critically important aspects of a good life. He instead embraced a conception of *minimalist autonomy* that referred to:

> a person's ability to reflect independently and critically upon basic commitments, values, desires, and beliefs, be they chosen or unchosen, and to enjoy a range of meaningful life options from which to choose, upon which to act, and around which to orient and pursue one's life projects. Minimalist autonomy understood as self-determination encompasses both evaluative capacities and a real ability to act on one's evaluations, if necessary adopting new commitments, changing one's values, altering previous desires, or revising old beliefs from a spectrum of meaningful possibilities. (p. 105)

Minimalist autonomy, which equates autonomy not with relentless rationality and egoistic individualism but with sovereignty and self-determination, is concerned less with what type of life a person chooses to live and more so with the process through which one makes such an important decision. In other words, this conception of autonomy is compatible with multiple ways of life, including those characterized by deep commitment to community, tradition, and/or devout religious belief. Though individuals with well-developed capacities for autonomy will most likely choose lives that allow them to exercise their autonomy, they are nevertheless free to autonomously choose lives as members of communities that do not hold autonomy among their highest values.

Reich (2002) suggested that, because the capacity for autonomy is such an important component of human freedom but does not automatically emerge within individuals, the state has an obligation to promote its development. Public schools, he suggested, offer particularly promising avenues for state-sponsored development of autonomy. Thus, the young citizen's right to the type of education that prepares him or her for autonomous decision making as an adult requires that the state guarantee access for all children—in line with Gutmann's (1987) conception of the democratic threshold and her principle of nondiscrimination—to this type of education even when it means going against the interests of parents or cultural groups who do not place a high value on private autonomy.[6] This is not to say that parents (or communities) have no rights or legitimate interests in the education of children but only that these rights ought to be limited insofar as they conflict with the child's right to an autonomy-facilitating education. Warnick's (2013) limited conception of parental rights reflected these sentiments:

1. Parents have a right to participate in shaping school policies that affect their children.
2. Parents have a right to invite, that is, to expose, their children to their own way of life and to persuade them to adopt that life as their own.
3. Parents have a right to engage in practices with their children that are essential to exposing the children to their own ways of life.
4. Parents do not have the right to restrict the exposure of children to only their own way of life. Children have rights to be exposed to multiple perspectives on important issues. (p. 51)

Additionally, respect for individual liberty and emancipatory insights from Fletcher's (2000) conception of autonomy as authenticity requires restraints on the powers of the state. It must be prohibited from imposing what Gutmann (1987) called overly determinant or repressive educational conditions upon students. For example, the state should not indoctrinate students into particular religions or coerce anyone to adopt what Rawls (1971) called comprehensive doctrines. Because the conception of private autonomy that we have described leaves open the realistic possibility of an individual choosing to live in an illiberal community, it cannot reasonably be considered a comprehensive doctrine. Further, because private autonomy is developed in students through a process of exposure to a wide range of perspectives, it cannot reasonably be said that students are indoctrinated into it as one might be into a comprehensive doctrine. Furthermore, mere exposure to an idea or perspective is clearly different from indoctrination into it.

In summation, if we value adult members' autonomous choices to live in illiberal groups, and capacities for autonomous decision making are not automatically developed, it follows that liberal, democratic societies have responsibilities to promote the development of citizens' capacities for autonomy and establish and maintain the conditions necessary for them to be able to exercise these capacities. Adult citizens, then, can choose to live nonautonomous lives but should not be permitted by the state to block children's access to an autonomy-facilitating education. In the pages that follow, we analyze the standards and the prevalent critiques outlined above through this public–private autonomy lens.

Assessment of the Standards

In our analysis, we found that the Common Core effectively promotes private autonomy but could be improved to increase the development of students' capacities for public autonomy. The CCSS lays out a general vision of what it means to be a literate person in the 21st century. Particularly, the standards are designed to cultivate students who demonstrate a range of characteristics relating to critical thinking and autonomous decision making—the basis of the conception of private autonomy to which we refer throughout this article.

Unlike most state standards that grant peripheral treatment to critical thinking, while focusing on content knowledge and basic skills, the CCSS set higher benchmarks encouraging students to actively participate in processes that require the use of higher order thinking. They aim to develop students who habitually perform the critical reading and thinking necessary to carefully navigate the staggering amount of information available to learners in the 21st century. They also direct students to consider multiple perspectives, engage in a process of evaluating these perspectives according to multiple sources of evidence, and examine how biases (including their own) influence this process. This type of reading and thinking aligns with the growing body of literature calling for disciplinary literacy within the classroom and is part of a larger effort to expose students to ideas that broaden their perspectives and enrich their lives.

An important, but certainly not the only, characteristic of an autonomy-facilitating P–12 education is that it helps prepare students who can function successfully in the environments in which they find themselves when they leave school. For many, this will mean entering directly into the workforce. For others, this will mean matriculating into some form of higher education. The Common Core standards, in fact, are designed primarily to enhance students' abilities to find success in these—college and career—realms of human experience. Thus, private autonomy and critical thinking, certainly beneficial to navigating challenges faced in the realms of college and career, are central foci. However, the literacy and critical thinking skills and understandings students are expected to demonstrate also have wide applicability outside the classroom or workplace. To this point, the standards are designed to help students become independent people who reflexively demonstrate the "cogent reasoning and use of evidence that is essential to both private deliberation and responsible citizenship in a democratic republic" (CCSSI, 2013).

---

[6]Though, unlike us, Gutmann believed the state should be willing to grant opt-outs for students whose parents object to their participation in school activities that might expose them to ideas that could potentially undermine their religious beliefs (e.g., comprehensive sex education, the scientific theory of evolution, positive depictions of other religious groups) to prevent fundamentalists from withdrawing from public education.

The CCSS aim to develop students beyond low-level thinkers, asking them to critique as well as comprehend. They are intended to cultivate students who are "engaged and open-minded—but discerning—readers and listeners . . . [who] work diligently to understand precisely what an author or speaker is saying, but they also question an author's or speaker's assumptions and premises and assess the veracity of claims and the soundness of reasoning" (CCSSI, 2013). Accordingly, these students develop critical dispositions and place a high value on the use of evidence in argumentation and in informed decision-making. For instance, they "cite specific evidence when offering an oral or written interpretation of a text. They use relevant evidence when supporting their own points in writing and speaking, making their reasoning clear to the reader or listener, and they constructively evaluate others' use of evidence" (CCSSI, 2013). The ability to evaluate propositions according to evidence provides helpful applications to citizenship and to individual pursuits.

Rather than accepting an author's arguments uncritically, students are called upon to evaluate the author's supporting evidence, assess the author's credibility, and consider the date and setting in which the work was written. Specifically, students are asked to "trace and evaluate the argument and specific claims in a text, distinguishing claims that are supported by reasons and evidence from claims that are not" and to "delineate and evaluate the argument and specific claims in a text, assessing whether the reasoning is sound and the evidence is relevant and sufficient; recognize when irrelevant evidence is introduced" (CCSSI, 2013). Keenly aware of how an author's biases can influence his or her writing, CCSS encourage students to assess how point of view and purpose shape the content and style of a text. For instance, students are required to cite strong and thorough textual evidence to support their analysis of an author's writing as well as inferences drawn from a text. Students are called upon to compare and contrast multiple authors' perspectives or interpretations of particular ideas or events and "integrate information from diverse sources, both primary and secondary, into a coherent understanding of an idea or event, noting discrepancies among sources" (CCSSI, 2013).

When such analysis leads to confusion or conflicting points of view on an issue, students are asked to "identify where the texts disagree on matters of fact or interpretation," determine an author's point of view or purpose in a text, and "analyze how the author acknowledges and responds to conflicting evidence or viewpoints" (CCSSI, 2013). Again, cultivating in students a desire to seek out and examine multiple perspectives as part of the process of forming their own views on a particular issue is of immense value to autonomy development and enhances the quality (and hopefully, the outcomes) of democratic deliberation.

Though explicit references to democratic education are limited within the standards, this is not to say that the standards fail to emphasize the development of individuals and groups capable of participating in the public sphere as rational, deliberative citizens—the very essence of public autonomy. Specifically, the standards direct students to consider multiple perspectives, engage in a process of evaluating these perspectives according to multiple sources of evidence, and examine how biases (including their own) influence this process—skills and dispositions that are central to deliberative democracy. Further, the standards consistently encourage various forms of discourse among diverse partners in the classroom. In this sense, students are expected to participate in a dialogue that is representative of ideal political discourse among adult citizens in a productive pluralist democracy. Such an aim—though only one example of how the standards mirror many of the aims of a democratic education—provides students with the opportunity to develop into citizens who recognize value in the voices of their peers and understand appropriate means for engaging in a deliberative community. Nevertheless, the standards' explicit focus is on preparing students for college and career, not necessarily citizenship. The standards do not, in our view, give adequate attention to developing the knowledge, skills, and dispositions relating to students' capacities for public autonomy.

Assessment of the Critiques

As we have already discussed, rhetoric in opposition to the Common Core includes critiques from a range of perspectives, with some arguments warning that adoption of "national standards" will lead to a significant loss of state and local influence over curriculum and, thus, sacrifice the interests of students, parents, and other members of school communities to those of distant special interest groups with influence at the federal policymaking level. These arguments typically stem from concern that CCSS will eventually lead to a centralized, federal government monopoly over public education, which critics contend will inevitably lead to less competition and poorer academic performance by American students as well as potential loss of voice for already marginalized groups. Though exaggerated, these claims likely reflect the concerns of a significant portion of the American population, and they deserve to be taken seriously by scholars, policymakers, and curriculum developers.

While we remain unconvinced that state adoption of Common Core will serve as a Trojan horse, leading to an inevitable takeover of public education by the federal government, concerns over the increasing centralization of public school decision making have some legitimacy. Arguments relating to the loss of local control, a very limited component of public autonomy, are also probably overstated, but, again, there is likely at least a kernel of truth behind them. That is, full implementation of any form of nationally benchmarked standards (even if they vary to a degree from state to state) would inevitably drown out a significant portion of local influence over what to teach in the public schools and how to teach it. Yet, as we have seen at various points in the history of the United States, when human rights are at odds with local decision making, it is often appropriate for local decision making to give way. If one believes that every child has the right to an autonomy-facilitating education, as we do, and observes inequities from one community to another in regard to children's access to this type of education, then it follows that some limited centralization of educational policymaking is appropriate.

Any loss to various aspects of public autonomy (e.g., local control or opportunities for public input into policy decisions) arising from adoption or implementation of CCSS could be mitigated by greater gains in private autonomy and other knowledge, skills, and dispositions relating to the capacity for public autonomy. This is not to say, however, that local values and voices should be ignored. In fact, the standards' design leaves much room for local influence into which content sources are selected for use in the classroom. Thus, only certain components of local control will be undermined and only minimal aspects of local cultures will be marginalized—those illiberal aspects that would undermine the development of students' autonomy—and this would be something to celebrate rather than dread. Further, if private autonomy is a necessary but not sufficient component of public autonomy, as we have argued, then liberal democratic societies might even value some loss of other aspects of public autonomy in education if it led to more private autonomy for students and thus contributed to more public autonomy in areas outside of education. Given the fact that much space remains for local communities to shape what goes on in their schools, it is conceivable that conversations about educational policy and curriculum might actually improve as their capacities for public autonomy improve in the long run.

Critics of the Common Core often conflate implementation efforts with the standards themselves. While due consideration of standards implementation is of crucial importance for sound educational policymaking, this conflation is ultimately unproductive. Au's (2013) concerns, for instance, that the standards will require adoption of autonomy-inhibiting standardized tests does not implicate the actual content of the standards but rather the practice of high-stakes testing, which is a different matter altogether.[7] Equally misguided are critics who point to, as evidence of the problematic nature of the Common Core, faulty activities, texts, or lesson plans created by companies more concerned with politics or profits than educational outcomes or teachers struggling to implement the standards. The process of resource selection and curriculum development should be guided by teachers' professional expertise and subjected to appropriate democratic constraints—that is, if excessively political texts and highly problematic supplemental materials are selected for use in the classroom, parents and communities should have meaningful opportunities to challenge these decisions and their concerns ought to be taken seriously. Poorly constructed implementation efforts do not reflect upon the quality or content of the standards themselves. If Common Core critics wish to enhance the credibility of their arguments, they should either explicitly state that they are addressing implementation efforts or actually address the standards in their analyses, which would require that they modify those aspects of their arguments that are unsupported by or directly in conflict with available evidence.

Furthermore, the CCSS do nothing to prevent any state from developing its own unique policies of education. Not only can states independently determine how the CCSS should be implemented, they are also free to make changes to existing standards. New York serves as an example of a state that has made significant changes and additions to CCSS, whereas Kansas chose to simply change the name (Porter, McMaken, Hwang, & Yang, 2011). The CCSS do in some sense restrict individual states and districts but only from educating in such a way as to hinder students' consideration of a range of reasonable perspectives—strongly suggesting adherence to Gutmann's (1999) principle of nonrepression (p. 46). Similarly, states that adopt CCSS are required to ensure that all schools are afforded the resources necessary to provide students meaningful opportunities to acquire the skills they will need to participate in the democratic process (again, relating to Gutmann's conception of a democratic threshold and principle of nondiscrimination).

The conservative critiques of Common Core do not focus on the capacities component but only the opportunity component of public autonomy. That is, they give little indication that critics are concerned about how or whether young citizens will develop necessary capacities for public autonomy. Thus, their critiques rest on the claim that local communities are losing some degree of control over the public schools. This is true, but only in a very limited sense. If the Common Core really does have the power to influence political control over school policy, the only foreseeable cultural losses for conservatives (or other groups) would be those aspects of their culture that run against

---

[7]The new Every Child Succeeds Act is an attempt to address these important—albeit separate—issues.

the development of children's autonomy—which, we believe, would represent constructive developments.

Similarly, most components of the multiculturalist argument also exaggerate the threats of the Common Core to public autonomy. If teachers can select much of the content based on their own professional expertise and the needs and interests of their students, which the standards clearly allow, it is unlikely that the CCSS would resemble anything akin to neoconservative cultural imperialism. Furthermore, as far as content is concerned, existing state standards (especially in the more ideologically conservative states) seem no less likely than so-called national standards to silence or marginalize minority perspectives. In fact, because they focus on critical thinking skills rather than canonical content, the Common Core standards are *less* likely than many states' standards to marginalize minority perspectives. Ultimately, these criticisms of the Common Core reflect only a superficial understanding of autonomy—that is, they generally only consider potential threats to local control or opportunities for public deliberation over policy rather than a more comprehensive view that considers both the opportunity *and* capacity components of public autonomy.

However, there are some aspects of the standards that might be revised to address the most compelling component, in our view, of the multiculturalist argument: the concern that the Common Core ELA standards' list of recommended texts does an inadequate job of representing non-mainstream voices. Fletcher's (2000) insights about the positive role of community and culture in the formation of identity are particularly salient in this regard—for, if a liberal, democratic society is to justly and effectively respond to the challenges of multiculturalism and religious pluralism, it must make serious efforts to include a wide range of minority perspectives on the public school curriculum. Such an inclusive list of texts would likely yield benefits to the development of autonomy in students from cultural minority groups who would be more likely to see positive aspects of their communities reflected in the curriculum as well as students from mainstream groups who would be exposed to a wider range of possibilities. Likewise, if Fletcher's insights were better reflected in the standards themselves—that is, if the standards contained explicit references to the importance of community, culture, and religion/worldview in the individual's life, students' autonomy interests would likely be furthered and forces contributing to cultural loss blunted.

We also agree with Singer's (2013) contention that the standards should have a stronger, or rather a more explicit, focus on democratic citizenship. The CCSS are problematic in this respect because, although they are well-designed to develop students' critical thinking skills and help them become individually empowered, they give inadequate attention to other components of democratic education such as the development of their capacities for deliberation and the disposition of mutuality. While the standards call upon students to listen to and assess other people's points of view, certainly both dialogue and discourse require more than carefully listening to another person or assessing the veracity of their claims. This shortcoming represents a major problem to those concerned about the development of students' capacities for public autonomy, and we would like to see revisions of the standards that give more attention to these important components of democratic education.

Conclusion

The driving purpose of the Common Core State Standards is to "insure that all students are college and career ready" (CCSSI, 2012). While the skills needed for success in college and career in a 21st century, interconnected world transfer easily to the arena of democratic citizenship, greater emphasis on the latter would certainly communicate an important message to young people. These potential shortcomings of the Common Core could be easily addressed without undermining the key aims of existing standards. By placing a greater emphasis on democratic citizenship, losses to local control over public school standards would be mitigated by overall gains in public autonomy relating to students' enhanced ability and motivation for democratic participation. Thus, adding the third component of citizenship to the college and career foci of the Common Core would greatly improve the standards, better promote students' development of capacities for public autonomy, and likely yield innumerable benefits for both individuals and society.

References

Au, W. (2013). Coring social studies within corporate education reform: The Common Core State Standards, social justice, and the politics of knowledge in U.S. schools. *Critical Education* 4(5), 1–16.

Bauerlein, M. & Stotsky, S. (2012). Common Core's ELA Standards place college readiness at risk. (Pioneer Institute white paper.no. 89). Boston, MA: Pioneer Institute.

Berry, S. (2014, May 22) Teacher: White 'privilege' makes Common Core necessary. *Breitbart.* Retrieved from http://www.breitbart.com/big-government/2014/05/22/teacher-common-core-necessary-because-as-a-white-male-i-ve-been-given-a-lot-of-privilege-i-didn-t-earn

Common Core State Standards Initiative. (2010). Reactions to the March 2010 draft Common Core State Standards: Highlights and themes from the public feedback. Last accessed June 1, 2016. Retrieved from http://www.corestandards.org/assets/k-12-feedback-summary.pdf

Common Core State Standards Initiative. (2012). Mission statement. Retrieved from http://www.corestandards.org

Common Core State Standards Initiative. (2013). *English Language Arts Standards*. Retrieved from http://www.corestandards.org/ELA-Literacy

Creppell, I. (2012). Toleration, politics, and the role of mutuality. In M. S. Williams & J. Waldron (Eds.), *Toleration and its limits* (pp. 315–359). New York: New York University Press.

Dewey, J. (1985). *Democracy and education 1916*. J. A. Boydston, & P. Baysinger (Eds.). Carbondale: Southern Illinois University Press.

Fletcher, S. (2000). *Education and emancipation*. New York, NY: Columbia University Press.

Gangi, J. & N. Benfer (2014). How Common Core's recommended books fail children of color. In V. Strauss, How Common Core's recommended books fail children of color. *Washington Post*. https://www.washingtonpost.com/news/answer-sheet/wp/2014/09/16/how-common-cores-recommended-books-fail-children-of-color/

Goldsworthy, H., & Sam, C. (2015). Twitter and the Common Core: Understanding emerging narratives through discourse. Unpublished paper presented in session.

Graebe, H. (2013, June 3) Common Core: Bad for teachers and students. *RedState.com*. Retrieved from http://www.redstate.com/freedomworks/2013/06/03/common-core-bad-for-teachers-and-students/

Gutmann, A. (1987). *Democratic education*. Hoboken, NJ: John Wiley & Sons, Ltd.

Gutmann, A. (1999). *Democratic education* (Revised edition). Princeton, NJ: Princeton University Press.

Habermas, J. (1984). *The theory of communicative action* (vol. I) (T. McCarthy, Trans.). Boston, MA: Beacon Press.

Habermas, J. (1995). Reconciliation through the public use of reason: Remarks on John Rawls's political liberalism. *The Journal of Philosophy, 92*(3) 109–131.

Kurtz, S. (2013, May 31). Tea Party revives to fight Common Core. *National Review Online*. Retrieved from http://m.nationalreview.com/corner/349808/tea-party-revives-fight-common-core-stanley-kurtz

McCluskey, N., Evers, W., & Stotsky, S. (2013). Stop the rush to the Common Core. *NY Daily News*. Retrieved from http://www.nydailynews.com/opinion/stop-rush-common-core-article-1.1385630

National Council for the Social Studies. (2010). Revitalizing civic learning in our schools. Retrieved from http://www.socialstudies.org/positions/revitalizing_civic_learning

Paul, R. (2013). "Common Core" nationalizes and dumbs down public school curriculum. *The Free Foundation*. Retrieved from http://www.the-free-foundation.org/tst5-27-2013.html

Pearson, P. D., & Hiebert, E. H. (2012). Understanding the common core state standards. *Teaching with the Common Core Standards for English Language Arts, Grades 3–5*, 1.

Porter, A., McMaken, J., Hwang, J., & Yang, R. (2011). Common core standards the new US intended curriculum. *Educational Researcher, 40*(3), 103–116.

Ravitch, D. (2013). Why I cannot support the common core standards. Diane Ravitch's blog. Retrieved from http://dianeravitch.net/2013/02/26/why-i-cannot-support-the-common-core-standards/

Rawls, J. (1971). *A theory of justice*. Cambridge, MA: Harvard University.

Rawls, J. (1996). *Political liberalism*. New York, NY: Columbia University Press.

Rawls, J. (2005). *Political liberalism*. New York, NY: Columbia University Press. (Original work published 1993)

Reich, R. (2002). *Bridging liberalism and multiculturalism in American education*. Chicago, IL: University of Chicago Press.

Robbins, J. (2013). Uncommonly bad. *Academic Questions* 26(1). Retrieved from https://www.nas.org/articles/the_common_core_state_standards_two_views.

Russo, A. (2013). Common what?: What is Common Core and why is everyone—right, left—so mad about it? *Slate.com*. Retrieved from http://www.slate.com/articles/double_x/doublex/2013/09/common_core_either_you_re_against_this_new_push_for_academic_standards_and_single.html

Scott, R. (2013). A republic of republics: How common core undermines state and local autonomy over K-12 education. (Pioneer Institute white paper no. 102.) Boston, MA: Pioneer Institute.

Singer, A. (2013a, July 30). What's missing from Common Core is education for democracy. *Huffington Post*. Retrieved from http://www.huffingtonpost.com/alan-trisinger/whats-missing-from-common_b_3673244.html

Singer, A. (2013b, August 30). What does a Common Core/Danielson lesson plan look like? *Huffington Post*. Retrieved from http://www.huffingtonpost.com/alan-singer/what-does-a-common-coreda_b_3804493.html

Smith, A. C. (2013, July 27). Florida GOP feels conservative backlash over Common Core. *Tampa Bay Times*. Retrieved from http://www.tampabay.com/news/politics/stateroundup/florida-gop-feels-conservative-backlash-over-common-core/2133569

StudentsFirst.org (2013). Common Core State Standards: Establishing rigor for all students. *StudentsFirst Policy Publication*. Sacramento, CA: StudentsFirst.org. Retrieved from http://edref.3cdn.net/bdc3e16de9f639f2ec_2um6vbfh7.pdf

Taylor, C. (1994). *Multiculturalism: Examining the politics of recognition*. Princeton, NJ: Princeton University Press.

The Aspen Institute (2012). Pedagogy and the CCSS. Retrieved from http://colegacy.org/news/wp-content/uploads/2013/07/Pedagogy-and-the-CCSS.pdf

Warnick, B (2013). *Understanding student rights in schools: Speech, religion, and privacy in educational settings*. New York, NY: Teachers College Press, Columbia University.

Critical Thinking

1. How would you characterize the aims and purpose of CCSS as curricular standards?
2. What are the strengths and weaknesses of the critiques of CCSS?
3. Distinguish between a priority of public autonomy and individual autonomy.

Internet References

Preparing America's Students for Success
http://www.corestandards.org/

The Debate Over Common Core
https://www.cbsnews.com/news/the-debate-over-common-core/

The Four Essentials of Democratic Education
http://www.ascd.org/research-a-topic/democratic-education-essentials.aspx

What is Democratic Education?
http://democraticeducation.org/index.php/features/what-is-democratic-education/

BENJAMIN J. BINDEWALD is an assistant professor of social foundations at Oklahoma State University.

RORY P. TANNEBAUM is an assistant professor of education in social studies at Merrimack College.

PATRICK WOMAC is an assistant professor of social studies education at the University of Maine.

Bindewald, B.J., Tannebaum, R.P., Womac, P. (2016) "The Common Core and Democratic Education: Examining Potential Costs and Benefits to Public and Private Autonomy." Democracy and Education, 24 (2), Article 4. Used by permission of Democracy and Education.

Article Prepared by: Sheron Fraser-Burgess, *Ball State University*

Digital Literacy: The Quest of an Inclusive Definition

JAMES K. NJENGA

Learning Outcomes

After reading this article, you will be able to:

- Reconsider the assumptions on which digital literacy is predicated.
- Use global contexts to theorize critical digital literacy
- Bring in full focus the way socioeconomic welfare and development mediate the possibilities of using digital technologies to enact socioeconomic emancipation

Introduction

Digital technologies are major drivers of globalisation and related economic competitiveness, which in turn, have become powerful forces in the social context (Avgerou 2010; Czerniewicz, Ravjee & Mlitwa 2006; Garrido et al. 2012). This makes digital literacy (DL) essential for progress in the contemporary era (Pangrazio 2016). Digital technology-based competitiveness has been studied in business for a long time (Roztocki & Weistroffer 2016). However, little has been done on societal competitiveness. To the general masses, the ubiquity of digital technologies has been credited not only for the accelerated rate of globalisation and economic competition, but also for their social impacts and controversies, at both the individual and societal levels (Baase 2012). The digital technologies view of economic competition and competitiveness requires individuals to have DL, which is synonymous with the ability of individuals to participate in the economy through skills and creativity enabled by the digital technologies (Klecun 2008). Globalisation involves the reorganisation of social and economic relations, interdependences and interconnectedness (Avgerou 2010). As a corollary to this, globalisation would need digital technologies that facilitate *universally*[1] accessible, reliable and inexpensive communication. Not withstanding the potential benefits of globalisation and economic competitiveness, there are concerns on the use of digital technologies related to, among others, 'antisocial, anticommunity effects', threats to security and privacy, challenges to intellectual property as well as the exacerbation of the existing inequalities between the haves and have-nots' (Baase 2012:5).

Furthermore, there is growing and valid scepticism on the digitally influenced socio-economic liberation. Three main observations that drive this scepticism are identified from the existing research. Firstly, there is a lack of commensurate socio-economic development arising from the use of digital technologies among the poor and marginalised communities (Cibangu, Hepworth & Champion 2017; Watkins 2011). Socio-economic developments among the poor and the marginalised still remain largely incomparable with the developments among the affluent members of the society, even when the poor are perceived to be using digital technologies (Alam & Imran 2015; Haugh & Talwar 2016; Klecun 2008). Secondly, the macro-level nature of empirical studies on the outcomes of digital technology use is more often than not focused on economic improvements, and not the whole socio-economic development and well-being at the micro-level, with direct impact on the individuals and societies (Cibangu et al. 2017; El-Darwiche et al. 2012; Roztocki & Weistroffer 2016). While the macro-level focus (often on gross domestic product [GDP],

---

[1] Here it means that digital artefacts are designed to meet the needs of most users, while their costs are plummeting, making it possible for many to own or access these devices. Of course, in Africa this remains to be a challenge and a major point requiring ongoing research.

the labour market and international esteem) is welcomed, it may have the proclivity to leave out the other critical factors that are essential for socio-economic development. Such factors include a population's education, political stability and social liberties, the standard of living and general health (Harris 2016; Roztocki & Weistroffer 2016). Harris (2016) attributes this to either a lack of genuine interest on the side of researchers or the possibility that researchers are chasing other interests such as publication and citation counts. Thirdly, the narrative of digital technologies and the development they bring about, where the micro-level is concerned, is often based on 'areas of interventions' rather than on the 'approaches or models that cut across different policy areas' (James 2005:286). This creates a chasm between actual field experiences and the processes which are 'created and changed over time' (James 2005:286). While these interventions are valuable in their own rights, the failure to identify multiple possible pathways that emerge as individuals and communities engage with these technologies would fail to capture the parties' responses to the changes over time (Bar, Weber & Pisani 2016; Boeri 2016; Sassen 2002).

Combined, these three views suggest an outcome- and impact-orientated approach to digital technologies, and by extension, DL which include and benefit even the marginalised and impoverished sections of the society. The benefits arise through the fruitful interaction of the communities with the digital technologies, when the outcomes of appropriation (i.e. local improvements, adaptations, experimentation and innovations) are realised by the indigenous population (James 2005). Appropriation is enhanced through competencies aimed at achieving better and more fulfilling lives (Cibangu et al. 2017:41). Certainly, the socio-economic pursuits associated with the progress in technology are neither new nor only applicable to digital technologies (Balasubramanian & Mahajan 2001). For instance, Behrent's (2013) essay on *Foucault and Technology* discusses the societal and technological reconfigurations that were happening in France (and in other parts of the world) after the Second World War, with specific emphasis on the power dynamics. Behrent (2013) notes that Foucault's work, while largely philosophical, was set to conceptualise the complexity of the evolving relationship between 'objects and machines' within a system of power. In this conceptualisation, relations 'refer not to tools, machines, or the application of science to industrial production, but rather to methods and procedures for governing human beings' (Behrent 2013:56). That is, the focus on DL should also be concerned with the processes that create the required change in the relationship between the individuals and society on one side, and the digital technologies on the other side.

Digital literacy, as a concept, has been viewed from a number of dimensions that do not seem to converge (Brown, Czerniewicz & Noakes 2016; Buckingham 2016). This ends up with overlapping and competing often divergent definitions (Helsper & Eynon 2013). The definitions have moved from the classical view of literacy as 'being able to read and write', to other forms of *literacies* which seem to put the prevalent or dominant theme to the digital technology or the use of digital technology as adopted by the researcher. However, there seems to be concurrence: that the original focus of DL should be on the essential competencies of the present-day citizens' success in today's highly competitive and globalised market, which often require the performance of basic tasks using technology (Buckingham 2016). The competency-based view of literacy, traditionally approached literacy as being able to write, read and deal with information, also includes competencies in using the different digital technologies (Burton et al. 2015). Consequently, there is an emergent view that what is required is a holistic view of the multiple literacies or *transliteracies* (Burton et al. 2015; Stornaiuolo, Smith & Phillips 2017) which are essential in a world dominated by dynamic perspectives on electronic media and technology (Buckingham 2016). These literacies enable individuals to appropriately respond, in socially recognised ways, to even future challenges through sharing and creating knowledge and eventually participating in the society (Merchant 2007). According to this emergent view, these multiple literacies cover both the mastery of information and communication technology (ICT) skills and generic and critical skills required to engage in social practices across boundaries of culture, institutions, countries and territories (Buckingham 2016; Burton et al. 2015; Lankshear & Knobel 2007). The mastery is informed by changes in task requirements, technology and knowledge.

This view is in agreement with Labbo, Reinking and McKenna's (1998) typification of the DL process as encompassing aspects of lifelong learning, social context, the multiplicity of competencies and ability to assemble and produce knowledge while pursuing other goals. That is, the embeddedness of digital technologies requires a critical view of DL which, among others challenges and addresses the ideological concerns and the social and educational inequalities (Pangrazio 2016). The concerns and inequalities inhibit or promote individual practice and at the same time prioritise technical proficiency, thereby forming new norms and living without conscious awareness (Pangrazio 2016).

However, as much as the promises of digital technologies need to be acknowledged, it is important to note that they cannot completely displace older technologies. Rather, the digital technologies need to be appropriated alongside the existing technologies (Michailova 2011). If digital technologies do not replace the older technologies, then the intellectual traditions of the other disciplines and their view on literacy will still remain important (Goodfellow 2011; Hinrichsen & Coombs 2013; Littlejohn, Beetham & McGill 2012). In addition, the dynamism and inseparability of digital technologies and the society can favour, invite, shape or even constrain their use in society, as well as the conceptualisation of DL. That is, in addition to learning the operational and functional uses of technologies, users and user societies should be able to make informed decisions on the use of these technologies, based on their contexts and needs measured against outcomes and consequences of their use (Lankshear & Knobel 2007; Moje 2009). Therefore, there is a need for clear distinctions between the digital technologies and the meaning derived from their uses, as well as the outcomes and consequences of the digital technologies from those of the technologies' uses (Lankshear & Knobel 2007; Moje 2009). These distinctions require individuals to be empowered to take advantage of the positive outcomes while avoiding or mitigating the negative consequences (Amichai-Hamburger et al. 2008; Maton 2008).

Importance of Context

Following from the main approach in this article, the context is dynamic and inseparable from the issue of DL (Michailova 2011), and at the same time, it provides 'situational opportunities and constraints' that change 'occurrence and meaning' of behaviour and relationships (Johns 2006:386). That is, the DL should not be abstracted or idealised; rather, its meaning should be derived from its contexts. At the core of the contextualised definition is the compelling evidence that digital technologies and globalised networks not only promote and facilitate the movement of and interaction between people, languages and works of art, but that they also do so on a very large and fast scale. This is to the extent that people's daily lives and routines have become characterised by these movements and interactions (Stornaiuolo et al. 2017). However, the above context does not speak to all parts of the world or society. For instance, the majority of people in Africa are poor (Pangrazio 2016). Their context should be understood from their history, culture and power (Garrido et al. 2012). They have very limited control over changes in their lives (Garrido et al. 2012). Without contextualised definition, DL is seen as another way of propagating the already existing digital divide, where skills create new inequalities (Alam & Imran 2015) arising from the 'variation in sophistication of use and user expertise' (Reynolds 2016:737). Indeed, the focus of the digital divide has shifted from access to digital technologies to the skills and capabilities required in appropriating these technologies (Alam & Imran 2015; Baase 2012; Buckingham 2007).

Consequently, concerns have been raised about the broad definition and understanding of DL in relation to the context of use of these technologies. For instance, Pangrazio (2016) laments about a narrow focus on the 'digital', which lacks an understanding of what would make DL applicable in other contexts and media. Contextualisation is placing the DL within the cultural, historical, geographical, social and political realms of the individuals' concerns, and with the aim of achieving outcomes that may include life fulfilment or material satisfaction (Long et al. 2014). This process also involves bridging the gap between the providers and recipients of DL (Long et al. 2014), and addressing issues of redresses and resource redistribution to deal with historical inequities (Czerniewicz et al. 2006).

Regrettably, the available definitions seem to fall into two, almost mutually exclusive, positions. One focuses on the production of digital materials and the other on the consumption aspects. This subsequently limits the development of an inclusive framework that would meet the needs of the intended audience. Using the production–consumption continuum, DL is then characterised on progressive levels of competence: with production being the topmost. According to this view, the rural and the marginalised are depicted as mere consumers, whose only role is limited to the use of both the technologies and their products. The challenge with this view is that while consumption is not bad, socio-economic development is dependent on how the use of these technologies and their products is beneficial to this group of people, as they move from simple consumption to actual production.

Still, these views of DL seem to have reduced DL to a competence or a skill of using a digital technology, discarding the original meaning of literacy, the ability to read and write (Buckingham 2007). This reduction in meaning is problematic. Defining DL without the context of use, reduces it to just mere competences, skills or abilities to use a digital technology whether for production of consumption. This reduction conceives of DL as possessing the basic skills required to perform given operations using digital technologies, while ignoring aspects of learning, 'problem solving, critical thinking, creativity, self-regulation' as well as the understanding of culture, a context of use of the digital technologies (Burton et al. 2015:152). By extension, a complete definition of DL should include the understanding of the contextual aspects—social, economic and cultural—of use of the digital technologies, as well as the critical aspects of learning—problem solving, critical thinking, creativity and self-regulation.

These contextual aspects are important as engagements in and with the digital technology simultaneously traverse space and time—whose understanding also requires reconfiguration. That is, the context-informed definition of DL is aware of the fact that the context of use of the digital technology requires mutually constitutive actions, social interactions, cultural and economic exchanges which interactively and dynamically shape, and are shaped by the digital technologies (Casey & Bruce 2011). Therefore, 'digital literacy encompasses the purpose, setting and practices in which technology is used' (Casey

& Bruce 2011:77). That is, a variety of context of use should be considered when defining DL (Martin 2008).

Digital Technologies' Interaction with Society (and also Society's Interaction with Digital Technologies)

Technologies and their use traverse both space and time; this brings along affordances that increase the dynamism in both the society and the digital technologies. As much as we appreciate these affordances, we also ought to recognise the constraints which these digital technologies put on the society (Zammuto et al. 2007). Any explanation of one will invariably involve the enactment of their entwined forms and functions in a cyclical relationship that also involves their contexts of use—as they both dynamically inform each other. The time, space or context disparity means that despite the perceived pervasiveness of the digital technologies, their use may vary depending on, among others, the technologies' purposes and their interactions with society.

The difference between the social model of DL and the competency-based model of literacy has been documented in the literature (Buckingham 2007; Lankshear & Knobel 2008). Buckingham (2007:48) notes that this issue is complex and needs to be fully addressed in terms of its aims as well as what DL actually entails, including 'systematic awareness of how digital media are constructed, and of the unique "rhetorics" of interactive communication'. To address this complex issue, there has been ongoing research and debates on digital technology, society and social change and their relationships, as well as the social change that includes critical theories, view of technology (Brey 2003; Sassen 2002). Brey (2003:54) argues that technology and society are co-constructed or 'deeply interwoven' and 'their meanings and functions and even (according to social constructivists) their contents are continually open to renegotiation by users and others'. There is therefore a need to reframe the digital technologies, to understand their impact on social development (Boeri 2016) while recognising the 'embeddedness and the variable outcomes of these technologies for different social orders' (Sassen 2002:365). The reframing should allow participants to 'recognize, interpret, and evaluate underlying ideologies' of linked information (Labbo et al. 1998:282) and could change our perception of DL.

As part of the reframing, the social constructivist view of DL drives the social determinism agenda, which seeks to place the 'human as an autonomous agent who holds a productive purpose driving technology use' (Reynolds 2016:737). Technology, and by extension DL, is therefore, shaped by individuals' participation in political, economic and socio-cultural practices (Hinrichsen & Coombs 2013). That is, technology and DL are never neutral. This is opposed to the technology determinism which views technology as value-neutral, having its own logic of making things happen independent of its 'socio-cultural context', and that everyone should adopt (or adapt to its consequences) because of its universally positive impacts (Hinrichsen & Coombs 2013). The technology deterministic view of DL is inadequate in that it would limit it to the skills required to use technology that currently exists, without recognising the ever-changing nature of technology and society, as it uses the technology (Reynolds 2016) and the more meaningful outcomes from the use of such technology (Watkins 2011). The social constructivist view therefore is seen as a way of having a definition of DL which does not go with the changes in technology, and one that holds that individuals have autonomy and agency (Reynolds 2016). However, the social constructivist view is not without limitations. Its most conspicuous limitation is its focus on actors 'directly relating or interacting with the technology-in-use'; this pre-occupation, therefore, leaves non-users out of the picture, even if they are affected by this technology (Müller & Tworek 2016:106). Lamentably, these non-users are usually the impoverished and the marginalised who constitute the majority of the population.

With this in mind, DL and approaches to DL cannot be placed in universalised contexts. Consequently, any definition of literacy that is afforded by the digital technologies should attend to how digital technologies and society interact (Leonardi & Barley 2010), while at the same time being aware of the fact that the literacies may be used differently in multiple contexts and even in different social structures (Tunçalp & Tun 2016). Therefore, this calls for a definition or an understanding of DL as meaning-making practices that vary, depending on, among others, the settings, communities and identities in the digital environment (Chase & Laufenberg 2011). To this end, O'Brien and Scharber (2008:66–67) view DL as 'socially situated practices supported by skills, strategies, and stances that enable the representation and understanding of ideas using a range of modalities enabled by digital tools'.

The Distinction between a Tool and Its Use

Combining context of use and of interaction between technology and society, there is a suggestion that an inclusive definition of DL should entail 'practices' which are socially recognised. That is, the technology, knowledge and skills triad, and the continuous changes in them, should be organised for ease of understanding of the people (Lankshear & Knobel 2007). However, this fails to capture the intended outcomes and the consequences of the practice. Therefore, there is a need to distinguish between the tool and the meaning derived from using the tool. There is also a need to distinguish the outcomes and consequences of the tool from those of its use. According to Moje (2009), distinctions:

> … between the tool (the media) and the norms or conventions that shape meaning making of the symbols offered via the tool (literate practices) are not only worth noting but are also worth distinguishing so that we can better understand the relative outcomes or consequences of each. (p. 349)

In the classical diffusion of innovation, the innovation-decision process is depicted as a cognitive process that individuals go through, from the time they become aware of an innovation to the time they make a final decision and a commitment to adopt or reject the innovation (Rogers 2003). However, in contemporary use of innovation, there is a further step of appropriation: ownership that could spur new uses (different from those originally intended), and especially new innovations that may arise in the course of use (Bar et al. 2016). They define appropriation as a:

> … contest for control over a technological system's configuration, as users, designers, and manufacturers battle over who can use that technology, at what cost, under what conditions, for what purpose, and with what consequences. (Bar et al. 2016:618)

The conditions, for DL, include capabilities of the indigenous people to better their lives through the appropriation (Cibangu et al. 2017; James 2005). However, appropriation relies heavily on recognising how ideology and power are manifested in the innovation (Bhatt & de Roock 2013), as well as imagining multiple distinctive future uses or purposes of the innovation that are different from the innovation's actual or originally intended use (Müller & Tworek 2016).

At the end, the new determined use of the innovation could be different in not only having new tweaks and new service offerings, but also significantly new social, economic and practical opportunities. In extending this view, Bar et al. (2016) have argued that the success of the adoption of an innovations lies in understanding four main things (which they call assumptions):

[1]technology is not neutral and a technology's architecture forms relationships between stakeholders that have social, economic and political implications; [2]adoption of technology is not for adoption sake, but it is aimed at making a difference in the adopter's life; [3]past the adoption, the adaptations to the technology which occur take many forms; and [4]cultural adaptations are 'uniquely creative' because, among other reasons, they challenge the original power structure that was embedded in the technology.

Following the appropriation route, then, defining DL should recognise the social, economic and political learning and the dialogues which take place to make meaning of the technology and to repurpose the technology to shape the outcomes and consequences of its use in a uniquely creative way. At the same time, this recognition extends to the outcomes and consequences not initially intended or imagined by the creators of the original technology.

As a Process of Empowerment

Digital literacy becomes a process of empowerment; it empowers an individual not only to use a tool but also to take advantage of the positive outcomes of the tool (or its use) while at the same time avoiding any negative consequences. Empowerment is aimed at linking an individual to the 'wider social and political environment' (Amichai-Hamburger et al. 2008:1776). Maton (2008) defines empowerment as:

> … a group-based, participatory, developmental process through which marginalized or oppressed individuals and groups gain greater control over their lives and environments, acquire valued resources and basic rights, and achieve important life goals and reduced societal marginalization. (p. 5)

It is a process of removing unjust inequalities that inhibit the majority or big groups of people from exercising choices, choices that disrupt the status quo at various levels—individual, group, organisational and community (Amichai-Hamburger et al. 2008; Haugh & Talwar 2016).

In most cases, the unjust inequalities are historical, often arising from either demographic characteristics or their physical or emotional difficulties (Riger 1993). Thus, a DL view of empowerment could be described as a means through which individuals acquire 'mastery and control over their lives, and a critical understanding of their environment' (Zimmerman et al. 1992:708). In order to influence their social, economic and political conditions (Gomez & Baron-Porras 2011) by acquiring or strengthening the necessary psychological resources in order to respond appropriately to their environment (Amichai-Hamburger et al. 2008). Thus, the empowerment is meant to capacitate someone to understand both the ideological dimensions and the cultural forms that encompass selective interests, and the relationships between what is happening in and with the individual and what is happening in the world (Mayo 1995).

The critical aspects of empowerment arising from these definitions can be classified into two broad categories: individual empowerment and community empowerment. Individual empowerment is seen as a participatory developmental process that is aimed at achieving goals—often enhancing an individual's capacities to control and influence, among others, their economic, political, social and psychological capacities in order to increase self-sufficiency and decrease external dependence (Christens et al. 2016; Gomez & Baron-Porras 2011; Mayo 1995; Rappaport et al. 1995). As a parallel, community empowerment is also a participatory developmental process, but its goals differ in that they are about increasing community participation, reinforcing shared identification and increasing collaborative control by delegating or distributing power to the powerless (Riger 1993). By implication, even the empowerment process discussed here is dynamic. The activities within the process and indeed the individuals' goals, expectations and outcomes are in flux.

From the individual's perspective, goals attainment is the drive towards empowerment, and therefore enhancing the strengths and competencies is akin to acquiring the necessary resources towards the goals (Amichai-Hamburger et al. 2008). The process individuals go through in determining their goals is critical. In this process, individuals have to systematically go through and identify the causes of powerlessness and their interconnection to other individuals, groups and systemic factors that should be collectively addressed to facilitate empowerment (Bradbury & Reason 2003). Zimmerman (1995) proposes a *nomological* framework of psychological empowerment, consisting of interpersonal, cognitive and behavioural components that could be applicable in this case. The interpersonal component is concerned with an individual's perceptions of influencing the sociopolitical domain; the cognitive component is concerned with the skills and competencies required to exert this influence; and the behavioural domain is concerned with the actions required to exert this influence. Viewed from an empowerment perspective, DL is a process where individual strengths and competencies are enhanced to enable the individual to be proactive to social policy, social changes, economic emancipation and political consciousness (Amichai-Hamburger et al. 2008; Gomez & Baron-Porras 2011; Zimmerman et al. 1992). Social policy and social change relate to the individual's standing in society, while economic emancipation deals with decisions on earning and spending an income (Haugh & Talwar 2016). Political consciousness involves a critical reflection of the information available (Parrott & Madoc-Jones 2008).

Conclusion

In this study, an argument has been presented for an elaborate and inclusive definition of DL. This elaborate and inclusive definition should be contextually placed within the socio-economic context of use of the digital technologies, while weighing on the outcomes and consequences of these technologies and their use. In the argument, the contextual aspects inform the simultaneous engagement of the contexts with the digital technologies across time and space. This engagement continuously requires reconfiguration as new understanding of the interplay between the context, the digital technologies, the individual and the society, through the mutually constitutive actions, social interactions, cultural and economic exchanges (Casey & Bruce 2011). In so doing, the view of DL captures the purpose of use of the digital technologies, the setting or the contexts as well as the practices that emanate in the use of digital technologies. Perhaps, the greatest challenge here would be the variety and uniqueness of context and social structures within these contexts, and the digital technologies as well as their use. To deal with this challenge, O'Brien and Scharber's (2008:66–67) view of DL as 'socially situated practices supported by skills, strategies, and stances that enable the representation and understanding of ideas using a range of modalities enabled by digital tools', is recommended. The range of modalities being enabled by these technologies, could cover the issues of appropriation of these technologies, as well as the social, economic and political changes on the one hand, and the technologies on the other hand.

Of course, this view requires us to reframe the understanding of DL based on the impact of the DL and the digital technologies on, among others, the social development, while at the same time recognising the inherent iterative interplay between literacy, technology and society. In focusing on the impacts, we place value on the way society and individuals within the society 'recognize, interpret, and evaluate underlying ideologies in various types of hypertextually linked information' (Labbo et al. 1998:282), which also changes the participants' view of DL. On empowerment, the focus is on the eventual outcome, or the intended outcome of the DL, and placing it within means through which individuals dynamically master and gain control over their lives. Individuals therefore need to not only have a critical understanding of the environment, but they should also be able to benefit from the environment. In this way, they will also be able to fulfil the self-interest of improving their lives.

References

Alam, K. & Imran, S., 2015, 'The digital divide and social inclusion among refugee migrants: A case in regional Australia', *Information Technology & People* 28, 344–365. https://doi.org/10.1108/ITP-04-2014-0083

Amichai-Hamburger, Y., McKenna, K.Y.A. & Tal, S.-A.A., 2008, 'E-empowerment: Empowerment by the Internet', *Computers in Human Behavior* 24, 1776–1789. https://doi.org/10.1016/j.chb.2008.02.002

Avgerou, C., 2010, 'Discourses on ICT and development', *Information Technologies and International Development* 6, 1–18.

Baase, S., 2012, *A gift of fire: Social, legal and ethical issue for computing technology*, 4th edn., Pearson Education, Upper Saddle River, NJ.

Balasubramanian, S. & Mahajan, V., 2001, 'The economic leverage of the virtual community', *International Journal of Electronic Commerce* 5, 103–138. https://doi.org/10.1080/10864415.2001.1104421

Bar, F., Weber, M.S. & Pisani, F., 2016, 'Mobile technology appropriation in a distant mirror: Baroquization, creolization, and cannibalism', *New Media & Society* 18, 617–636. https://doi.org/10.1177/1461444816629474

Behrent, M.C., 2013, 'Foucault and Technology', *History and Technology* 29, 54–104. https://doi.org/10.1080/07341512.2013.780351

Bhatt, I. & De Roock, R., 2013, 'Capturing the sociomateriality of digital literacy events', *Research and Learning Technology* 21, 21281. https://doi.org/10.3402/rlt.v21.21281

Boeri, N., 2016, 'Technology and society as embedded: An alternative framework for information and communication technology and development', *Media, Culture & Society* 38, 107–118. https://doi.org/10.1177/0163443715607845

Bradbury, H. & Reason, P., 2003, 'Action research', *Qualitative Social Work* 2, 155–175. https://doi.org/10.1177/1473325003002002003

Brey, P., 2003, 'Theorizing modernity and technology', in T.J. Misa, P. Brey & A. Feenberg (eds.), *Modernity and technology*, pp. 33–71, MIT Press, Cambridge.

Brown, C., Czerniewicz, L. & Noakes, T., 2016, 'Online content creation: Looking at students' social media practices through a connected learning lens', *Learning, Media & Technology* 41, 140–159. https://doi.org/10.1080/17439884.2015.1107097

Buckingham, D., 2007, 'Digital media literacies: Rethinking media education in the age of the Internet', *Research in Comparative and International Education* 2, 43–55. https://doi.org/10.2304/rcie.2007.2.1.43

Buckingham, D., 2016, 'Defining digital literacy', in B. Bachmair (ed.), *Medienbildung in Neuen Kulturräumen*. VS Verlag für Sozialwissenschaften, pp. 59–71, Wiesbaden. https://doi.org/10.1007/978-3-531-92133-4_4

Burton, L.J., Summers, J., Lawrence, J., Noble, K. & Gibbings, P., 2015, 'Digital literacy in higher education: The rhetoric and the reality', in M.K. Harmes, H. Huijser & P.A. Danaher (eds.), *Myths in education, learning and teaching*, pp. 151–172, Palgrave Macmillan, London. https://doi.org/10.1057/9781137476982_9

Casey, L. & Bruce, B.C., 2011, 'The practice profile of inquiry: Connecting digital literacy and pedagogy', *E-Learning Digital Media* 8, 76–85. https://doi.org/10.2304/elea.2011.8.1.76

Chase, Z. & Laufenberg, D., 2011, 'Embracing the squishiness of digital literacy', *Journal of Adolescent & Adult Literacy* 54, 535–537. https://doi.org/10.1598/JAAL.54.7.7

Christens, B.D., Winn, L.T. & Duke, A.M., 2016, 'Empowerment and critical consciousness: A conceptual cross-fertilization', *Adolescent Research Review* 1, 15–27. https://doi.org/10.1007/s40894-015-0019-3

Cibangu, S.K., Hepworth, M. & Champion, D., 2017, 'The impact of mobile phone uses in the developing world: Giving voice to the rural poor in the Congo', *International Journal of Information Communication Technologies and Human Development* 9, 20–48. https://doi.org/10.4018/IJICTHD.2017040102

Czerniewicz, L., Ravjee, N. & Mlitwa, N., 2006, *ICTs and the South African higher education landscape*, Council on Higher Education, South Africa, Pretoria.

El-Darwiche, B., Sharma, A., Singh, M. & Samad, R.A., 2012, *Digitization in emerging economies: Unleashing opportunities at the bottom of the pyramid*, Strategy, Beirut.

Garrido, M., Sey, A., Hart, T. & Santana, L., 2012, *Literature review of how telecentres operate and have an impact on e-inclusion*, European Commission, Seville.

Gomez, R. & Baron-Porras, L.F., 2011, 'Does public access computing really contribute to community development? Lessons from libraries, telecentres and cybercafés in Colombia', *The Electronic Journal of Information Systems in Developing Countries* 49, 1–11. https://doi.org/10.1002/j.1681-4835.2011.tb00346.x

Goodfellow, R., 2011, 'Literacy, literacies and the digital in higher education', *Teaching in Higher Education* 16, 131–144. https://doi.org/10.1080/13562517.2011.544125

Harris, R.W., 2016, 'How ICT4D research fails the poor', *Information Technology for Development* 22, 177–192. https://doi.org/10.1080/02681102.2015.1018115

Haugh, H.M. & Talwar, A., 2016, 'Linking social entrepreneurship and social change: The mediating role of empowerment', *Journal of Business Ethics* 133, 643–658. https://doi.org/10.1007/s10551-014-2449-4

Helsper, E.J. & Eynon, R., 2013, 'Distinct skill pathways to digital engagement', *European Journal of Communication* 28, 696–713. https://doi.org/10.1177/0267323113499113

Hinrichsen, J. & Coombs, A., 2013, 'The five resources of critical digital literacy: A framework for curriculum integration', *Research & Learning Technology* 21, 21334. https://doi.org/10.3402/rlt.v21.21334

James, J., 2005, 'The global digital divide in the Internet: Developed countries constructs and third world realities', *Journal of Information Science* 31, 114–123. https://doi.org/10.1177/0165551505050788

Johns, G., 2006, 'The essential impact of context on organizational behavior', *The Academy of Management Review* 31, 386–408. https://doi.org/10.5465/AMR.2006.20208687

Klecun, E., 2008, 'Bringing lost sheep into the fold: Questioning the discourse of the digital divide', *Information Technology & People* 21, 267–282. https://doi.org/10.1108/09593840810896028

Labbo, L.D., Reinking, D. & McKenna, M.C., 1998, 'Technology and literacy education in the next century: Exploring the connection between work and schooling', *Peabody Journal of Education* 73, 273–289. https://doi.org/10.1080/0161956X.1998.9681895

Lankshear, C. & Knobel, M., 2007, 'Researching new literacies: Web 2.0 practices and insider perspectives', *E-Learning & Digital Media* 4, 224–240. https://doi.org/10.2304/elea.2007.4.3.224

Lankshear, C. & Knobel, M., 2008, 'Introduction. Digital literacies: Concepts, policies and practices', in *Digital literacies: Concepts, policies and practices*, pp. 1–16, Peter Lang Publishing, New York.

Leonardi, P.M. & Barley, S.R., 2010, 'What's under construction here? Such social action, material, and power in constructivist studies of technology and organizing', *Academy of Management Annals* 4, 1–51. https://doi.org/10.1080/19416521003654160

Littlejohn, A., Beetham, H. & McGill, L., 2012, 'Learning at the digital frontier: A review of digital literacies in theory and practice', *Journal of Computer Assisted Learning* 28, 547–556. https://doi.org/10.1111/j.1365-2729.2011.00474.x

Long, L.-A., Chamberlain, S. & Gagnaire, K., 2014, 'The 80–20 Debate: Framework or fiction? How much development work is standardized across geographies, and how much is customized for local conditions', *Innovations* 9, 87–96. https://doi.org/10.1162/inov_a_00219

Martin, A., 2008, 'Digital literacy and the "digital society"', in C. Lankshear & M. Knobel (eds.), *Digital literacies – Concepts, policies and practices*, pp. 151–176, Peter Lang Publishing, New York.

Maton, K.I., 2008, 'Empowering community settings: Agents of individual development, community betterment, and positive social change', *American Journal of Community Psychology* 41, 4–21. https://doi.org/10.1007/s10464-007-9148-6

Mayo, P., 1995, 'Critical literacy and emancipatory politics: The work of Paulo Freire', *International Journal of Educational Development* 15, 363–379. https://doi.org/10.1016/0738-0593(95)00021-T

Merchant, G., 2007, 'Writing the future in the digital age', *Literacy* 41, 118–128. https://doi.org/10.1111/j.1467-9345.2007.00469.x

Michailova, S., 2011, 'Contextualizing in international business research: Why do we need more of it and how can we be better at it?', *Scandinavian Journal of Management* 27, 129–139. https://doi.org/10.1016/j.scaman.2010.11.003

Moje, E.B., 2009, 'Standpoints: A call for new research on new and multi-literacies', *Research in the Teaching of English* 43, 348–362.

Müller, S.M. & Tworek, H.J.S., 2016, 'Imagined use as a category of analysis: New approaches to the history of technology', *History and Technology* 32, 105–119. https://doi.org/10.1080/07341512.2016.1218957

O'Brien, D. & Scharber, C., 2008, 'Digital literacies go to schools: Potholes and possibilities', *Journal of Adolescent & Adult Literacy* 52, 66–68. https://doi.org/10.1598/JAAL.52.1.7

Pangrazio, L., 2016, 'Reconceptualising critical digital literacy', *Discourse Studies in the Cultural Politics of Education* 37, 163–174. https://doi.org/10.1080/01596306.2014.942836

Parrott, L. & Madoc-Jones, I., 2008, 'Reclaiming information and communication technologies for empowering social work practice', *Journal of Social Work* 8, 181–197. https://doi.org/10.1177/1468017307084739

Rappaport, J., Altman, D., Arbor, A. & Zimmerman, M.A., 1995, 'Psychological empowerment: Issues and illustrations', *American Journal of Community Psychology* 23, 581–599. https://doi.org/10.1007/BF02506983

Reynolds, R., 2016, 'Defining, designing for, and measuring "social constructivist digital literacy" development in learners: A proposed framework', *Educational Technology Research and Development* 64, 735–762. https://doi.org/10.1007/s11423-015-9423-4

Riger, S., 1993, 'What's wrong with empowerment', *American Journal of Community Psychology* 21, 279–292. https://doi.org/10.1007/BF00941504

Rogers, D.E.M., 2003, *Diffusion of innovations*, 5th edn., Simon & Schuster, New York.

Roztocki, N. & Weistroffer, H.R., 2016, 'Conceptualizing and research the adoption of ICT and the impact on socioeconomic development', *Information Technology for Development* 22, 541–549. https://doi.org/10.1080/02681102.2016.1196097

Sassen, S., 2002, 'Towards a sociology of information technology', *Current Sociology* 50, 365–388. https://doi.org/10.1177/0011392102050003005

Stornaiuolo, A., Smith, A. & Phillips, N.C., 2017, 'Developing a transliteracies framework for a connected world', *Journal of Literacy Research* 49, 68–91. https://doi.org/10.1177/1086296X16683419

Tunçalp, D. & Tun, D., 2016, 'Questioning the ontology of sociomateriality: A critical realist perspective', *Management Decision* 54, 1073–1087. https://doi.org/10.1108/MD-07-2014-0476

Watkins, C.S., 2011, 'Digital divide: Navigating the digital edge', *International Journal of Learning Media* 3, 1–12. https://doi.org/10.1162/ijlm_a_00072

Zammuto, R.F., Griffith, T.L., Majchrzak, A., Dougherty, D.J. & Faraj, S., 2007, 'Information technology and the changing fabric of organization', *Organization Science* 18, 749–762. https://doi.org/10.1287/orsc.1070.0307

Zimmerman, M.A., 1995, 'Psychological empowerment: Issues and illustrations', *American Journal of Community Psychology* 23, 581–599. https://doi.org/10.1007/BF02506983

Zimmerman, M.A., Israel, B.A., Schulz, A. & Checkoway, B., 1992, 'Further explorations in empowerment theory: An empirical analysis of psychological empowerment', *American Journal of Community Psychology* 20, 707–727. https://doi.org/10.1007/BF00942234

Critical Thinking

1. How does digital literacy stand in relationship to digital technologies?

2. What factors distinguish global and development contexts from first world countries in terms of the environment for socioeconomic liberation?
3. If scholars deviate from an idealized version of digital literacy to a definition rooted in the context, what is the pathway to becoming a means of empowering its population?

Internet References

Digital literacy
https://www.tolerance.org/frameworks/digital-literacy

How to Teach Digital Literacy in the Classroom
https://www.aeseducation.com/how-to-teach-digital-literacy-in-the-classroom

What is digital literacy?
https://www.thetechedvocate.org/what-is-digital-literacy/

Njenga, James. (2018). Digital literacy: The quest of a inclusive definition. Reading & Writing. 9. 10.4102/rw.v9i1.183.

UNIT

Prepared by: Sheron Fraser-Burgess, *Ball State University*

Teaching English Language Learners

Since 1972, the US Commission on Civil Rights introduced legislation that would create a better learning environment for non-native speakers of English. The articles included in this unit celebrate the benefit of such instruction for these students and the academic goals of education and pedagogy.

The concepts of culture and diversity encompass all the customs, traditions, and institutions that people develop as they create and experience their history and identity as a community. In the United States, very different cultures coexist within the civic framework of a shared constitutional tradition that guarantees equality before the law. So, many people are united as one nation by our constitutional heritage. Some of us are proud to say that we are a nation of immigrants. Our country is becoming more multicultural with every passing decade. As educators, we have a unique opportunity to encourage and educate our diverse learners. The articles in this unit reflect upon all the concerns mentioned above. You can establish a classroom that is a place of caring and nurturing for your students, multicultural-friendly, equitable, and free from bigotry, where diverse students are not just tolerated but are wanted, welcomed, and accepted. Respect for all children and their capacity is the baseline for good teaching. Students must feel significant and cared for by all members of the classroom. Our diverse children should be exposed to an academically challenging curriculum that expects much from them and equips them for the real world.

The number of children (ages 5–17) who speak a language other than English at home has grown from 4.7 million in 1980 to 11,994,000 in 2012 (Annie E. Casey Foundation). Among these children, the percentage who speak English with difficulty is now around 2.5 million or around 5 percent. If we compare these students by age, the youngest had the most difficulty speaking English; while 7 percent of children ages 5–9 and only 4 percent of adolescents ages 14–17 spoke English with difficulty (U.S. Department of Education, National Center for Education Statistics, 2012).

On average, Hispanic students never perform as well as other students, not even in kindergarten. In some states, the Hispanic school-age population has nearly doubled since 1987 and is approaching one-half of all students. Unfortunately, these students are more likely to attend a hyper-segregated school, where the population is 90–100 percent minority, and they are less likely to read or do math at grade level or earn a college degree. In fact, they drop out of high school at higher rates than all other categories of the student population (Coleman and Goldenberg, 2010).

These data appear to indicate that teachers and schools are making an impact on second language acquisition of students who do not speak English at home. The articles in this unit focus on the concept that caring, culturally responsive instruction from teachers with positive attitudes who look for student's assets can and will help English language learners (ELLs) be successful learners in school.

A shift in our thinking can make a powerful difference in how we approach and teach students who are ELLs. To begin with, we might consider new ways to think and talk about students from other countries and cultural backgrounds. For example, we might consider that students who are ELLs have experiences that make them culturally different but not culturally deficient. The Network School in New York City has a graduation rate that is more than double the other schools in the city. There are lessons to be learned from those teachers who view their students who are ELL as assets.

A request from a general education middle school teacher to an ELL teacher caused them to consider how they might meet the needs of more ELL students and their teachers. As school populations of students who speak other languages has increased, schools have not been able to find nor can they afford to hire as many ELL teachers as administrators need or want. Therefore, teachers are beginning to form groups to support each other as they work to teach and nurture ELL students.

Early Childhood classrooms are particularly interesting when young ELL or ESL students arrive. They are most likely dual language learners. While they are learning the language which they will use in school, they are continuing to learn their first language at home. These students may present a challenge to classroom teachers unless their teachers understand how to use each language to complement the learning of the other language.

Schools in rural areas have seen a rise in drop-out rates and corresponding drop in graduation rates for students who are ELL. Research data tell us that there is a positive correlation between ELL parent engagement, especially engagement with teachers, and the academic achievement of their children who are ELL. Some of the barriers to parent participation are identified as language, cultural differences, job schedules, and lack of transportation. With the rise in non-English speaking citizens in rural communities and the unsatisfactory drop-out and graduation outcomes, researchers were interested in discovering what factors influenced ELL parent–teacher relationships and interactions from the viewpoint of the parents. The results of this study offer valuable suggestions for teachers everywhere to consider.

References

Annie E. Casey Foundation, (N.D.). Data Center: Children who speak a language other than English at home. Author. Retrieved on 20 June 2014 from http://datacenter.kidscount.org/data/tables/81-children-who-speak-a-language-other-than-english-at-home?loc51&loct51#detailed/1/any/false/868,867,133,38,35/any/396,397.

Coleman, R. & Goldenberg, (2010). *What Does Research Say about Effective Practices for English Learners?, Kappa Delta Pi Record*, Winter 2010.

U.S. Department of Education, National Center for Education Statistics. (2012). *The Condition of Education 2011* (NCES 2011-045), Indicator 6.

Article

Prepared by: Sheron Fraser-Burgess, *Ball State University*

Becoming Sociocultural Mediators
What All Educators Can Learn from Bilingual and ESL Teachers

SONIA NIETO

Learning Outcomes

After reading this article, you will be able to:

- Characterize the professional labor of bilingual and ESL teachers.
- Be clear about the way that these pedagogical strategies translate into lessons from which teachers who are not similarly trained but teach English Language Learners (ELL) can learn.
- Ascertain the reasons that learning certain bodies of knowledge and building bridges with students can better position nonspecialist teachers to increase ELL student learning.

In the past several decades, those who speak languages other than English have become a growing presence in the United States, even in areas where they had not previously been concentrated. In fact, in the past three decades their numbers have almost tripled, from 23 to 60 million (Gándara, 2015). U.S. schools have felt the major impact of this growing population. Currently, about 9.1 percent, or 4.4 million students in U.S. classrooms, are classified as ELLs (English Language Learners), or emergent bilinguals (U.S. Department of Education, 2014).[1]

Many emergent bilingual students, although not all, are immigrants or refugees; others were born in the United States and speak only, or primarily, their native language until they arrive at school. Although some are in bilingual and ESL classrooms with teachers who have gained the necessary knowledge and expertise to teach them, many are in regular English-medium classrooms. Some receive no special language assistance at all. The growing numbers of emergent bilingual students make it imperative that all teachers learn how to competently teach them. Yet, over 80 percent of U.S. teachers are White, monolingual English speakers. A good number have had little or no training in how to teach these students, and many have had limited experience with diversity, including language diversity (Aud et al., 2012).

On the bright side, most bilingual and ESL teachers have received the necessary preparation for working with the growing number of emergent bilingual students. Mining the knowledge and practices of these teachers means learning from what they value and what they do. In this article, I focus specifically on how what I call non-specialist teachers (i.e., those who are neither bilingual nor ESL teachers) can benefit from the practices of bilingual and ESL teachers, and how teacher educators can incorporate this knowledge in their curriculum and pedagogy. To do so, I use examples from research I have done over many years to examine how bilingual and ESL teachers engage with students of diverse language backgrounds through curriculum, pedagogy, outreach to families, and engagement in the community (Nieto, 2005, 2010, 2013, 2015).

There are two major lessons that non-specialist teachers of emergent bilingual students can learn from bilingual and ESL teachers: one is that they need to learn certain bodies of knowledge, and the other is that they need to build bridges with their students by developing affirming dispositions about language, culture, and difference. My examples come from

---

[1] In this article, I use the term *emergent bilinguals* instead because it focuses on what students can become rather than on what they do not know (Bartlett & García, 2011).

teachers who teach students of diverse language backgrounds at different grade levels and in a variety of settings around the country. Next, I give some examples of non-specialist teachers who embody some of these lessons from bilingual and ESL teachers. I end the article with what this information implies for teacher education.

Learning to Teach Emergent Bilingual Students

Bilingual and ESL teachers have to learn an impressive amount to be successful with students of diverse language backgrounds. They need to learn, for instance, about first and second language acquisition. They need to become familiar with research in language education that points to effective practices and policies. They need to learn how to work effectively with families. They need to learn sociocultural knowledge about the students they teach. Some of this knowledge comes from their studies, and some of it is developed as a result of their work in the classroom. Some examples follow.

Becoming Resources for Non-specialist Teachers

There are many ways in which bilingual and ESL teachers can become resources for their non-specialist colleagues. For example, several teachers I've interviewed over the years have mentioned that a good number of the non-specialist teachers with whom they work know little about their students' trajectory as second language learners. These teachers may incorrectly think, for instance, that learning another language is a fairly quick and painless process, that it takes just some grammar and vocabulary lessons before students are ready to enter a "mainstream" classroom. Obviously, this misperception is even built into state and federal laws that mandate a quick transition—generally a year—from limited English knowledge to English-only classrooms.

A group of bilingual, dual language, and ESL teachers I interviewed in California several years ago described how they served as resources for their colleagues. Many of the teachers had themselves been immigrants and they understood in a visceral way what their students go through. For these teachers, being resources for their colleagues meant serving as models, either through their teaching practices or in their relationships with students and families. In the specific case of teachers working with Latino/a students, Leticia Ornelas spoke about the responsibility of Latino/a teachers to speak up when other staff members expressed negative ideas about the students and their families. Leticia said, "That's us! That's the way that we grew up!" (Nieto, 2013, p. 86). She said she didn't remember her own parents going to any parent meetings, or even understanding the reasons for doing so, but she explained this didn't mean they didn't value education. In fact, the opposite is true: many immigrants realize that education is their only way out and they constantly remind their children of this fact. This support for education is something all teachers need to understand.

Another teacher, Angela Fajardo, brought up the many sacrifices that families make so that their children can get a good education. "Our students' parents work in hotels; they work at the airport. They have night shifts. How can you tell me these parents don't care when they are working all hours for their children?" (Nieto, 2013, p. 86). Explaining these things to their colleagues, Leticia said, might help them be more understanding and sensitive. This can happen through activities as simple as hallway conversations when non-specialist teachers might have questions, or in more formal settings such as professional development sessions in which bilingual and ESL teachers share their knowledge and experiences. It can also happen through newsletters and other less formal activities.

Building Bridges

One of the most significant roles a teacher can have is being a bridge, that is, connecting students' worlds of home and school in meaningful and constructive ways. A bridge is a good metaphor for teachers' work as sociocultural mediators. A bridge helps connect two areas that otherwise might be hard to reach. A bridge also introduces us to new terrains and new adventures. In addition, a bridge makes going back and forth easy. Rather than the expectation that students need to "burn their bridges"—that is, forget and reject their native language and ethnic culture—they can instead become bilingual and bicultural. When teachers act as bridges, they send a message to their students that their identities are worthwhile. This is a valuable disposition for all teachers to have.

Dispositions are values put into practice. They do not come as a prepackaged curriculum, nor are they a specific pedagogy or set of strategies. Dispositions are also not about creating a "feel-good" curriculum or lowering standards. Dispositions—although not easily taught—can nevertheless be learned through experience and practice. These dispositions include being open to learning about their students, having empathy and solidarity for them, being respectful of their families and communities, and having a passion for social justice; dispositions I have written about in a previous book (Nieto, 2013). For many bilingual and ESL teachers, these kinds of dispositions are often second nature, sometimes because of their own lives as immigrants, at other times because of their personal experiences with diversity, their work in different cultural settings, or in other ways. Developing these dispositions can go a long way in creating strong bonds of caring and respect between teachers and students.

More than anything else, becoming a competent teacher of emergent bilingual students means learning to be a sociocultural mediator, that is, using students' cultures and language to open new possibilities for them *while at the same time* supporting their emerging bilingualism and biculturalism rather than forcing them to what Alejandro Portes and Ruben Rumbaut have called a "premature assimilation" (Portes & Rumbaut, 2006). This is easier said than done, especially for teachers who have had little personal or professional experience with students of diverse language backgrounds. Becoming a sociocultural mediator entails two different, but complementary, practices: first, it means taking students someplace else—in the case of emergent bilinguals, teaching them English and helping them adapt to the culture and traditions of their new country; and second, it means encouraging them to honor what they already know and who they are. In essence, this means eschewing the assimilation imperative and instead, in the words of Margaret Gibson, teaching them "accommodation without assimilation" (Gibson, 1988). A few examples from bilingual and ESL teachers follow.

Strengthening Academic and Personal Bonds

Bilingual and ESL teachers know all too well that forging strong relationships with students is essential if students are to connect with school and learning. A number of years ago I interviewed Angeles Perez, a 4th grade bilingual teacher in the Sheldon Independent School District in Houston, Texas. Angeles was her students' "biggest fan," she said unapologetically. She worked hard at cultivating the teacher-student relationship both academically and socially. For example, she helped her students develop their own learning goals, saying, "I pride myself on getting them to set their goals and they're not low goals, they're high goals" (Nieto, 2013, p. 39). She was thrilled when her students reached their goals, and then she helped them set new goals. Angeles pushed her students hard and they reaped the benefits of her demands when, for instance, one of her students won the school Spelling Bee—in English—unprecedented for a student in a bilingual class.

Angeles also created strong bonds with her students on a personal level. No student in her class remained invisible. She made it a point, for instance, to stand by the door each morning to greet each student personally. At the end of the day, she said, "they run to give me a hug and it's the best feeling because they care so much about me. They work for me because they know I work for them. I love them" (Nieto, 2013, p. 38). But it's often just little things that count. Angeles also instituted "hanging out with Ms. Perez time" for the last ten minutes of the school day as a way to learn more about each student's interests and experiences.

A number of humorous examples of building bridges come from some of the ESL and bilingual teachers I interviewed several years ago in the Los Angeles area. Leticia Ornelas, a bilingual teacher in the Montebello school district in California, arrived from Mexico when she was a child. She spoke about building bridges with her students in numerous ways. She explained that she had instituted something she called "Lotion Day" in her classroom on Fridays, saying,

> My skin gets dry, so I put lotion on, and because kids notice everything you do, one day they said, "You know, you don't share your lotion with us." I said, "Oh, no! You didn't notice that!" So I said, "You want some of my lotion?" and they said, "Yeah!" (Nieto, 2013, p. 84)

She continued, "So I gave it to a little girl, and now I have this long line of students every Friday." A simple gesture as seemingly insignificant as sharing lotion with one's students can go a long way in relating to them, especially students new to this country who may see their teachers as unapproachable.

Angela Fajardo also had a humorous example of building bridges. She spoke about a group of students who hadn't passed the California exit exam. Exasperated, one day she asked them, "What do I have to do for you to learn this?" They were quick to respond, "Feed us, just feed us!" (Nieto, 2013, p. 86). Thereafter, Angela kept a stocked refrigerator and a microwave in her classroom. The metaphor of food as sustenance is an apt one because food is a tangible demonstration of a commitment to nurturing students' intellects, bodies, and souls.

Unlike the other ESL and bilingual teachers featured until now, Nina Tepper, who recently retired after many years in the classroom, is not Hispanic. But as an ESL teacher, she learned early on that ESL and bilingual teachers are most successful when they draw on students' cultural backgrounds and experiences to make learning more meaningful. This meant that she needed to learn about the students she taught, about their identities, their communities, and their realities.

Nina wrote about many of the strategies she used to bring students' lives into the curriculum and pedagogy. She often asked students to write about themselves and, in an essay she wrote shortly after retiring, she recounted the final author party in her classroom in which students had written essays about an important lesson they had learned in their lives. Through tears and laughter, and knowing they were in a safe space, the students described significant incidents they might not have been able to talk about elsewhere. She wrote, "Each story is unique and each story tells of the complicated lives with which our students come to us. Without searching for their stories, I would never have known, and what assumptions might I have made?" (Tepper, 2015, p. 37).

Nina also wrote about having her students imagine the future and their role in it by bringing *all* of themselves into it without having to completely change who they are. This is another key lesson for nonspecialist teachers to learn, that is, that students' cultures should be viewed as an asset rather than as a deficit or something to be discarded because in this way, they can envision themselves as significant players in the future. In her essay, Nina wrote,

> When teachers validate each child's culture and experience, when teachers inject facts and stories that connect the past and present to the future, when teachers design real opportunities for students to work collectively with others, students can then explore how their lives are woven into the fabric of society and begin to imagine how they too can contribute to our world (Tepper, 2015).

Validating students' experiences in school sounds simple enough to do, but given the current focus on accountability, standardization, and rigid pre-packaged curricula that has swept the nation in the past three decades, it can be difficult to accomplish. Teachers must find ways to bring students' experiences and realities into school, sometimes putting aside school or district mandates, instead using creative approaches to integrating these issues into the curriculum.

Non-specialist Teachers Learning from Bilingual and ESL Teachers

We have seen several examples of what bilingual and ESL teachers value and what they do to create strong bonds—academic and personal—with their students. What can other teachers learn from them?

Starting Where Kids Are At

A veteran of 42 years in the classroom, Mary Ginley, now retired, taught students of all backgrounds both in Massachusetts and in Florida: children of privilege in a wealthy community, immigrant children in an impoverished community, and children of diverse backgrounds in a socioeconomically mixed community. Through it all, she has thought long and hard about what it means to reach all her students. In a journal entry she wrote for a class she took with me in the 1990s, Mary pondered how to be an effective teacher for all her students. At the time, she was teaching in a socioeconomically disadvantaged community with a growing Puerto Rican population. As the excellent teacher she always was, Mary questioned her own awareness and understanding:

> My philosophy has always been—start from where they are and go together to someplace else. Still, when more and more Puerto Rican children entered my classroom, I had trouble starting from where they were, because I didn't know where they were and it was hard for them to tell me (Ginley, 1999a, p. 75).

Mary was always introspective, an important quality in teachers working with students who are not like them. Being introspective means constantly questioning what one is doing, and whether it is enough to reach all students. As Mary progressed in her understanding of her growing Puerto Rican student body, she mused,

> Every child needs to feel welcome, to feel comfortable. School is a foreign land to most kids (where else in the world would you spend time circling answers and filling in the blanks?), but the more distant a child's culture and language are from the culture and language of school, the more at risk that child is. (Ginley, 1999b, pp. 85–86)

That is, rather than using the term "at risk" to blame families, children, and culture, she correctly placed the onus of being "at risk" on schools and society in general. And although she agreed that it's important for teachers to be warm, friendly, and nice, she also discovered that it wasn't enough because,

> We have plenty of warm friendly teachers who tell the kids nicely to forget their Spanish and ask mommy and daddy to speak to them in English at home; who give them easier tasks so they won't feel badly when the work becomes difficult; who never learn about what life is like at home or what they eat or what music they like or what stories they have been told or what their history is. Instead, we smile and tell them to listen to our stories and dance to our music. We teach them to read with our words and wonder why it's so hard for them. We ask them to sit quietly and we'll tell them what's important and what they must know to "get ready for the next grade." And we never ask them who they are and where they want to go (Ginley, 1999b, p. 86).

Mary Ginley's powerful caution that being nice is not enough is an important reminder to all teachers that learning about students and their communities is essential for all teachers, not just specialists in ESL and bilingual education. The kinds of dispositions Mary developed through her many years of teaching also demonstrate that knowledge of second language acquisition, cultural difference, and the sociopolitical context of education are all key areas of learning for non-specialist teachers who work with emergent bilingual students.

Learning Another Language

One lesson from bilingual and ESL teachers is to learn the native language of their students. But why should non-bilingual and non-ESL teachers learn another language? After all, they aren't expected to teach in a language other than English, and also they may have few emergent bilingual students in their classes. Also, it is not always practical for them to learn another language, especially if they have a number of languages represented in their classroom. Nevertheless, teachers can at the very least learn key vocabulary in several of the languages their students speak, and they can label objects in the room with these languages. They can also encourage their same-language students to work together in small groups, using their native languages to do some of their work. This can be a good transition to an all-English classroom, as well as a significant message that their language is worthwhile and important for them to keep using. Stocking the classroom library with books in a variety of languages gives the same message, as is encouraging the school librarian to do the same.

There are other good reasons for learning another language. Bill Dunn, a teacher of English and social studies at a vocational high school in Massachusetts, provides a powerful example of why it's important for non-specialist teachers to learn another language. Bill, a former student of mine, had experienced vicarious second language learning over a couple of decades as a result of his school district undergoing a dramatic increase in the number of Spanish-speaking students in the city (Dunn, 1999). Bill decided, he said, to "come out of the closet as a Spanish speaker," because he realized he was understanding a great deal of what his Spanish-speaking students were saying. Thus began Bill's journey to learn the language. He immersed himself in it, taking a class, watching TV shows, reading the Spanish language newspaper, and sitting in on a bilingual class in his school. He also kept a journal documenting his experiences.

Bill was frustrated and disappointed when he took a test in Spanish in a bilingual class in his school and couldn't answer most of the questions. What really shocked him, he said, was that he didn't understand two-thirds of the questions. Always a thoughtful and caring teacher, Bill became a more effective and understanding one as well because, being in the position of a second-language learner, he began to understand what his students went through. He wrote, "I thought of all those kids in the lower tracks who are condemned to answering questions that they don't understand at the end of countless chapters that they don't comprehend" (Dunn, 1999, p. 150). Bill became restless, began to take books from the shelf, wanted to talk to his neighbors and, because he became very tired, even contemplated putting his head on the desk. Bill began to understand these and other behaviors of his students who were learning English.

Another benefit of Bill's foray into learning Spanish was that he began to understand and appreciate the Puerto Rican community and Spanish speakers in ways he hadn't before. He wrote,

> [There] are things about Puerto Rican people and culture that I admire very much. I would also have to admit that I did not always admire these things because I did not understand them at first. This is a good lesson not only for second-language learning but for any situation where different cultures come in contact. It takes time to build understanding (Dunn, 1999, p. 151).

At the end of the semester, Bill wrote, "I now know from personal experience that second-language acquisition is a slow and difficult process, yet in most American schools we demand that nonnative-English speakers achieve fluency in a short period of time" (p. 174). This kind of understanding is not always easy to come by, but learning a second language is almost guaranteed to make it happen.

Developing Solidarity with Students

A high school English teacher in Athens, Georgia, a state that has seen an unprecedented increase in its Latino immigrant population in the past three decades, Matt Hicks wrote about his dawning awareness of the difficult daily experiences faced by his undocumented immigrant students. "Over time," he wrote in an essay in my most recent book (Nieto, 2015), "I became more and more conscious of their status-specific struggles" (Hicks, 2015, p. 132). As both a teacher and coach, Matt was becoming more engaged in their lives. He also began to welcome—and learn from—conversations about his students' experiences. As a result, he became an activist, attending rallies with his students to protest, for example, Georgia House Bill 87, modeled after Arizona's SB 1070, the most restrictive state legislation against the immigration of undocumented people into the United States.

Matt also worked inside the school to create spaces of inclusion for students who have generally been excluded. One of his students, Uma, worked with Matt to create a guide that provided students and their advocates with information about colleges to which they could apply, as well as available scholarships, admissions questions, and more. As the state's Latino immigrant student population increased, including the number of undocumented youngsters, he sent the guide to counselors around the state.

In another move to advocate for his students, Matt asked Uma to help him use the school's enrichment period to teach a class from the guide. "We gave the course a vague, innocuous name," he wrote, "and from there we used our relationships with other kids to bring together 15 aspiring, college-bound, undocumented students . . ." (Hicks, 2015, p. 134). At the end of the year, seven of the students who took the class were admitted to at least one college, no small feat for students who are generally excluded from attending college because of a lack of access to in-state tuition and financial aid. Three students earned 6 scholarships, an even greater accomplishment. Matt's engagement led him to become a strong advocate for his undocumented students. He explained how his engagement extended beyond his curriculum and pedagogy; it was about "coming into full humanity," the title he gave his essay:

> This work was more than just something I made plans for each week. It was no longer an abstraction or intellectual pursuit. It was close to my heart each night as I prepared for school. It was what brought me there each day. These kids brought me there each day (Hicks, 2015, p. 135)

Implications for Teacher Education

Although different in many ways, the teachers whose stories illuminate this article developed academic and personal relationships with their students by:

- Engaging their students in conversations about their identities and realities
- Creating curricula centered on their students' lives
- Developing a caring pedagogy
- Promoting respectful relationships with family members and communities
- Understanding that it is not only what they teach, but also whom they teach that matters

The experiences of the teachers highlighted in this article also suggest a number of lessons for teacher education and professional development. Teacher educators and professional developers can change some of the courses they teach to include the kind of content that bilingual and ESL teachers must learn to gain teacher certification. They can, for instance, require that all teachers, not just those preparing to specialize in bilingual and ESL education, take courses that include linguistics, first and second language acquisition, culture, and family outreach and relationships. They can also require practicum activities such as learning how to connect with students' families and caregivers, learning about and visiting social service agencies and other community organizations, and attending school board meetings. These and other related activities, although not identical to the preparation of bilingual and ESL teachers, will at least give non-specialist teachers more of the knowledge they need to be successful teachers of emergent bilingual students.

In addition, although teachers' values and dispositions cannot necessarily be taught, they can be learned. In their professional development, most bilingual and ESL teachers learn about creating learning environments that focus on inclusive and nurturing practices, and that embody high expectations. Rather than offer only courses with a singular focus on methods—although some methods courses are necessary—courses that focus on respectful and caring relationships, outreach to families, and the sociocultural realities of the children with which they will be working can help future and practicing teachers learn about their students and the communities in which they teach in more meaningful ways.

Taking courses in other departments besides education is also essential. Naturally, courses in the discipline they plan to teach are fundamental, but to give students a broader perspective, equally important are courses in history, literature, sociology, anthropology, psychology, and other arts and the social sciences. In addition, preservice teachers should be given the opportunity to have extended and relevant field experiences in the kinds of communities in which they will be working. These experiences rather than solidify existing biases—as long as they're combined with critical discussions and other experiences in their teacher education programs—can help challenge biases.

Finally, preparing future teachers to work in collaboration with specialist teachers in ESL and bilingual education can put them in good stead for the realities of today's classrooms where more than ever, emergent bilingual students will be a big part. Instead of isolating ESL and bilingual teachers into tracks that never connect with other preservice teachers, the goal should be to have them together with non-specialist teachers as much as possible.

Conclusion

It is unfortunately too often the case that emergent bilingual students feel alienated and invisible in English-medium classrooms (Bartlett & Garcia, 2011). This is not the way it has to be, however. With the help of specialists who work with emergent bilingual students, namely, ESL and bilingual teachers, other educators can learn important lessons about how to go about teaching and reaching emergent bilingual students.

The changes needed to help emergent bilingual students transition into English-medium classrooms are about both policy and practice. Policies include making time for other staff members to learn about what it takes to teach emergent bilinguals, developing outreach efforts with families, providing the resources (books and other materials) that teachers need to use with these students, and others. Naturally, administrators, policymakers, teacher educators, and the general public need to do the lion's share of changing the policies that make it difficult for all students to feel a sense of power and inclusion in our public schools. Classroom practices, however, are mainly the purview of teachers who, in spite of rigid curricular mandates, can nevertheless make meaningful changes in their classrooms. Teachers often believe they have little power to make change, but all educators can take solace from the teachers highlighted in this article as well as many others like them, to understand that they too can make a substantive difference in the lives of their students through their curricula, pedagogy, outreach efforts, and activism.

The stories in this article illustrate what can happen when teachers, working in tandem with students, families, colleagues, administrators, and others—and sometimes even when working alone—take seriously the challenge to provide young people of all backgrounds with the kinds of affirming practices too often missing in our nation's classrooms and schools.

References

Aud, S., Hussar, W., Johnson, F., Kena, G., Roth, E., Manning, E., Wang, X., & Zhang, J. (2012). *The condition of education 2012*. NCES 2012-045. Washington, DC: U.S. Department of Education, National Center on Education Statistics. http://nces.ed.gov/pubsearch

Bartlett, L., & García, O. (2011). *Additive schooling in subtractive times: Bilingual education and Dominican immigrant youth in the Heights*. Nashville, TN: Vanderbilt University Press.

Dunn, B. (1999). Mi semester de español: A case study on the cultural dimension of second-language acquisition. In S. Nieto, *The light in their eyes: Creating multicultural learning communities* (pp. 146–152). New York, NY: Teachers College Press.

Gándara, P. (2015). Rethinking bilingual instruction. *Educational Leadership*, 72(6), 60–64.

Gibson, M. (1988). *Accommodation without assimilation: Sikh immigrants in an American high school*. Ithaca, NY: Cornell University Press.

Ginley, M. (1999a). Start from where kids are at. In S. Nieto, *The light in their eyes: Creating multicultural learning communities* (p. 75). New York, NY: Teachers College Press.

Ginley, M. (1999b). Being nice is not enough. In S. Nieto, *The light in their eyes: Creating multicultural learning communities* (pp. 85–86). New York, NY: Teachers College Press.

Hicks, M. (2015). Coming into full humanity through teaching, sharing, and connecting. In S. Nieto (Ed.), *Why we teach now* (pp. 131–137). New York, NY: Teachers College Press.

Nieto, S. (2005). Public education in the twentieth century and beyond: High hopes, broken promises, and an uncertain future. *Harvard Educational Review*, 75(1), 57–78.

Nieto, S. (2010). *The light in their eyes: Creating multicultural learning communities*. 10th anniversary edition. New York, NY: Teachers College Press.

Nieto, S. (2013). *Finding joy in teaching students of diverse backgrounds: Culturally responsive and socially just classrooms in U.S. classrooms*. Portsmouth, NH: Heinemann.

Nieto, S. (2015). *Why we teach now*. New York, NY: Teachers College Press.

Portes, A., & Rumbaut, R. (2006). *Immigrant America: A portrait* (3rd ed.). Berkeley, CA: University of California Press.

Tepper, N. (2015). Staying true to why I teach. In S. Nieto (Ed.), *Why we teach now* (pp. 36–44). New York, NY: Teachers College Press.

U.S. Department of Education, National Center for Education Statistics. (2014). *The condition of education 2014* (NCES 2014-083), English Language Learners. Available at http://nces.ed.gov/fastfacts/display.asp?id=96

Critical Thinking

1. Of what importance is bilingual and ESL teaching being a resource for nonspecialist teachers in terms of communicating the values and norms of students' cultures?

2. Draw conclusions about the substance of the sociocultural mediation that bilingual and ESL teachers can be doing?

3. What kind of teacher education can be learned from this collaboration?

Internet References

Classroom Accommodations for the ESL Student
https://www.ed.gov.nl.ca/edu/k12/curriculum/guides/esl/classroom_accommodations.pdf

ColorinColorado
http://www.colorincolorado.org/ell-strategies-best-practices

ESL Teacher Career Guide
https://www.teachercertificationdegrees.com/careers/esl-teacher/

SONIA NIETO is a professor emerita of Language, Literacy, and Culture in the College of Education at the University of Massachusetts Amherst, Amherst, Massachusetts.

Nieto, Sonia. "Becoming Sociocultural Mediators: What All Educators Can Learn from Bilingual and ESL Teachers." Issues in Teacher Education, v26 n2 p129–41 Sum 2017. Used by permission of Caddo Gap Press.

Article

Prepared by: Sheron Fraser-Burgess, *Ball State University*

ESL and Classroom Teachers Team Up to Teach Common Core

Collaboration may be the new norm for teachers of ELL students.

LESLI A. MAXWELL

Learning Outcomes

After reading this article, you will be able to:

- Separate the scope of the task of content area teachers from that of ESL teachers.
- Delineate the curricular implications that the Common Core Standards impose on ELL.
- Envision the benefits of teacher collaboration for assisting students in navigating these standards.

It started with a simple after-school conversation last spring between two teachers.

Barbara Page, a veteran English-as-a-second-language teacher, and Meredith Vanden Berg, an 8th grade science teacher, were discussing a student from Somalia who had just arrived from a refugee camp in Yemen and landed at their ethnically diverse middle school in Beaverton, Ore.

Ms. Vanden Berg wanted to know what more she could do to help the girl—who was just beginning to learn a few words of English—understand what was going on in her science classroom.

"I don't like when I see students staring off into space when I'm teaching and I know it's because of the language," said Ms. Vanden Berg. "I needed to take a look at my own practice. What could I be doing to convey the core concepts without completely losing her?"

That discussion was the spark for what has evolved into a much closer collaboration between ESL and content teachers at the 600-student Meadow Park Middle School as they fully embrace the Common Core State Standards in English/language arts and mathematics this academic year. Along with their math teacher colleague, Allison Shultz, Ms. Vanden Berg and Ms. Page have begun picking apart the standards, stripping them down to the essential concepts, simplifying the language, and developing strategies that all of them can use to support English-learners in both content and ESL classes.

It's a kind of collaboration and discussion that educators say needs to happen at schools across the country as teachers now stand on the front lines of helping an increasingly diverse student population meet the demands of the new standards. Every student, whether a native English-speaker or a second-language learner, is expected to engage in conversation and discourse in the classroom, read and understand complex texts, and make effective oral and written arguments, among other high-level language practices in the new standards.

Both Ms. Shultz and Ms. Vanden Berg credit Ms. Page with helping them better understand how their own language of instruction can pose a major barrier to students whose English proficiency is still low.

"I really see now how much we as content teachers take for granted," said Ms. Vanden Berg. "It takes a lot of freaking words to explain the periodic table or an atom."

Shifting Relationships?

The nation's roughly 45,000 ESL teachers—many of whom split their time among schools with little chance to co-teach or plan with content teachers—have expertise and strategies that experts say all teachers will need to ensure that English-learners are not shut out of the rigorous, grade-level content that the common core envisions will prepare all students for college and careers. Special education teachers, too, say schools need to foster closer collaboration between them and content teachers to support students with special needs.

But what role will ESL teachers play in this groundbreaking shift to the common core? Will there be a broader move to co-teaching or tighter collaboration between ESL teachers and their academic-content colleagues? What, if any, common-core professional development are ESL teachers receiving, and how is their expertise being tapped?

Earlier this year, the TESOL International Association, the professional organization for teachers who specialize in working with English-learners, raised those issues and more during a convening of ESL professionals who work in school systems in and around Washington. There was strong consensus among the group that ESL teachers, in addition to working directly with students, need to be deployed as consultants to content teachers who will need guidance on how best to support English-learners.

"If held to the same high and rigorous standards as their peers, the learning curve for English-learners is going to be longer and higher than most of their peers and therefore, the teachers who teach them need to be much better equipped," said Rosa Aronson, the executive director of the Alexandria, VA-based TESOL group. "What ESL teachers bring to the table is deep understanding of how language is acquired, the importance of teaching academic language, and the cultural issues for students who are English-learners. They are often closer to their students and families than content teachers and can be strong advocates for these students."

ESL Teacher Status

In many schools, ESL educators have not traditionally been seen as being as central to the enterprise of teaching students as their subject-matter peers, said Aída Walqui, the director of teacher professional development for WestEd, a San Francisco-based research group.

Often itinerant among schools, ESL teachers may serve multiple grade levels and are viewed by their content-area colleagues as being solely responsible for developing students' language skills. They are likely to spend their instructional time with English-learners in stand-alone classrooms in the so-called "pullout" approach, though some districts, such as St. Paul, Minn., partner ESL and content teachers to keep English-learners in mainstream classrooms for all or most of the day.

ESL teachers are also less likely to become principals and take on other leadership roles in their schools than their content-area colleagues, Ms. Walqui said.

All of that, said Ms. Walqui, makes elevating and recasting the role of the ESL teacher even more challenging.

"This is a major dilemma," she said. "What should the role of the ESL teacher be in this dramatically shifting environment of the common core?"

Ms. Walqui argues that ESL teachers themselves, as well as their content-area peers, need to reconceptualize what language is and evolve from their concentrated focus on vocabulary and grammar or on how to make a request or express a hypothesis.

"Students are too often engaged in the production of sentences with vocabulary they have learned," Ms. Walqui said. "But a sentence is an isolated unit of language that would never really count as deep engagement with academic work, which is what the common core is all about."

Content All Day

Deep engagement with content is how a network of 16 high schools that specialize in serving recently arrived immigrants in California, New York, and Virginia, approaches instruction for English-learners.

"Every single teacher is a teacher of language and content," said Claire Sylvan, the executive director and president of the Internationals Network for Public Schools, based in New York City. "If you want these students to learn rigorous academic content and gain dexterity in the new language, you better be doing more than 15 minutes a day of English-language instruction and better be doing rigorous content all day long."

In the Internationals network schools, students with varying levels of English proficiency, as well as those in different grade levels, are purposely mixed in classrooms. That way, more-experienced students help "acculturate" the newer arrivals, and a team of teachers sticks with the same group for two full years. That team—consisting of math, science, English/language arts, and social studies teachers, at least one of whom is also an ESL expert—share responsibility for the same cohort of students over time.

Each school is autonomous, but the network provides hundreds of digital lesson plans and other resources that integrate language instruction with content. Any teacher among the 16 schools can tap those, said Ms. Sylvan.

"All the units our teachers have developed are designed to have students using their language in group projects, talking with each other, and actively engaged in discourse, no matter how imperfect it may be," Ms. Sylvan said.

While most of the teachers working in the International schools are not necessarily trained in second-language acquisition or how to work with English-learners when they are hired, Ms. Sylvan said principals screen aggressively for prospective faculty members who are willing to learn.

'Push-in' Model

At another New York City school, John J. Pershing Middle School, where 40 percent of the 1,300 students are English-learners, Marcus Artigliere and his team of six fellow ESL teachers are working together, and with their core-content peers, to craft common-core lessons in English/language arts and math that outline explicit supports and "scaffolds" for ELLs, based on their proficiency levels.

They are doing that at the same time the school is shifting from pulling its ELL students out of mainstream classes for explicit language instruction to a "push-in" model in which the ESL teachers are always in the classrooms with content teachers.

"We think this is the only way that the shift to the common core is going to work for our English-learners," said Mr. Artigliere, who is also an instructional coach at the Brooklyn school. "The goal is that you have the ESL professional right in the room to model for content teachers how you scaffold the content for English-learners."

In Broward County, Fla., where state law requires all academic content teachers to have some training in the theories and practice of teaching second-language learners, the district's curriculum and instruction team has created an open-source trove of digital professional-development resources around the common core, in addition to face-to-face training. The district has produced a series of webinars to address particular instructional shifts in the new standards. Each of those also has a companion webinar specifically targeting teachers who work with ELLs, said David Shelley, the district's curriculum supervisor for literacy. Teachers in school-based professional learning communities watch the webinars together and engage in discussions about strategies and supports they can use for all students.

"All of our teachers, whether they are mainstream content teachers or ESL teachers, are getting this professional development and are doing it together," said Vicky B. Saldala, the director of the district's English-as-a-second-language department.

Ms. Saldala's team wrote a "best practices" document for English-learners meant for all teachers in need of understanding what types of classroom activities and supports work best for ELLs at different proficiency levels and in different subject areas. It also breaks down which supports are most effective across the four language domains of speaking, listening, reading, and writing, she said. Thirteen percent of Broward's 265,000 students are English-learners.

Principal's Role

Key to any type of meaningful collaboration and inclusion of ESL professionals in the rollout of the common core, said Ms. Aronson, are principals and district administrators willing to give faculty members the time and space to work together.

"The principal especially plays a huge role for encouraging and facilitating an inclusive school culture that promotes ESL teachers and content teachers working together, but unfortunately, they are the ones who often erect the biggest barriers to this," she said.

At Beaverton's Meadow Park Middle School, Principal Toshiko Maurizio is backing the work of the three teachers who have taken the lead in devising common-core support strategies for the school's English-learners. She has carved out staff-development time for them to collaborate and share their work.

Their work is particularly challenging because ESL teachers like Ms. Page do not work alongside content teachers in the classroom. English-learners are pulled out for language instruction as part of their school day, and they are grouped based on proficiency levels, not grade level.

To help cross those barriers, Ms. Page created a Google document that all teachers in her school can access to write what key concepts they want their ELL students to understand in an upcoming lesson or unit. She plans her language instruction around those core-content requests, though she says it's an imperfect process.

"I'm really working on my juggling skills," Ms. Page said. "Folding in the core content at grade level into language instruction is really tough, especially when you are working with students at different grade levels. We don't have it all figured out, but we are trying. We are committed."

Critical Thinking

1. What can be learned about the challenges that CCS present for ELL from the Oregon school?
2. How are these challenges differently nuanced in the Broward and New York examples?
3. Describe the "push-in" strategy.

Internet References

For Teachers of English Learners, Common Core Means Double the Work
   https://hechingerreport.org/for-teachers-of-english-learners-common-core-means-double-the-work/

The Common Core State Standards and English Learners: A Resource Page
   https://www.tesol.org/advance-the-field/standards/the-common-core-state-standards-and-english-learners

---

Maxwell, Lesli A. "ESL and Classroom Teachers Team Up to Teach Common Core." Education Week, October 28, 2013. Used by permission of Editorial Projects in Education.

Article

Prepared by: Sheron Fraser-Burgess, *Ball State University*

A Better Chance to Learn: Bilingual Bicultural Education

UNITED STATES COMMISSION ON CIVIL RIGHTS

Learning Outcomes

After reading this article, you will be able to:

- Describe the United States Commission on Civil Rights' policy position on the subject of the educational rights of students from minority language backgrounds.
- Describe the United States Commission on Civil Rights' support for programming in bilingual-bicultural education.
- Explain how the U.S. Supreme Court's decision in *Lau v. Nichols* (1974) affected the rights of limited English proficiency (LEP) students in the public schools.

Appearing in the third edition of *Notable Selections in Education* (now known as *Classic Education Sources: Education*), this excerpt introduces the history of focused bilingual-bicultural programs in the United States, stemming from the 1964 Civil Rights Act Title VI to provide special language programs for those children speaking a non–English native language and belonging to an identifiable "minority" group.

From Fred Schultz's introduction in *Notable Selections in Education*: "In May 1975 the United States Commission on Civil Rights issued a thoroughly documented, in-depth statement on the history of the education of language minority students in the United States and on how the struggle of language minority students to achieve equality of educational opportunity is linked to the broader struggle for equality in the field of education. The commission specifically discussed the direct relationship between the United States Supreme Court decision in *Brown v. Board of Education of Topeka, Kansas* (1954) and various federal court decisions involving the educational rights of limited English proficiency (LEP) students. The commission's document was distributed to all public school districts that had or were putting into place either bilingual educational programs or English as a Second Language programs for language minority children. This document, *A Better Chance to Learn: Bilingual Bicultural Education*, is excerpted in the following selection. In it, the commission clarifies how the Supreme Court decision in *Lau v. Nichols* (1975) is based on Fourteenth Amendment 'equal protection of the laws' precedents, which had led the Court to declare in *Brown* that segregated schools are 'inherently unequal.' The historical precedents for bilingual educational programs in the United States are also reviewed in the document." (Schultz, 2001, p. 236)

. . .

No public institution has a greater or more direct impact on future opportunity than the school. Between the ages of 6 and 16, American children spend much of their time in school. Early educational success or failure dictates to a large extent a student's expectations for the future, including whether he or she will seek postsecondary education and thus have a wide range of economic options available following formal schooling. The importance of an equal opportunity to public education was underscored in the case of *Brown v. Board of Education* and was followed in the 1960's by civil rights activity to end segregated schools. Similarly, much of the effort to overcome discrimination against limited or non-English speaking persons in the 1970's has been focused on schools.

The term "language minority" is used in this report to refer to persons in the United States who speak a non-English native language and who belong to an identifiable minority group of generally low socioeconomic status. Such language minority groups—including Mexican Americans, Puerto Ricans, Native Americans, and Asian Americans—have been subject to discrimination and limited opportunity. The emphasis given attainment of an education places them at a further disadvantage, since the public school does not appear to have met the needs of language minority groups.

Not only have many language minority children been subject to segregated education, low teacher expectations, cultural incompatibility with dominant culture-oriented curricula, and the educational neglect experienced by minority children in general, many also face a unique and equally severe form of discrimination which results from lack of proficiency in the language of instruction. In January 1974, the Supreme Court affirmed in *Lau* v. *Nichols* that school districts are compelled under Title VI of the Civil Rights Act of 1964 to provide children who speak little or no English with special language programs which will give them an equal opportunity to an education. The form such assistance should take is the subject of debate among educators, concerned language minority parents, and others.

There is little disagreement that learning English is essential to economic and social mobility in this monolingual English speaking society. The main controversy surrounds the issue of how language minority children can be taught English in a manner so that they do not fall so far behind in subject matter instruction that they cannot recover. Questions also have been raised concerning what methods are best for teaching English to language minority students; whether the learning of English alone will equalize educational opportunity and what role, if any, should be played by the native language and culture in the educational process.

Bilingual bicultural education is instruction using the native language and culture as a basis for learning subjects until second language skills have been developed sufficiently; it is the most widely discussed of approaches to providing language minority children with an equal educational opportunity. On the one hand, it has been hailed as a sound educational approach that overcomes the incompatibility between language minority students and the monolingual English public school. On the other, it has been criticized as failing to provide language minority students with sufficient English skills and as fostering ethnic separateness.

In this report, the Commission examines the extent to which bilingual bicultural education is an effective educational approach for increasing the opportunity of language minority students. In undertaking this study, the Commission assessed the educational principles behind bilingual bicultural education but did not analyze findings from existing bilingual bicultural programs, since few reliable evaluation data are available.

Because of the Commission's civil rights jurisdiction, this report concentrates primarily on bilingual bicultural education as a means for overcoming a denial of equal educational opportunity. However, another valuable objective of bilingual bicultural education is the enrichment of the education of children of all socioeconomic levels and racial/ethnic groups through learning two languages and two cultures....

The Need Today

Although the height of immigration has long since passed, a large proportion of Americans still have a native language that is other than English. According to the 1970 census, 33.2 million Americans, or roughly 16 percent of the population, speak a language other than English as a native tongue. Spanish, German, and Italian speakers are the most numerous, in that order. Spanish is the only one of the three which has experienced substantial growth in the number of speakers since 1940, largely owing to increased immigration from Latin America.

Although persons of Mexican origin are native to the Southwest, the number of Spanish speaking persons in this country has grown noticeably since 1920. In the 1920's two factors contributed to a major influx of Mexican immigrants: a socially disruptive revolution in Mexico and the agricultural development of the Southwest United States and the subsequent need for labor. Between 1920 and 1973, 1,480,887 or more than 60 percent of all Mexican immigrants came to the United States.

Similarly, since 1920, Puerto Ricans have migrated in greater numbers, stimulated by the crowded living and bad economic conditions of Puerto Rico and the need in urban areas for low-paid, unskilled workers. The Puerto Rican migration swelled from 7,000 in 1920 to 852,061 in 1970.

Between 1920 and 1973, 215,778 Central Americans and 487,925 South Americans immigrated to this country. By 1973, Spanish origin persons numbered 9,072,602 nationwide and constituted the second largest minority group in the United States at roughly 4.4 percent of the total American population.

Immigration continues to be a major source for increasing the size of American language minority communities. Asian groups, for example, have experienced rapid increases in size since restrictive legislation barring or limiting their entry was repealed. In the less than 10 years since 1965, when all immigration quotas were liberalized, 654,736 or more than one-third of all Asian immigrants since 1820 have entered the United States. In 1973 more Asians immigrated than any other group. Other language minority groups, including Italians, Greeks, French Canadians, and Portuguese, have been part of a steady stream of language minorities coming to this country.

The 1970 census estimates that 31 percent of the 760,572 Native Americans counted speak a Native American tongue as their first language. Unlike the other groups, the survival of Native American languages is primarily the result of their continued use by existing groups and geographic isolation, rather than of replenishment through immigration.

Although precise data are not available on the numbers of limited or non-English speaking children currently in school, at the present time, the U.S. Office of Education estimates that at least 5 million need special language programs. The Census Bureau reports that 4.5 million Spanish speaking children under 20 years of age speak Spanish at home. An estimated 259,830 Asian American children speak little or no English, and some 56,493 Native American children speak a Native American language as a first language.

Unlike earlier non-English speaking children in this country, these children face an increasingly technical, skills-oriented society. There has been a shift in jobs from manual labor to skilled occupations. Although there is no direct correlation between years of schooling and ability to perform many jobs, educational level has become one frequently employed means of differentiating job applicants from one another.

Educators have known for many years that language minority children have difficulty succeeding in English monolingual schools. As early as 1930 it was documented that, in Texas, overageness and dropout rates were higher for Mexican American children than for either black or white students, and that most Mexican American children never progressed beyond third grade. In addition, while approximately 95 percent of Anglo children were enrolled in schools, only 50 percent of Mexican American children were. The causes were considered at the time to include lack of English language knowledge, low socioeconomic status, and inaccurate measuring instruments.

Although some scattered attempts were made to improve the education of Mexican American children from 1920–1940, no large scale effort was undertaken to alter the effects of education on them. A number of questions were raised about the education of non-English speaking children, including whether children would suffer less language handicap in school if first instruction in reading were in their native language. In the 1940's one researcher called for action to be taken by the Texas Department of Education, teacher training institutions, and schools to better meet the needs of Spanish speaking students. In 1946, the First Regional Conference on the Education of Spanish-speaking People in the Southwest was held in Austin, Texas. Recommendations included an end to segregated schools for Spanish speaking children, improved teacher training, and more efficiency in teaching English.

That public education continued to neglect the needs of language minority students for another 20 years is evident in the fact that recommendations of the 1964 Orange County Conference on the Education of Spanish Speaking Children and Youth were almost identical to those developed 18 years before. Nearly three decades after the First Regional Conference on the Education of Spanish-speaking People compiled information on the difficulties experienced by Mexican American students, the U.S. Commission on Civil Rights conducted a five-year Mexican American education study. It revealed that problems of segregation, teacher training, and language difficulty are still severe for Mexican American students in the five Southwestern States. In addition, the Commission's State Advisory Committees have examined the problems of Puerto Ricans, Native Americans, and Asian Americans. All of these studies document the continuing failure of public schools to provide language minority children with a meaningful education.

Compared with the median number of 12.0 school years completed for whites, the median is 8.1 for Mexican Americans, 8.6 for Puerto Ricans, 9.8 for Native Americans, and 12.4 for Asian Americans. The Commission's Mexican American Education Study shows that 40 percent of Mexican Americans who enter first grade never complete high school. As of 1972, the dropout rate for Puerto Ricans in New York City from 10th grade to graduation was 57 percent. In New England, 25 percent of the Spanish speaking student population had been retained in grade for at least 3 years; 50 percent, for at least 2 years. Only 12 percent were found to be in the correct grade for their age group. The dropout rate for Native Americans in the Southwest between grades 9 and 12 is 30.6 percent. For Navajos, the largest Native American tribe, the median educational level achieved is fifth grade.

Academic achievement scores recorded for language minority groups in the 1966 Coleman report show that they lag significantly behind majority group Americans. By the 12th grade the Mexican American student is 4.1 years behind the national norm in math achievement; 3.5, in verbal ability; and 3.3, in reading. The Puerto Rican student is 4.8 years behind the national norm in math; 3.6, in verbal ability; and 3.2, in reading. The Asian American student is 0.9 years behind the norm in math; 1.6, in verbal ability; and 1.6, in reading. Studies indicate that the longer language minority students stay in school the further they fall behind their classmates in grade level achievements. On tests of general information—including humanities, social sciences, and natural sciences—the median 12th grade score is 43.3 for Mexican Americans, 41.7 for Puerto Ricans, 44.7 for Native Americans, and 49.0 for Asian Americans as compared to a median score of 52.2 for whites.

In the 1960's there was a growing recognition that language minority children needed some manner of special assistance if they were to have an opportunity to succeed in school. Where efforts were made to provide such assistance, they usually took the form of supplemental English language development, or what is commonly known as the English as a Second Language (ESL) approach. In 1968, the Bilingual Education Act provided funds to support a few bilingual programs, which were to use the children's native language and culture for instruction while they were learning English. Since 1971, Massachusetts, Texas, Illinois, and New Jersey have enacted mandatory bilingual education laws.

The first expression of Executive policy in the area of equal educational opportunity for language minority students came in 1970 when the Department of Health, Education, and Welfare (HEW) issued its May 25 Memorandum, which required federally-funded school districts to provide assistance for language minority children. The memorandum indicated that failure to provide such assistance, where needed, would be considered a violation of Title VI of the Civil Rights Act of 1964.

In *Lau* v. *Nichols*, the Supreme Court affirmed that interpretation of Title VI's scope, stating:

> Under these state-imposed standards there is no equality of treatment merely by providing students with the same facilities, textbooks, teachers, and curriculum; for students who do not understand English are effectively foreclosed from any meaningful education.
>
> Basic English skills are at the very core of what these public schools teach. Imposition of a requirement that, before a child can effectively participate in the educational program, he must already have acquired those basic skills is to make a mockery of public education. We know that those who do not understand English are certain to find their classroom experiences wholly incomprehensible and in no way meaningful.
>
> ...It seems obvious that the Chinese-speaking minority receives less benefits than the English-speaking majority from respondents' school system which denies them a meaningful opportunity to participate in the education program....

Both HEW and the Supreme Court declined to prescribe for school districts the type of assistance program which would provide language minority children with equal benefits in the attainment of an education, leaving the ultimate decision to the local districts themselves. Many school districts are faced with determining what constitutes that equality of educational opportunity. If we assume that the goal of public education is to provide basic skills and knowledge needed for participation in American society, then equal educational opportunity means that all students should have the same chance to acquire those skills and knowledge. In considering ESL and bilingual bicultural education—the two major approaches to meeting the needs of language minority children—it is important, therefore, to examine their overall potential for providing such an education....

Conclusion

The Commission's basic conclusion is that bilingual bicultural education is the program of instruction which currently offers the best vehicle for large numbers of language minority students who experience language difficulty in our schools.

Many language minority children, including Mexican Americans, Puerto Ricans, Native Americans, and Asian Americans, face two obstacles in attaining an education. Not only may they be the target of discrimination because they belong to identifiable minority groups, they also may not understand English well enough to keep up with their English speaking counterparts.

Under *Lau* v. *Nichols*, the Supreme Court has held that school districts receiving Federal funds cannot discriminate against children of limited or non-English speaking ability by denying them the language training they need for meaningful participation in the educational process. In this report, the Commission has examined whether the bilingual bicultural education approach is an effective means of providing that opportunity. Primary emphasis was placed on the educational principles which support the use of the native language in educating children, in nurturing positive self concept, and in developing proficiency in English. However, consideration was also given the effect on successful learning of the attitudes toward language minority groups in this country.

Critical Thinking

1. What sorts of bilingual-bicultural programs are best for language minority students?
2. Should students in the United States who do not know how to speak or read English receive special help in learning English?
3. How do you discuss this topic with those members of the community who support English First?

Internet References

National Association for Multicultural Education
www.nameorg.org

The National Association for Bilingual Education
www.nabe.org

Teachers of English to Speakers of Other Languages
www.tesol.org

From A Better Chance to Learn: Bilingual-Bicultural Education by United States Commission on Civil Rights, 1975

UNIT

Prepared by: Sheron Fraser-Burgess, *Ball State University*

Twenty-First Century Learning Technology and Integration

Technology has been a change agent in education. After experiencing early motion pictures in 1913, Thomas Edison declared that books would become obsolete in schools because we would be able to learn everything from movies. Most recently, we have heard similar claims about digital books from advocates of Kindle, Nook, iPad, and other e-readers and sellers of audio books. What is really happening in our schools? Are textbooks disappearing? Is everyone connected? Are our students sitting all day laboring over a keyboard and staring at a screen? In this unit, we will explore both the potential of the digital technology and the challenges of using this technology for teaching and learning.

There are significant trends noted by Bitter and Pierson (2002) that continue to be important to this discussion even now, thirteen years later. The first is the shift in demographics within our student population. We are seeing an increased numbers of students who do not live in traditional family structures, who have special needs at both the high and low ends of achievement, who are English Language Learners, or who live in poverty. For many of these students, the ability to access sophisticated technology may not exist in their homes or neighborhoods. Hence, schools are the only place where they can be exposed to and learn about the usage of technology. These students, many of whom will need technology to access the curriculum, will pose a considerable challenge to public schools. An additional challenge, according to Bitter and Pierson, will be the acceleration of technological change that correspondingly increases the pace of change in our knowledge base. Keeping up in one's field of expertise or areas of interest has become a full-time job of its own.

In most schools, regardless of where the school is regionally or economically, most teachers who use computers do so because computers make their jobs easier and help complete tasks more efficiently. The computer can do things the teacher cannot, or is unwilling to, do. We use them to keep digital grade books that will correctly calculate final grades in a flash; search for information to use in lectures; create photos and clip art to illustrate our PowerPoints; obtain lesson plans to meet state standards; and communicate with peers down the hall, the principal, and even with parents. But too often, the teacher's computer may be the only computer in a classroom. There may be a computer lab down the hall or a few computers in the media center, but very few schools have laptops or handhelds for all students. So almost 100 years ago, Thomas Edison may have been a bit hasty to declare books a thing of the past. In the *Education* 98/99, we published an article, *The Silicon Classroom* by Kaplan and Rogers (1996) in which they declared that schools were rushing to spend billions on computers without a clue on what to do with them. In present day classrooms, we continue to see the challenges that schools face in implementing computer usage in the classroom. These issues are economic, social, and philosophic. Why haven't we seen greater strides made to bring every school into the digital age? We hope the articles presented in this unit will challenge you to consider how you should and will use technology to remove barriers to the curriculum within your content area.

How do we respond when confronted with the accusation that too many teachers and schools are using 19th century methods to teach 21st century students? Some see a rebellion happening in schools as students are unable to relate to the teaching methods and materials presented in most classrooms. This is a non-violent rebellion, but it is nonetheless disturbing to see students who are not fully engaged in active learning experiences and frustrated in their desires for more.

If we are in the middle of a rebellion or revolution, even a non-violent one, we will need weapons to take into battle. The article on collaborative technology provides an interesting array of weapons, or rather technology tools, that are easily accessible to teachers and their students. Most of us know about Google Docs, but how does that software and other Web 2.0

applications support students' ability to meet Common Core Standards?

In an effort to make the most of face-to-face classroom time, many teachers are flipping their classes. Rather than looking for reasons and rationales for why students were failing, teachers should look for solutions. One teacher found her solution by *flipping*. This article is a good place to start if you are not sure what flipping a classroom means. Others are looking at collaborative online tools to support learning in and out of the classroom. Thinking in new ways has helped teachers in the specials such as physical education, art, and music integrate technology into teaching, learning, and assessing.

With the increasing diversity of students in our classroom, we need to provide more and more assistive technology to meet their needs. If we look around we can find technologies that will work for *all* students. Calculators may be available in math and even in science classes, but what about their use in social studies and language arts classes where students may want to average grades or percentages in class elections. Digital cameras can be used to document notes on the board from class discussions, posters they need to remember, or even a slide from a multimedia presentation. Dictionaries allow students with disabilities, who are ELL, or even gifted, to look up a definition of a new word (Melville, 2005).

The articles in this section explore the technical, social and pedagogical aspects of incorporating technology in classrooms. As a group, they focus on technology not as an end in itself but as a means to a desirable and valued end. For example, the research article on standards-based technology integration draws upon the TPACK model to prose a more contextualized framework for emergent bilinguals. On this reading, the affordances of the various platforms can be utilized to escalate English language learning.

Hopefully, the articles in this unit will stimulate your imagination to consider using more technology in your classroom or using what you have more creatively.

References

Bitter, G. & M. Pierson. 2002. *Using Technology in the Classroom*. Boston, MA: Allyn and Bacon.

Melville, E. (2005). Cell Phones: Nuisance or Necessity. *Teaching Today*. Retrieved on 15 May 2012 from http://privateschool.about.com/gi/o.htm?zi=1/XJ&zTi=1&sdn=privateschool&cdn=education&tm=26&gps=234_220_1066_560&f=l20&tt=13&bt=1&bts=1&zu=http%3A//www.glencoe.com/sec/teachingtoday/educationupclose.phtml/52

Article

Prepared by: Sheron Fraser-Burgess, *Ball State University*

Standards-based Technology Integration for Emergent Bilinguals

BRIANA RONAN

Learning Outcomes

After reading this article, you will be able to:

- Distinguish between achieving technical knowledge mastery and technology integration.

- Use the criteria of whether emergent bilinguals are able to thoughtfully use technology to enhance their reading, writing, speaking, and listening skills as a standard of its effectiveness

- Delineate the revised TPACK framework for emergent bilinguals.

Today's educators serve the United States public-school system at a time of considerable curricular, technological, and demographic change. In 2010, the Common Core State Standards in Math and English Language Arts significantly altered the curricular landscape of K-12 classrooms. On the heels of this reform came the adoptions of English Development/Proficiency Standards and Next Generation Science Standards.

These new standards are not only more academically rigorous, but they also call for teachers to prepare students for successful learning with 21st century tools. Increased expectations for technology integration have resulted in school districts seeking ways to improve their Internet infrastructure and provide 1:1 computing devices for all students.

Such standards reform and technology demands have also come at a time of significant demographic change in the U.S., particularly in states like California, where emergent bilingual students comprise over 22% of the K-12 public school population and represent over 60 language groups (California Department of Education, 2015b). Teachers of emergent bilinguals are often faced with unique changes to support their students in meeting the new content and English language standards while also gaining equitable access to technology.

This article aims to address this challenge by presenting a standards-based framework for supporting technology integration with emergent bilingual students. The framework adapts a leading model for technology integration, the Technological, Pedagogical, and Content Knowledge (TPACK) model, and aligns it with English Language Development (ELD) and International Society for Technology in Education (ISTE) standards. The article also discusses exemplar activities, technologies, and essential planning questions to aid teachers in designing technology-integrated lessons for a multicultural, multilingual student population.

Theoretical Framework: TPACK Model

In developing a framework for technology integration for emergent bilinguals, it helps to examine existing frameworks and models. The leading model in the field of education is the TPACK framework. Mishra and Koehler (2006) developed this framework in an effort to address a significant oversight in technology integration. They noted that all too often teacher training and professional development tend to emphasize the technical functions of technology.

For example, how does a device turn on/off, create student accounts, access reporting options, or connect to peripheral devices? This emphasis on technological knowledge is prioritized to the exclusion of how the technology can be used in concert with content knowledge and pedagogical knowledge. Thus, TPACK was proposed as an effort to apply a much-needed theoretical basis for understanding what constitutes effective technology integration (Mishra & Koehler, 2006).

The TPACK framework builds on the work of Shulman (1986), who sought to integrate two previously separate and discrete bodies of knowledge—content knowledge and pedagogical knowledge. Shulman was concerned with how content can be best organized, adapted, and represented to learners through pedagogical techniques and strategies.

The result of this intersection was Pedagogical Content Knowledge (PCK). Shulman (1986) conceptualizes PCK as including "the most regularly taught topics in one's subject area, the most useful forms of representation of those ideas, the most powerful analogies, illustrations, examples, explanations, and demonstrations—in a word the ways of representing and formulating the subject that make it comprehensible to others" (p. 9). When teachers develop a sophisticated understanding of PCK, they are better prepared to anticipate and address their students' struggles and misconceptions.

When teachers can do all of this with the aid of technology, then they add another unified body of knowledge to their toolbox: TPACK. This body of knowledge lies at the intersection of technological knowledge, content knowledge, and pedagogical knowledge (see Figure 1). The TPACK model is not about learning the newest and most popular digital tool, but rather how teachers can use such digital tools to represent content in new ways, enhance particular instructional approaches or strategies, and build on existing knowledge in order to improve or enhance understanding of content and pedagogy.

For teachers of emergent bilinguals, TPACK includes developing a deep understanding of English Language Development as a content area (content knowledge), various pedagogical techniques to support teaching ELD (pedagogical knowledge), and effective use of technology and digital tools to facilitate students' language development (technological knowledge). One aim of this article is to discuss what counts as TPACK for English Language Development, specifically how it is defined within California's English Language Arts/English Language Development Framework (California Department of Education, 2015a).

Pedagogical Language Knowledge

Unlike other content areas, such as math, science, social studies, or even English Language Arts, English Language Development is not a subject area that all students receive in schools. Rather, it is reserved for emergent bilinguals, students who learn English as an additional or new language. The California Department of Education considers ELD to be a "specialized instructional support" that fosters academic English development and full access to the other core subjects (California Department of Education, 2015a, p. 10). Given its unique position and purpose in the curriculum, ELD requires a PCK that is quite distinct from other disciplines.

Traditionally, educational linguists have considered knowledge of second language acquisition theories and linguistic features and structures of English, such as syntax, semantics, and phonology to be essential in teaching ELD (Freeman & Freeman, 2004). However, more recent reviews of PCK for ELD/ESL educators have noted that such decontextualized, linguistic knowledge bases are often insufficient in supporting students' access to the core academic curriculum (Galguera, 2011; Bunch, 2013).

Instead, a newer perspective argues for the development of Pedagogical Language Knowledge (PLK) which is defined as the "knowledge of language directly related to disciplinary teaching and learning and situated in the particular (and multiple) contexts in which teaching and learning take place" (Bunch, 2013, p. 307). PLK distinguishes itself from PCK in that it emphasizes the integration of language with content area teaching and learning.

A PLK vision of ELD instruction includes teaching students to identify and analyze key linguistic features and structures of disciplinary texts, such as comparative clauses in math problems or the passive voice in social studies and science informational texts. This same emphasis on language is a hallmark of the Common Core State Standards in Math and ELA.

These newer standards are considerably more language and literacy-focused than previous standards, requiring students to engage in purposeful meaning-making with a variety of complex text individually and in collaboration with others (Bunch, 2013; California Department of Education, 2015a).

When California revised its English Language Development Standards in 2012, it did so in an effort to align with and support the language demands of the Common Core State Standards. The revision resulted in several significant shifts in its definition of PLK. Rather than seeing language development as a set of grammatical rules to be mastered by an individual learner, the new framework situates language as a resource for interactive, meaning-making in a social context (California Department of Education, 2015a).

Prior to these new standards, ELD was often taught in isolation from the core content with standards organized by reading, writing, listening, and speaking skills. In the new framework, ELD instruction draws to and from the content area and the standards are organized by communicative modes and linguistic processes.

The California ELD standards are organized in two main parts (see Appendix A). Part I of the ELD standards, "Interacting in Meaningful Ways," focuses on the communicative functions of English. It consists of three main communicative modes: Collaborative, Interpretive, and Productive. The second part of the ELD standards, "Learning How English Works," focuses on linguistic forms and structures of the English Language. Part II of the standards consists of three main linguistic processes:

countries. There are a number of organizations, like iLEARN, that match classrooms from around the world to work on common projects. Alternatively, colleagues at different schools in the same state or school district can set-up similar class-to-class relationships using video-conferencing platforms.

When designing collaborative activities for students, it is important for teachers to keep in mind the technological knowledge and language skills of each member, so that all students have an opportunity to contribute to the work of the group.

Conclusion

When educators plan ways to integrate technology into their instruction for emergent bilingual students, it is essential that they keep in mind the unique characteristics and needs of the students and their classroom context. The activities and technologies discussed in this article are merely presented as starting points for consideration. In evaluating whether a particular activity or technological tool will benefit their students, a teacher might consider the following questions:

What are my learning goals for my classroom community? How do these goals/tools relate to content knowledge standards, ISTE standards, and ELD standards?

Then one might ask:

What are my students' prior knowledge and experience with this particular content/tool? How can it build on their linguistic repertoires?

Finally, one might consider the available technology in the classroom.

To what extent does available technology build and expand on my students' knowledge and help achieve my learning goals?

If the technology doesn't provide a meaningful difference in how the content is represented or the nature of the work that students engage in, then one might consider if technology is really necessary or if other forms of technology are needed.

However, when considered thoughtfully and carefully, technology integration can provide rewarding and motivating experiences for teacher and students alike. For emergent bilingual students in particular, technology integration can be a valuable vehicle for fostering creativity, self-expression, and academic achievement.

References

Bunch, G. C. (2013). Pedagogical language knowledge: Preparing mainstream teachers for English learners in the new standards era. Review of Research in Education, 37(1), 298–341.

California Department of Education. (2015a). English language arts/English language development framework for California public schools. Sacramento, CA: Author.

California Department of Education. (2015b). Facts about English learners in California. Retrieved from http://www.cde.ca.gov/ds/sd/cb/cefelfacts.asp

California Department of Education. (2012). California English language development standards: Kindergarten through grade 12. Sacramento, CA: Author.

Cummins, J. (2005). A proposal for action: Strategies for recognizing heritage language competence as a learning resource within the mainstream classroom. Modern Language Journal, 585–592.

Freeman, D. E., & Freeman, Y. S. (2004). Essential Linguistics: What you need to know to teach reading, ESL, spelling, phonics, and grammar. Portsmouth, NH: Heinemann.

Galguera, T. (2011). Participant structures as professional learning tasks and the development of pedagogical language knowledge among preservice teachers. Teacher Education Quarterly, 38(1), 85–106.

Harris, J., Hofer, M., Blanchard, M., Grandgenett, N., Schmidt, D., van Olphen, M., & Young, C. (2010). "Grounded" technology integration: Instructional planning using curriculum-based activity type taxonomies. Journal of Technology and Teacher Education, 18(4), 573–605

International Society for Technology in Education. (2016). ISTE standards for students. Retrieved from https://www.iste.org/standards/standards/for-students

Mishra, P., & Koehler, M. J. (2006). Technological pedagogical content knowledge: A framework for teacher knowledge. Teachers College Record, 108(6), 1017.

National Governors Association Center for Best Practices, Council of Chief State School Officers. (2010). Common core state standards for English language arts and literacy in history/social studies, science, and technical subjects. Washington DC: Authors.

Polly, D., Mims, C., Shepherd, C. E., & Inan, F. (2010). Evidence of impact: Transforming teacher education with preparing tomorrow's teachers to teach with technology (PT3) grants. Teaching and Teacher Education: An International Journal of Research and Studies, 26(4), 863–870.

Ronan, B. (2017). Digital tools for supporting English language learners' content area writing. In M. Carrier, R. M. Damerow, and K. M. Bailey (Eds.), Digital language learning and teaching (93–103). New York, NY: Routledge.

Rymes, B., Flores, N., & Pomerantz, A. (2016). The common core state standards and English learners: Finding the silver lining. Language, 92(4), e257–e273.

Shulman, L. (1986). Those who understand: Knowledge growth in teaching. Educational Researcher, 15(2), 4–14.

Appendix A

California English Language Development Standards (California Department of Education, 2012)

Part I: Interacting in Meaningful Ways

A. Collaborative
1. Exchanging information and ideas via oral communication and conversations
2. Interacting via written English (print and multimedia)
3. Offering opinions and negotiating with or persuading others
4. Adapting language choices to various contexts

B. Interpretive
5. Listening actively and asking or answering questions
6. Reading closely and explaining interpretations and ideas from reading
7. Evaluating how well writers and speakers use language to present ideas
8. Analyzing how writers use vocabulary and other language resources

C. Productive
9. Expressing information and ideas in oral presentations
10. Writing literary and informational texts
11. Supporting opinions or justifying arguments and evaluating those of others
12. Selecting and applying varied, precise vocabulary and other language resources

Part II: Learning About How English Works

A. Structuring Cohesive Texts
1. Understanding text structure and organization
2. Understanding cohesion

B. Expanding and Enriching Ideas
3. Using verbs and verb phrases
4. Using nouns and noun phrases
5. Modifying to add details
6. Connecting and Condensing Ideas
7. Connecting ideas within sentences by combining clauses
8. Condensing ideas within sentences using a variety of language resources

Appendix B
ISTE Standards for Students
(International Society for Technology in Education, 2016)

1. Empowered Learner: Students leverage technology to take an active role in choosing, achieving and demonstrating competency in their learning goals, informed by the learning sciences.
2. Digital Citizen: Students recognize the rights, responsibilities and opportunities of living, learning and working in an interconnected digital world, and they act and model in ways that are safe, legal and ethical.
3. Knowledge Constructor: Students critically curate a variety of resources using digital tools to construct knowledge, produce creative artifacts and make meaningful learning experiences for themselves and others.
4. Innovative Designer: Students use a variety of technologies within a design process to identify and solve problems by creating new, useful or imaginative solutions.
5. Computational Thinker: Students develop and employ strategies for understanding and solving problems in ways that leverage the power of technological methods to develop and test solutions.
6. Creative Communicator: Students communicate clearly and express themselves creatively for a variety of purposes using the platforms, tools, styles, formats and digital media appropriate to their goals.
7. Global Collaborator: Students use digital tools to broaden their perspectives and enrich their learning by collaborating with others and working effectively in teams locally and globally.

Critical Thinking

1. What challenges are characteristic to ELL that technology can address?
2. Relate the benefits of a collaboration with platforms like Google Doc for achieving technology integration with emergent bilinguals.
3. How do Web 2.0 platforms supersede the limitations of the TPACK model?

Internet References

A Standards-Based Technology Integration Path at Towson University
https://www.citejournal.org/volume-4/issue-1-04/general/a-standards-based-technology-integration-path-at-towson-university/

ISTE Standards
https://www.iste.org/standards

BRIANA RONAN is an assistant professor in the School of Education at California Polytechnic State University, San Luis Obispo.

Article

Prepared by: Sheron Fraser-Burgess, *Ball State University*

Utilizing Technology in Physical Education: Addressing the Obstacles of Integration

The use of technology to enhance the educational experience has become a standard within all content areas. Physical education is not exempt from this standard, although implementation of technology use has been difficult because of the unique nature of the physical education classroom environment. The authors discuss the obstacles that teachers and administrators face while integrating technology into the physical education environment, as well as approaches that can be taken to overcome those obstacles.

BETH PYLE AND KERI ESSLINGER

Learning Outcomes

After reading this article, you will be able to:

- Justify reasons to overcome the roadblocks to integrating technology into physical education.
- Develop a lesson plan with two appropriate implementations of technology.

Technology and physical education (PE) are often considered at opposite ends of the educational spectrum—one sedentary and the other requiring movement. Tony Hall, in his keynote lecture given at the *International Association of Physical Education in Higher Education 2011 Conference*, addressed this very dilemma, suggesting that interactive technology needs be a solution to, rather than a reason for, "the serious contemporary educational and societal problems of inactivity, hypokinetic, and sedentary living" (Hall, 2012, p. 106). However, establishing or crossing the bridge with technology on one side and PE on the other can be difficult because of two major roadblocks—those from the perceptions of administrators and those self-imposed by physical educators. These roadblocks are not insurmountable, but they do require a plan, resting on the important idea that technology should enhance teaching, not replace it (Juniu, 2011).

Administrative Roadblocks

Administrators and faculty technology committees often overlook the technology needs of PE. This oversight is not necessarily intentional but more often occurs because they are unaware of the technology possibilities within PE or because of financial restraints. Administrators may not consider the gymnasium a classroom. For instance, an interactive whiteboard is often out of the question in a gymnasium because of Internet capabilities, wiring, and safety concerns and because the gym is a multipurpose facility—often used for lunch, assemblies, interscholastic competitions, band and choral concerts, and so forth. Although having a separate classroom for PE would be ideal, it is rarely the reality, and many do not see retrofitting an older gymnasium with technology as being cost effective.

Self-Imposed Roadblocks

Even as administrators often overlook how technology and PE can be partnered, physical educators may also overlook obvious links that could create this needed relationship.

Most physical educators recognize the positives of technology in education but may not know how to implement them into the curriculum without taking away from activity time. Utilizing technology without adequate prep time for teachers to master its use may result in technology taking away from student learning and activity time (Sinclair, 2002). The key to maximizing the positive effects of technology in PE is to enlarge the physical educator's knowledge base. By starting small and enlisting the help of colleagues—with more than one person making an effort—the PE teacher can share and lessen frustration during the learning curve. For instance, creating a web page for PE on the school's website is a viable first step. Successfully implementing one piece of technology within PE will affirm its importance. It is also imperative that physical educators make administrators and technology committee members aware of the technology needs within PE.

Teacher Preparation

In teacher education, technology is frequently an area in which all student teachers must demonstrate competence. Teacher-preparation universities need to address how they are preparing future teachers in PE (Liang, Walls, Hicks, Clayton, & Yang, 2006) and emphasize the need for teacher candidates to meet technology standards (Southern Regional Education Board, n.d.). For instance, in Kentucky, technology is one of ten standards on which teacher candidates are evaluated. The candidate must display his or her ability to implement technology to (a) support instruction; (b) access and manipulate data; (c) enhance professional growth and productivity; (d) communicate and collaborate with colleagues, parents, and the community; and (e) conduct research (Kentucky Teacher Standards, 2008). The National Council for Accreditation of Teacher Education (NCATE) also emphasizes the importance of technology for teachers and for student learning.

Technology in PE

Technology can be implemented in a number of areas within the teaching of PE: unit and lesson plan preparation; classroom management; communication with parents and students; instruction and feedback; and assessment. However, too often physical educators implement technology only to meet the standards without discovering the how, why, and when to best use the technologies available ("Does Technology," 2012). Technology should be used to enhance student learning, to save time, and to motivate the student and the teacher. Technology should not be used just to meet state or district requirements. The challenge is how to find best uses of technology for PE.

Class preparation. The most common and accessible way for PE teachers to use technology is in their preparation for the school year. Numerous websites to which teachers can refer are available in this area: www.pecentral.com; www.aahperd.org/naspe; www.braingym.com; www.pe4life.org; www.letsmove.gov; and www.spark.org. At these sites, physical educators can find inspiration for units, outlines, lesson plans, and national and state standards as well as new ideas to augment their knowledge and experiences. In addition, physical educators from around the United States and the world can collaborate, share ideas, and problem solve, thereby further expanding their knowledge bases. Sharing via the Internet is also a valuable tool for new teachers as they prepare for their classes.

Classroom management. Keeping students meaningfully active is the primary goal of physical educators, but this is sometimes a difficult task. Music is a great addition to physical activities, useful for getting the students moving faster, keeping them motivated and moving, or calming them down. Software such as *GarageBand* (www.apple.com/ilife/garageband)—a tool that can create, write, or edit music as well as record songs—is advantageous to use in PE (Miller, n.d.). It allows a PE teacher to create musical loops with sound effects that the teacher then plays to signal students to move from station to station. For example, one piece of music can designate time for working at a station; a sound effect can signal equipment return at that station; another piece of music can then cue transition from one station to another; and a sound effect can signal students to begin the next station. This musical loop can be repeated until the students have moved through all the stations. Because the music is set up on a continuous loop, the PE teacher no longer needs to turn the music off and on manually or remotely to signal student rotation but can move freely about the gym, providing instruction and immediate feedback as well as monitoring off-task behavior.

Communication. A PE web page is a great technology tool with which to keep students, parents, colleagues, administrators, school board members, and the community informed. Daily PE routines, special events, review worksheets, exams, PE policies, and so forth can all be communicated to stakeholders via the Internet. Also, having an area on the web page for parents and other viewers to submit questions and concerns provides an additional opportunity for communication. PE advocacy is yet another reason for such a web page. Links to community recreation opportunities and tips on health and wellness can promote lifetime physical activity for the entire family.

However, a PE web page is only valuable if its contents are up-to-date; reading information that is 2 years old will not give others, including administrators, the impression that technology is important. PE teachers must have a systematic strategy in place to keep information current. For example, the organizational concept of *only handle it once* can be utilized to ensure timely information. PE teachers can write their units and assignments right into their web page while they plan, rather than having to plan, transfer, and update.

Instruction and feedback. Physical educators are often their own worst enemies when it comes to technology because they sense that technology operates against the very soul of their mission: to help students be physically active! *Technology and PE* appears to be an oxymoron, but the terms can complement each other. Video game consoles such as Wii (Nintendo, 2013), pedometers, heart rate monitors, iPads, active apps, interactive whiteboards, digital video recorders, and so forth can all be used to help students understand the relationships among the key components of physical education: motor skills, fitness, and physical activity. For example, a PE teacher may use a camcorder to record, share, and critique a student's performance. In their research, Banville and Polifki (2009) found a student's ability to learn and perform motor skills increased with the use of digital video recorders. Furthermore, digital videos are teacher friendly because they can be recorded and played back without any interruption to instructional time (Banville & Polifko, 2009).

Another application of technology to enhance instruction and feedback is to make available videos of appropriate skill performance and game play. Such videos can be used during the teaching, review, and assessment portions of a PE unit. Every day brings a new app for nutritional tracking, video feedback, PE rules, workout routines, and so forth. The number of apps and the rate at which they are hitting the market is astounding. Many schools are now providing iPads for each student or portable learning labs, so the possibilities of using apps for direct instruction and feedback are limitless.

Assessment. Although much of the physical skill assessment done in PE is time consuming by nature, technology can be a time saver if used properly (Graham, Holt-Hale, & Parker, 2013). For instance, to save precious in-class time for physical activity, teachers can assess cognitive knowledge with exams given online outside of class time; feedback on these exams can be immediate. Another advantage is that record keeping for student attendance and grades can be linked directly to the teacher's grade-reporting system for easy access and distribution from various mobile devices such as tablets, iPads, or smart phones. Students can also utilize these devices to self-assess motor performance by analyzing their skills immediately through videos. In addition, using software such as MovieMaker (Microsoft, 2013), students can showcase the application of their PE knowledge and skill through the creation of instructional and performance movies. Technology makes this type of authentic assessment more meaningful for the student and the teacher (Kovar, Combs, Campbell, Napper-Owen, & Worrell, 2012).

Conclusion

Despite the roadblocks, a partnership of technology and PE is workable and beneficial for all involved. Frustrated by early failures with technology, many physical educators may give up or under-utilize technology just to say they are using it. The ability to understand technology may appear to some a natural-born trait; however, just like the acquisition of any skill-related endeavor in PE, time on task makes the difference. Once they invest the time and effort to learn technology, teachers who use it for unit and lesson plan preparation, classroom management, communication with parents and students, instruction and feedback, and assessment can save enormous amounts of time and energy. Truly, developing and improving the partnership between technology and PE is vital for student learning and needs to be a priority for all stakeholders—physical educators, administrators, classroom teachers, parents, and students.

References

Apple, Inc. (2013). GarageBand [Computer software]. Cupertino, CA: Author. Available from http://www.apple.com/ilife/garageband/

Banville, D., & Polifko, M. F. (2009). Using digital video recorders in physical education. *Journal of Physical Education, Recreation & Dance,* 80(1), 17–21. doi:10.1080/07303084.2009.10598262

Does technology in physical education enhance or increase the time available to engage in physical activity? (2012), *Journal of Physical Education, Recreations & Dance,* 83(7), 53–56.

Graham, G., Holt-Hale, S. H., & Parker, M. (2013). *Children moving: A reflective approach to teaching physical education.* New York, NY: McGraw-Hill.

Hall, T. (2012). Emplotment, embodiment, engagement: Narrative technology in support of physical education, sport and physical activity. *Quest,* 64(2), 105–115. doi:10.1080/00336297.2012.669324

Juniu, S. (2011). Pedagogical uses of technology in physical education. *Journal of Physical Education, Recreation & Dance,* 82(9), 41–49. doi:10.1080/07303084.2011.10598692

Kentucky Education Professional Standards Board. (2008). *Kentucky teacher standards.* Retrieved from http://www.kyepsb.net/teacherprep/standards.asp

Kovar, S. K., Combs, C. A., Campbell, K., Napper-Owen, G., & Worrell, V.J. (2012). *Elementary classroom teachers as movement educators.* New York, NY: McGraw-Hill.

Liang, G., Walls, R. T., Hicks, V. L., Clayton, L. B., & Yang, L. (2006). Will tomorrow's physical educators be prepared to teach in the digital age? *Contemporary Issues in Technology and Teacher Education,* 6(1), 143–156.

Microsoft, Inc. (2013). MovieMaker [computer software]. Redmond, WA. Retrieved from http://windows.microsoft.com/en-us/windows-live/movie-maker#tl=overview

Miller, A. (n.d.). Podcasting tool: GarageBand [web page]. Retrieved from https://sites.google.com/site/adammillerphysedandhealth/podcast

Nintendo of America, Inc. (2013). Wii [Video game system]. Redmond, WA: Author. Retrieved from http://www.nintendo.com/wii

Sinclair, C. (2002). A technology project in physical education. *Journal of Physical Education, Recreation & Dance,* 73(6), 23–27. doi:10.1080/07303084.2002.10607823

Southern Regional Education Board. (n.d.). *Technology standards for teachers.* Retrieved from http:/www.sreb.org/page/1380/

Critical Thinking

1. Review the roadblocks mentioned in the article. Then develop an argument for using technology to overcome two of the administrative and two of the self-imposed roadblocks.

2. Use the websites in the article and mentioned here to find at least three technologies (software or devices) to support your teaching. Write a letter to your principal or school board explaining how these tools would enhance students' skills and help them develop a healthy lifestyle.

3. To help your principal/school board understand the practical use of technology in physical education and support your request for technology, develop one or two lesson plans using the technology you have requested.

Internet References

iPhys-Ed.com
http://www.iphys-ed.com/technology-in-pe
PE Central
http://www.pecentral.org/
The PE Geek
https://thepegeek.com/

Pyle, Beth; Esslinger, Keri. From Delta Kappa Gamma Bulletin Winter 2014. Copyright ©2014 by Delta Kappa Gamma Society. Used with permission.

Article

Prepared by: Sheron Fraser-Burgess, *Ball State University*

Implications of Shifting Technology in Education

JANET HOLLAND AND JOHN HOLLAND

Learning Outcomes

After reading this article, you will be able to:

- Assess the changing trends in technology.
- Reflect on your gaps in technological knowledge and skills.
- Implement research-based technology practices.

Instructional Gaps

While talking to an engineer volunteering to work with middle and high school students on a robotics competition, he expressed his surprise at how the students did not have a basic understanding of simple everyday concepts like clockwise and counterclockwise. A school nurse complained how sick students came into her office and when handed a phone to call their parents, they did not know how. At a recent workshop presentation for middle and high school students they were told to e-mail the information to the group leader then to their own account. It was surprising how many did not know how to do it. How can this be happening in this day and age? Were the students not taught the knowledge and skills through authentic experiences, did they not have access to the technology, are they using different terms or formats for communications? These events cause one to wonder what the root causes might be and to think about whether they need to be addressed. If so, how, especially when considering ourselves to be in this technologically advanced era?

Shifting Technologies

From simple observations, reading magazines, newspapers, and Internet articles, to watching the TV news we are seeing many new technologies arrive and old ones go away, so it is important to reflect on what we are gaining and losing in the shuffle. Think about the recent losses of or declines in the markets for stopwatches, calculators, compasses, print cameras, network TV, portable radios, tapes, CDs, DVDs, GPS units, big box games, rolodex organizers, maps, books, magazines, newspapers, travel agents, and greeting cards; just to name a few. Locally the large bookstores and news stands have disappeared, video stores closed, office supply store stocks dwindle, no local printing presses anymore, even the local newspaper is making deep cuts in hardcopy, while working to develop an online presence.

Radios and TVs are being challenged at every turn to keep people interested in their nearly real time media. We have a younger generation often more interested in what the Internet has to offer than the traditional entertainment options. The newer media offers a more personalized, interactive method of learning, socializing, and entertainment on a reduced or no cost basis.

The major greeting card companies are slowly reducing employees. This is happening as digital card use continues to grow with the added features of audio, video, and animation provided at a reduced or no cost basis. The selling of card stock paper for self-printed cards, again demonstrates the digital shift towards increasing user control. We are seeing traditional magazines and books going to digital formats. According to various popular press articles, more books are being sold as e-texts than as hard copy or paperback combined. Learners now have small, compact, increased access using mobile devices. The subsequent increase in self-publication software and apps provides a way for anyone to publish then share globally within a richer media platform while bypassing editor restrictions.

It seems like the current level of expectation to produce more at a faster pace has resulted in writing being shorthanded in most of our everyday communications. Elementary classroom teachers have been discussing whether students still need to know how to physically write with everything going digital today. Though typing electronically is quick, voice command typing is even faster. In addition, digital writing offers the support of immediate spelling and grammar checking. It is not fool proof and still requires a good foundation in writing basics. With the decline of writing checks for bill payments and an increase in electronic banking transactions, it is also reducing the need for handwriting. So, when reflecting on how handwriting has been so centrally necessary to building and preserving our culture, it takes a shift in mindset to see it should still be preserved even if performed electronically. I believe we can all agree, no matter what medium is used, students still need to have the knowledge and command of effective two-way communication skills including recording their thoughts, knowledge, opinions, discoveries, and inventions in a clear and concise way.

No sooner do we have to decide whether to save writing skills, and then smartphones arrive with their heavy and direct affect on new technology shifts. Most students are now packing an impressive set of apps used for learning, sharing, and even entertainment, all in their pocket with access at an all time high. One smartphone app called TuneIn (2012) currently advertises access to over 70,000 radio stations and two million podcasts with listeners from 230 countries. Talk about seductive and personalized, just shake your phone and it will locate similar stations, how sweet is that? It is only logical to see where this could be headed with continued growth. How long until our cars are standard equipped with this expanded access? Imagine the possibilities of students having this type of access to timely International news and the ability to hear reports in different languages, as we become a more global society.

Many of the older technology declines are directly attributable to technology shifts with quick direct open access through the Internet, for personal e-mail, chat, social media, new and improved software, tools, mobile devices, and apps. As a result, digital alternatives are quickly taking the place of our more traditional tools with the lure of small, mobile, quick, easy to use devices, improved quality, with increased user control and choice. It is not a bad thing, but there are implications, whether it is simply a new medium, or whether we might be missing some of the underlying bits of important knowledge needed to carry us forward in a digital era.

Technology Growth Areas

Where are consumers spending their money in the tech sector? According to CNN Money (2012), the "7 Fastest-Growing tech companies" include Cirrus Logic, making circuit components for tablets, Biadu China's search engine with a custom personalized homepage based on the users' search patterns, Apple's voice recognition phone, IGI Photothonics fiber lasers, 3D Systems creating three dimensional parts found in smartphones and other devices produced, Priceline online international travel booking, and Acme Packet security gateways reflecting the incredible growth and profits within the industry. The same consumer desires mentioned earlier are also reflected here with fast-personalized searches, shifts toward voice-activated communications, use of mobile devices, and increasing globalization.

Growth of technologies in the workplace are expanding to improve innovations and to expand the bottom line. The Deloitte Technology Trends annual report called "Elevate IT for digital business" (2012) examines actionable practices used to achieve improvements within five major technology forces over the past several years: analytics, mobility, social, cloud, and cyber security. Areas targeted for growth include; social business, gamification, mobility, user empowerment, cloud services, big data, geospatial visualization, digital identities, measured innovation, and outside-in architecture. Author's Cearley and Claunch (2012) (*The Top 10 Technology Trends for 2012*) point to Gartner's annual list reflecting the tremendous growth in mobile computing in the workplace. The top 10 strategies include, "media tablets and beyond, mobile-centric applications and interfaces, contextual and social user experiences, Internet of things, app stores and marketplaces, next-generation analytics, big data, in-memory computing, extreme low-energy servers, and cloud computing" (Cearley & Claunch, 2012, p. 1). It looks like one can find different items when looking at the various listings but it is easy to see major overlapping trends in mobile and social technologies. The current workplace knowledge-based economies are requiring more high-level creative thinking skills with workers adept in problem solving within expanded global markets.

Oftentimes, areas of growth in the workplace extend into the educational arena at some point in time. The "NMC Horizon Report > 2012 K-12 Edition", research from the Consortium of School Networking (CoSN), and the International Society for Technology in Education (ISTE) provides a list of the top emerging technologies, trends, and challenges impacting teaching, learning, and creative inquiry over the next five years. Within one year it is anticipated adoption will increase for, cloud computing, collaborative environments, mobiles, apps, and tablet computing. In two to three years adoption of digital identity, game-based learning, learning analytics, and personal learning environments is anticipated. From four to five years, augmented reality, natural user interfaces, semantic applications, and tools for assessing twenty-first century learning skills. Key trends are reflecting the shift towards more access, mobility, online, hybrid, and authentic active challenge-based collaborative learning models to develop leadership and creativity (NMC Horizon Report, 2013, p. 1).

According to authors Trucano, Hawkins, and Iglesias in EduTech (2012) blog article called "Ten trends in technology use in education in developing countries that you may not have heard about" provides a list of instructional technology trends in developing countries including, "tablets, social learning networks, translations, the great firewall of . . . everywhere, earlier and earlier, special needs, e-waste, open data, big brother data, getting school leadership on board, going global locally" (Trucano, Hawkins, & Iglesias, 2012, p. 1). The list reflects the trend towards increasing mobility and social learning within globalized learning environments.

With the release of mobile broadband wireless multiport Internet access, gaining Internet access on the go is ever more accessible, not only at home and from hotels, but literally traveling in the passenger seat riding the highways of America. It is arguably a step forward when exercising the potential for Internet access while becoming an effective use of what would normally be down time, now used productively. This is not to advocate working 24/7 but to create flexibility for hectic schedules. In the next section, we will examine some of the current best research-based instructional practices to see how they can be aligned with the use of new technologies.

Literature-Based Current Best Educational Practices

New technologies offer a great way to invigorate instruction, whether in traditional classrooms, online, or in blended learning environments. We are finding many new digital tools allow learners to actively research, collaborate, innovate, and share their ideas. Collaborative tools can be used to increase knowledge acquisition quickly and efficiently while making global connections for broader perspectives. Providing meaningful integration of new technologies through the careful selection of quality tools aligning to best instructional practices can alter how learners and instructors engage with concepts and each other to achieve powerful learning. The following sections provide some background knowledge on the current best instructional practices found in the research literature used as the bases for aligning instructional needs directed towards technology enhanced teaching and learning.

Mobility

One of the biggest trends in education is the ability to be mobile. *Time* magazine. April 1 (2013) states the percentage of U.S. phones that are smartphones has reached 57%. According to Apple's released reports, more than 40 billion apps were downloaded for the iPhone, iPad and the iPod Touch, in 2012. It is hard to deny the success realized with approximately 83 million iPads sold by the third fiscal quarter of 2012 (Nations, 2013). To put their impact into perspective, iPads have now surpassed Mac OS sales with the new mobile iOS (Caulfield, 2011). These sales reflect the strong consumer demand for this new media. There are many iPad contenders such as Amazon, Archos, Disgo, Acer, Asus, HTC, Google, Android, Motorola, Toshiba, BlackBerry, Sony, Samsung, Microsoft, Dell, Vizio, HP, and the e-book readers including the Kindle, Kobo, and Nook. Users are drawn to the sleek design, small portable size, long battery life, in store support, inexpensive, intuitive natural interface, with a vast number of quality content apps to run on the mobile devices, as well. Learning can then be extended beyond the classroom to working from home, on the go, and in the field. "We really have reached the point where we do have magic, and thus we have the opportunity to ask what we should do with it" (Quinn, 2012, p. 3). In the corporate environment educational applications range from training, performance support, increased access, and collaboration to learning. In the educational setting, learners are gaining new content, communicating, capturing information, analyzing data, presenting, sharing, and even using location based activities. "To have mobile learning work well, power has to shift from instructors and managers to the learners themselves" (Woodill, 2011, p. 165). It is a self-directed or do-it-yourself (DIY) approach to learning.

Problem-Based Learning

Problem-Based Learning is an instructional method in which learners, usually working in teams, are given complex authentic problems or challenges and are asked to solve them. This approach is often used to increase learner interactions by working together collaboratively. Teams determine the needs, and work through the steps to solve the problem. Barrows (1986) describes problem-based learning as a way to motivate students' solutions through self-directed explorations while gaining additional practice. Problem-solving models of instruction are based on contributions from Dewey (1916, 1938). Dewey defined a problem as anything giving doubt or uncertainty. His active learning experiences included providing an appropriate learning topic, which was important and relevant.

Inquiry Learning

The researchers Bigge and Shermis (2004), Holcomb (2004), Joyce and Calhoun (1998), Van Zee 2001), and others define inquiry learning as capitalizing on students' interests in discovering something new or finding alternatives to unsolved questions or problems. Learners often work together to conduct research, experiment, synthesize, classify, infer, communicate, analyze, draw conclusions, evaluate, revise, and justify findings. In inquiry learning, students are responsible for problem solving, discovery, and critical thinking in order to construct new knowledge through active experiences. "Inquiry teaching requires a high degree of interaction among the learner, the teacher, the materials, the content, and the environment. Perhaps the most crucial aspect of the inquiry method is that it allows both students and teachers to become persistent askers, seekers, interrogators, questioners, and ponderers" (Orlich, Harder, Callahan, Trevisan, & Brown, 2007, p. 296).

Motivating Learning

Keller's (1983) ARC (attention, relevance, confidence, satisfaction) model of motivation provides insight into providing motivating instructional learning environments. In general, gaining attention involves capturing learner interest, stimulating inquiry, and maintaining it. Relevance includes identifying learner needs, aligning them to appropriate choices and responsibilities, and building on prior experiences. Confidence includes building positive expectations, support, competence, and success. Satisfaction includes providing meaningful opportunities to apply new knowledge and skills, reinforcement, and positive accomplishments. In Gagne (1985) "Conditions of learning" he indicated it is necessary to gain students' attention before they will be able to learn. Ongoing studies in the field of educational motivation continued to expand with additional research by Wlodkowsky (1999), Brophy (1983, 1998), and others. They determined that additional traits of motivated learners include the desire to learn, work, meet a need, personal value, reach a goal, complete tasks, engaging, curiosity, successful effort or ability, achievement, and personal responsibility. In a constructivist framework, motivation includes both individual and group generated knowledge and concepts.

Communications and Collaborations for Learning

In the learning environment building professional relationships through collaborating, coaching, and mentoring are all social interactions directed towards learning to share ideas, give and receive feedback, and offer support (Carr, Herman, Harris, 2005). The concepts of social learning can be traced to Bruner (1961) and Vygotsky (1978) and others. Quality instructional design directed towards technology-enhanced learning requires a great deal of student interaction. Promoting learner-to-learner interactions can increase engagement through negotiations, reflections, and shared understandings. The interactions allow students to expand viewpoints and build social connections to each other. Dialogue directed towards learning can provide students a way to expand ideas, extend concepts, and apply theory in authentic ways to solve challenges. "The focus of this work is ongoing engagement in a process of purposeful inquiry designed to improve student learning" (Carr, Herman, Harris, 2005, p. 1–2). "Collaboration forms the foundation of a learning community online-it brings students together to support the learning of each member of the group while promoting creativity and critical thinking" (Palloff, Pratt, 2005, p. xi). Some of the constructivists contributing to social learning included Piaget (1969), Jonassen (1995), and Brookfield (1995). Social presence creates the "feeling of community and connection among learners, has contributed positively to learning outcomes and learner satisfaction with online courses" (Palloff, Pratt, 2005, p. 7). Researchers finding a strong connection between social presence and improved learning, interaction, and satisfaction include Picciano (2002), Gunawardena and Zittle (1997), Kazmer (2000), and Murphy, Drabier, and Epps (1998). With the wide range of collaborative tools available for communications and collaboration, it forms the perfect foundation for social interactions and collaboration directed towards learning.

Multimedia Rich Learning

Multimedia refers to the use of text, graphics, sound, video, animation, simulation, or a combination of media. By appropriately aligning rich media to the content message, it can provide additional clarity and increase student focus rather than detract from it. Using a variety of media can increase interest and motivation while allowing unique opportunities to reach diverse learners. Mayer conducted many studies from comparing lessons presenting content with words, to lessons presenting content with words and relevant visuals (R. C. Clark & Mayer, 2003; Mayer 2001). The results have consistently demonstrated the positive impact of appropriate instructional visual selections. "Rich media can improve learning if they are used in ways that promote effective cognitive processes in learners" (Reiser & Dempsey, 2007, p. 315). Whether an educator prescribes to the learning principles of Skinner in the 30's by changing behavior, the 70's cognitive psychology focus on memory and motivation, the 80's constructivist focus on real world application, or a mixture of approaches, multimedia, used effectively, can help students to learn. Some media considerations include: gaining and keeping attention, memorability using an appropriate speed, level of difficulty, comprehension, placement, easy access, media matching the purpose, image content value, discovery, and level of interaction to improve effectiveness. "Ultimately good learning environments begin with the principles of learning and instruction, but require evaluation, revisions, and fine tuning to balance these competing values and ensure that the benefits are accrued for all intended learners" (Alessi & Trollip, 2001, p. 41). Multimodal learning can include a wide range of multimedia and interactive tools used to engage learners, thereby providing multiple modes of interfacing within the system.

Diverse Learners

Students learn in different ways and have unique abilities and preferences on how they best acquire new information. The exceptionalities in intellectual ability, communications, sensory, behavioral, physical, and combinations sometimes require special learning accommodations. One benefit digital tools can provide is the unique interface differing from traditional computing with gesture controlled navigation, the offering of computer-assisted programs, ability to increasing the size and contrast for text, images, audio, audio readers, audio text recording, audio commands, video media, interactive and collaborative tools to target specific learning needs. In addition, there is an increase in multi-language support. This can include assistance for both special needs, low and high, as well as the ever-increasing diversity of learners from all over the world joining our classes and workplaces.

Globalization

With the tremendous increase in travel, immigration, and communication technologies the world is becoming more diverse, connected, and interdependent. Globalization has accelerated the exchange of ideas and perspectives thereby increasing the overall knowledge base. Current digital tools provide increased opportunities for extending content and perspectives to transform knowledge into innovative. Using integrated curriculums, team teaching, and media rich instructional technologies, and forming partnerships, and fostering innovation, we can create knowledge and skills to prepare learners to work in future markets. Success in global markets, as we are now experiencing, demands successful interactions with a diverse, wide range of individuals and cultures. It begins with intercultural knowledge, skills, and respect for our combined contributions and strengths. As educators, we need to become international stewards sharing insights and preparing learners for the future. The dramatic increase in mobility and digital communications now "connects people and facilitates transnational understanding" in ways not previously possible (Bryan & Vavrus, 2005, p. 184). As a result, the international information infrastructure allows learners to interact and share multimedia resources easily with anyone across the globe. Current technology tools easily allow for original creations and global sharing.

It seems like it would be beneficial to offer classes on global language basics including key functional survival skill words through the use of immersive practice with multiple-languages. Subsequently, providing the potential to foster international relationships, travel, and commerce needed for an increasingly global society.

Active Hands-On Learning

Hands-on refers to the learning activity involving practice on actual equipment, or in this case digital tools. The learning activity is designed with the goal of promoting the transfer of knowledge through application. In an active learning environment students are active, working in teams, and socialization is directed toward learning productively. "Students must be actively involved in the learning process if their classroom experience is to lead to deeper understandings and the building of new knowledge. Students (and adults, as I have discovered) need to hear it, touch it, see it, talk it over, grapple with it, confront it, question it, laugh about it, experience it, and reflect on it in a structured format if learning is to have any meaning and permanence" (Nash, 2009, p. xi). The dialogue provides time for learners to digest new information, exchange ideas, and engage with others in authentic, active hands-on ways for expanded perspectives, and memorable learning experiences.

Creative Learning

Open-ended digital tools allowing for original solutions to problems or challenges provide the perfect environment for creative thinking. Students can demonstrate understanding through a wide variety of digital resources to present and share their unique solutions. It is critical to develop learners who can think beyond the box and lead us to new innovations. Simply reading and testing over material will not develop the creative, original thinking needed to move our society forward. Instructors often use Bloom's Taxonomy (1956) to ensure inclusion of high-level knowledge and skills as can be found in original creative work.

Learning New Content with Practice

The main consideration when selecting content resources is the relevance to the desired topic, and how clear the main ideas are communicated to learners. Providing learners with a graphic organizer is a nice way to show what will be studied by providing a brief overview of the content. By isolating facts, concepts, and generalizations, it makes it easier to understand new content. The higher level of knowledge integration teaches learners how items are related, similar, different, and how to compare so they can understand more complex relationships. Interactions with the content and others can provide additional practice to better retain new information. Some instructional activities are designed to provide learners with opportunities for review of previously learned information through repetition. Some digital tools provide the needed practice activities by using repetition to ensure retention into long-term memory. It is important to identify the objectives and align them with the learning activity.

Feedback, Support, and Assessment

By providing learners with timely information about their actions they will know how they compare to the desired level of criteria. "We should ensure that they receive feedback about their success and failure, are appropriately resourced with support to ultimately succeed, and ideally can share tasks and learning with one another" (Quinn, 2012, p. 24). Learner feedback can take many different forms such as traditional instructor exams with rating scales or comments for students. Another alternative is to use student self-evaluations using checklists or rubrics for individual or group work to learn to monitor their own success. Sometimes instructors will also use checklists or rubrics for evaluation and providing student feedback. Instructors can use a pretest to assess learners' current level of knowledge, diagnostic test to assess areas of strengths and weakness, formative assessments to measure ongoing progress, and summative letter grade assessments to make judgments on the quality and completion of projects. The data gathered by the instructor can be used to monitor learning and make adjustments as needed as the course progresses or for changes to be made before teaching the lesson, unit, or module again. It is important to identify the desired learning of "behaviors, activities, and knowledge you will be evaluating" (Orlich, Harder, Callahan, Trevisan, & Brown, 2007, p. 332). Instruction can include the teaching of knowledge, performance skills, and attitudes such as found in collaborative group work. Another consideration is whether the learning goal aligns to standards and provides feedback in this regard to students, parents, instructors, and administrators, as needed.

Objectives for Learning

Mager's (1975) model for objectives, indicates quality objectives including the following three elements: 1) statement of the conditions or context of performance, 2) statement of the task, and 3) measurable way to evaluate the performance. Meaningful objectives are the backbone for instructors to create learning activities designed for knowledge to be retained, transferred, and applied to similar situations. It is accomplished by providing a specific statement of what learners will be able to do when they complete the lesson. A measureable performance objective statement describes the behavior students will demonstrate at the end of the lesson, the conditions under which they will be demonstrated, and the criteria for acceptable performance. Identifying the objectives becomes the guiding force for the selection of appropriate digital tools to get to the desired learner outcomes.

Flipped Classroom

Flipped classrooms are a more recent trend used to transform the way instructors are providing information by inverting traditional classroom lectures into online video and screencast presentations, so learners can view them prior to attending class. At home, learners can watch step-by-step explanations of concepts with visual examples to better understand complex concepts. The digital presentations allow each student to learn at their own pace with the ability to pause and replay as much as needed, on their own personal schedule when they are the most receptive to learning, to acquire the needed foundation knowledge. Class time is then flipped, so students complete homework and practice activities applying the new concepts in class. When attending class, students are engaged in student-to-student interactions, collaborations, and critical thinking with the instructor serving as a facilitator to support learners, as needed. The classroom is transformed into an active, authentic, learning environment where students can deal with complex issues related to the content topic. The Flipped classroom can be an alternative to traditional lecture-based models or can be used as a blended learning environment to engage student learning. Screencast technology is often used to leverage learning outside of class, so a teacher can spend more time facilitating project-based learning during class. This is most commonly being done using teacher-created videos that students view outside of class time. Then, the learners spend class time on problem solving, thereby increasing interactions between students and instructors. With the tremendous growth and availability of mobile devices, learners have ever improving abilities to view the videos on their own time. As noted, this just keeps increasing the chances the class time can be spent on problem-based collaborative learning.

Emerging Technologies

On a *CBS This Morning* show segment called "Gadgets and Gizmos Galore" with Brian Cooley, he reported on the 2013 Las Vegas, NV, International Consumer Electronics Show. He talked about how we are starting to move into a post-mobile era.

It does not mean getting rid of mobile devices but rather seeing a merger of devices such as computers, phones, TV, and tablets so we will not be thinking about what device we are using. One example of this trend is the movement towards hybrids such as the Phablet, where the phone and tablet are combined. Cooley also talked about exciting developments through body gesturing such as Vuzix's®™ eye motion control, Leap Motion's®™ sensor on the device screen controlled by hand movements, and InteraXon's®™ Muse headband reading brainwaves for device control. Within ten years we may no longer be using the mouse and touchscreen technology. It seems like the new devices will have the potential to increase usability access for diverse learners while being a more tactile and engaging way to interact with technology resources.

Conclusions and Future Implications

When searching the literature for recommendations practitioners could consider, when dealing with shifting technologies and the pursuit of quality learning environments within the K-12 setting, a Freakonomics podcast provides some insight. Stephen Dunbar's (2011) podcast tells about how the New York City Department of Education pilot program called "School of One" personalized educational plans so each individual student has a chance to excel. Dunbar interviewed the program founders Joel Rose, Chris Rush, and chancellor Joel Klein. They implemented a technology algorithm, similar in concept to what is used to personalize Pandora radio, to analyze how each individual student learns the best. Based on the analysis results, learning was customized the next day to maximize learning efficiency. The learning modality was also aligned to how each individual student learned best; whether alone, in small or large groups, synchronously or asynchronously to practice learning concepts. One shared success story pertained to a student who initially took ten to twelve exposures to learn, but after targeting how this individual student learned best, the number of exposures was reduced to two to three. Rather than guessing what students have learned, it is statistically analyzed at the individual level to ensure it is happening through personalization. Along the same line, the U.S. Department of Education report (2012) states

> The realization of productivity improvements in education will most likely require a transformation of conventional processes to leverage new capabilities supported by information and communications technologies. In sum, rigorous evidence is needed to support effective practices to foster the adoption of efficient, effective paths to learning.

We have three sets of insightful recommendations for higher education. They include "growth, even with the accompanying pains, is generally welcome because it provides energy, new ideas, and attention to innovations. Often, however, a snazzy new technology becomes the sole focus, not the ideas or innovative uses that lead to improved learning" (Wilson, 2005, p. 1). It is important to consider instructional needs alongside new and emerging technologies aligned to desired outcomes. If we do not, we may find ourselves marching towards obsolescence as we fail to adapt to changing educational goals, objectives, and new technologies. "Most universities are using the same methods to teach all of the same stuff. This is very dangerous as the world is changing so quickly that entire fields and bodies of knowledge risk being outdated/outmoded very quickly" (Moravec, 2013, p. 1). Moravec goes on to state we "need to stop behaving as consumers of education, but become creators, producers, and prosumers. At the same time, learning needs to become more immersive and personally-meaningful (subjective experiences) to each learner" (Moravec, 2013, p. 2). In a video interview with Douglas Rushkoff, he makes a good comment about how students need to ask themselves the following questions. "Am I learning? Am I becoming a smarter more innovative human being? That's what's going to serve you in the real job market of tomorrow. By the time the corporation has told the city college what skills it wants from its future workers you are going to graduate and those skills will have changed anyway" (Rushkoff, 2013, p. 3). The factory and banking models are no longer relevant and students are now demanding interactive, relevant learning experiences, as they well should.

Recommendations for business training include actionable improvements to add measurable value to the company. With the influx of digital natives into the workplace, social technology use is increasing. "Leading enterprises today are applying social technologies like collaboration, communication and content management to social networks—the connected web of people and assets that impact on a given business goal or outcome—amplified by social media from blogs to social networking sites to content communities. Yet it's more than tools and technology. Businesses are being fundamentally changed as leaders rethink their core processes and capabilities with a social mindset to find new ways to create more value, faster" (Ramsingh, 2012, p. 1). According to author Ron Zamir, keeping "learners engaged and motivated in training through rich media, bite-sized content and gamification are essential for creating training that is both palatable to the learner and creates real workplace change" (Zamir, 2013, p. 1). Zamir's goal is to design innovative solutions to create better training using new technologies "not just simply rehashing old, unchanged content" (Zamir, 2013, p. 1). Other current trends found from the Training Zone (2013) website include the integration of rich media, mobile learning, online learning, conferencing, and the shift to globalization. It is critical to first know the learners and organizational goals to better meet their needs. The best training is personalized, accessible, and engaging in both the training and support materials offered. The technology itself is not the magic bullet, it is what you do with it to reach the business goals. The training is a means to an end, with the end resulting in a positive impact.

Integrating quality research-based instructional practices as new technologies are released is one way to fight against knowledge gaps at all levels. When one analyzes the learning needs, goals, and objectives, then selects and aligns the best tools to accomplish the tasks, one increases opportunities for exceptional learning.

Looking at where we need to be going with technology infused education, *eSchool News* has an article called eSN Special Report: Keeping students on a path to graduation. The author states "educators are determined to find that relevance by giving students more of the skills they'll need to succeed in a globally competitive economy—the so-called "twenty-first-century skills" such as problem solving, critical thinking, communication, and collaboration" (Nastu, 2012, p. 1). By integrating technology through meaningful applications, learners are more likely to stay the course needed for college and future careers. Students tend to learn best through the application of concepts to functions via meaningful work tasks, integrating those concepts through authentic relevant connections.

With so many tremendous technological shifts happening, we need to be mindful of the missing bits of information which still need to be taught. Ask people from all walks of life what is missing, what are we no longer teaching that needs to be included no matter what medium is used? Keeping in mind, the knowledge and skills valued by our society are also in a state of flux.

The concepts of collaboration and social interactions directed towards learning can continue to play a great role in the digital transitions. Could we be at a point where we think those brains, properly educated and trained to collect data, to think about problems through deeper root cause evaluation processes might be ready to start coming up with solutions to issues, concerns, and problems? Could we be ready to embrace a little change? Might we be ready to start exploring ways to maximize the potential of each individual? This article points to the need to conduct various needs analyses, identify relevant learning goals and align them to current best research-based instructional practices, no matter what technologies are selected, while staying flexible and adaptable to the changes that are sure to come.

A story by Sugata Mitra from NPR's Ted Radio called Unstoppable Learning is a wonderful example of the resilience of learners. He found by putting computers in villages in rural India, that the residents who had never seen computers before, with absolutely no resources to teach them taught themselves how to use them. My favorite quote was "you gave us a machine that only works in English, so we taught ourselves English to use it" (Mitra, 2013). By providing challenges then standing back to watch we will be amazed at what the human spirit of inquiry is capable of learning.

In looking at the New Horizons Report (2013) for K-12, Higher Education, and online resources for new and emerging technologies in industry, there are some very exciting new developments happening from augmented reality, wearable technologies, 3D printing, and much more. It will be fun to see how these technologies can be used effectively to have a positive impact on learning.

Closing suggestions for future researchers include: continue to examine effective ways to personalize instruction, examine goals and learners, tailor instruction or training specifically to the learner. Then, we may find the keys to additional innovations in teaching, training, and learning.

References

Alessi, S., Trollip, S. (2001). *Multimedia for learning: Methods and development,* 3rd Edition. Allyn & Bacon, A Pearson Education Company, Needham Heights: MA.

Bryan, A., & Vavrus, F. (2005). The promise and peril of education: The teaching of in/tolerance in an era of globalization. *Globalization, Societies and Education,* 3(2), 183–202. Doi:10.1080/14767720500167033

Carr, J., Herman, N., & Harris, D. (2005). *Creating dynamic schools through mentoring, coaching, and collaboration.* Association for Supervision and Curriculum Development, Alexandria: VA.

Caulfield, B. (2011). Apple now selling more iPads than Macs; iOS eclipses Dell and HP's PC Businesses. Retrieved March 17, 2013 from http://www.forbes.com/sites/briancaulfield/2011/07/19/apple-didnt-just-sell-more-ipads-than-macs-ios-has-now-eclipsed-dell-and-hps-pc-business-too/

Cearley, D., Claunch, C. (2012). The top 10 technology trends for 2012. Retrieved Jan. 12, 2013 from: http://www.junctionsolutions.com/gartner-insights-the-top-10-technology-trends-for-2012/

CNN Money, 7 Fastest-Growing tech companies, Retrieved Nov. 2, 2012 from http://money.cnn.com/gallery/technology/2012/09/06/fastest-growing-tech-companies.fortune/index.html

Cooley, B. (2013). CBS This Morning, Gadgets and gizmos galore. Retrieved Jan. 8 from: http://www.cbsnews.com/video/watch/?id=50138517n

Deloitte, (2012). Tech trends 2012: Elevate IT for digital business. Retrieved Jan. 12, 2013 from: http://www.deloitte.com/view/en_US/us/Services/consulting/technology-consulting/technology-2012/index.htm?id=us_google_techtrends_02212&gclid=CIuI7Nqb47QCFYp_QgoduSsAcw

Dunbar, S. (2011). How is a bad radio station like our public-school system? A Freakonomics Radio Podcast Encore. Retrieved May 21, 2013 from: http://www.freakonomics.com/2011/12/21/how-is-a-bad-radio-station-like-our-public-school-system-a-freakonomics-radio-podcast-encore/

Hawkins, R. (2010). 10 global trends in ICT and education. Retrieved Jan. 12, 2013 EduTech: A World Bank Blog on ICT use in Education from: http://blogs.worldbank.org/edutech/10-global-trends-in-ict-and-education

Mitra, S. (2013). Unstoppable learning. NPR, Ted Radio Hour. Retrived May 23, 2013 from: http://www.npr.org/2013/04/25/179010396/unstoppable-learning

Moravec, J. (2013). The university of the future: Marching toward obsolescence? Education Futures. Retrieved May 21, 2013 from: http://www.educationfutures.com/2013/04/08/uni-future/

Nash, R. (2009). The active classroom: Practical strategies for involving students in the learning process. Corwin Press, Thousand Oaks: CA.

Nastu, J. (2012). eSN Special Report: Keeping student on a path to graduation, *eSchool News,* Retrieved Nov. 2, 2012 from: http://www.eschoolnews.com/2011/02/22/esn-special-report-keeping-students-on-a-path-to-graduation/?ast=95&astc=8784

Nations, D. (2013). How many iPads have been sold? Retrieved March 17, 2013 from: http://ipad.about.com/od/iPad-FAQ/a/How-Many-iPads-Have-Been-Sold.htm

New Media Consortium (2013). NMC Horizon Report. K-12 Education Edition and Higher Education Edition. Retrieved May 21, 2013 from: http://www.nmc.org/publications

Orlich, D., Harder, R., Callahan, R., Trevisan, M., & Brown, A. (2007). Teaching strategies: A guide to effective Instruction, 8th Edition. Houghton Mitllin Company, Boston: MA.

Palloff, R., Pratt, K. (2005). *Collaborating online: Learning together in the community.* Jossey-Bass, A John Wiley & Sons Inc. Imprint, San Francisco: CA.

Quinn, C. (2012). *The mobile academy mlearning for higher education.* Jossey-Bass a John Wiley & Sons, Inc. Imprint, San Francisco: CA.

Ramsingh, K. (2012). Reimagining business with a social mindset. Deloitte Tech Trends. Retrieved May 21, 2013 from: http://deloitteblog.co.za.www102.cpt1.host-h.net/2012/03/28/reimagining-business-with-a-social-mindset-%E2%80%93-deloitte-tech-trends-2012/

Reiser, R. & Dempsey, J. (2007). *Trends and issues in instructional design and technology,* Second Edition. Pearson, Merrill Prentice Hall, Upper Saddle River: NJ.

Rushkoff, D. (2013). Education in present shock: An interview with Douglas Rushkoff. Education Futures. Retrieved May 21, 2013 from: http://www.educationfutures.com/2013/05/03/education-in-present-shock-an-interview-with-douglas-rushkoff/

Training Zone (2013). Learning Technologies 2013. Retrieved May 25, 2013 from: http://www.trainingzone.co.uk/features/Technology

Trucano, M., Hawkins, R., & Iglesias C. (2012). Ten trends in technology use in education in developing countries that you may not have heard about, EduTech: A World Bank Blog on ICT use in Education Retrieved Jan. 12, 2013 from: http://blogs.worldbank.org/edutech/some-more-trends

Tuneln Radio, Retrieved Nov. 2, 2012 from http://tunein.com/press/

U.S. Department of Education (2012). Understanding the implications of online learning for educational productivity. Office of Educational Technology. Retrieved May 21, 2013 from: http://www.ed.gov/edblogs/technology/research/

Wilson, B. G. (2005). Choosing our future. Retrieved May 21, 2013 from: http://carbon.ucdenver.edu/~bwilson/ChoosingOurFuture.html

Woodill, G. (2011). *The mobile learning edge: Tools and technologies for developing your teams.* The McGraw-Hill Companies, New York: NY.

Zamir, R. (2013). Corporate training trends in 2013. Retrieved May 25, 2013 from: http://www.allencomm.com/2013/02/corporate-training-trends-in-2013/

Critical Thinking

1. The sections on shifting technologies and technology growth discuss an array of changes and new devices/software coming to market. Which of these new technologies will have the most impact on your personal life? Explain why and how it will impact your personal life.

2. Some sections of the article provide an overview of the current best educational practices. Which of these practices will have the most impact on your teaching practices? Do not consider finances, but think about your content area or grade level and technology expertise. Explain why and how it will impact your teaching. Now consider if and how your answers to these two questions are similar.

3. In their conclusion the authors ask, ". . . what is missing, what are we no longer teaching that needs to be included no matter what medium is used?" Ask two to three teachers with different years of teaching experience this question and include your own answer. Reflect on the implications of your findings.

Internet References

Center for Implementing Technology in Education
http://www.cited.org/

International Society for Technology in Education
http://www.iste.org/

U.S. Department of Education: Use of Technology in Teaching and Learning
http://www.ed.gov/oii-news/use-technology-teaching-and-learning

Holland, Janet; Holland, John, "Implications of Shifting Technology in Education", TechTrends, May/June 2014. Copyright ©2014 by Association for Educational Communications and Technology (AECT). Used with permission.

Article

Prepared by: Sheron Fraser-Burgess, *Ball State University*

Assistive Tech for Everyone?

MICHELLE R. DAVIS

Learning Outcomes

After reading this article, you will be able to:

- State reasons why all technology should be available to all students all the time.
- Explain safeguards that should be put in place to ensure all students have equal access to, and appropriate devices for, high stakes testing.
- Identify the barriers to accessing technology that still remain in our schools and workplaces.

As students with disabilities in Virginia's Fauquier County district take online assessments, they have access to a toolbox of technologies that can make it easier to show what they know. An optic mouse can help magnify text; a text-to-speech tool provides a spoken version of exam questions; and various switches and joysticks, for those unable to use a mouse and keyboard, can be merged with the assessment.

But even students who don't have individualized education programs, or IEPs, have digital learning enhancements at their disposal in Virginia's online testing world, said Mary Wills, the 11,000-student district's director of testing. They have access to an electronic yellow highlighter that never runs out of ink, an electronic pencil for note-taking or math calculations, and an eliminator tool that narrows down the answers for multiple-choice questions.

"These tools are for all kids, not just for those with special needs," Ms. Wills said.

Assistive technologies and accommodations, once seen as primarily for students with disabilities, are now merging into the broader testing world, especially as more states and districts embrace online testing. Computer-based exams provide an opportunity to allow all students to tap into accommodations that could aid comprehension and focus.

"There are all types of interventions that came out to address the needs of students with disabilities, but anyone can benefit from them and should have the opportunity to use those accommodations if they want them," said Kimberly Hymes, the senior director of policy and advocacy for the Council for Exceptional Children, an Arlington, Va.-based advocacy group for students with disabilities. "Technology allows us to have those types of interventions readily available."

That philosophy is based on the concept of "universal design for learning," or UDL, she said. UDL calls for students to be presented with information and content in different ways and for providing multiple options to show understanding. The approach is intended to help all students, not just those with disabilities, Ms. Hymes said.

The Common-Core Effect

Some states, such as Virginia, have been doing online testing for years and have more experience with using assistive technologies and accommodations on assessments for students with disabilities, and for all students. But as the requirements for Common Core State Standards go into place, more districts in many states are going to be confronted with the issue. The two major coalitions developing online tests—the Smarter Balanced Assessment Consortium and the Partnership for Assessment of Readiness for College and Careers, or PARCC—are working to allow assistive devices for students with disabilities who need them and to provide other learning-enhancement tools to all students, said Brandt Redd, the chief technology officer for Smarter Balanced.

For specialized devices intended to help students with disabilities, for example, the coalition has developed a list of certified technologies that can work seamlessly with the online tests, such as certain input devices for students with motor-skills impairments or some text-to-speech readers, he said. Smarter Balanced's assistive technology certification process requires companies to pay $5,000 to have the coalition certify their devices work with the tests. Companies can also try out their devices with the assessment using Smarter Balanced's training tests online for free, but that does not provide certification.

Assistive "devices are allowed as long as the student uses it in regular instruction," Mr. Redd said. "We want to make sure no one is bringing in a device to artificially inflate" achievement.

It's also important that a student isn't using a device he or she had no experience with before test day, Mr. Redd said. The goal of the test is to measure academic abilities, not how adept the student is with technology.

Zoom Function

Smarter Balanced is approaching assistive technologies and supports from a three-tiered perspective. Some of those technologies—such as highlighters and zoom functions—will be available to all students. Others will be available to students who have had their uses approved by educators and other designated adults, such as translation tools for English-language learners or an English pop-up glossary. Still others, such as tools for translation into Braille, will be for students with IEPS that require those accommodations.

Parcc is approaching accommodations for its assessment in a similar way, said Jeffrey Nellhaus, the coalition's director of policy, research, and design. Supports embedded into the tests for all students include a magnifier and the option to change font size or background colors. Text-to-speech tools will be available to all students on tests in selected areas, Mr. Nellhaus said, but will be available for students with visual impairments on all parts of the test.

For math, that will be particularly helpful. "We want to make sure we're just measuring their ability to do the math, not their ability to read," he said.

Parcc doesn't require certification for assistive devices, but will produce a list of devices that work with their test as well as a list of technical guidelines for devices.

However, several advocacy groups have criticized PARCC for its failure to have all accommodations ready for its field testing this spring. In January, the National Federation of the Blind filed a lawsuit against PARCC, saying its upcoming field testing doesn't provide access for blind students who use Braille, representing a violation of the Americans with Disabilities Act. PARCC and the group have since settled the suit, with PARCC pledging to have Braille accommodations available for the practice test in spring 2014.

Patti Ralabate, the director of implementation for the Center for Applied Special Technology, or cast, said her group, based in Wakefield, Mass., and others are watching to make sure supports for all students are provided and are not limited to small groups.

She's also eager to see whether devices not on certified lists are ultimately permitted.

"There are all kinds of issues around integrating assistive-technology devices with whatever technology is used to give the test," she said. Ms. Ralabate said it's important all accessability measures are working for the field test so that "all populations are taken into account."

The National Center and State Collaborative, one of two coalitions developing alternative assessments for students with severe cognitive disabilities, is pilot and field testing assessments with a high focus on assistive technologies, said Rachel Quenemoen, the project director. To ensure assistive devices work with assessments, the collaborative borrowed the most commonly-used devices to run compatibility checks and will work to resolve any barriers to the use of assistive devices before operational testing in the spring of 2015, she said.

Even aside from the common core, assistive technologies are blurring the lines between what students with disabilities get versus the rest of the student population.

In the 10,400-student Janesville, Wis., school district, for instance, many of the assistive technologies used are available for all students based on the concepts of universal design for learning, said Kathy White, an assistive-technology specialist for the district.

Word-prediction software, for example, which suggests words visually and aloud as students write, is one of the most commonly used assistive technologies in the district, according to Ms. White. It can help students with disabilities struggling to spell or conceptualize an idea, but it can also help an on-grade-level student writing about a historical period who needs unfamiliar vocabulary, or a kindergartner who wants to use a big word but doesn't know how to spell it.

Having such technologies available to all students takes away the stigma that can arise when it's just students with disabilities who use them, Ms. White said.

"I've seen a dramatic shift in the way these students look at technology," she said, referring to students with disabilities. "They used to say they didn't want to use it because they'd be different. Now we know everyone learns in a different manner."

Uneven Access

Districts also have to consider expenses. Some costs for assistive devices are down, because the technologies are now built into the assessments—like a text reader for example—or because the technology is getting cheaper. But that's not the case for everything, said Ms. Hymes.

Of course, the reality is that even as districts embrace assistive technologies and accommodations for more students, that approach doesn't necessarily carry over to students' experiences with state tests.

In the 210,000-student Houston school district, officials have taken up the UDL philosophy. Houston opted for laptops instead of tablets for its 1-to-1 computing initiative in part because that choice allows all students, including those with disabilities, to use the same technology, with some add-ons, said Sowmya Kumar, the assistant superintendent for special education. All students can also use Kurzweil software, a text-to-speech tool with built-in study aids, including a dictionary, a thesaurus, and an idea-organizing tool.

But on state tests, the majority of students who don't have IEPS won't have access to assistive technologies or accommodations. It's a practice that Ms. Kumar hopes to see shift in the near future.

Critical Thinking

1. What is the conceptual framework and research behind allowing the use of technology by all students?
2. Name the leaders who make a priority of providing access to technology and discuss what they have accomplished.
3. What do you think remain the primary barriers to access for all students?

Internet References

Center for Applied Special Technology
http://cast.org/

Edutopia
http://www.edutopia.org/

Go2web20
www.go2web20.net

No Limits 2 Learning: Celebrating Human Potential through Assistive Technology
www.nolimitstolearning.blogspot.com

Michelle R. Davis, "Assistive Tech for Everyone?," Editorial Projects in Education, 2014, pp. 16–18. Copyright ©2014 by Editorial Projects in Education. All rights reserved. Used with permission.

UNIT

Prepared by: Sheron Fraser-Burgess, *Ball State University*

Special & Exceptional Education

Education that aims to be inclusive should seek to accommodate the full spectrum to learner's abilities. This claim is a basic tenet of multicultural education. Multicultural education is a term that has come to stand for educational reform to promote cultural diversity. Discourse about the reasons for multicultural education generally has not been framed in terms of its moral value for schooling. Scholars of multicultural education appeal to the political/social ideal of social justice. In education theory, advocating for the rights of children with disabilities or exceptional students fall under this umbrella of education for social justice. Multicultural education is predicated on the history of schools as being spaces that are ideally calibrated for students who fit within the majority on all the identity categories. Special education functions as one type of schooling intervention that enables educational equality in a diverse society.

Students who are marginalized based on membership in groups that are stigmatized, underserved or simply incongruent with dominant ways of life face the possibilities of being overlooked. In this way, schools can become avenues to replicate the social hierarchies of the society within which it is embedded. The prevalence of autism has shattered this clear distinction. Schools that value multicultural education commit equitable education.

Now more than ever, it has become imperative to address the needs of special and exceptional students. One in 57 students has been diagnosed as autistic, which challenges the firm mainstream versus minority separation. In the face of the growing numbers of children who need interventions and social services in order to successfully navigate the school setting, public education must now find cost-effective ways to meeting the needs of every student. Another logistical layer of this mandate is resolving the mainstream versus special education issue. This state of affairs raises questions that the included articles address. What is the best classroom possible for each student? To what extent are the needs and interests of students at the high ability level of the spectrum being served adequately? In the classroom economy of accountability, how can students who are successful be motivated to further fulfill their potential? Are there tools now available through technological advancement that can assist or make possible the accommodations that are required.

Reference

Banks, J. & Banks, C. Eds. (2010). *Multicultural education: Issues & perspectives* 7th ed. Hoboken, NJ: John Wiley & Sons

Article

Prepared by: Sheron Fraser-Burgess, *Ball State University*

Inclusive Education: Lessons from History

How has education evolved from exclusion to inclusion, from judgment to acceptance, and from disability to difference?

BARBARA BOROSON

Learning Outcomes

After reading this article, you will be able to:

- Know the types of exclusion that has characterized American public education for the last century.
- Grasp the meaning and nature of the struggle for equal rights for students who are labeled as disabled as a matter of extending civil rights to this population.
- Recognize that educational accommodations and removal of the stigma of differences is an ongoing battle in American society.

One of the central principles of our melting pot in the United States has been to greet diversity with inclusivity: *Give me your tired, your poor, your huddled masses yearning to breathe free.* In practice, however, the meaningful inclusion of individuals who are different from the majority has been fraught in many ways. Learning about the evolution of the education system and its treatment of students who are different in terms of race, gender, or ability can guide us as educators to lead the way forward.

In America's earliest days, children born with disabilities were the source of shame and guilt among families, often stashed away in institutions. As described by The Anti-Defamation League (2005):

The stigmatization of disability resulted in the social and economic marginalization of generations of Americans with disabilities, and like many other oppressed minorities, left people with disabilities in a severe state of impoverishment for centuries. In the 1800s, people with disabilities were considered meager, tragic, pitiful individuals unfit and unable to contribute to society, except to serve as ridiculed objects of entertainment in circuses and exhibitions.

Even into the late 20th century, 1.8 million students with disabilities in the United States were excluded entirely from the public education system (Duncan, 2015).

In 1975, the federal Education for All Handicapped Children Act (EHA) required public schools to guarantee a free, appropriate public education to students with disabilities. But the question of what constituted appropriate education was left to the courts (Esteves & Rao, 2008). And despite the legislation, the inclusion of individuals with special needs was considered by many educators to be of questionable worth, a drag on teachers' time and an intrusion—a threat to the status quo (West, 2000).

In the 1980s, activists began to lobby for a broader civil rights statute. As a result, the Americans with Disabilities Act (ADA) was passed in 1990, ensuring equal access and equal treatment for people with disabilities. Since then, the EHA has been reauthorized and renamed numerous times. The current version, the Individuals with Disabilities Education Improvement Act, together with the ADA, the Every Student Succeeds Act, and other legislation, aim to ensure that the concepts of access and appropriateness are interpreted and applied consistently. All students are now guaranteed an education that is not only accessible, but also free, appropriate, timely, nondiscriminatory, meaningful, measureable, and provided in the least-restrictive setting.

Today more than 90 percent of all students with disabilities receive education in mainstream schools, and more than half are included in the general classroom for at least 80 percent of the day (Snyder, de Brey, & Dillow, 2016).

Although the signing of these federal laws imposed immediate legislative mandates to ensure equal access for and treatment of people with disabilities, long-standing assumptions, stereotypes, and pedagogical practices have persisted. Practically, educators still struggle to balance the acute needs of a few with the ongoing needs of the whole. Philosophically, educators and advocates today explore the implications of a semantic or paradigmatic shift from *disabled* to *different*. In more practical terms, the education community continues to worry that students with special needs will detract from the integrity of the competitive classroom environment.

Exclusion by Race: Separate but Unequal

We've been here before. Up until the mid-19th century, virtually all slave codes in the United States prohibited the education of black Americans (Marable & Mullings, 2003). At the time, it was widely thought that educating those who were believed to be inferior would be not only a waste of resources, but also a threat to the dominant majority.

The late 19th century brought the Jim Crow laws, which legally mandated racially segregated education in many states under the veil of "separate but equal." The separateness was strictly enforced—the equality, not so much. It wasn't until 1954 that segregation was declared unconstitutional in *Brown v. Board of Education*. But it was another 10 years before the Jim Crow laws were finally eradicated by the Civil Rights Act of 1964, which forbade discrimination on the basis of race.

Even so, entrenched biases persisted in many communities, and black students faced harassment and often abuse as they matriculated into previously all-white schools. Jason Sokol (2008) describes how some white Southerners felt as desegregation began to take hold:

> The civil rights struggle threatened to hoist African Americans up and out of [the] social "place" that whites had created for them. White Southerners would find blacks in their schools and neighborhoods, their restaurants, and polling places.... Many whites denounced the "Civil Wrongs Bill," holding that such federal laws imperiled their own rights. They clung to the notion that rights were finite, and that as blacks gained freedom, whites must suffer a loss of their own liberties. On the precarious seesaw of Southern race relations, whites thought they would plummet if blacks ascended. (p. 62)

Just as many educators and families today fear the intrusion of students who are differently abled into general education classrooms, many white Americans believed that black students would be a drag on teachers' time and energy, and would dilute the dignity and integrity of a homogenous learning environment.

Exclusion by Gender: The Fight for Coeducation

Dipping back in time again, it is important to remember that early American education was an exclusive privilege not of white *people*, but more specifically of white *males*. In the early 19th century, girls and young women who were lucky enough to have access to education were generally taught only homemaking skills, such as needlework, cooking, and etiquette (Forman-Brunell, 2001).

It was 200 years after the first American colleges were founded before white women were allowed to partake in postsecondary education, and even then, only sort of. By means of a familiar "separate but equal" version of segregated education, women were granted admission to *coordinate colleges* that were loosely affiliated with men's colleges, providing only limited access to university resources and opportunities.

By the beginning of the 20th century, white women were allowed to enroll in historically male-only colleges. As was the case when black students first entered historically white-only schools, women encountered prejudice and discrimination from their peers and instructors. Many professors disapproved of the admission of women, asserting that women were constitutionally incapable of higher-level academic work and often refusing to acknowledge women's presence in their classes. The situation for black women was even more repressive. Just as some educators today doubt the academic potential of students with learning or functional differences, many considered women to be constitutionally inferior and unworthy of the investment of robust academic resources or opportunity. A dramatic shift would later occur in 1972 with the passage of Title IX of the Education Amendments Act, which protects students from discrimination on the basis of gender.

Where does this fear and resistance of others come from? Again it seems the dominant majority of white men felt somehow unsteady on their lofty perch—they believed that the act of lifting up others would topple the towering world of privilege they had created. So the status of black Americans and women was perpetuated as less-than, a disadvantage, a flaw, a predictor of incapacity, or incompetence—a disability.

Next Steps for Inclusive Educators

At this point in our development as inclusive educators, we have moved past legally exclusionary practices. But perhaps we, too, feel uncertain at the helm of classes that already struggle to stay afloat, even before students with significant learning differences come onboard. A paradigm shift could help us change course.

First, let's look closely at the language we use. As inclusive educators, many of us are still in a self-conscious phase of adjustment, bumping up against remnants of old stumbling blocks. Consider this historical parallel: As women took their place in previously male-only classrooms, the term *coeducation* became an uncomfortable catchphrase. Although coeducation means "the education of both sexes together at the same time," women were considered to be the physical manifestations of the coeducation movement. While men were called *students*, women were called *coeds*. The message was that women were on campus only because of the coeducation movement; they were not really students. Although coeducational status is no longer something that colleges and universities need to shout from the rooftops of their hallowed halls, the term *coed* still lingers.

Similarly, as inclusive educators, it's time to move past the self-congratulatory phase of celebrating our "integrated" schools and classrooms. Our public schools are expected to be inclusive of students of all fluid varieties of gender, race, and ability. So let's acknowledge that students who come from other classrooms or programs are not "inclusion kids," and the teachers who come with them are not "inclusion teachers." Every student in every classroom is an inclusion kid. Every teacher in every classroom is an inclusion teacher. These students and teachers are not here because of the inclusion movement; *we* are all here because we embrace difference and diversity.

At the same time, we must be careful never to slip into an oversimplified illusion that we're all the same, as has happened before. When Martin Luther King, Jr. shared his dream that black Americans would be judged not "by the color of their skin but by the content of their character," much of white America tried obligingly to be colorblind. The well-intentioned effort to treat race as irrelevant was meant to draw attention to commonalities. Instead, as Monnica Williams (2011), psychologist and director of the Laboratory for Culture and Mental Health Disparities, explains, "[colorblindness] helped make race into a taboo topic that polite people cannot openly discuss. And if you can't talk about it, you can't understand it."

Valuing the Difference

In this context, let's look at the vigorous movement toward inclusion for students on the autism spectrum. In the 1990s, the term *neurotypical* was coined by some in the autism community to describe people who are *not* on the autism spectrum. From the notion of neurotypicality sprang a broader movement toward neurodiversity, which seeks to portray natural variations in neurological functioning as benign and inclusive, implying that all neurological functioning lies on a spectrum. In this sense, every one of us, different as we are, has a place on the same universal, neurodiverse spectrum.

In this inclusive light, we can view differing abilities from a more open, accepting perspective. Peter Smagorinsky (2011) asks:

> Whose rules provide the center of gravity for considering what counts as appropriate behavior? Why are those who don't understand or follow those rules viewed as being in deficit, or having a *disorder*? Do folks on the spectrum have a *dis*order? Or do they simply follow their *own* order? (p. 1716)

Many proponents of the neurodiversity movement believe that Autism Spectrum Disorder and other neurological and neurodevelopmental differences should no longer be considered deficits that need to be cured or treated. Instead, neurodiversity advocates maintain that all kinds of neurofunctioning are valid. They encourage the neurotypical community to meet folks on the autism spectrum where they are and to stop trying to change them.

These concepts present us with challenges that go beyond semantics. As our lexicon shifts from *disability* to *difference*, how do we address the reality of varied abilities? How do we honor different kinds of academic achievement even as we are expected to bring all students to standardized or "normalized" academic expectations? How do we balance the neutrality of *difference* with the practical reality of *disability*? Simon Baron-Cohen (2013), director of the Autism Research Centre in Cambridge, England, suggests,

> Autism is both a disability *and* a difference. We need to find ways of alleviating the disability while respecting and valuing the difference. (p. 367)

Meeting Students Where They Are

Universal Design for Learning (UDL) takes us a long way toward finding that balance. UDL is based on the notion that rather than forcing students into a one-size-fits-all learning style, educators must provide varied and flexible options for learning, along with appropriate supports and accommodations. Our inclusive goal is to meet students where they are and as they are and to lead them to be resourceful, knowledgeable, goal-oriented, and motivated learners. UDL strategies can help us acknowledge differences, differentiate instruction, and guide students to maximize their potential, while still leaving room for students' individuality to shine.

According to UDL's principles, we must incorporate diverse strategies for engagement, representation, and action and expression. To provide students with an engaging learning environment, for instance, keep classroom decorations to a minimum. Classrooms can be colorful and attractive without being overwhelmingly distracting to students with special needs. Consider posting large swaths of plain, brightly colored paper on the wall to keep things cheerful while giving students' eyes a place to rest.

In terms of representation, present new information in clear context so all students can assimilate it in ways that are personally meaningful to them. By positioning new concepts on a timeline or in a Venn diagram, for example, we help students make their own associations between new concepts and prior knowledge. Like using hashtags on social media, this makes it easier for them to retrieve information when they need it.

Offer and accept a variety of ways for students to express their knowledge. Many students assimilate far more knowledge than they are able to demonstrate through conventional means. Whenever possible, let students choose to speak, write, act, sing, dance, pantomime, illustrate, videotape, collage, montage, podcast—or whatever vehicle drives them.

The Inclusive School

And spread awareness. Creating a school culture of meaningful inclusivity starts by drawing in classroom paraprofessionals, teachers in special areas, coaches, and bus and building staff. Provide adults in the school community with information about specific disabilities and actionable tips to support students so that all learners and teachers will be comfortable together.

Champion difference. Fill your school and classroom libraries with biographies of people who exemplify all kinds of difference: Helen Keller, Harvey Milk, and Malala Yousafzai, to name a few. Choose read-aloud books that highlight protagonists who stand out for their differences: *Chrysanthemum* by Kevin Henkes, in which the main character is a feisty individualist; the *Joey Pigza* series by Jack Gantos, in which the spunky protagonist has ADHD; *Wonder* by R.J. Palacio, in which the beauty of the narrator shines through his facial deformity; and *Out of My Mind* by Sharon Draper, in which the brilliant, nonverbal narrator gives voice to cerebral palsy.

Considering disabilities to be differences that are as neutral as race and gender may be a false equivalence. But by viewing the classroom through the lens of neurodiversity, we can see that diverse learners do not dilute the dignity and integrity of a homogenous learning environment. Rather, diverse learners breathe energy, openness, and vitality into our classrooms and curriculum, so that for future generations, diversity will be mainstream, and appreciation of differences will be the one thing we all have in common. **EL**

References

Anti-Defamation League. (2005). A brief history of the disability rights movement. Retrieved from http://archive.adl.org/education/curriculum_connections/fall_2005/fall_2005_lesson5_history.html

Duncan, A. (2015). *Forty years of the Individuals with Disabilities Education Act (IDEA)*. Washington, DC: U.S. Department of Education.

Esteves, K., & Rao, S. (2008). *The evolution of special education: Retracing legal milestones in American history*. Alexandria, VA: National Association of Elementary School Principals.

Forman-Brunell, M. (Ed.). (2001). *Girlhood in America: An encyclopedia in two volumes*. Santa Barbara, CA: ABCCLIO.

Marable, M., & Mullings, L. (Eds.). (2003). *Let nobody turn us around: Voices of resistance, reform, and renewal*. New York: Rowman & Littlefield.

Smagorinsky, P. (2011). Confessions of a mad professor: An autoethnographic consideration of neuroatypicality, extranormativity, and education. *Teachers College Record, 113*(8), 1701–1732.

Snyder, T. D., de Brey, C., & Dillow, S. A. (2016). *Digest of Education Statistics 2014* (NCES 2016-006). Washington, DC: National Center for Education Statistics, Institute of Education Sciences, U.S. Department of Education.

Sokol, J. (2008). White Southerners' reactions to the civil rights movement. In *Free at last: The U.S. Civil Rights Movement* (pp. 62–64). Washington, DC: U.S. Department of State, Bureau of International Information Programs.

Solomon, A. (2013). *Far from the tree: Parents, children, and the search for identity*. New York: Scribner.

West, J. (2000). *Back to school on civil rights: Advancing the federal commitment to leave no child behind*. Washington, DC: National Council on Disability.

Williams, M. (2011, December 27). Colorblind ideology is a form of racism. *Psychology Today*. Retrieved from www.psychologytoday.com/blog/culturally-speaking/201112/colorblind-ideology-is-form-racism

Critical Thinking

1. How has the mantra of the Statue of Liberty arguably been at odds with the treatment of children born with disabilities in public education?

2. What contiguities are there with the treatment of women, blacks and other minoritized children?
3. What changes would acceptance and tolerance of difference broadly defined mean for American public education?

Internet References

Inclusive Education for Children with Disabilities

https://plan-international.org/education/inclusive-education-children-disability

Inclusive Education: What It Means, Proven Strategies, and a Case Study

https://education.cu-portland.edu/blog/classroom-resources/inclusive-education/

BARBARA BOROSON (barbaraboroson@gmail.com, www.barbaraboroson.com) has worked in the field of autism spectrum education for 25 years in clinical, administrative, and advisory capacities. She is the author of *Autism Spectrum Disorder in the Inclusive Classroom: How to Reach and Teach Students with ASD* (Scholastic, 2nd edition, 2016).

Boroson, Barbara. "Inclusive Education: Lessons from History." Educational Leadership, Vol 74, No 7, April 2017, pp 18–23. Used by permission of ASCD.

Article

Prepared by: Sheron Fraser-Burgess, *Ball State University*

Text-to-Speech: Not Just for Special Education Students!

KRISTINE NAPPER

Learning Outcomes

After reading this article, you will be able to:

- Define techquity.
- Link technologies with advancing literacy.
- Deduce the efficacy of text-to-speech technologies for all students.

I'm a middle school ESL teacher who accidentally picked up a reputation for being "techy." But I'll tell you a secret—I'm not even that into technology. I kicked and screamed through my edtech class as an undergrad.

I am, however, a big believer in a concept I call "techquity." Instead of doing the same old things on new devices and getting the same results, I believe technology can be used to create more equitable opportunities for all students.

We all have students reading below grade level. Students with learning disabilities, developing English proficiency, poor instruction, low attendance, and other factors, share the struggle of being unable to navigate grade-level text. While there's no magical solutions to complex issues, text-to-speech (TTS) is a tool that I find makes a powerful difference for tasks that involve reading.

Accessing Content

The right to learn in school shouldn't be limited by low literacy. Some of my lowest readers are also some of my brightest students. They might not decode well, but they can memorize, comprehend, analyze, connect, evaluate, apply... In short, they can think! When students can't independently read a text about World War II, shouldn't they still get to learn about World War II? Low readers often starve for more information and depth than remedial texts typically provide. TTS breaks down barriers to content.

Stretching Text Endurance

Although most of my students have enough skills to at least slog through assigned reading, for many it's an exhausting process. They wrestle with each word, grasping for meaning.

Since making TTS available, I've noticed a pattern. Many students start an assignment reading on their own. As they fatigue, they pop in some headphones and continue reading with TTS. In a pre-techquity world, these same tired students would give up or turn into behavior problems. Now they're staying engaged with text for longer, and adjusting strategies to fit their own learning needs.

Easing Text Anxiety

Conversely, some reluctant readers use the same strategy in reverse. These are the students that say they're "too lazy" to start a task, which is usually covering up insecurity about their abilities. Using TTS sounds easier and less threatening, so they're willing to get started. Once they get into the text, they often turn off TTS, preferring to continue at their own pace without the robotic voice. The technology lowers their affective filter enough to gain some reading momentum. Then, if they don't need it anymore, they naturally stop using it.

Unlearning Helplessness

"Ms. Napper, what does this word mean?"

"Which word?"

"Co... cone.... cone-see-kwee...I don't know how to say it!"

"How can you figure it out?"

At this point, they listen with TTS, and the next thing out of their mouth will either be, "Consequence! Oh, yeah, I know that word," or "What does consequence mean?"

I'm so tired of students waiting for teachers to hold their hands. TTS allows them to be independent learners, using tools to get information. While I'll happily help my students when they need it, they have to put in enough effort to at least ask a good question. If they can figure out the answer themselves, even better! It's empowering for kids who are used to being spoon-fed.

Helps With Writing

For years I've told students to read their writing aloud before declaring it finished, but it's never been very effective. Kids either feel awkward and refuse to do it, or they rush through reading it the way they want it to sound, rather than as it's written. I'm seeing better results now that I tell them to listen to their own words via TTS. Kids who've never voluntarily used a period or comma in their life can hear how confusing the text sounds without punctuation. Those who can't see the need for editing, can often hear it.

But How Will They Ever Learn To Read?

Let me be very clear—TTS does *not* replace reading instruction. My original intention was solely to provide access to content. However, I'm finding that it also supplements learning to read — which makes sense. Does anyone ever worry that reading to a child will become a crutch, keeping them from learning to read? Of course not; we encourage it as a way to promote literacy.

Most TTS highlights as it reads, drawing the eye along. It allows students to have meaningful interactions with text throughout the day, instead of dedicating that time and energy to avoidance. I've met 6th grade students who I secretly expected to continue needing TTS forever. Two years later, I have the joy of watching them surpass my expectations, voluntarily reading out loud in class without any technology.

Dropping The Stigma

When I started experimenting with TTS, I only offered it to the one or two students in a class with the highest reading needs. It opened doors for them... when they actually used it. They were self-conscious about peers seeing them using something "special."

As I started imagining TTS benefitting more students, I changed my approach. Now I introduce it to the whole class as something we can all keep in our toolbox. "*Some of our brains learn better by listening while we read. If that's you, this might help. Some of you will want to use it a lot of the time. Some might just use it occasionally, when the reading is challenging or you're tired. Some will find it too distracting. Do whatever works for your brain!*"

Just like that, the stigma is gone! Kids easily accept that our brains learn differently, and that doesn't make one style better or worse than another. They've taken ownership of how, when, and if they use TTS, and they're handling the responsibility beautifully.

Critical Thinking

1. What differences can text-to-speech technologies bring in academic performance?
2. What kind of results should be evaluated to determine that special needs children are being well served?
3. Why is unlearning helpless a possible outcome of techquity interventions?

Internet References

How Do You Level the Digital Playing Field?
https://tiie.w3.uvm.edu/blog/equity-and-technology-in-schools/#.XURjLC2ZMnU

How Technology Can Boost Equity in Education
https://www.theeducatoronline.com/k12/news/how-technology-can-boost-equity-in-education/237978

KRISTINE NAPPER is a middle school teacher of English Language Learners in Beaverton, OR. She uses her own experience of living with a physical disability to inform her work, uniquely suiting her to work with dual-identified students. She's driven by a desire to promote student equity as well as a love of laughing with kids every day.

Napper, Kristine. "Text-to-Speech: Not Just For Special Education Students!" https://medium.com/inspired-ideas-prek-12/text-to-speech-not-just-for-special-education-students-39e7e9aa444b. Used by permission.

Article

Prepared by: Sheron Fraser-Burgess, *Ball State University*

Mobile Apps the Educational Solution for Autistic Students in Secondary Education

AGATHI STATHOPOULOU, ET AL.

Learning Outcomes

After reading this article, you will be able to:

- Ascertain the promise of mobile technologies for student learning in high school and secondary education.
- Recognize the convergences of familiarity and utility that mobile apps and hardware present for engaging autistic students.

1 Introduction

Our knowledge and understanding of academic success and failure, ability and disability can be considered as cultural constructions. This is because the dominant group in a society defines the features of the culture that differentiate 'those who can' and 'those who can't' and cultural understandings of difference are reflected not only in the beliefs and attitudes of people, but also in the reactions and behaviour of individuals [1] and especially in the beliefs and attitudes of educators [2].

Traditionally, education has been offered in classes where students can interact directly with their educators, making teachers physical presence basic teaching pylon [3]. Undoubtedly, in recent years the dominant culture of education has been oriented to computers causing substantial issues, mostly conflicts between informal learning with personal devices and traditional classroom education [4]. The wide distribution of computers and communication technologies has made every learning process easier. Since the arrival of mobile phones in the 1980s, they have been widely used by people of all ages all around the world. It could be said that the whole world is becoming mobile; mobile phones are not only communication devices, but also portable and private pieces of technological equipment [5]. Mobile learning represents a new technological trend that is ubiquitous in education, powerful, highly portable and endowed with multimedia capabilities bringing a new dimension to curriculum delivery [6]. There is great potential in using mobile devices to transform the way we learn by changing the traditional class-room to one that is more interactive, engaging and successful. Provided the possibility of teaching without being restricted by time and place, enabling learning to continue after class is over or outside the classroom in places where learning occurs naturally. Furthermore, provide the connection between educators and learners on a more personal level with digital devices that they use on a regular basis, while sensing technologies enable learning to be personalized and customized to the needs of individual learner [7].

Since then a new revolutionary approach of teaching with mobile devices equipment begins. Internet connections have created a way for a new form of electronic learning, called mobile learning, internet-enabled mobile devices can help students to access learning resources and online courses, anywhere and at any time [8].

In the last decade most adults and adolescents in developed countries use mobile phones and mobile devices, and for many people in developing countries a mobile device can be the easy way for long distance communication. Additionally, in a parallel educational development to the spread of personal technology, schools, colleges and universities have experimented with handheld technology for educational reasons, including classroom response practice, data probes, and digital assistant tools. Universities allow students to bring laptop computers to lectures and some schools are now providing pupils with tablet computers. As personal mobile technologies for learning become more widespread, studies are begging to show evidence of the value of incorporating mobile devices in teaching and learning [4] parallel with traditional ways of learning [9].

In these new conditions a new generation of educators is created who have been oriented in the rapid and analytical transmission of information and the easier understanding by students created. Digital learning is a flexible learning in a digital world. Flexible learning is the focus of a new wave of interest. There is more flexibility to meet the needs of the learner, through adaptability to different needs of the learner, learning patterns and settings, and media combinations. Indeed, it would appear that wherever one looks, institutions are rushing headlong to embrace the Knowledge Media and to adopt new, open and distant learning practices [10].

2 Mobile Application in High and Secondary Education

The last decade, we have observed an impressive increase in the use of mobile learning technologies especially in high schools globally. A new educational environment has been created into the classroom with digital media. These devices have attracted interest, by the educational community mainly due to their versatile learning capabilities [11]. Every new version of these devices brings innovative features that make them more convenient and affordable, and new apps that make learning procedure easier become available continually.

Mobile apps are increasingly becoming ubiquitous, penetrating and transforming everyday social views and practices. These practices can be accompanied with text documents in different formats, audiovisual contents with videos, applications, and social networks. Smartphones are no longer only a tool for communication, but in many cases have become an instrument of people's social and work life, and possibly, a powerful instrument in academic life. Therefore, middle and higher education in developed and developing countries are now trying to establish the use of smartphones in the learning process from different perspectives and teaching learning methods [13]. Mobile devices such as smartphones and tablets are gaining popularity due to their relatively strong computing capability built into small sizes and their internet connectivity. The possibility of various types and easy-to-use mobile software applications allows users to investigate alternative learning and communication methods. Mobile apps also are now gaining increasing role and popularity across educational research. It is estimated that by 2015, 80% of people accessing the internet will do it through cell phones. Mobile technologies are now gaining increased attention and popularity across education sectors, which has led to innovation in mobile app design [14].

In addition, in the last decade a prevalence of mobile technologies among college students is estimated. In fact, the majority of students' smartphones and tablets are reportedly used for academic purposes. Furthermore, many educators in secondary schools emphasize in the creative, student-centered pedagogical approaches facilitated by mobile apps, while others stress the role of online communication and collaboration in creating well-informed and well-connected global citizens. The latest generation of smart phones has became tools for supporting learning—inside and outside the classroom .Mobile applications also have significant potential to be used in literacy performance and in mental health interventions with adolescents [15].

Undoubtedly, mobile apps provide the greatest possibility for effective integration of technological hardware into language learning. These devices are technologically superior to usual mobile phones, running on advanced operating systems such as iOS (Apple), Android (Google) and Symbian (Nokia) which allow the use of high-resolution touch-screen interfaces and smartphone-specific applications [16]. Also, they are usually owned by the students themselves, at a relatively low-cost [17]. These mobile apps features mean that smartphones have the potential to become significant devices not only in language learning, but also in general the ability to learning ability access [18].

Mobile apps are rapidly growing in importance and can be used for various functions. They have been used widely especially in educational inquiry. One educational direction for which mobile apps were used was training to read and pronounce the verses of the Holy Quran. There are apps that offer students the opportunity to read and explain the Quran, and search for a particular word or phrase in the text as well as listening to verses of the Holy Quran. Recent study aimed to declare the relationship between the behavioral factors and perceived usefulness of using the mobile to revel application "Say Quran" for studying the Quran on students' perceived performance, satisfaction and behavior [19]. In this research, students of the Islamic University had been asked to use the apps to help them on study the Quran. The results from this study provide evidence that there is a positive relationship between the mobile application "Say Quran" and students' perceived performance, satisfaction and behavior while engaged in studying the Holy Quran [15].

The Spanish National University of Distance Education published a study regarding the benefits of smartphones in higher education. The ambition of this research was to assess the value of a specific didactic mobile application and the utility to enhance student learning in university issues in ubiquitous environments and develop universal competencies according to the European Higher Education Field [20]. The main aim of the study was to reveal and assess students' perceptions regarding the capabilities of smartphones and apps in improving learning processes in university subjects were assessed. The conclusions demonstrate that the use of apps developed specifically for university subjects is highly valued by students as a new format which equally supports and enhances learning practices that not only provide further opportunities to establish connections and relations with their subjects, but also foster collaborative work among students and professors.

To underline collaboration and support real world skills, universities are experimenting with digital education policies that allow for more flexibility in interactions between students when working on projects and assessments [21]. In this context, many Universities around the world have begun implementing mobile learning with smartphones. For example, students at the University of Phoenix study in over 200 institutions simultaneously as well as online. With the university's mobile app, students can view their course materials, flag and mark posts even when they are offline, and participate in class discussions, gaining required participation points out of anywhere. In addition to the standard mobile apps Stanford University offers shuttle times, an event catalog, an online directory, and boasts a mobile learning research department, thereby giving students a chance to read case studies regarding mobile learning. The Stanford Mobile Inquiry Learning Environment program allows students to use their devices to create, collaborate, and evaluate questions regarding educational topics, essentially becoming a research lab in students' pockets. At Florida International University, by means of one of its apps, offered to students the availability of library resources and access all video content [22], [23].

In addition, mobile applications have potential for helping students increase their physical activity, since little is known about the behavior change techniques via installed application, as recent research showed [24]. Furthermore, mobile apps have important use in psychological health inquiry. Study reveal results in which the installation of a specific application in a mobile phone provides a cognitive behavioral therapy intervention for the treatment of depression [25]. Lately, there are an increasing number of mobile apps available for adolescents with mental health problems and an increasing interest in assimilating mobile health into mental health services. Researchers have systematically searched for relevant publications, which describe mental health apps (targeting depression, bipolar disorder, anxiety disorders, self-harm, suicide prevention, conduct disorder, eating disorders and body image issues, schizophrenia, psychosis, and insomnia) for mobile devices for use by adolescents younger than 18 years [26].

Furthermore, there is a widely acceptable opinion that iPad applications are being used as an added tool for learning within educational environments improving the academic skills of students. A recent pilot study investigated the competence of iPad applications in improving the literacy and overall academic skills [27]. Results reveal that while statistical significance was not obtained, practical significance was found for the use of iPad applications to support learning in the literacy skill area of spelling knowledge and number concept. Also, the iPad applications that were chosen for this project were selected with several key criteria in mind and were mainly focused on the key academic concepts. Besides, they were developmentally appropriate for children with several levels of difficulty through which children could move independently, according to their needs and they provided positive or neutral feedback to children's responses. For the intervention condition, the applications gave multiple opportunities for the child to learn about and practice at least one of the skill areas [28].

Taking the above into consideration, many researchers have also focused on using mobile learning for assessing mathematic in secondary students. Firstly, K-Nect project, targets secondary at-risk students to focus on increasing their mathematics skills through mobile smartphones [29]. MobileMath offers several methods to help students learn mathematical skills. Learners learn through learning by doing by practicing their skills in the games. The learners therefore engage in direct experience and focus on learning reflection to increase their knowledge, skills, and values. MobileMath uses various personalization rules for creating the recommendations for the learners, assisting them in choosing activities and making navigation easy. Also, consists of several features such as games, lessons, tutorials, examples and quizzes, which offer a different strategy for learning the topic. The algebra content is embedded into the game itself in a way that an algebraic skill is required for playing each game while there are games for finding factors, adding and subtracting directed numbers, factorization and solving equations [28].

3 Supporting Secondary Students with Autism with Mobile Applications

Autism spectrum disorder is a lifelong, neurodevelopmental condition that affects approximately 1% of students [30]. It is also characterized by core impairments in social reciprocity, social communication and flexibility, a constellation of associated difficulties, including problems with executive function, sensory sensitivity, emotional and behavioural regulation, language, motor control and eating [31]. In most European countries the majority of children diagnosed with autism attend mainstream school [32]. Studies and evidence from the empirical literature, suggests most of the children with autism face considerable challenges and difficulties in mainstream school settings. Many educational researches have shown that children with autism are at elevated risk of being bullied at school [33] for having emotional and behaviour problems [34], and for showing lower-than-expected academic attainment given their high IQ [35]. There appear to be substantial barriers to the successful integration of students with autism into mainstream schools, and a better understanding of these barriers is needed to promote inclusion [36].

Furthermore, high schools are large, complex environments that often face of lack cohesion. High school tends to be more impersonal, competitive and complicated than middle school [37]. Undoubtedly, high school teachers have few of opportunities to interact regarding all the students' needs. In a single day, a high school student may have seven different classes, with a different teacher and group of each peers. In addition, students in high school are expected to be independent in their academic functioning with greater demands on their planning and organizational skills [38]. Within educational environment, difficulties in the areas of social interaction and courses's performance can put students with autism at risk for social and educational isolation [39]. Information and communication technologies (ICTs) have opened new ways to help students with autism especially in high school. These technologies allow creation of truly teaching models suitable for autism and offer clinicians and teachers different support to work with [40]. The enthusiasm surrounding the use of new technologies (e.g. smartphones, tablets) to support adolescents with autism may be due to the tension of children with autism for such devices. Screen-based technology use is a primary and preferred discretionary activity for the majority of adolescents with autism [41], [42]. Researchers found that 98% of the teens with autism surveyed spent approximately 5 h per day on a computer during summer months, primarily engaged in playing video games and surfing the web. A study that compared the screen-based technology use of adolescents with autism to their typical siblings found that participants on the spectrum were heavier users [42]. Information and communication technology-based interventions can be classified into three main categories. First, iPod and iPad apps aim to facilitate specific aspects of social life. Second, serious games can be described as 'digital' games and equipment with an agenda of educational design. Finally, ICT interventions include the use of robots with students with autism [43]. Of course, beyond entertainment, the importance is found in educational software that, through mobile apps, can teach autistic students in main stream high school [44].

In the last five years there has also been growing interest in the use of mobile technology by children with autism. Study evaluate the use of a specific app with multiple prompt levels, indicating its potential to increase efficacy in completion of novel tasks and transitioning within and between tasks.

Educational researchers also used standardized measurement tools to measure the efficacy of a mobile app as cognitive aid in a sample of high school students with autism, indicating positive initial outcomes. Reports on the use of mobile technology are also being published specifically to support social skills development [28]. Mobile apps also offer the opportunity to modify the educational environment, for example by eliminating or reducing information that might distract attention from the main task, and allowing children to work at their own pace. Multi-touch tablets have been found to be appealing for children with autism, resulting in benefits such as increased motivation, attention and learning compared to traditional methods.

4 Methodology of Our Research

4.1 Purpose of Our Research

The aim of our study was to investigate whether the performance of autistic students in high school can be improved with the mobile apps use with specific educational software.

4.2 Main Research Question

The main research question that we were concerned about was whether mobile apps use allows cognitive access in all courses, targeting to entering the university.

4.3 Data collection

For the purposes of our research a small questionnaire was given to high school teachers on completing for the mobile apps educational results using by autistic students.

4.4 Participants

The survey involved on a group of high school teachers. Out of the 124 participants, 50 were men and 74 were women.

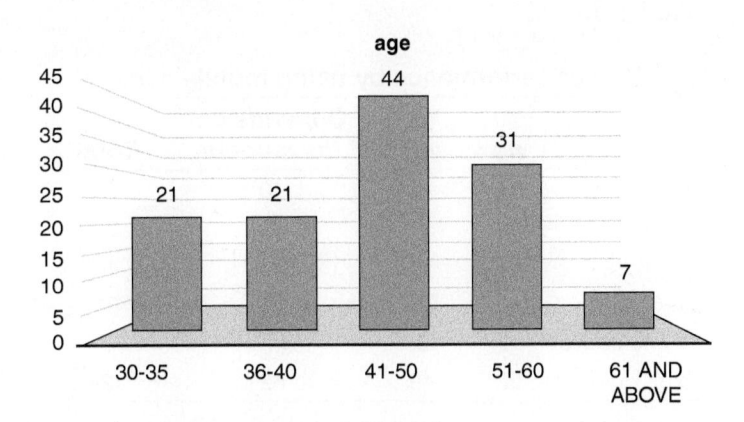

Figure 1 Graph 1. Age of participants

training in ICTs

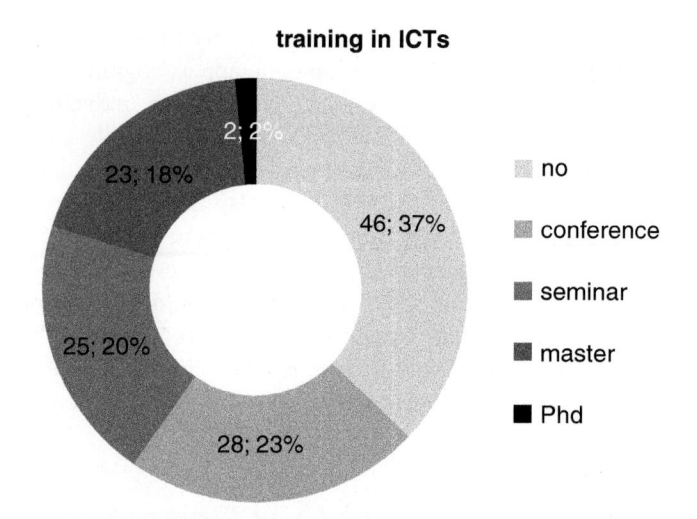

Figure 2 Graph 2. Teachers training in ICTs

4.5 Procedure
We collected our data from February of 2018 to May of 2018 with 124 participants, who are educators in high schools in Athens. Moreover, to each participant was given an Android-based cell phone with an online structured questionnaire developed by us.

4.6 Statistical analysis
Statistical analysis of the data was carried out with the SPSS 23 statistical package. The frequency of teacher's age and teacher training in ICTs were calculated. We found the Correlations between all variables using the Pearson Chi-Square. Our results are presented in the form of text.

4.7 Results
Research question 1: Whether the age of teachers influence their views about using mobile apps by autistic students.

Table 1.

Higher performance by using mobile apps

	no	yes	Depends on the student	Total
30–35	3	5	13	21
36–40	4	7	10	21
41–50	1	18	25	44
51–60	10	8	13	31
61 and above	4	2	1	7
Total	22	40	62	124

$X^2 = 41,759$, df = 16, p = 0,000.

The value of the Pearson Correlation Coefficient between the variable 'index age' and the variable: "index higher performance by using mobile apps" was statistically significant.

Conclusion
The purpose of our study was to examine how can the opportunity to high school students with autism to claim equal access to knowledge as do the other students be offered, by using supportive educational procedures, and especially mobile apps. In this effort 124 participants, who are educators in high school in Athens enrolled. Concerning the research questions, the results show an important correlation between the age of educators and their views about the digital education practice of autistic students. Especially, the 41–50 year olds' are more positive than their colleagues, and they also point out the capabilities of each student. In addition the data that concern teachers' response "depends on the student" especially correlated with teachers' ICTs training, are particularly important. In our research the majority of responses "depends on the student" which states the decisive role of the individual educational profile of each autistic student, plays a catalytic role.

Furthermore, well-designed mobile apps offer consistent and clearly defined tasks and visually cued instructions that can reduce misunderstandings caused by multiple verbal instructions [45] and thus promote independent educational functioning. In high schools, the complex academic environment can increase demands on organizational skills, planning skills and working memory for any student, but especially for students with autism. Recent developments in handheld devices with tools like portable checklists and reminder alarms can help increase independence in completing tasks [46]. In addition to previous research, this study revealed the educators' views that high school students with autism may use mobile apps in a variety of supportive educational ways. In many studies, participants reported using technology apps in school to increase their independence, reduce their anxiety, and improve their social opportunities. They also reported bringing technology tools with them to school every day but entry find barriers to its use through school and classroom restrictions on technology use [47].

References
[1] Carrington, S. (1999). Inclusion needs a different school culture. International Journal of Inclusive Education, 3(2), 257–268, http://dx.doi.org/10.1080/136031199285039

[2] Skiba, R. J. (2002). Special Education and School Discipline: A Precarious Balance. Behavioral Disorders, 27(2), 81–97, https://doi.org/10.1177/019874290202700209

[3] Smith, K.A., Sheppard, S.D., Johnson, D.W &. Johnson, R.T. (2005). "Pedagogies of Engagement: Classroom-Based Practices. Journal of Engineering Education, 94(1), 87–101 https://doi.org/10.1002/j.2168-9830.2005.tb00831.x

[4] Sharples, M., Taylor, J. & Vavoula, G. (2013). A Theory of Learning for the Mobile Age:Learning through conversation and exploration across contexts. R. Andrews and C. Haythornthwaite. The Sage Handbook of E-learning Research, Sage publications, 221–247, https://telearn.archives-ouvertes.fr/hal-00190276

[5] Fu, F.-L., Su, R.-C. & Yu, S.-C. (2009). 'E Game Flow: A scale to measure learners'enjoyment of e-learning games', Computers & Education, 52(1), 101–112, http://www.sciencedirect.com/science/article/pii/S0360131508001024 https://doi.org/10.1016/j.compedu.2008.07.004

[6] Melhuis. K. & Falloon, G.(2010). Looking to the future:-M-Learning with the I-pad., 1–16.

[7] Chu, H. C., Hwang, G. J., Tsai, C. C., & Tseng, J. C. (2010). A two-tier test approach to developing location-aware mobile learning systems for natural science courses. Computers & Education, 55(4), 1618–1627. https://doi.org/10.1016/j.compedu.2010.07.004

[8] Büyükbaykal, C. I. (2014). Communication Technologies and Education In the Information Age. Procedia - Social and Behavioral Science, 636–640.

[9] Motamedi,V. & Sumrall, W. J. (2000). Mastery learning and contemporary issues in education. Action in Teacher Education, 22(1), 32–42.

[10] Colis, B. & Moonen, J. (2001). Flexible learning in a digital world: Experiences and expectations. London: Kogan-Page 10.

[11] Litchfield, A. J., Dyson, L. E., Lawrence, E. M., & Bachfischer, A. (2007). Directions for mlearning research to enhance active learning. In Annual Conference of the Australasian Society for Computers in Learning in Tertiary Education. Centre for Educational Development, Nanyang Technological University.

[12] Johnson, L., Adams Becker, S., Estrada, V., & Freeman, A. (2014). NMC horizon report: 2014 higher education edition. Austin, Texas: The New Media Consortium.

[13] Vázquez-Cano, E. (2014). Mobile Distance Learning with Smartphones and Apps in Higher Education. Educational Sciences: Theory and Practice, v14 (4), pp1505–1520. Retrieved January 28, 2015, from http://files.eric.ed.gov/fulltext/EJ1045122.pdf https://doi.org/10.12738/estp.2014.4.2012

[14] Hsu, Y. C., Rice, K., & Dawley, L. (2012). Empowering educators with Google's Android App Inventor: An online workshop in mobile app design. British Journal of Educational Technology, 43, E1-E5. doi:10.1111/j.1467-8535.2011.01241.x Johnson

[15] Stathopoulou, A., Karabatzaki, Z., Drigas, A. et al. (2018). «Mobile assessment procedures for mental health and literacy skills in education». International Journal of Interactive Mobile Technologies, 12 (3), 21–36. https://doi.org/10.3991/ijim.v12i3.8038

[16] Kukulska-Hulme, A. (2009). Will mobile learning change language learning? ReCALL, 21(2), 157–165 https://doi.org/10.1017/S0958344009000202

[17] Johnson, L., Smith, R., Willis, H., Levine, A., & Haywood, K. (2011). The 2011 Horizon Report. Austin, Texas: The New Media Consortium.

[18] Barrs, K. (2011). Mobility in learning: The feasibility of encouraging language learning on smartphones. Studies in Self-Access Learning Journal, 2(3), 228–233.

[19] Alqahtani, M. & Mohammad, H. (2015). Mobile Applications' Impact on Student Performance and Satisfaction. The Turkish Online Journal of Educational Technology, 14(4), 102–112.

[20] Vazquez-Cano, E. (2014). Mobile Distance Learning with Smartphones and Apps in Higher Education, Educational Sciences: Theory & Practice, 14(4), 1505–1520.

[21] Johnson, D., Means, T., & Khey, D. (2013). A State of flux: Results of a mobile device survey at the University of Florida. Educate Review online (May 6, 2013). Retrieved from http://www.educause.edu/ero/article/state-flux-results-mobiledevice-survey-university-florida

[22] Johnson, L., Adams Becker, S., Estrada, V., & Freeman, A. (2014). NMC horizon report: 2014 higher education edition. Austin, Texas: The New Media Consortium.

[23] Dahlstorm, E., Warraich, K. (2013). Student mobile computing practices, 2012: Lessons learned from Qatar (Research Report). Louisville, CO: EDUCASE Center for Applied Research. Retrieved from http://educase.edu/ecar

[24] Smith, J., J. Morgan, P., J. Plotnikoff, R., C., Dally, K., A., Salmon, J., Okely, A., D., Finn, T., L. & Lubans, D. R. (2014). Smart-Phone Obesity Prevention Trial for Adolescent Boys in Low-Income Communities: The ATLAS RCT, PEDIATRICS 134(3), 723–731. https://doi.org/10.1542/peds.2014-1012

[25] Watts, S., Mackenzie, A., Thomas, C., Griskaitis, A., Mewton, L., Williams, A. & Andrews, G. (2013. CBT for depression: A pilot RCT comparing mobile phone vs. computer. BMC Psychiatry 13:49 https://doi.org/10.1186/1471-244X-13-49

[26] Grist, R., Porter, J. & Stallard, P. (2017). Mental Health Mobile Apps for Preadolescents and Adolescents: A Systematic Review, Journal of medical internet research, 19(5), 176. https://doi.org/10.2196/jmir.7332

[27] Hutchison, A., Beschorner, B., & Schmidt-Crawford, D. (2012). Exploring the use of the iPad for literacy learning. The Reading Teacher, 66(1), 15–23. https://doi.org/10.1002/TRTR.01090

[28] Karabatzaki, Z., Stathopoulou, A., Drigas, A., et al. (2018). «Mobile application tools for students in secondary education. An evaluation study». International Journal of Interactive Mobile Technologies. 12(2), 142–161.

[29] Franklin, T., & Peng, L. W. (2008). Mobile math: Math educators and students engage in mobile learning. Journal of Computing in Higher Education, 20(2), 69–80. https://doi.org/10.1007/s12528-008-9005-0

[30] Baird G, Simonoff E, Pickles A, et al. (2006). Prevalence of disorders of the autism spectrum in a population cohort of

children in South Thames: The Special Needs and Autism Project (SNAP). The Lancet 368(9531), 210–215 https://doi.org/10.1016/S0140-6736(06)69041-7

[31] American Psychiatric Association (APA) (2013). Diagnostic and Statistical Manual. 5th ed. Washington, DC: APA

[32] Department for Education (2012). Special Educational Needs in England. London: Department for Education

[33] Sterzing PR, Shattuck PT, Narendorf SC, et al. (2012). Bullying involvement and autism spectrum disorders: prevalence and correlates of bullying involvement among adolescents with an autism spectrum disorder. Archives of Pediatrics & Adolescent Medicine 166(11), 1058–1064 https://doi.org/10.1001/archpediatrics.2012.790

[34] Kaat, A.J., Gadow, K.D. & Lecavalier, L. (2013). Psychiatric symptom impairment in children with autism spectrum disorders. Journal of Abnormal Child Psychology 41(6), 959–969. https://doi.org/10.1007/s10802-013-9739-7

[35] Jones CRG, Happé F, Golden H, et al. (2009). Reading and arithmetic in adolescents with autism spectrum disorders: peaks and dips in attainment. Neuropsychology 23(6), 718–728. https://doi.org/10.1037/a0016360

[36] Mandy, W., Murin, M., Baykaner, O., Staunton, S., Hellriegel, J., Anderson, S., & Skuse, D. (2016). The transition from primary to secondary school in mainstream education for children with autism spectrum disorder. Autism: The International Journal of Research and Practice, 20, 5–13. https://doi.org/10.1177/1362361314562616

[37] Corcoran, T., & Silander, M. (2009). Instruction in high schools: The evidence and the challenge. The Future of Children, 19(1), 157–183 https://doi.org/10.1353/foc.0.0026

[38] Rosenthal, M., Lawson, R., Dixon, E., Wallace, G., Wills, M., Yerys, B., & Kenworthy, L. (2013). Impairments in real-world executive function increase from childhood to adolescence in autism spectrum disorders. Neuropsychology, 27(1), 13–18. https://doi.org/10.1037/a0031299

[39] Humphrey, N., Lewis, S. (2008). 'Make me normal': The views and experiences of pupils on the autistic spectrum in mainstream secondary schools. Autism, 12(1), 23–46. https://doi.org/10.1177/1362361307085267

[40] Josman, N., Ben-Chaim, H., Friedrich, H. & Weiss P. (2008). Effectiveness of virtual reality for teaching street-crossing skills to children and adolescents with autism. Int j Disabil 8 (7), 49–56. https://doi.org/10.1515/IJDHD.2008.7.1.49

[41] Kuo, M., Orsmond, G., Coster, W. et al. (2013) Media use among adolescents with autism spectrum disorder. Autism 18(8), 914–923. https://doi.org/10.1177/1362361313497832

[42] Mazurek MO, Shattuck PT, Wagner M. et al. (2012) Prevalenceand correlates of screenbased media use among youths with autism spectrum disorders. Journal of Autism and Developmental Disorders 42: 1757–1767. https://doi.org/10.1007/s10803-011-1413-8

[43] Grossard, C., Palestra, G., Xavier, J., Chetouani, M., Grynszpan, O., Cohen, D. (2018). ICT and autism care: state of the art. Current Opinion in Psychiatry: Child and Adolescent psychiatry, 31(6), 474–783. doi: 10.1097/YCO.00000000000004553

[44] Capo B and Orellana A (2011) Web 2.0 technologies for classroom instruction: high school teachers' perceptions and adoption factors. Quarterly Review of Distance Education 12(4), 235–253.

[45] Grynszpan O, Weiss PL, Perez-Diaz F. et al. (2014) Innovative technology-based interventions for autism spectrum disorders: a meta-analysis. Autism 18(4): 346–361. https://doi.org/10.1177/1362361313476767

[46] Palmen, A, Didden, R. & Verhoeven, L. (2012) A personal digital assistant for improving independent transitioning in adolescents with high-functioning autism spectrum disorder. Developmental Neurorehabilitation 15(6), 401–413 https://doi.org/10.3109/17518423. 2012.701240

[47] Hedges, S.H., Odom, S.L., Hume, M. & Sam, A (2017).: Technology Use as a Support Tool by Secondary Students with Autism. Autism, 1–10, https://doi.org/10.1177/1362361317717976

Critical Thinking

1. What do mobile apps offer as tools for digital learning for general education?
2. From the autistic student's perspective, explain the appeal of the various mobile technologies.

Internet References

An International Survey of Parental Attitudes to Technology Use by Their Autistic Children at Home
https://link.springer.com/article/10.1007/s10803-018-3798-0

Technology use as a support tool by secondary students with autism
https://files.eric.ed.gov/fulltext/EJ1167404.pdf

The transition from primary to secondary school in mainstream education for children with autism spectrum disorder
https://journals.sagepub.com/doi/pdf/10.1177/1362361314562616

AGATHI STATHOPOULOU is Partner of Institute of Informatics & telecommunications, Net Media Lab-Brain & Mind R&D, N.C.S.R. "DEMOKRITOS" Department of Psychology. She is a teacher in Secondary Education with a specialization in Greek philology. She holds PhD in Stress Disorder & Adolescent Psychology. She has participated in many educational seminars and conferences as a keynote speaker and as instructor. She has taught at the Department of Special Education of University of Athens and at the Department of Greek Literary of Democritus University of Thrace. She has written one book, and articles in scientific journals.

ZOE KARABATZAKI is a School Advisor at the 21st Preschool Educational Region of Athens. She holds a PhD on Educational Sciences (Special Education). She has participated in many educational seminars and conferences as a keynote speaker and as instructor. Furthermore, she has taken part in research programs that were supported by many universities of Greece. She has written two books, chapters in collective volumes, articles in scientific journals and educational notes. She has taught at the Department of Special Education of UTH (University of Thessaly), at the Department of Education and Early Childhood of UOA and the Department of Greek Literary of Democritus University of Thrace. She is also a scientific associate at Net Media Lab, Brain & Mind R&D of N.C.S.R. 'Demokritos'.

DIMOSTHENIS TSIROS hold an MSc in Special Education. He is teacher in secondary Education with a specialization in physic.

SPIRIDOYLA KATSANTONI holds a PhD in Special Education. She has taken part in research projects and seminars. At the current period is serving as a special educator at the Center for Diagnosis, Differentiation and Support, where pupils with special educational needs are assessed. She is also a scientific associate at Net Media Lab, Brain & Mind R&D of N.C.S.R. 'Demokritos.'

ATHANASIOS DRIGAS is a director of research at N.C.S.R. Demokritos. He is the Coordinator and founder of Net Media Lab, Brain & Mind R&D since 1996. From 1985 to 1999, he was the Operational manager of the Greek Academic network. He has been the Coordinator of Several International Projects, in the fields of ICTs, and e-services (e-learning, e-psychology, e-government, e-inclusion, e-culture, etc). He has published more than 300 articles, 7 books, 25 educational CD-ROMs and several patents. He has been a member of several International committees for the design and coordination of Network and ICT activities and of international conferences and journals. (e-mail: dr@iit.demokritos.gr).

Stathopoulou, Agathi et al. "Mobile Apps the Educational Solution for Autistic Students in Secondary Education." International Journal of Interactive Mobile Technologies, Vol 13, No 2 (2019). Used by permission.

5 Strategies for Inclusivity in Special Education

KAREN ACHTMAN

Learning Outcomes

After reading this article, you will be able to:

- Recognize ways that teaching for special needs relates to inclusive education for all students.
- Identify teaching dispositions that support inclusive education.

Like I suppose many of us, I knew I wanted to go into education. However, where I am in my career now is nowhere what I expected or anticipated when I began my journey 10 years ago. I earned degrees in elementary and special education knowing how much differentiation teachers are required to do nowadays. As a classroom teacher, I was drawn to my lower leveled students—those that needed more support to be successful, were behind grade level, but wanted to be like their peers. I took a leap to leave the classroom and take on the role as a special education teacher. For the past year plus, I have been teaching at a therapeutic day school for students on the Autism Spectrum Disorder. Students in my classroom range in age and academic levels. My classroom is organized like a typical classroom, but I do a lot of small group instruction to support their various needs and abilities.

Inclusive education is near and dear to my heart. I truly believe all students should have the opportunity to learn and be successful in the classroom. Though I make accommodations and modifications on a daily basis, differentiation benefits all students. Here are some easy tips to incorporate in the classroom that support multiple students!

1. Clear Expectations and Schedules

We've all been there—you know what you want students to do, but after you give instructions blank faces are staring back at you. Give clear expectations of what you want students to do to complete an activity: what are the directions, where can they work, what should the voice volume be, what should they do if they need help. Giving the directions orally and writing them on a board or projecting them are helpful ideas for students who have different modes of learning.

Some students benefit from individual directions they can refer to. I often post an agenda for the session and check off tasks as we complete them, so students know what they can expect next. If there are going to be schedule changes, preview them in advance in case some students struggle with the change. Being clear will help students know exactly what to do and focus more energy on the activities than figuring out what is going on.

2. Set Reasonable Goals

When I create IEP goals, I think, "what skills will this student need to be successful in the future?" While my criteria is different than if I was at a public school, I do think it's important to think about what will truly benefit the student. Is it more important someone can solve multi-digit operation problems or be able to use a calculator? If a student can access information if someone reads it to him, then should we focus on comprehension in addition to fluency? If handwriting is an issue, can he type or dictate to complete his work and share his ideas? Are there social skills that can be incorporated into an activity? It may be hard to think past the current moment, but it's also important to think what skills does this child need to be successful longterm.

3. Be a Team Player

It truly takes a group of teachers and therapists to support all aspects of a child. I'm fortunate to have a social worker, speech-language pathologist, occupational therapist, and behavior analyst in addition to paraprofessionals to support my students. Each person brings a unique perspective to the conversation. Together, you can make a difference. Don't be afraid to reach out and ask for advice or a question. Since each person has a different background, she may notice something different or have a new strategy to try. Collaboration is worth the time to help your classroom run more smoothly.

4. Be Flexible

Days never go as planned as there are many things out of your control. Maybe your students take longer to grasp a concept, so you have to spend more days teaching than originally planned. Maybe something is going on at home and a student is upset; as a result, you scrap your lesson because having a social and emotional conversation takes priority. Maybe a topic is challenging and the student gets frustrated; you give them a break and find a new way to teach the topic the following day. Maybe the student has trouble sitting still and needs extra sensory input and misses some of the activity. Maybe there are a lot of staff absent on a certain day and your plan period is cancelled so you can support instruction. While some of the situations are frustrating, it's not worth getting upset—remember, your job is to support these students. Have faith that the work will get done. Build relationships with your students and support them in whatever ways are needed in the moment.

5. Stay in the moment. Have a fresh start each day

There are going to be good days and bad days. There are going to be unexpected bumps in the road and challenging moments. As hard as it may be, get through it, reflect on what you can do next time, and keep going. Even when I have days that it seems everything goes wrong, I try to find at least one positive that happened. Even when I am frustrated with how a student behaved, I remember that the next morning is a new day and to give him a fresh start. As much as we support these students, we don't know or understand everything that is going on in their lives. It is our job to be their cheerleader and support them. There is something good in every day.

As teachers, it seems that our workload never stops but don't forget your main priority is to educate your students. Look for ways that you can incorporate new ideas or strategies into your classroom that support all your students. Feel free to comment below with additional ideas you use to support your students.

Critical Thinking

1. What is the significance of attending to learning outcomes in implementing learning strategies?
2. What are common characteristics of the steps to inclusive special education?

Internet References

Educator Voices: Where the Art of Teaching Meets the Science of Learning
https://www.mheducation.com/prek-12/explore/art-of-teaching.html

Special Education Degrees: Your Guide to a Career in Special Education
https://www.special-education-degree.net/what-are-inclusive-special-education-programs/

KAREN ACHTMAN is a special education teacher at Giant Steps in Illinois. This is her seventh year teaching in both elementary and special education classrooms. Karen graduated from Syracuse University with a degree in Inclusive Elementary and Special Education. She is passionate about teaching all students at their ability levels and finding a way for them to be successful.

"Achtman, Karen. "5 Strategies for Inclusivity in Special Education." https://medium.com/inspired-ideas-prek-12/5-strategies-for-inclusivity-in-special-education-609ccdacfdb7. Used by permission of the author."

Article

Prepared by: Sheron Fraser-Burgess, *Ball State University*

Education of All Handicapped Children Act

U. S. Congress, Public Law 94–142

Learning Outcomes

After reading this article, you will be able to:

- Summarize the legendary public law for special education—94-142—considered as one of the most basic facts that should be known by all educators.
- Identify the terms "IEP" and "FAPE."
- Identify IDEA, the re-naming legislation that was passed in 1990.

Now known as the Individuals with Disabilities Education Act (IDEA), the Education of All Handicapped Children Act required states to provide a Free Appropriate Public Education (FAPE) for all individuals with disabilities between the age of 3 and 21. The program was designed to meet the individual needs of each child with an Individualized Education Plan (IEP) and to provide an education to prepare students for employment and independent living. Originally passed in 1975, the act was renamed in 1990 to reflect the preferred use of the term "disability" rather than handicap. The legislation included three fundamental purposes: (1) to assure that all children with disabilities receive free public education designed for their unique needs; (2) to protect the rights of children with disabilities and their parents and guardians; (3) to assist states in providing for the effective education of all children with disabilities. When enacted in 1975, "more than half of the disabled children in the United States did not receive appropriate educational services which would enable them to have full equality of opportunity." Today, nearly all children with disabilities receive a free public education.

. . .

Statement of Findings and Purpose

SEC. 3. (a) Section 601 of the Act (20 U.S.C. 1401) is amended by inserting "(a)" immediately before "This title" and by adding at the end thereof the following new subsections:

"(b) The Congress finds that—

"(1) there are more than eight million handicapped children in the United States today;

"(2) the special educational needs of such children are not being fully met;

"(3) more than half of the handicapped children in the United States do not receive appropriate educational services which would enable them to have full equality of opportunity;

"(4) one million of the handicapped children in the United States are excluded entirely from the public school system and will not go through the educational process with their peers;

"(5) there are many handicapped children throughout the United States participating in regular school programs whose handicaps prevent them from having a successful educational experience because their handicaps are undetected;

"(6) because of the lack of adequate services within the public school system, families are often forced to find services outside the public school system, often at great distance from their residence and at their own expense;

"(7) developments in the training of teachers and in diagnostic and instructional procedures and methods have advanced to the point that, given appropriate funding, State and local educational agencies can and will provide effective special education and related services to meet the needs of handicapped children;

"(8) State and local educational agencies have a responsibility to provide education for all handicapped children, but present financial resources are inadequate to meet the special educational needs of handicapped children; and

"(9) it is in the national interest that the Federal Government assist State and local efforts to provide programs to meet the educational needs of handicapped children in order to assure equal protection of the law.

"(c) It is the purpose of this Act to assure that all handicapped children have available to them, within the time periods specified in section 612(2) (B), a free appropriate public education which emphasizes special education and related services designed to meet their unique needs, to assure that the rights of handicapped children and their parents or guardians are protected, to assist States and localities to provide for the education of all handicapped children, and to assess and assure the effectiveness of efforts to educate handicapped children."

(b) The heading for section 601 of the Act (20 U.S.C. 1401) is amended to read as follows:

"SHORT TITLE; STATEMENT OF FINDINGS AND PURPOSE".

Definitions

SEC. 4. (a) Section 602 of the Act (20 U.S.C. 1402) is amended—

(1) in paragraph (1) thereof, by striking out "crippled" and inserting in lieu thereof "orthopedically impaired", and by inserting immediately after "impaired children" the following: ", or children with specific learning disabilities,";

(2) in paragraph (5) thereof, by inserting immediately after "instructional materials," the following: "telecommunications, sensory, and other technological aids and devices,";

(3) in the last sentence of paragraph (15) thereof, by inserting immediately after "environmental" the following:", cultural, or economic"; and

(4) by adding at the end thereof the following new paragraphs:

"(16) The term 'special education' means specially designed instruction, at no cost to parents or guardians, to meet the unique needs of a handicapped child, including classroom instruction, instruction in physical education, home instruction, and instruction in hospitals and institutions.

"(17) The term 'related services' means transportation, and such developmental, corrective, and other supportive services (including speech pathology and audiology, psychological services, physical and occupational therapy, recreation, and medical and counseling services, except that such medical services shall be for diagnostic and evaluation purposes only) as may be required to assist a handicapped child to benefit from special education, and includes the early identification and assessment of handicapping conditions in children.

"(18) The term 'free appropriate public education' means special education and related services which (A) have been provided at public expense, under public supervision and direction, and without charge, (B) meet the standards of the State educational agency, (C) include an appropriate preschool, elementary, or secondary school education in the State involved, and (D) are provided in conformity with the individualized education program required under section 614(a) (5).

"(19) The term 'individualized education program' means a written statement for each handicapped child developed in any meeting by a representative of the local educational agency or an intermediate educational unit who shall be qualified to provide, or supervise the provision of, specially designed instruction to meet the unique needs of handicapped children, the teacher, the parents or guardian of such child, and, whenever appropriate, such child, which statement shall include (A) a statement of the present levels of educational performance of such child, (B) a statement of annual goals, including short-term instructional objectives, (C) a statement of the specific educational services to be provided to such child, and the extent to which such child will be able to participate in regular educational programs, (D) the projected date for initiation and anticipated duration of such services, and (E) appropriate objective criteria and evaluation procedures and schedules for determining, on at least an annual basis, whether instructional objectives are being achieved.

"(20) The term 'excess costs' means those costs which are in excess of the average annual per student expenditure in a local educational agency during the preceding school year for an elementary or secondary school student, as may be appropriate, and which shall be computed after deducting (A) amounts received under this part or under title I or title VII of the Elementary and Secondary Education Act of 1965, and (B) any State or local funds expended for programs which would qualify for assistance under this part or under such titles.

"(21) The term 'native language' has the meaning given that term by section 703(a) (2) of the Bilingual Education Act (20 U.S.C. 880b–1 (a) (2)).

"(22) The term 'intermediate educational unit' means any public authority, other than a local educational agency, which is under the general supervision of a State educational agency, which is established by State law for the purpose of providing free public education on a regional basis, and which provides special education and related services to handicapped children within that State.".

(b) The heading for section 602 of the Act (20 U.S.C. 1402) is amended to read as follows:

Eligibility

"SEC. 612. In order to qualify for assistance under this part in any fiscal year, a State shall demonstrate to the Commissioner that the following conditions are met:

"(1) The State has in effect a policy that assures all handicapped children the right to a free appropriate public education.

"(2) The State has developed a plan pursuant to section 613 (b) in effect prior to the date of the enactment of the Education for All Handicapped Children Act of 1975 and submitted not later than August 21, 1975, which will be amended so as to comply with the provisions of this paragraph. Each such amended plan shall set forth in detail the policies and procedures which the State will undertake or has undertaken in order to assure that—

"(A) there is established (i) a goal of providing full educational opportunity to all handicapped children, (ii) a detailed timetable for accomplishing such a goal, and (iii) a description of the kind and number of facilities, personnel, and services necessary throughout the State to meet such a goal;

"(B) a free appropriate public education will be available for all handicapped children between the ages of three and eighteen within the State not later than September 1, 1978, and for all handicapped children between the ages of three and twenty-one within the State not later than September 1, 1980, except that, with respect to handicapped children aged three to five and aged eighteen to twenty-one, inclusive, the requirements of this clause shall not be applied in any State if the application of such requirements would be inconsistent with State law or practice, or the order of any court, respecting public education within such age groups in the State;

"(C) all children residing in the State who are handicapped, regardless of the severity of their handicap, and who are in need of special education and related services are identified, located, and evaluated, and that a practical method is developed and implemented to determine which children are currently receiving needed special education and related services and which children are not currently receiving needed special education and related services;

"(D) policies and procedures are established in accordance with detailed criteria prescribed under section 617(c); and

"(E) the amendment to the plan submitted by the State required by this section shall be available to parents, guardians, and other members of the general public at least thirty days prior to the date of submission of the amendment to the Commissioner.

"(3) The State has established priorities for providing a free appropriate public education to all handicapped children, which priorities shall meet the timetables set forth in clause (B) of paragraph (2) of this section, first with respect to handicapped children who are not receiving an education, and second with respect to handicapped children, within each disability, with the most severe handicaps who are receiving an inadequate education, and has made adequate progress in meeting the timetables set forth in clause (B) of paragraph (2) of this section.

"(4) Each local educational agency in the State will maintain records of the individualized education program for each handicapped child, and such program shall be established, reviewed, and revised as provided in section 614 (a) (5).

"(5) The State has established (A) procedural safeguards as required by section 615, (B) procedures to assure that, to the maximum extent appropriate, handicapped children, including children in public or private institutions or other care facilities, are educated with children who are not handicapped, and that special classes, separate schooling, or other removal of handicapped children from the regular educational environment occurs only when the nature or severity of the handicap is such that education in regular classes with the use of supplementary aids and services cannot be achieved satisfactorily, and (C) procedures to assure that testing and evaluation materials and procedures utilized for the purposes of evaluation and placement of handicapped children will be selected and administered so as not to be racially or culturally discriminatory. Such materials or procedures shall be provided and administered in the child's native language or mode of communication, unless it clearly is not feasible to do so, and no single procedure shall be the sole criterion for determining an appropriate educational program for a child.

"(6) The State educational agency shall be responsible for assuring that the requirements of this part are carried out and that all educational programs for handicapped children within the State, including all such programs administered by any other State or local agency, will be under the general supervision of the persons responsible for educational programs for handicapped children in the State educational agency and shall meet education standards of the State educational agency.

"(7) The State shall assure that (A) in carrying out the requirements of this section procedures are established for consultation with individuals involved in or concerned with the education of handicapped children, including handicapped individuals and parents or guardians of handicapped children, and (B) there are public hearings, adequate notice of such hearings, and an opportunity for comment available to the general public prior to adoption of the policies, programs, and procedures required pursuant to the provisions of this section and section 613.

Critical Thinking

1. What is the significance of the terms "individuals" and "individualized"?
2. What title would now be more appropriate for IDEA?
3. Discuss the evolution from "mainstreaming" to inclusion education.

Internet References

The IDEA Partnership
www.ideapartnership.org

The Families and Advocates Partnership for Education Project
www.fape.org

From Public Law 94–142, 94th Congress by U.S. Congress, 1975.

UNIT

Prepared by: Sheron Fraser-Burgess, *Ball State University*

Ethics & Community Engagement

Schools are nested within the broader societal context; however, discourse about schools can take place as if the school building is on an island. Related to this image is the isolated functioning of all of its standard aspects (classrooms, building maintenance, school board meetings, etc.) in isolation from the substantive engagement with community. To not consider the families whom the school serves overlooks a significant source of knowledge that can help children learn. In this area, a paradigm shift is taking place in K–12 education that relates to the role of family engagement in schools. A focus on community engagement presupposes that the families and the community in which they embedded are a rich resource for children. Gonzalez, Moll & Amanti (2009) refer to this reservoir as funds of knowledge upon which schools can draw. Amatea (2012) maintains that leveraging children's cultural background for classroom learning is the necessary trait of the optimal relationship among schools, families and the community. This collaborative relationship is a paradigm of relationship where families are valued for unique strengths, practices and lived experiences with it is associated. Families become capable partners in educating their children. Foregrounding community engagement takes for granted the value of the family and community and undertakes the task of strengthening the relationship through curricular and extracurricular activities.

Family collaboration is in contrast with a deficit approach that is characteristic of the separation paradigm of relationships between families and schools. On this view, schools are self-contained and autonomous spaces in which learning takes place. There is also the assumption that learning requires diminishing the influence of one's language, history, and culture. Ironically, separation can co-occur with an authentic desire to transform the social conditions, which many vulnerable families face. Predominantly black and brown communities can confront a set of converging factors that include economic disadvantage, underemployment, and subpar schools. A separation paradigm holds that the best interventions are found in the classrooms and through teacher-centered learning. In contrast, culturally responsive instruction truly mines the child's background and the caregivers as their first teachers to scaffold learning.

Paying attention to schools' ability to incorporate and draw on the hopes, dreams and aspiration of their children's families is part of a broader conversation about teaching ethics. Bringing an ethical prism to the education world imposes standards of good and right action as norms by which teaching practices and education policies can be evaluated. It is dramatic contrast to educational accountability only in terms as being relative to students' performance on standard tests. Ethical frameworks can evaluate the extent to which schools are spaces that protect the rights of parents and other caregivers, promote human flourishing and advance democratic virtues among all stakeholders. The articles included in this unit both recognize increasing prominence of family engagement and, in the Dewey article, show the longstanding dependence among democracy, community and the education. At the university level, the town-gown relationships can be evaluated on whether community engagement in terms of promotes true partnership. For example, are these relationships reciprocal in power and knowledge transfer? The article on the K–12 setting offers an ethical model in which trust and community was fostered among stakeholders.

References

Amatea, E. (2012). *Building culturally responsive family school relationships*. 2nd Edition. New York, NY: Pearson.

Gonzalez, N., Moll, L. C., and Amanti, C. (2009). *Funds of Knowledge: Theorizing Practices in Households, Communities, and Classrooms*. New York: Routledge.

Article

Prepared by: Sheron Fraser-Burgess, *Ball State University*

The Next "Evolution" of Civic Learning

TANIA D. MITCHELL

Learning Outcomes

After reading this article, you will be able to:

- Link democratic engagement with civic learning initiatives.
- Ascertain the pedagogical best practices of civic learning in higher education.

Civic learning and democratic engagement are near ubiquitous in higher education, with postsecondary institutions embracing their responsibility to prepare students for active and informed participation in their communities. This work, aimed at civic renewal, seeks to develop graduates who will do their part to ensure a robust democracy.

Scholars and practitioners have spent much of the last thirty years outlining best practices and identifying the outcomes that result when these practices are implemented. Civic learning initiatives have been shown to yield higher grade point averages, a greater acceptance of diversity, and a desire to contribute to the common good. And while we have seen an expansion of programs, opportunities, and experiences in colleges and universities that promote civic learning and democratic engagement, data from the Student Experience in the Research University (SERU) survey still show that nearly 45 percent of the college students responding to the survey (N = 19,728) report spending zero hours contributing to the community.

Despite its pervasiveness, there is still a significant gap in the reach of civic learning initiatives. So, the initiatives profiled in this issue represent an important step in the work to ensure a broader reach and a deeper connection to civic learning and demonstrate that civic opportunities and motivations exist across our institutions.

Civic learning and democratic engagement are multidisciplinary, interdisciplinary, and transdisciplinary—allowing for these initiatives to thrive in multiple spaces on our campuses. Centering this work within departments and academic units allows faculty to embrace the civic dimensions of their disciplines. It creates linkages between civic learning and civic professions—supporting students in understanding how they might contribute to the public good through occupations connected to their academic studies. It also generates ongoing opportunities for students and instructors to engage in dialogues that might emerge, persist, and evolve as they encounter each other in classes throughout their academic careers.

And while this deepening of civic learning through academic departments and majors ensures that students will be challenged to reflect on the civic possibilities for their lives as college students and after, it does not yet ensure that our improved civic opportunities on campus yield civic benefits beyond our institutional walls. We know our students will benefit, but what will it mean for the communities where this work most often happens?

Civic learning initiatives should aim not only to support students in understanding their civic responsibility and the civic possibilities for our increasingly diverse democracy, but should also aim to be responsive to the social and community concerns that limit civic engagement. These initiatives should also work to alleviate those concerns with the recognition that full and inclusive engagement in civic life shapes the robust democracy we seek.

Therefore, as we consider the spaces in our own institutions where these kinds of engaged departments might thrive, let us ensure we are also considering the ways we might engage so that our communities also thrive.

- Are we creating spaces and opportunities to build civic leadership and civic agency in our communities as well as in our student body?
- Do community members believe us when we say we want to help? Why or why not?

- Are our civic efforts responsive to issues identified by community members?
- Do we engage the members of the community most impacted by the issues we are addressing?
- Are the actions we are taking those that communities have asked of us?
- Do community members (co-)lead those efforts?
- Are we acting in ways that truly effect change on those community-identified issues?

It feels important that the next "evolution" of civic learning asks not only how we do this work well in our institutions, but how we ensure these efforts yield the best possible civic outcomes—not just for our students, but also for the communities where this work happens.

Critical Thinking

1. What kinds of classroom practices have been found to promote deep civic learning?
2. What hangs on the quest for the best possible civic outcomes in the future?

Internet References

Civic Learning and Democratic Engagement
https://www.naspa.org/focus-areas/civic-learning-and-democratic-engagement

Civic Learning and Engagement in Democracy
https://www.ed.gov/civic-learning

How Civic Engagement Impacts Student Learning and Student Success
http://www.aasa.org/content.aspx?id=37858

Mitchell, Tania D. "The Next 'Evolution' of Civic Learning." Peer Review: Emerging Trends and Key Debates in Undergraduate Education, 2017. Used by permission of Association of American Colleges & Universities.

Article

Prepared by: Sheron Fraser-Burgess, *Ball State University*

Democracy in Education

JOHN DEWEY

Learning Outcomes

After reading this article, you will be able to:

- Explain the importance of "freedom of intelligence."
- Identify Dewey's three most powerful motives of human activity.
- Describe a basic conception of cultural rather than political democracy.

No brief statement can fully convey the importance and significance of John Dewey's work for the field of education. An academic philosopher who became most interested in education beginning in the early 20th century when faced with questions of how to best educate his children, Dewey's professional writings helped to define pragmatism as a dominant American philosophical tradition of the 20th century and to establish the foundations for progressive education. Today, *Experience and Education* is typically viewed as his most popular work and *Democracy and Education* as the most profound education-related publication, seen he said, "as the closest attempt he had made to summarize his 'entire philosophical position'." (Westbrook, 1991, p. 168)

John Dewey (1859–1952), in his role as head of the Department of Philosophy, Psychology, and Pedagogy at the University of Chicago, established in 1896 an experimental school that became one of the most important laboratory schools in the country. After his move to Columbia University in 1904, he continued to work with professors at Teachers College (the related education college of Columbia) and to write in the field of educational foundations.

Excerpts from Dewey's publications prove difficult to extract even though I do not fully agree with Justice Oliver Wendell Holmes who described Dewey's writing as what "God would have spoken had He been inarticulate but keenly desirous to tell you how it was." (Dykhuizen, 1973, p. 214) (1.) No mere selection can adequately portray Dewey's work. "Readers seeking a balanced and judicious overview of Dewey's vast educational ruminations are advised to turn directly to Dewey's writings." (Jackson, 1998, p. 165) Students of education would be well served, however, to also read one of the many biographies that have appeared, notably Jay Martin's *The Education of John Dewey*. (Martin, 2002) Instead of including a book excerpt in *Classic Edition Sources: Education*, a self-inclusive article from the *Elementary School Teacher* journal has been selected. Written shortly after Dewey's popular education book, *The School and Society,* and during a most active time as an educational administrator, "Democracy in Education" articulates Dewey's view of the most powerful motives of human activity.

(Note 1.) Although it should be noted that Holmes also gave praise; after reading *Experience and Nature* "he felt as though he had for the first time seen the universe 'from the inside'." (Ryan, 1995, p. 20)

. . .

Modern life means democracy, democracy means freeing intelligence for independent effectiveness—the emancipation of mind as an individual organ to do its own work. We naturally associate democracy, to be sure, with freedom of action, but freedom of action without freed capacity of thought behind it is only chaos. If external authority in action is given up, it must be because internal authority of truth, discovered and known to reason, is substituted.

How does the school stand with reference to this matter? Does the school as an accredited representative exhibit this trait of democracy as a spiritual force? Does it lead and direct the movement? Does it lag behind and work at cross-purpose? I find the fundamental need of the school today dependent upon its limited recognition of the principle of freedom of intelligence. This limitation appears to me to affect both of the elements of school life: teacher and pupil. As to both, the school has lagged behind the general contemporary social movement; and much that is unsatisfactory, much of conflict and of defect, comes from the discrepancy between the relatively undemocratic organization of the school, as it affects the mind of both teacher and pupil, and the growth and extension of the democratic principle in life beyond school doors.

The effort of the last two-thirds of a century has been successful in building up the machinery of a democracy of mind. It has provided the ways and means for housing and equipping intelligence. What remains is that the thought-activity of the individual, whether teacher or student, be permitted and encouraged to take working possession of this machinery: to substitute its rightful lordship for an inherited servility. In truth, our public-school system is but two-thirds of a century old. It dates, so far as such matters can be dated at all, from 1837, the year that Horace Mann became secretary of the state board of Massachusetts; and from 1843, when Henry Barnard began a similar work in Connecticut. At this time began that growing and finally successful warfare against all the influences, social and sectarian, which would prevent or mitigate the sway of public influence over private ecclesiastical and class interests. Between 1837 and 1850 grew up all the most characteristic features of the American public-school system: from this time date state normal schools, city training schools, county and state institutes, teachers' associations, teachers' journals, the institution of city superintendencies, supervisory officers, and the development of state universities as the crown of the public-school system of the commonwealth. From this time date the striving for better schoolhouses and grounds, improved text-books, adequate material equipment in maps, globes, scientific apparatus, etc. As an outcome of the forces thus set in motion, democracy has in principle, subject to relative local restrictions, developed an organized machinery of public education. But when we turn to the aim and method which this magnificent institution serves, we find that our democracy is not yet conscious of the ethical principle upon which it rests—the responsibility and freedom of mind in discovery and proof—and consequently we find confusion where there should be order, darkness where there should be light. The teacher has not the power of initiation and constructive endeavor which is necessary to the fulfilment of the function of teaching. The learner finds conditions antagonistic (or at least lacking) to the development of individual mental power and to adequate responsibility for its use.

I. As to the teacher.—If there is a single public-school system in the United States where there is official and constitutional provision made for submitting questions of methods of discipline and teaching, and the questions of the curriculum, text-books, etc., to the discussion and decision of those actually engaged in the work of teaching, that fact has escaped my notice. Indeed, the opposite situation is so common that it seems, as a rule, to be absolutely taken for granted as the normal and final condition of affairs. The number of persons to whom any other course has occurred as desirable, or even possible—to say nothing of necessary—is apparently very limited. But until the public-school system is organized in such a way that every teacher has some regular and representative way in which he or she can register judgment upon matters of educational importance, with the assurance that this judgment will somehow affect the school system, the assertion that the present system is not, from the internal standpoint, democratic seems to be justified. Either we come here upon some fixed and inherent limitation of the democratic principle, or else we find in this fact an obvious discrepancy between the conduct of the school and the conduct of social life—a discrepancy so great as to demand immediate and persistent effort at reform.

The more enlightened portions of the public have, indeed, become aware of one aspect of this discrepancy. Many reformers are contending against the conditions which place the direction of school affairs, including the selection of text-books, etc., in the hands of a body of men who are outside the school system itself, who have not necessarily any expert knowledge of education and who are moved by non-educational motives. Unfortunately, those who have noted this undemocratic condition of affairs, and who have striven to change it, have, as a rule, conceived of but one remedy, namely, the transfer of authority to the school superintendent. In their zeal to place the center of gravity inside the school system, in their zeal to decrease the prerogatives of a non-expert school board, and to lessen the opportunities for corruption and private pull which go with that, they have tried to remedy one of the evils of democracy by adopting the principle of autocracy. For no matter how wise, expert, or benevolent the head of the school system, the one-man principle is autocracy.

The logic of the argument goes farther, very much farther, than the reformer of this type sees. The logic which commits him to the idea that the management of the school system must be in the hands of an expert commits him also to the idea that every member of the school system, from the first-grade teacher to the principal of the high school, must have some share in the exercise of educational power. The remedy is not to have one expert dictating educational methods and subject-matter to a body of passive, recipient teachers, but the adoption of intellectual initiative, discussion, and decision throughout the entire school corps. The remedy of the partial evils of democracy, the implication of the school system in municipal politics, is in appeal to a more thorough going democracy.

The dictation, in theory at least, of the subject-matter to be taught, to the teacher who is to engage in the actual work of instruction, and frequently, under the name of close supervision, the attempt to determine the methods which are to be used in teaching, mean nothing more or less than the deliberate restriction of intelligence, the imprisoning of the spirit. Every well graded system of schools in this country rejoices in a course of study. It is no uncommon thing to find methods of teaching such subjects as reading, writing, spelling, and arithmetic officially laid down; outline topics in history and geography are provided ready-made for the teacher; gems of literature are fitted to the successive ages of boys and girls. Even the domain of art, songs and methods of singing, subject-matter and technique of drawing and painting, come within the region on which an outside authority lays its sacrilegious hands.

I have stated the theory, which is also true of the practice to a certain extent and in certain places. We may thank our heavens, however, that the practice is rarely as bad as the theory would require. Superintendents and principals often encourage individuality and thoughtfulness in the invention and adoption of methods of teaching; and they wink at departures from the printed manual of study. It remains true, however, that this great advance is personal and informal. It depends upon the wisdom and tact of the individual supervisory official; he may withdraw his concession at any moment; or it may be ruthlessly thrown aside by his successor who has formed a high ideal of "system."

I know it will be said that this state of things, while an evil, is a necessary one; that without it confusion and chaos would reign; that such regulations are the inevitable accompaniments of any graded system. It is said that the average teacher is incompetent to take any part in laying out the course of study or in initiating methods of instruction or discipline. Is not this the type of argument which has been used from time immemorial, and in every department of life, against the advance of democracy? What does democracy mean save that the individual is to have a share in determining the conditions and the aims of his own work; and that, upon the whole, through the free and mutual harmonizing of different individuals, the work of the world is better done than when planned, arranged, and directed by a few, no matter how wise or of how good intent that few? How can we justify our belief in the democratic principle elsewhere, and then go back entirely upon it when we come to education?

Moreover, the argument proves too much. The more it is asserted that the existing corps of teachers is unfit to have voice in the settlement of important educational matters, and their unfitness to exercise intellectual initiative and to assume the responsibility for constructive work is emphasized, the more their unfitness to attempt the much more difficult and delicate task of guiding souls appears. If this body is so unfit, how can it be trusted to carry out the recommendations or the dictations of the wisest body of experts? If teachers are incapable of the intellectual responsibility which goes with the determination of the methods they are to use in teaching, how can they employ methods when dictated by others, in other than a mechanical, capricious, and clumsy manner? The argument, I say, proves too much.

Moreover, if the teaching force is as inept and unintelligent and irresponsible as the argument assumes, surely the primary problem is that of their improvement. Only by sharing in some responsible task does there come a fitness to share in it. The argument that we must wait until men and women are fully ready to assume intellectual and social responsibilities would have defeated every step in the democratic direction that has ever been taken. The prevalence of methods of authority and of external dictation and direction tends automatically to perpetuate the very conditions of inefficiency, lack of interest, inability to assume positions of self-determination, which constitute the reasons that are depended upon to justify the régime of authority.

The system which makes no great demands upon originality, upon invention, upon the continuous expression of individuality, works automatically to put and to keep the more incompetent teachers in the school. It puts them there because, by a natural law of spiritual gravitation, the best minds are drawn to the places where they can work most effectively. The best minds are not especially like to be drawn where there is danger that they may have to submit to conditions which no self-respecting intelligence likes to put up with; and where their time and energy are likely to be so occupied with details of external conformity that they have no opportunity for free and full play of their own vigor.

I have dwelt at length upon the problem of the recognition of the intellectual and spiritual individuality of the teacher. I have but one excuse. All other reforms are conditioned upon reform in the quality and character of those who engage in the teaching profession. The doctrine of the man behind the gun has become familiar enough, in recent discussion, in every sphere of life. Just because education is the most personal, the most intimate, of all human affairs, there, more than anywhere else, the sole ultimate reliance and final source of power are in the training, character, and intelligence of the individual. If any scheme could be devised which would draw to the calling of teaching persons of force of character, of sympathy with children, and consequent interest in the problems of teaching and of scholarship, no one need be troubled for a moment about other educational reforms, or the solution of other educational problems. But as long as a school organization which is undemocratic in principle tends to repel from all but the higher portions of the school system those of independent force, of intellectual initiative, and of inventive ability, or tends to hamper them in their work after they find their way into the schoolroom, so long all other reforms are compromised at their source and postponed indefinitely for fruition.

2. As to the learner.—The undemocratic suppression of the individuality of the teacher goes naturally with the improper restriction of the intelligence of the mind of the child. The mind, to be sure, is that of a child, and yet, after all, it is mind. To subject mind to an outside and ready-made material is a denial of the ideal of democracy, which roots itself ultimately in the principle of moral, self-directing individuality. Misunderstanding regarding the nature of the freedom that is demanded for the child is so common that it may be necessary to emphasize the fact that it is primarily intellectual freedom, free play of mental attitude, and operation which are sought. If individuality were simply a matter of feelings, impulses, and outward acts independent of intelligence, it would be more than a dubious matter to urge a greater degree of freedom for the child in the school. In that case much, and almost exclusive, force would attach to the objections that the principle of individuality is realized in the more exaggerated parts of Rousseau's doctrines: sentimental idealization of the child's immaturity, irrational denial of superior worth in the knowledge and mature experience of the adult, deliberate denial of the worth of the ends and instruments embodied in social organization. Deification of childish whim, unripened fancy, and arbitrary emotion is certainly a piece of pure romanticism. The would-be reformers who emphasize out of due proportion and perspective these aspects of the principle of individualism betray their own cause. But the heart of the matter lies not there. Reform of education in the direction of greater play for the individuality of the child means the securing of conditions which will give outlet, and hence direction, to a growing intelligence. It is true that this freed power of mind with reference to its own further growth cannot be obtained without a certain leeway, a certain flexibility, in the expression of even immature feelings and fancies. But it is equally true that it is not a riotous loosening of these traits which is needed, but just that kind and degree of freedom from repression which are found to be necessary to secure the full operation of intelligence.

Now, no one need doubt as to what mental activity or the freed expression of intelligence means. No one need doubt as to the conditions which are conducive to it. We do not have to fall back upon what some regard as the uncertain, distracting, and even distressing voice of psychology. Scientific methods, the methods pursued by the scientific inquirer, give us an exact and concrete exhibition of the path which intelligence takes when working most efficiently, under most favorable conditions.

What is primarily required for that direct inquiry which constitutes the essence of science is first-hand experience; an active and vital participation through the medium of all the bodily organs with the means and materials of building up first-hand experience. Contrast this first and most fundamental of all the demands for an effective use of mind with what we find in so many of our elementary and high schools. There first-hand experience is at a discount; in its stead are summaries and formulas of the results of other people. Only very recently has any positive provision been made within the schoolroom for any of the modes of activity and for any of the equipment and arrangement which permit and require the extension of original experiences on the part of the child. The school has literally been dressed out with hand-me-down garments—with intellectual suits which other people have worn.

Secondly, in that freed activity of mind which we term "science" there is always a certain problem which focuses effort, which controls the collecting of facts that bear upon the question, the use of observation to get further data, the employing of memory to supply relevant facts, the calling into play of imagination, to yield fertile suggestion and construct possible solutions of the difficulty.

Turning to the school, we find too largely no counterpart to this mental activity. Just because a second-handed material has been supplied wholesale and retail, but anyway ready-made, the tendency is to reduce the activity of mind to a docile or passive taking in of the material presented—in short, to memorizing, with simply incidental use of judgment and of active research. As is frequently stated, acquiring takes the place of inquiring. It is hardly an exaggeration to say that the sort of mind-activity which is encouraged in the school is a survival from the days in which science had not made much headway; when education was mainly concerned with learning, that is to say, the preservation and handing down of the acquisitions of the past. It is true that more and more appeal is made every day in schools to judgment, reasoning, personal efficiency, and the calling up of personal, as distinct from merely book, experiences. But we have not yet got to the point of reversing the total method. The burden and the stress still fall upon learning in the sense of becoming possessed of the second-hand and ready-made material referred to. As Mrs. Young has recently said, the prevailing ideal is a perfect recitation, an exhibition without mistake, of a lesson learned. Until the emphasis changes to the conditions which make it necessary for the child to take an active share in the personal building up of his own problems and to participate in methods of solving them (even at the expense of experimentation and error), mind is not really freed.

In our schools we have freed individuality in many modes of outer expression without freeing intelligence, which is the vital spring and guarantee of all of these expressions. Consequently we give opportunity to the unconverted to point the finger of scorn, and to clamor for a return to the good old days when the teacher, the representative of social and moral authority, was securely seated in the high places of the school. But the remedy here, as in other phases of our social democracy, is not to turn back, but to go farther—to carry the evolution of the school to a point where it becomes a place for getting and testing experience, as real and adequate to the child upon his existing level as all the resources of laboratory and library afford to the scientific man upon his level. What is needed is not any radical revolution, but rather an organization of agencies already found in the schools. It is hardly too much to say that not a single subject or instrumentality is required which is not already found in many schools of the country. All that is required is to gather these materials and forces together and unify their operation. Too often they are used for a multitude of diverse and often conflicting aims. If a single purpose is provided, that of freeing the processes of mental growth, these agencies will at once fall into their proper classes and reinforce each other.

A catalogue of the agencies already available would include at least all of the following: Taking the child out of doors, widening and organizing his experience with reference to the world in which he lives; nature study when pursued as a vital observation of forces working under their natural conditions, plants and animals growing in their own homes, instead of mere discussion of dead specimens. We have also school gardens, the introduction of elementary agriculture, and more especially of horticulture—a movement that is already making great headway in many of the western states. We have also means for the sake of studying physiographic conditions, such as may be found by rivers, ponds or lakes, beaches, quarries, gulleys, hills, etc.

As similar agencies within the school walls, we find a very great variety of instruments for constructive work, or, as it is frequently, but somewhat unfortunately termed, "manual training." Under this head come cooking, which can be begun in its simpler form in the kindergarten; sewing, and what is of even greater educational value, weaving, including designing and the construction of simple apparatus for carrying on various processes of spinning, etc. Then there are also the various forms of tool-work directed upon cardboard, wood, and iron; in addition there are clay-modeling and a variety of ways of manipulating plastic material to gain power and larger experience.

Such matters pass readily over into the simpler forms of scientific experimentation. Every schoolroom from the lowest primary grade up should be supplied with gas, water, certain chemical substances and reagents. To experiment in the sense of trying things or to see what will happen is the most natural business of the child; it is, indeed, his chief concern. It is one which the school has largely either ignored or actually suppressed, so that it has been forced to find outlet in mischief or even in actually destructive ways. This tendency could find outlet in the construction of simple apparatus and the making of simple tests, leading constantly into more and more controlled experimentation, with greater insistence upon definiteness of intellectual result and control of logical process.

Add to these three typical modes of active experimenting, various forms of art expression, beginning with music, clay-modeling, and story-telling as foundation elements, and passing on to drawing, painting, designing in various mediums, we have a range of forces and materials which connect at every point with the child's natural needs and powers, and which supply the requisites for building up his experience upon all sides. As fast as these various agencies find their way into the schools, the center of gravity shifts, the régime changes from one of subjection of mind to an external and ready-made material, into the activity of mind directed upon the control of the subject-matter and thereby its own upbuilding.

Politically we have found that this country could not endure half free and half slave. We shall find equally great difficulty in encouraging freedom, independence, and initiative in every sphere of social life, while perpetuating in the school dependence upon external authority. The forces of social life are already encroaching upon the school institutions which we have inherited from the past, so that many of its main stays are crumbling. Unless the outcome is to be chaotic, we must take hold of the organic, positive principle involved in democracy, and put that in entire possession of the spirit and work of the school.

In education meet the three most powerful motives of human activity. Here are found sympathy and affection, the going out of the emotions to the most appealing and the most rewarding object of love—a little child. Here is found also the flowering of the social and institutional motive, interest in the welfare of society and in its progress and reform by the surest and shortest means. Here, too, is found the intellectual and scientific motive, the interest in knowledge, in scholarship, in truth for its own sake, unhampered and unmixed with any alien ideal. Copartnership of these three motives—of affection, of social growth, and of scientific inquiry—must prove as nearly irresistible as anything human when they are once united. And, above all else, recognition of the spiritual basis of democracy, the efficacy and responsibility of freed intelligence, is necessary to secure this union.

Critical Thinking

1. Do you agree with Justice Oliver Wendell Holmes' description of Dewey's writing?
2. What is Dewey's conception of democracy and education?
3. How would this text be written for educators of the 21st century?

Internet References

The Center for Dewey Studies
www.siu.edu/~deweyctr

The John Dewey Society
http://doe.concordia.ca/jds/

The Museum of Education, University of South Carolina
www.ed.sc.edu/museum/dewey_movietone.html

DEWEY-L
http://people.cas.sc.edu/burket/dewey-l.html

From The Elementary School Teacher, December 1903.

UNIT

Prepared by: Sheron Fraser-Burgess, *Ball State University*

Identity & Intersectionality in Education

The construct of identity has gained increasing prominence in conversations about educational equity and achievement. In the early 1970s, multicultural education promoted political pluralism such that culture, race and ethnicity served as important components of school curriculum. In its most developed form, multicultural education presented pluralism as a cross-curricular task that was a social justice imperative. It could be argued that, in the quest for equity, identity supersedes multicultural education as a cohesive theorization of difference in education. While multicultural education relates to culturally responsive or culturally relevant education, it has allowed primarily for curricular attention to be given to differences of race, ethnicity and even geographic region. In contrast, invoking identity has provided greater discursive space for seeking equity for sexual minorities and LGBTQ causes. The structuring of multicultural education in terms of static categories and binaries (race, religion, gender, abilities, etc.) was less able to accommodate the emerging acknowledgement of gender and sexual fluidities.

Where race and ethnicity can be associated with specific cultural backgrounds, it can be linked with a sense of a belonging to a group. The term identity offers a comparable category with which there can be such an association. The divergent conceptions of identity allow for discussion as to whether its various forms are fixed, binary or essentialist. As sexually and other minoritized groups have sought for political recognition and accommodations through, for example, curriculum that acknowledges same sex partnerships or transgender identity, that such appeals were a form of identity politics became part of the discourse about group rights. It signals that LGBTQ activism represents a fight for the power to disrupt the hegemony of Judeo-Christian norms in order to affect a more inclusive representation of forms of life. In the context of identity politics, controversies centered around the social basis of identity ascriptions and the related norms, especially in light of emergent identity constructions (e.g. mixed race, queer, diasporic) as exemplifying identity fluidity.

In the quest for anti-oppressive education, practice and policy, the term intersectionality has also grown to represent complex interrelationships that there can be among the various ways that persons experience being a member of multiple groups. Crenshaw (2009) first proposed intersectionality to represent the unique experiences of overlapping minoritized group membership as a location of oppression. For example, the oppression that a black woman experiences is distinct from the individual barriers based on race or identity alone. One of the articles included in this section tackles identity issues from the vantage point of teacher preparation. It underscores that growing to advocate for the equitable treatment of members of LGBTQ community can be cultivated through the right sets of experiences. Particularly for future teachers, it is especially important that they be equipped to the create spaces of acceptance where every student believes that they are valued as persons. In the face of the recent Supreme Court decision in the case Obergefell v. Hodges on June 26, 2015, that struck down all state bans on **same-sex marriage**, **legalized** it in all fifty states, and required states to honor out-of-state same-sex marriage licenses, it has become even more incumbent upon schools, as a democratic institution, to be assimilate these families into the mainstream rather than continuing to keep them on the margins by default.

References

Crenshaw, K. (2009). Mapping the margins; Intersectionality, identity politics, and violence against women of color (E. Taylor & D. Gillborn, Eds.). In G. Ladson-Billings (Ed.), *Foundations of critical race theory in education* (pp. 213–247). NY: Routledge.

Fraser-Burgess, S. (2018). Identity Politics and Belonging. In P. Smeyers (Ed.), *International handbook of philosophy of education* (pp. 851–865). Cham, Switzerland: Springer International Publishing.

Hall, S. and DuGay, P. (Eds.) (2000). *Questions of cultural identity*. London: Sage Publications.

Nieto, S. & Bode, P. (2018) *Affirming diversity: The sociopolitical context of multicultural education* 7th Hoboken, NJ: Pearson.

Article

Prepared by: Sheron Fraser-Burgess, *Ball State University*

Building LGBTQ Awareness and Allies in Our Teacher Education Community and Beyond

LAURA-LEE KEARNS, JENNIFER MITTON KUKNER, AND JOANNE TOMPKINS

Learning Outcomes

After reading this article, you will be able to:

- Summarize the need for building awareness among teacher candidates in higher education teacher education programs.
- Interrupt and respond to instances of bullying and harassment in schools and elsewhere.
- Discuss issues faced by pre-service teachers who want to do the right thing, but have concerns when mentor teachers oppose such actions.

Introduction

Research has demonstrated that over 75% of Lesbian, Gay and Bi-sexual youth and 95% of Transgendered students do not feel safe at school compared to 20% of heterosexual students (Taylor et al., 2011, 47). The current bullying discourse does not often highlight the vulnerability of sexual minority youth. According to the *First National Climate Survey on Homophobia in Canadian Schools* (Taylor et al., 2009) "homophobic and transphobic bullying are neither rare nor harmless but major problems that schools need to address" (p. 2). The Canadian Charter of Human Rights and Freedoms, provincial equity policies, school and school board policies and curricula emphasize "human rights and diversity" however, "LGBTQ students feel unsafe, insulted or harassed," on a daily basis (Taylor as cited in Petz 2011). Compounding this issue is the reality that LGBTQ youth hear and see a lot of homophobia and transphobia in schools, and they don't see adults in leadership positions interrupting this type of discrimination (Goldstein et al., 2007; Kumashiro 2002; Taylor et al., 2011). This is particularly regrettable as research also shows that "the climate is significantly better in the schools that have taken even modest steps to combat homophobia" (Taylor, 2011, para 4). To that end, we are trying to promote anti-oppressive pedagogy as part of our approach to teaching and learning in our faculty of education.

Here we share the impact of a training program, Positive Space I (PSI) and Positive Space II (PSII), two three-hour workshops, that have been integrated into mandatory education classes, Sociology of Education and Inclusion I, which help to promote pre-service teachers' understandings of and abilities to create safe spaces for LGBTQ youth. The purpose of our study is to explore the impact of this training program, and to consider challenges and best practices to build awareness and allies in our own higher-education context, as well as to help create better learning communities for LGBTQ youth and allies in schools. Our Positive Space Training program is also critical as many future teachers are not prepared to address "issues of homophobia and heterosexism in the classroom" (Stiegler, 2008, p. 117). By honouring our students and helping them become "activists" who may help advance "academics and social justice" (Kumashiro, 2002, p. 13), we hope to better inform not only our own practice but also that of the field of higher education.

Our teacher education faculty is situated within St. Francis Xavier University in rural Atlantic Canada. Our Bachelor of Education is a two-year program, with approximately 240 students. Prior to 2009, PS I & PS II were voluntary. Since 2009 it has been institutionalized as part of our B.Ed program in courses that discuss issues around power and privilege, and interlocking forms of oppressions. Positive Space I features awareness building with a focus on language and terminology and Positive Space II focuses on becoming an ally, which gives the opportunity for preservice educators to witness and role play educators interrupting heteronormativity. Recognizing that "a lack of a solid Canadian evidence base has been a major impediment faced by educators who need to understand the situation of . . . LGBTQ students in order to respond appropriately" (Taylor et al., 2009, p. 2), sharing our work is timely and necessary. As a further impetus, we also recognize that in addition to feeling unsafe, rural LGBTQ youth have been shown to experience more hostile climates than their urban counterparts compounded by fewer resources and supports, including a lower prevalence of Gay Straight Alliances (GSAs), supportive staff, inclusive curricula, and comprehensive anti-bullying policies (GLSEN Report, 2012).

Data Collection

This paper describes the Positive Space training program and its relationship to our teacher education program. It highlights findings from workshop evaluations of Positive Space I and II provided by participants 2010–2012, incorporates findings from pre- and post-training on-line surveys in 2011–2012, and follow-up interviews with individuals and a small focus group in 2013.

Themes Arising from the Data
On the Need to Create LGBTQ Awareness

There is a broad range of awareness and understanding of LGBTQ realities among our pre-service teachers. In the presurvey at the very beginning of their B.Ed in September, in response to the question, "*Have you ever had any previous training in LGBTQ issues?*" 84% of respondents said "No". Of the 16% who said "Yes", some said they had friends or parents who identified as LGBTQ. And others had taken Positive Space training as part of women's studies programs. In response to the question, "*When you were in school, was there a Gay Straight Alliance (GSA)?*" 13% said "Yes", 74% said "No" and 16% wrote that they were unsure. In response to "*Have you ever had the experience of participating in any LGBTQ event?*" 24% said "Yes", and 76% said "No" (Pre-Training Electronic responses Fall 2011). For those who said "Yes", the events listed included mostly Pride parades and same sex weddings. Although workshop feedback and pre-survey data showed that some pre-service educators self-identified as allies who wanted more critical discussions on these issues, we found it surprising that a majority of pre-service teachers would not have had the opportunity to engage with the LGBTQ community. All of this information is insightful, as it indicates that both formally and informally pre-service educators need support and explicit LGBTQ training to engage with anti-oppressive pedagogy.

Positive Impact of the Training

The training proved to be important on multiple levels. Many participants said it helped with their confidence in terms of awareness about the challenges some LGBTQ individuals face. As one participant shared, the training "opened my eyes to issues I hadn't thought of before . . . [I didn't] recognize the severity and impact [homophobia] might have [on LGBTQ youth]" (Interviewee 7). The training not only created more understanding about the challenges LGBTQ individuals face, it clarified language and terminology, and also helped people recognize and examine the privilege of heterosexuals. It created a way to discuss complex issues and also showed the importance of interrupting homophobia. One participant shared "my awareness of LGBTQ issues and comfort intervening when I witness a homophobic act is much greater since taking these Positive Space Training sessions" (Postsurvey electronic response—Winter 2012). Further, we learned that without this specific training, some pre-service educators may not have seen responding to the needs of LGBTQ or human rights advocacy as part of their professional responsibilities. As one interviewee shared, prior to the training "sexuality wasn't big on my radar for school because I was so worried about . . . [having] a good lesson" (Interviewee 8). The interviewees also shared that since many had not participated in GSAs in their own schools, they said the training was critical to understanding what they were and that everyone was welcome to be an ally. Certainly, pre-service educators found it is important to consciously name discrimination and weave ways to address homophobia in our program.

Lack of Understanding of What It Meant to Interrupt

Although the pre-service teachers we worked with emphasized the importance of learning more about how to create and sustain positive spaces for LGBTQ youth and allies in schools, a common thread emerging from follow-up focus group interviews was their lack of understanding of what it meant to interrupt situations of a discriminatory nature. For example, one pre-service teacher, in describing his action of crossing out the word 'gay' that had been negatively written over a Positive Space sticker in a school washroom, commented, "I don't know if that was appropriate but at least they [LGBTQ youth] don't have to see it . . . I guess that's a step in the positive direction."

Some of the pre-service teachers' uncertainty about interruptions and their seeming lack of understanding about the power of small actions, as seen in our previous example, may be connected to their prior experiences as learners in schools, or imagining that anti-discrimination actions need to be extraordinary, or their field placement experiences in which they witnessed few examples of anti-oppressive pedagogy. For us, these discussions helped us recognize that we need to highlight the power of small, ongoing interruptions as part of pre-service teachers' understanding of anti-oppressive pedagogy and the ways it might inform their work in schools.

Power Imbalance

Our follow-up interviews also showed that issues of power impact the sense of agency our pre-service teachers feel as they attempt to interrupt homophobia and transphobia. On one level there is a power imbalance between pre-service teachers and their cooperating teachers. They are student interns working alongside mentor teachers. The relationship is meant to be of mutual benefit. Though there is an imbalance the opinions of the licensed teacher hold some weight in the student's evaluation and potentially future employment prospects. It is a power relationship of which our pre-service teachers are highly aware: "the power structure is against us in a variety of ways. We want to have good references and . . . do a good job . . . all those things conflict depending on who your CT is. . . . my career is at stake" (Interviewee 4). This power dynamic can also be a problem for some pre-service teachers who want to interrupt homophobia when the cooperating teacher does not. One student explains: ". . . I had a student pass a note to another student and it had faggot written on it . . . And I couldn't think of a way to approach the class about it and my CT didn't want to deal with it . . ." (Interviewee 1). Reflecting back on the incident, the student teacher said "it's hard being a student teacher" and asked ". . . how do I make this work"? Though several pre-service teachers felt supported to act as an ally, others worried that their attempts to challenge homophobia and heteronormativity could be viewed negatively and felt limited to act as an ally.

The Gender Binary: Responding and Interrupting

It was clear that the gender binary, a system of overtly and covertly naming and stereotyping differences between boys and girls is learned and reproduced by schools. Our follow-up interviews showed our pre-service teachers grappling with just how *profound* this binary is instilled and trying to find ways to disrupt or work within it. For example, one interviewee in our focus group shared that she would try to show the grade primary class "non-gendered pictures" and the 5 and 6 year olds "would ask is this a boy or a girl and how can you tell" (Interviewee 3). The pre-service teacher would think to herself, "it doesn't matter it's just a [picture]". Yet she understood that "it was all the systems that they grew up with and what they were used to . . . boys wear pants and shirts . . . and . . . [to] try and break an entire system . . . It's really difficult." The boy and girl codes though deeply entrenched, were recognized by this pre-service teacher, who at least wanted to start doing "small things" to open up more possibilities. In her context, she "started asking 'are you a boy or are you a girl? It's your choice, I'll put down whatever you tell me you are.'" At the secondary level the importance of gender was also at the fore. One interviewee shared that in the social studies classroom there were more opportunities to discuss human rights, but in the physical education classroom, where there was still a lot of "boys vs girls" it was more challenging. This one student teacher had a transgender student in his class, so in order to respond, he asked the student which team s/he preferred to play on: "I'd let [James] play on the girls team if he wanted to" (Interviewee 8). Pre-service teachers are engaged in the gender binary in schools daily, some are trying to complicate it, disrupt it or simply adhere to it in different ways.

Implications: Continuing Our Work in Higher Education

Our study has substantiated some of what we know about the importance of including LGBTQ in higher education programs (Goldstein et al., 2007; Kitchen & Bellini, 2012; Taylor et al., 2009, 2011). Our research also shows that by taking part in the training, pre-service teachers felt they were more capable at supporting LGBTQ youth, colleagues, people and/or participating in GSAs. Key themes that emerged in our data and which we note as different from other studies is the lack of understanding that pre-service teachers had about small interruptions as being an important part of their anti-oppressive pedagogy. We also note how they were able to identify the gender binary as a presence in schools and curriculum, and the choices they made in such situations with actions that they felt enabled students to have broader choices about who they felt themselves to be. While we emphasize the positive impact of the training, we also note that participants expressed concerns about how much they were able to do in schools in relation to LGBTQ work, putting particular emphasis on a power imbalance between themselves and their cooperating teachers. Several participants also mentioned that they wanted more training opportunities, and in response we are planning a Positive Space III and IV. Our efforts will continue to focus on ways to support opportunities for future, early career, and experienced teachers to create inclusive spaces in schools.

Conclusion

As a result of positive space training teacher, candidates' awareness of LGBTQ issues has increased and they are developing a vocabulary to name heterosexism and identify instances in which they should intervene to interrupt homophobia and transphobia. Importantly they are developing the skills to proactively create inclusive environments. Results also indicate areas for further growth, particularly in pre-service teachers' sense of efficacy to act as allies. The opportunity for teacher candidates to understand how to incorporate anti-discrimination work in their teaching practice is a key component of school and education reform. Social justice policies and procedures exist in many school settings, but unless new teachers have the opportunity to explore and apply their grounded knowledge from professional development, these well-meaning policies are often neglected or ignored. We suggest that this particular program is an example of how to work towards the development of a pedagogy that does not oppress; one that truly embraces, celebrates, and honours all learners.

References

GLSEN (2007). *Gay-straight alliances; creating safer schools for LGBTQ students and their allies (GLSEN research brief).* New York: Gay, Lesbian and Straight Education Network.

Goldstein, T., Russell, V., & Daley, A. (2007). Safe positive and queering moments in teaching education and schooling: A conceptual framework. *Teaching Education, 18*(3), 183–199.

Kitchen J. & Bellini, C. (2012). Addressing lesbian, gay, bisexual, transgender, and queer (lgbtq) issues in teacher education: Teacher candidates' perceptions. *Alberta Journal of Educational Research, 58*(3), 444–460.

Kumashiro, K. (2002). *Troubling education: "Queer" activism and anti-Oppressive pedagogy.* New York, NY: Routledge.

Stiegler, S. (2008). Queer youth as teachers: Dismantling silence of queer issues in a teacher preparation program committed to social justice. *Journal of LGBTQ Youth, 5*(4), 116–123.

Taylor, C., Peter, T., Schachter, K., Paquin, S., Beldom, S., Gross, Z., & McMinn, T. L. (2009). *Youth speak up about homophobia and transphobia: The first national climate survey on homophobia in Canadian Schools. Phase one report.* Toronto, Canada: Egale Canada Human Rights Trust.

Taylor, C., & Peter, T., with McMinn, T.L., Elliott, T., Beldom, S., Ferry, A., Gross, Z., Paquin, S., & Schachter, K. (2011). *Every class in every school: The first national climate survey on homophobia, biphobia, and transphobia in Canadian schools. Final report.* Toronto, ON: Egale Canada Human Rights Trust. Available from http://www.egale.ca/index.asp?lang=E&menu=1&item=1489

Taylor, C. (2011). Homophobia creates hostile world for Canadian students [Press release]. University of Winnipeg. Retrieved from http://www.uwinnipeg.ca/index/uw-news-action/story.572/title.homophobiacreates-hostile-world-for-canadian-students

Critical Thinking

1. If you do not have an opportunity to discuss LGBTQ issues in your program, would you feel free to request that this information be provided?

2. Based on this article, what suggestions would you give professors who are considering introducing the topic in a class? What format should be used, online, face-to-face, or small group workshops? What specific topics should be discussed?

3. Write a scenario in which you tried to help a student who is being bullied, but your mentor teacher told you to stop intervening. What would you tell your mentor teacher and how would you respond to rejection of your ideas?

Internet References

American Civil Liberties Union-LGBT Youth
https://www.aclu.org/issues/lgbt-rights/lgbt-youth

Gay-Straight Alliance Network
https://www.gsanetwork.org

National Resource Center for Youth Development
http://www.nrcyd.ou.edu/lgbtq-youth

StopBullying.gov
http://www.stopbullying.gov

Welcoming Schools
http://www.welcomingschools.org

Kearns, Laura-Lee; Kukner, Jennifer Mitton; Tompkins, Joanne. From Collected Essays on Learning and Teaching, 2014. Copyright ©2014 by Society for Teaching and Learning in Higher Education. Used with permission.

Article

Prepared by: Sheron Fraser-Burgess, *Ball State University*

Here's What I Wish White Teachers Knew When Teaching My Black Children

AFRIKA AFENI MILLS

Learning Outcomes

After reading this article, you will be able to:

- Identify barriers to teachers being prepared to teach Black children well.
- Consider the significance of Black students' perspective and context in relation to the dominant curriculum.

Dear White Teachers of My Black Children:

I am a Black mom and I have two children who are now in high school. Raising them to be inquisitive, informed adults with a strong sense of identity and agency is an essential part of my life.

we have a long way to go before we're even close to treating all of our students equitably. I am also an educator, so I understand the deep importance of guiding and shaping all of our children. I'm also intimately aware of all the cultural complexity surrounding our work. I know, too, that we have a long way to go before we're even close to treating all of our students equitably. This is why I'm writing to you today. I have much to say about what I wish you had been able to do for my children when they were in your elementary and middle school classrooms, and what I hope you will do for all children of color entering your classrooms.

Because I'm an educator, I know well what you—or at least the vast majority of you— learned in your pre-K-12 education and in your teacher prep program and what you didn't learn.

As you grew up, you were most likely taught in school and at home that Abraham Lincoln was the great emancipator, that it was acceptable, right even, to refer to the people of the global majority as minorities, and that communities with higher percentages of Black families are in need of saving.

As a teacher, you most likely did not receive ongoing professional development about race and education in America. You're likely to have a vague understanding of issues of diversity and equity and inclusion with an insufficient understanding of culturally responsive teaching and learning.

In high school, college and your teacher prep program, you no doubt were taught something about race in America, but it's highly unlikely that you learned the truth about the Black experience. It's likely, for instance, that you've been taught little to nothing about the pre-enslavement contributions of Black people to the world, the horrors and impact of centuries of enslavement, post "Emancipation" Jim Crow laws and practices and the many ongoing racially based systemic injustices such as mass incarceration, housing discrimination, wealth disparities and lack of equal access to quality education, health care and more.

I didn't learn about these things in school either, but thankfully, my parents made sure I learned about these important aspects of American life and history that are absent from the textbooks and teacher's guides.

Because it's unlikely that you learned about all of these things in school or in your home, it's even more unlikely that you teach about these matters now.

We have talked extensively about these matters at home, but my children's school experiences would have been far more valuable if you would have introduced them to the lives and works of Ellen and William Craft, Katherine Johnson, Lewis Hayden, Ida B. Wells and Denmark Vesey. They wanted to hear you tell them the truth about The Black Panther Party, the reasons behind the FBI's surveillance of Martin Luther King, Jr., the painful facts about Columbus's experiences in the Americas and the meaning of Juneteenth. And they didn't want to just hear a few tidbits about these essential and complex aspects of American life during Black History Month.

What my children needed from you in school—what all students of color need from you in school—is a much deeper understanding of racial history and ongoing racial matters. What my children needed from you in school—what all students of color need from you in school—is a much deeper understanding of racial history and ongoing racial matters.

If, for instance, you teach a social studies unit on immigration and you have your students present about the countries of their ancestors, Black children need you to think more deeply about how this assignment feels for them.

This can also be a tough and painful assignment for other students of color—especially for First Nations people whose ancestral stories are overlooked and misrepresented. My guess is that you didn't think about all this in planning the unit. Going forward, I hope you will.

Because you were entrusted to partner with me in the education of my children, I wanted you to wonder how they felt when they saw Mount Rushmore or the face of Andrew Jackson on the twenty-dollar bill they handed you with their field trip permission slip. I wanted you to wonder how they felt in your class after hearing about yet another unarmed Black life erased from this world by police brutality—all because the melanin we see as so beautiful looks like danger to others.

Do you know how it felt for my children when you didn't say anything about racial injustices at the time of their occurrences? Do you know how it feels for your Black students today?

If your school is anything like the schools where I taught, you'll be expected to interact with your students' families at open houses, conferences, and literacy or math nights. On those nights, families are expected to come to school and are often judged harshly if they don't. I want you to think about this, think about why you are judging them harshly and what assumptions you are making.

During parent-teacher conferences, you will most likely not have a lot of time, so you'll probably default to talking *at* families about their children instead of engaging in dialogues *with* families as partners. I know it's hard. I've been there, too. But I'm asking you now, when it's time for conferences, when families show up to engage in conversation with you about the most precious people in their lives, please don't see your contract as a limitation. Use these moments as opportunities to connect, learn and share.

As you well know, the dominant culture in the United States tries to suppress conversations on race. There are numerous reasons for this, most of them related to the maintenance of the power status quo. I'm asking you to help break this damaging practice—especially among adults in your school.

There are certain conversations that take place in teachers' lounges about students and their families that I find both infuriating and heartbreaking. Too often, teachers are silent in the face of racist, prejudicial, biased or stereotypical comments. I know it's uncomfortable to confront a colleague. I want you to consider, however, how uncomfortable it makes my family and all other families of color to know that there are people who we've entrusted with the care and teaching of our children who think of them as less than—less important, less worthy of our love and attention.

When that moment arises next time—and it will arise—I want you to think of how uncomfortable the students are in that teacher's classroom, and I want you to speak up on their behalf. If a colleague says something derogatory about a child and/or that child's family, you must speak up. As Desmond Tutu said, "If you are neutral in situations of injustice, you have chosen the side of the oppressor."

Finally, I know it's tempting to think that because you teach in a school with a high percentage of Black students, racism isn't an issue for you. Please know that proximity doesn't equal awareness. That would be like a male teacher saying, "I can't be sexist because I have female students." Know, too, that racial colorblindness isn't really a thing. While it's right to treat children equitably, it's also important to understand how race shapes lives in a racist system.

By improving equity in schools, by becoming truly inclusive learning communities with an effective anti-racist curriculum, we improve both individual lives and equity and justice in society. We all breathe in the smog of oppression, and the only way to expel it is to read, listen, reflect, ask questions and become better as a result of what we learn. I'm here asking you as educators to help lead the way. By improving equity in schools, by becoming truly inclusive learning communities with an effective anti-racist curriculum, we improve both individual lives and equity and justice in society. I'm here for you and I'm rooting for you. As Lilla Watson said, "… your liberation is bound up with mine."

With love, respect and hope,
Afrika Afeni Mills
A Black Educator Mom

Critical Thinking

1. Where are the gaps in curriculum that can exclude Black students?
2. What are teacher practices that can exclude Black students?

Internet References

Culturally Responsive Teaching in Today's Classrooms
https://www2.ncte.org/blog/2018/01/culturally-responsive-teaching-todays-classrooms/

AFRIKA AFENI MILLS is the senior manager of Inclusive and Responsive Educational Practices with BetterLesson. She works with teachers, coaches, and administrators to transform instructional practices and empower all students to thrive.

Mills, Afrika Afeni. "Here's What I Wish White Teachers Knew When Teaching My Black Children." https://educationpost.org/heres-what-i-wish-white-teachers-knew-when-teaching-my-black-children/. Used by permission of the author.

UNIT STEM

Prepared by: Sheron Fraser-Burgess, *Ball State University*

Science, technology, engineering, and math (STEM) is an umbrella concept that has allowed for an allied understanding of these fields in education from kindergarten through college completion and for structuring and prioritizing these areas of the curriculum. This grouping permits conclusions to be drawn about education outcomes regarding the aggregate of the fields. This categorization makes possible a better understanding of the way that, for instance, girls are discouraged from pursuing careers in this field. The notion of STEM allows for the kinds of categorizations that focus on the task of schools as preparation for the world of work. High school STEM courses have been increasingly tasked with creating a school to career pipeline of students who are sufficiently trained in STEM areas to be prepared to enter apprenticeship programs. Typically, these opportunities are provided in the corporate setting. A STEM focus also exposes disparate outcomes for LatinX and African-American students. While Black and Brown students enter STEM programs at about the same percentage as White students, they are more likely to drop out of these programs (Reigle-Crumb, King & Irizarry, 2019). Another priority of STEM education has been positioning students to achieve maximum learning in these fields from pre-kindergarten and sustaining that learning through middle and high school. Innovative pedagogies such as maker spaces are intended to integrate science learning with creative technologies that focus tactile experiences and manipulatives that have the goal of "the build." The growth of robotics clubs and competitions is additional examples of extra-curricular activities that are increasing student engagement in robots and engineering more broadly. The last article considers the classroom culture that can pose as a barrier to the openness of children to technology at the earliest stages of their schooling. That the teacher's points of insecurity and lack of confidence transfers to a similar unease with children show the kind of intractable barriers to changing perceptions and teachers' comfort-level with technology.

Reference

Reigle-Crumb, C., King, B., Irizarry, Y. (2019). Does STEM stand out? Examining racial/ethnic gaps in persistence across postsecondary field. *Educational Researcher* 48(3), 133–144.

Article

Prepared by: Sheron Fraser-Burgess, *Ball State University*

Elements of Making
A Framework to Support Making in the Science Classroom

SHELLY RODRIGUEZ, ET AL.

Learning Outcomes

After reading this article, you will be able to:

- Define "making."
- Identify its six elements.
- Relate the design build process to scientific thinking.

Kyle Albernaz is a preservice chemistry teacher who wants to bring creativity and passion into his classroom. Back when he was a student himself, Kyle remembers a dichotomy between his fellow students: Those driven by logic were drawn to the sciences; the creative types, less so. Kyle wanted to blend the two worlds, and now, as a student teacher at Connally High School in Pflugerville, Texas, he has found a way, discovering that the activity known as "making" can bring creative learning experiences to his science students.

What is Making?

While there is no official definition, making is generally thought of as turning ideas into products through design, invention, and building. We define making as

- an iterative process of design and fabrication that draws on a do-it-yourself (DIY) mindset;
- allows for self-expression through the creation of a personally meaningful product shared with a larger community, and, like project-based instruction;
- can help students learn content as they design solutions and build products. These products can address real-world challenges or simply be items students are inspired to create.

"Many aspects of making are universal," Kyle says. "A lot of students enjoy creating something with their hands and seeing a finished product."

Support is growing for integrating making into STEM education (see *The National Science Foundation and Making* "On the web"). Making can help high school students explore science concepts and phenomena (Bevan 2017), yet, lacking training and experience, many science teachers are reluctant to add making to their curriculum. Blikstein and Worsley (2016) found those new to making require "a considerable amount of onboarding and facilitation" before adding making in their own teaching (p. 71).

We work to help preservice STEM teachers bring making into the classroom. These teachers need a solid understanding of what making is and how to involve their students in maker practices. To succeed at making, students need to:

- Learn to identify questions or personal interests that can lead to the creation of a product.
- Use appropriate tools safely.
- Practice elements of a maker mindset and put them into action.
- Connect their work to STEM disciplinary core ideas.
- Present their work publicly and contribute to the broader community.

This article describes six elements of making, provides a matrix to assist teachers, and offers a sample chemistry lesson for context.

Getting Started with the Elements of Making

The six elements of making are creating original, personally meaningful products; engaging in iterative design and fabrication;

developing a maker mindset; collaborating and connecting with community; sharing work; and using science and engineering. These elements are highlighted as a way to help science teachers unpack different facets of making. The section below expands on each element and provides suggestions for getting started with students.

1. Makers Create Original, Personally Meaningful Products

Making allows for self-expression and empowerment, driven by personal interests and creativity. The "What is a Maker?" video (see "On the web") is a good introduction.

How to start: Maker products reflect something personal about the maker. Thus, making helps students flourish and find their passion, though drawing inspiration from their experiences can take scaffolding. As students start to make, ask them to journal about and discuss with peers connections between what they are building and their own lives or communities. Over time, students will become more comfortable identifying their own interests and using them to find inspiration.

2. Makers Engage in Iterative Design and Fabrication

Makers select from various materials and know how to use assorted high- and low-tech tools safely, including hand and power tools, open-source programming languages, electronics, soldering, crafts, 3-D printers, laser cutters, and more. Like engineers, makers create prototypes, test their work, seek feedback from others, and continually revise and refine.

How to start: Building things that are tangible, useful, and complex can provide satisfaction and confidence for students. However, getting started can be challenging for those who have limited making experience. Consider collaborating with technology and engineering teachers to help establish best safety practices, teach tool skills, and manage technology-based projects. Also consult standards for using educational technology developed by the International Society for Technology in Education (see "On the web"). Start with projects and tools that you, as the teacher, are comfortable with. Review project websites, such as *instructables.com,* for initial ideas. Starting with step-by-step instructions can raise student confidence with fabrication skills. As students become more comfortable with making, they can make their own decisions about the equipment, materials, and revisions needed for their design.

3. Makers Demonstrate Characteristics of a Maker Mindset

A maker mindset promotes effort and persistence. Successful makers view failure as a chance to rethink and revise their work. Makers seek advice and feedback from others and are willing to change tack as needed. Because making is an internally motivated process, makers frequently demonstrate enjoyment in their work.

How to start: Learning persistence, flexible thinking, and a positive view of failure is a lifelong process. As a first step, have students discuss these traits and consider how they might be useful in their lives. Encourage a sense of playfulness and focus on your students' effort, persistence, and ability to incorporate feedback more than on the products they make. Overt attention to these areas will foster a maker mindset.

4. Makers Collaborate and Connect with Community

The maker community is characterized by a willingness to share ideas, tools, and designs. Makers connect in person and through digital forums to form vibrant communities where they display work, share resources, and reflect on lessons learned.

How to start: Fostering community starts in the classroom. Have students work together and share ideas as they make. Next, introduce students to the broader maker community by visiting a local maker faire or connecting via social media. Visit *www.makerfaire.com* to browse local and national events. Follow the maker faire twitter feed, *@makerfaire,* or *@MakerEDOrg,* the feed for the maker education initiative of *Make* magazine. Also see these groups' Facebook pages. Connecting to the larger maker community, students are exposed to various people and passions involved in making and may discover new ideas, role models, and personal inspiration.

5. Makers Share Their Work Publicly

By sharing their work, makers contribute innovative ideas and products to the broader community. Without sharing, the maker community and the advances it fosters could not exist.

How to start: Some students may be more confident sharers than others. Support students with in-class sharing activities like peer feedback and gallery walks. Then, consider bringing in outside feedback or publicly sharing work by exhibiting at a school event, library, or nearby maker faire. Encourage students to upload their projects, with their parents' permission, to sites like *makershare.com* or *instructables.com,* each of which welcomes contributions from users.

6. Makers Use Science and Engineering

Makers use science and engineering practices when they develop questions, make precise measurements, design solutions, test their products, and communicate information. However, for hobbyists and others making in informal settings, these practices may be more intuitive than explicit. Science teachers should bring science and engineering to the forefront.

How to start: Use the *Next Generation Science Standards* (NGSS Lead States 2013, see page 29) as a guide. Ask students to discuss connections to the standards throughout the project and draw attention to the science and engineering practices being employed. Explicitly link their work to the nature of science and engineering.

The Elements of Making matrix

We created the Elements of Making (EOM) matrix (Figure 1) to help science teachers engage with making at various levels. We hope this document, inspired by the National Research Council (NRC 2000), will help identify ways that making can be successfully incorporated into science teaching.

The matrix lists the six elements of making along the side. Teachers may choose to focus on one or all of these in a particular project or activity. The columns in the matrix describe varying degrees of scaffolding and a range of options to help science teachers support students. Science educators may land on different parts of the matrix, depending on their curricular goals, the nature of the project, the teacher's comfort with making, available resources, and the students' level of experience.

FIGURE 1 The Elements of Making matrix

MAKERS	SUPPORTED	EMERGING	DEVELOPING	SOPHISTICATED
Create original, personally meaningful product	Makers engage in a task provided by an outside source and/or build a product from a pre-existing model or template. Personal meaning is not a relevant factor in product creation.	Makers refine a task provided by an outside source and offer some modification to a pre-existing design or template. The design is connected to personal interests or experience in limited ways.	Makers choose from a possible set of tasks or define their own task. Makers offer noticeable modification to a pre-existing design or template. The modified design is connected to personal interests or experience. Makers can articulate this connection.	Makers define their own tasks and create personally meaningful products that are either completely original or significantly modify pre-existing designs. The designs are deeply connected to personal interests or experiences. Makers articulate the personal connection with clarity. Personal motivation pushes the makers to exceed project expectations.
Engage in iterative design and fabrication	Makers are given step-by-step procedures for product creation. Feedback is limited. No revisions are attempted. Makers are directed to specific tools, materials, and safety procedures.	Makers are given general procedures for product creation. Feedback is provided and the makers are directed to make specific modifications. Makers are given a limited choice of tools. Makers begin to develop an understanding of selected tools, materials, and safety procedures.	Makers are given limited procedures and support as needed. Makers are given feedback at several points and use this feedback to decide on modifications and refine their designs. Makers select their own tools. Makers demonstrate an understanding of tools, materials, and safety procedures as well as some skill in fabrication.	Makers engage in independent problem solving and regularly ask thought-provoking questions of themselves and others. Makers solicit support and feedback as needed. Makers develop models and work through multiple iterations of the product design. Makers demonstrate a deep understanding of tools, materials, and safety procedures. Makers show improving fabrication skills, and their end products display high-quality craftsmanship.

(Continued)

FIGURE 1 Continued

Demonstrate characteristics of a maker mindset	Makers are introduced to characteristics of a maker mindset, including but not limited to being playful, having a growth mindset, seeing failure as instructive, and embracing collaboration.	Makers identify one or more characteristics of a maker mindset and reflect on those areas. Makers are given specific reflection prompts.	Makers display several characteristics of a maker mindset. Makers reflect on those areas throughout the project. Makers are given broad guidelines to facilitate reflection.	Makers display characteristics of a maker mindset. Makers show flexible thinking and a willingness to try new strategies throughout the making process. Makers demonstrate persistent effort and use missteps as opportunities for growth. Makers consistently reflect on their work.
Collaborate and connect with community	Makers are directed to collaborate with others during the process of design, reflection, redesign, or presentation. Makers are given a template or prompts to facilitate discussion and idea sharing.	Makers are given opportunities to collaborate with others during the process of design, reflection, redesign, or presentation. Makers are given broad guidelines to facilitate discussion and idea sharing.	Makers solicit opportunities to collaborate with others. Evidence of collaboration is present in multiple facets of the project, including design, reflection, redesign, and/or presentation.	Makers solicit opportunities to collaborate with others both inside of the classroom and in the broader maker community. Evidence of collaboration is present in all facets of the project, including design, reflection, redesign, and presentation.
Present their work publicly	Makers present their work to someone else. Makers are given a template or specific prompts to support the discussion of their work and to seek feedback.	Makers present their work to a group. Makers are given broad presentation guidelines to support the discussion of their work and to seek feedback.	Makers present their work to multiple groups. Makers engage with the audience, can discuss the progression of their project, and seek feedback on their work. The presentation includes a prototype or functional product.	Makers present their work in multiple forums, including a presentation in a public space. Makers engage with the audience, are articulate, and can describe the making process from start to finish. Makers seek and respond to feedback. The presentation includes a high-quality product and documentation of prior iterations and designs.
Use science and engineering	Makers are given all connections to the science content and disciplinary core ideas. Makers are provided with a specific science or engineering practice to include in their work.	Makers are given possible connections to science content and disciplinary core ideas. Makers are directed to science and engineering practices as defined by the *NGSS* and asked to select a relevant practice to highlight in their work.	Makers are guided in forming connections to science content and disciplinary core ideas and can articulate connections. Makers demonstrate several science and engineering practices as defined by the *NGSS*. Makers can identify these practices in their work.	Makers independently draw complex connections to content, articulate ties between their work and disciplinary core ideas, and form interdisciplinary links to domains such as the arts, humanities, and mathematics. Makers demonstrate connections to multiple science and engineering practices as defined by the *NGSS*. Makers can describe these practices and identify them in their work.

Connecting to the *Next Generation Science Standards* (NGSS Lead States 2013)

Standards
HS-PS1 Matter and Its Interactions
HS-ESS2 Earth's Systems
HS-ETS1 Engineering Design

Performance Expectations

- The chart below makes one set of connections between the instruction outlined in this article and the NGSS. Other valid connections are likely; however, space restrictions prevent us from listing all possibilities.
- The materials, lessons, and activities outlined in the article are just one step toward reaching the performance expectations listed below.

HS-PS1-3. Plan and conduct an investigation to gather evidence to compare the structure of substances at the bulk scale to infer the strength of electrical forces between particles.

HS-ESS2-5. Plan and conduct an investigation of the properties of water and its effects on Earth materials and surface processes.

HS-ETS1-1. Analyze a major global challenge to specify qualitative and quantitative criteria and constraints for solutions that account for societal needs and wants.

DIMENSIONS	CLASSROOM CONNECTIONS
Science and Engineering Practices	
Planning and Carrying Out Investigations Plan and conduct an investigation individually and collaboratively to produce data to serve as the basis for evidence, and in the design: decide on types, how much, and accuracy of data needed to produce reliable measurements and consider limitations on the precision of the data (e.g., number of trials, cost, risk, time), and refine the design accordingly.	Students designing their exhibits for the water museum project based their models on observations and data from prior experiments. The design of the exhibit may need to be refined several times because making is an iterative process. Interactive water museum exhibits can allow visitors to carry out their own investigations about the properties of water.
Developing and Using Models Design a solution to a complex real world problem based on prioritized criteria and trade-offs that include a range of constraints including cost, safety, reliability, aesthetics, as well as possible social, cultural, and environmental impacts.	Students are given a real-world design challenge to construct an exhibit that models the properties of water for their water museum. In the design process students must think about the safety and reliability of an exhibit that other people may interact with. Students are given opportunities to improve upon their designs, which may include more aesthetically pleasing exhibits after their initial prototypes.
Disciplinary Core Ideas	
PS1.A: Structure and Properties of Matter The structure and interactions of matter at the bulk scale are determined by electrical forces within and between atoms.	Student exhibits explain various physical and chemical properties of water, such as specific heat capacity, refraction of light, expansion upon freezing, changes in density, and how these properties are essential to the role of water in Earth's surface processes.
ESS2.C: The Roles of Water in Earth's Surface Processes The abundance of liquid water on Earth's surface and its unique combination of physical and chemical properties are central to the planet's dynamics.	Students can design maker exhibits that show how the interactions of a large number of water molecules result in unique properties.

Crosscutting Concept

Structure and Function The functions and properties of natural and designed objects and systems can be inferred from their overall structure, the way their components are shaped and used, and the molecular substructures of its various materials.	Student exhibits can highlight the structure of water and the connection to concepts such as polarity. Exhibits can summarize observations of water's interaction with other water molecules (cohesion) via hydrogen bonding and water's interaction with polar and ionic compounds (adhesion).

A Classroom Example

In a sample lesson conducted by a preservice chemistry teacher, students are asked to build interactive exhibits for a local children's science museum. Student teams must use their knowledge about water—its structure, polarity, and properties—to design an interactive exhibit intended to get middle schoolers excited about water chemistry. Roles within each team include a materials manager, team lead, chemistry consultant, and design consultant. In their exhibit, students represent the property on a macroscopic and molecular level, ensure the product requires interaction from the user, and make an informative plaque so potential visitors can read information as well as interact with the exhibit.

The complete sample lesson plan (see "On the web") gives a general overview of the lesson, describes what students made, and shows how the activity aligns with disciplinary core ideas, science and engineering practices, and crosscutting concepts. The example also discusses how the EOM Matrix can be applied when analyzing this lesson. In addition, next steps are provided as suggestions for how the lesson could be modified to move toward more sophisticated making.

Advice

For this article we received advice from preservice teachers, mentors, and educators involved in making. They advise teachers not to be intimidated. While making may seem daunting, project options range from those taking a semester to complete to others that take only 45 minutes. Some projects use high-tech equipment, while others use common materials. Find what works best for you, jump in, make mistakes, and learn alongside students. Also remember that making is an excellent avenue for building useful products that support your community. By considering the needs of others, students can build empathy and develop confidence in their ability to create and contribute. In this way, making can reach beyond the walls of the science classroom to benefit the broader society.

Conclusion

The elements of making and the accompanying matrix are intended to provide scaffolding to support making in the science classroom. Making is built on a foundation of collaboration, shared resources, and community. In that spirit, we are sharing our experiences with making in STEM classrooms in the hopes of empowering other science teachers and their students with these practices.

. . .

References

Bevan, B. 2017. The promise and the promises of making in science education. *Studies in Science Education* 53 (1): 75–103.

Blikstein, P., and M. Worsley. 2016. Children are not hackers: Building a culture of powerful ideas, deep learning, and equity in the maker movement. In *Makeology: Makerspaces as learning environments*, vol. 1, ed. K. Peppler, E.R. Halverson, and Y.B. Kafai, 64–79. New York, NY: Routledge.

National Research Council (NRC). 2000. *Inquiry and the National Science Education Standards: A guide for teaching and learning*. Washington, DC: National Academies Press.

NGSS Lead States. 2013. *Next Generation Science Standards: For states, by states*. Washington, DC: National Academies Press.

Critical Thinking

1. What are the parallels between "making" and the scientific method?
2. How is creativity realized moving to fabrication?

Internet References

The Design Build Institute of America
https://www.dbiarockymountain.org/what_is_design_build.php
What is Design Build?
https://dbia.org/what-is-design-build/

SHELLY RODRIGUEZ is a clinical associate professor and the director of UTeach Maker.

JASON HARRON is a doctoral student at the University of Texas in Austin, Texas.

STEVEN FLETCHER is an associate professor at St. Edwards University in Austin, Texas.

HANNAH SPOCK is a science teacher at Montbello Career and Technical High School in Denver, Colorado.

Rodriguez, S., Harron, J., Fletcher, S., & Spock, H. (2018). Elements of making: A framework to support making in the science classroom. The Science Teacher, 85(2). Used by permission.

Article

Prepared by: Sheron Fraser-Burgess, *Ball State University*

Don't Ask Me Why: Preschool Teachers' Knowledge in Technology as a Determinant of Leadership Behavior

ANNA ÖQVIST AND PER HÖGSTRÖM

Learning Outcomes

After reading this article, you will be able to:

- Describe the underlying elements of implementing classroom technology.
- Define leadership behavior.
- Weigh the implications of the teacher's influence for pre-K student's confidence.

Today, children are growing up in an environment in which everyday technologies and advanced technologies are evolving at a rapid pace. Computers, mobile phones, and other advanced technologies are available in almost every home and workplace. The ability to communicate and apply new knowledge is necessary in a society characterized by a huge flow of information (Williams, 2002). To embrace and facilitate the use of all the technologies that children encounter in everyday life, it is essential that they have a basic understanding technology. In Sweden, the preschool educational mission addresses the importance and significance of integrating technology in the education of young children. In the new Swedish preschool curriculum, technology education is emphasized as one of the most significant pedagogical areas. It puts particular emphasis on the teacher's role, emphasizing that it is the preschool teacher's responsibility to stimulate and challenge children's interest in science and technology (Skolverket, 2016). Thus, as part of their leadership, it is crucial for preschool teachers to have the appropriate knowledge to distinguish and highlight technology in children's everyday lives to facilitate children's learning. Unfortunately, prior research has shown that many preschool teachers feel uncertain about what technology is and the extent of their knowledge on the topic (Plowman, Stephen, & McPake, 2010; Siu & Lam, 2005; Smith, 2001). According to a Swedish Schools Inspectorate quality report (Skolinspektionen, 2012), in-service preschool teachers express uncertainty and even fear regarding technology, viewing it as something unknown. For example, teachers seem to have different perceptions of what technology is and, in many cases, understand technology strictly as electrical equipment, such as computers and televisions (Skolinspektionen, 2012; Smith, 2001). Teachers commonly associate technology with high-tech artifacts and focus on the use of these artifacts rather than their structure or the process that led to their development (Siu & Lam, 2005). Furthermore, preschool teachers experience technology as complex and difficult to manage (Plowman et al., 2010; Siu & Lam, 2005; Skolinspektionen, 2012). This trend is worrisome. To date, prior research has focused on investigating preschool teachers' knowledge of technology. Less attention has been paid to the actual influence of preschool teachers' knowledge on their leadership behavior toward children, that is, how preschool teachers act toward children in technology-related activities and how this might affect learning outcomes for children. We propose that addressing this can provide new avenues through which to understand how to facilitate children's learning about technology. The aim of this article is to explore how preschool teachers' knowledge of, and approaches to, technology influence how they act toward children in different learning activities.

Technology is part of the preschool environment and provides the children with experiences of everyday phenomena. From there, children will have the opportunity to build their perceptions of how technology can be used, among other things, to facilitate and solve problems in everyday life (Skolverket, 2016). First and foremost, this includes their ability to discern the technical objects of everyday life and become acquainted with them. In this way, children are given opportunities to reflect on issues concerning the use, benefits, functions, materials, design, and construction of these objects (Skolverket, 2016). From a Swedish perspective, such situations are particularly interesting because the preschool curriculum considers creativity, play, and enjoyment in learning as the backbone of young children's education. A central activity in preschool is free play. Prior research has shown that through free play, children learn largely by participating. For example, studies concerning children's involvement and participation show that these contribute to their understanding of technology.

This highlights the importance of direct experience in stimulating children's learning (Turja, Endepohls-Ulpe, & Chatoney, 2009; Tu, 2006). Children have an innate curiosity that compels them to discover things for themselves, and when they do so, their first meeting with the science of technology occurs. By participating in technical activities, children develop their investigative skills and learn to discuss, reflect, and formulate thoughts and ideas (Tu, 2006).

However, it is worrisome when children's perceptions of technology are inadequate and their development of alternate perceptions does not change over time (Mawson, 2011). Preschool teachers' ability to enhance children's participation in technology use seems to largely depend on the teachers' own knowledge. Previous research indicates that the teacher's role and behavior are crucial in encouraging children in their learning about technology (Rohaan, Taconis, & Joechems, 2010; Siraj-Blatchford & MacLeod-Brudenell, 1999). Children who receive considerable support and guidance on how various phenomena work have more opportunities to develop technical skills (Mawson, 2011; Stables, 1997; Tu, 2006). In such situations, children need adults with the appropriate knowledge and experience to guide them further (Smith, 2001). Therefore, it is important that teachers get involved in activities controlled by children (e.g., free play) because it is in participating in such activities that children are driven by a strong motivation to achieve a specific goal (Parker-Rees, 1997). Turja, Endepohls-Ulpe, and Chatoney (2009) find that play prompts children to use their imaginations to experiment with alternative plans, solutions, and problem-solving and to combine things in new ways. Practices in which children are only offered materials (e.g., building blocks) without support and must decipher for themselves what these materials can be used for can be counterproductive. For example, if the children build something, the teacher usually does not ask the children if they really understand what they have done. Therefore, the visible result is the dominant criterion in the evaluation of successful technology education (Tu, 2006). Siu and Lam (2005) conclude that if children are to get a basic understanding of everyday technology, they must have an understanding of the process involved in, for example, the construction of a specific technical artifact. When the children need support or help in solving problems or in finding new ways to proceed, the teacher's role in encouraging and being supportive is crucial (Stables, 1997).

Altogether, previous research highlights the importance of introducing technology at an early age to offer children an advantage in school. An early introduction to technology can change children's perceptions of what technology is as they interact with it (Can-Yasar & Uyanik, 2012; Mawson, 2010; Milne & Edwards, 2013; Siraj-Blatchford, 2001; Siu & Lam, 2005). Teachers' knowledge of technology is crucial for encouraging and stimulating the development of children's knowledge of technology and their skills in its use. From a broader perspective, due to the growing need for technical skilled labor, it is important that preschool teachers are aware of how to challenge, stimulate, and motivate the children's learning of, and interest in, technology (Rohaan et al., 2010).

Theoretical Framework

The aim of the present study was to determine how preschool teachers' knowledge of, and approaches to, technology influence how they act toward children in different learning activities. To derive an understanding of how preschool teachers' actions contribute to children's learning about technology, the study used the path–goal theory framework (House, 1996). *Path–goal theory* is a theory of leader effectiveness that focuses on identifying the effects of the leader's behavior on the subordinates' outcomes. To the extent that subordinates lack support and resources required to accomplish goals, it is the leader's function to provide such support or resources (House, 1996). According to path–goal theory,

> The motivational functions of the leader consist of increasing personal pay-offs to subordinates for work-goal attainment, and making the path to these pay-offs easier to travel by clarifying it, reducing roadblocks and pitfalls, and increasing the opportunities for personal satisfaction en route. (House, 1971, p. 324)

Thus, an effective leader is one who assists subordinates with navigating paths that ultimately lead to organizationally desired and individually valued outcomes.

Path–goal theory has proven fruitful in the field of education. For example, Öqvist and Malmström (2016) employed the theory to expand the understanding of teachers' leadership behavior and its impact on students' educational motivation. From the students' point of view, the authors highlighted the usefulness of the theory to capture how levels of developmental leadership cause low levels of motivation among students. In the present study, path–goal theory helped to explain how preschool teachers' knowledge of technology influences their leadership behavior toward children in different learning activities. Accordingly, if the children need help with solving a problem to achieve a goal (e.g., a playful activity involving building something), the teacher needs to help, support, and motivate the children by clearing away obstacles and discussing possible solutions in order to improve their learning and performance. The children will be motivated to carry out the activity or task if they feel that they are competent and possess the right knowledge to take on and complete the activity. This presupposes that the preschool teacher, as the leader, provides a clear direction and gets involved in the children's goal achievement by supporting and helping the children in different ways. Through their leadership, preschool teachers can influence children's motivation and interest in solving a problem or completing a task (cf. Yukl, 2013). Csikszentmihalyi (1990) and Dörnyei and Ushioda (2011) show that problem solving leads to motivation. For preschool teachers, then, the challenge is to exhibit behavior that best meets the needs of the children.

Methodology
Sample
The present study adopted a qualitative embedded multiple case-study research design inspired by Eisenhardt (1989) and Yin (2003). Cases of preschool teachers' experiences were used to explore their knowledge of technology and how this influences their actions. The sample included data from 15 interviews with preschool teachers in northern Sweden. The first step in identifying participants was to locate teachers working in preschools. Through a directory of the preschools in various districts in the same municipality, 15 teachers were identified. The age of the teachers ranged from 28 years to 62 years with a mean age of 36 years. The range of experience in the field was from 3 years to over 30 years. The teachers worked in eight different preschools in the municipality. Letters were sent to all 15 preschool teachers through their workplaces; in these letters, they were informed about the study and were invited to participate. The preschool teachers contacted the researchers via e-mail or phone to set up a time for the interview. The names presented in the results are pseudonyms.

Data Collection
In-depth interviews were used to capture the preschool teachers' experiences and their view of reality (Silverman, 2013). For the data collection, an interview guide was developed to guide the researchers in capturing the teachers' experiences. The interviews were conducted with the teacher at their preschool in a room in which only the teacher and researchers were present. On average, each interview lasted about 1 hour. The interviews were recorded using a digital recorder and then transcribed. The amount of data recorded increased the potential of identifying fragmented and complex patterns in the preschool teachers' self-experienced narratives of technology in preschool (Mezias & Scarselletta, 1994). The number of interviews was considered sufficient to meet the study's aims. In other words, saturation was reached, and patterns were clear and validated (Yin, 2003).

Data Analysis
The idea behind this analysis was that social groups construct their own reality (Mumby & Clair, 1997), which is expressed through their representations and experiences (Fairclough, 1992). The approach applied presupposed that socially constructed institutions are produced and made real by the preschool teachers' storytelling and are reproduced in narrative form.

The data analysis was performed in a four-step interpretative process (see Figure 1) inspired by a microanalysis approach proposed by Corbin and Strauss (2015). The first step entailed interviewing the preschool teachers and transcribing the interviews. This involved gaining an initial understanding of the content, which facilitated the next step. The second step entailed manually coding the transcribed data. The coding followed an interpretive approach with repeated feedback between the theoretical framework and empirical data. Inspired by Corbin and Strauss (2015), words and phrases expressed in the preschool teachers' narratives were scanned. To help make sense of the data, a search was undertaken for statements and expressions related to technology that were associated with a set of guiding questions: (a) What are the main arguments about preschool teachers' knowledge of technology, (b) what kinds of technology-related activities are described, and (c) what actions toward children are described? The coding was subsequently grouped into patterns. The third step involved defining categories through the repeated analysis of patterns. The researchers met frequently to compare the emerging categories. Categories were identified with repetitive feedback between categories and patterns, thus following the recommendations of Denzin and Lincoln (2000) and Miles and Huberman (1994). In the fourth and final step, the categories were grouped to generate the basis for three different themes: *knowledge*, *planned activities*, and *unplanned activities* (see Figure 1). Consequently, typical aspects of the preschool teachers' statements were highlighted, illustrating the various themes. In this interpretive process, investigative triangulation between patterns, categories, and themes was used. To establish construct validity, narrative stories and quotes were used to present and illustrate these inductively generated results (Gibbert, Ruigrok, & Wicki, 2008; Yin, 2003). In this way, the researchers observed a high degree of consistency, which can underpin the internal validity of the results.

Results

The results describe the preschool teachers' knowledge of technology and how this influenced their actions toward children in planned and unplanned activities.

Limited Knowledge of Technology

Within the theme of *knowledge*, the preschool teachers' statements show their views on technology in relation to themselves and their profession. They faced difficulties in defining technology, with many relating it to computers, television, and other technical equipment. As to defining technology in preschool, they expressed that it is about solving problems of various kinds. Maria expressed the following:

> Technology is solving problems. I see a child in front of me who sits and builds a tower, and so it collapses, and everything is all about building the tower right. They need to know how to build it right. Problem solving.

The preschool teachers expressed that the goal of problem solving is that children should learn various technical skills to solve various problems. In problem solving, the child learns a skill, without the involvement of the teacher, explores, and tries out different procedures to finally reach a solution. The teachers also emphasized that the preschool environment offers, through a variety of materials, many challenges for children to work with different kinds of problem solving, both indoors and outdoors.

Besides problem solving, the preschool teachers defined technology as something that exists in everyday life in a substantial way and permeates the most basic needs. Sarah described the situation as follows:

> Technology in preschool exists everywhere in everyday life. When children wash their hands, I say to them that this is technology, and they learn what technology is. If I open the tap, the water comes out, and when I close the tap, the water stops. It is technology.

Sarah emphasized that technology appears in everyday situations. A common way of working with technology is by paying attention to the technology around the students, such as when they open the tap and water flows or when they close the tap and water stops flowing. Thus, focusing on such phenomena and attaching the word *technology* to them has become a strategy that the preschool teachers use when working with children to give them a basic understanding of technology in preschool.

Even when using such strategies and seeming pleased with them, the teachers also discovered problems with this way of teaching children about what technology is. Several preschool teachers expressed concerns about whether they were challenging the children in their learning process in everyday situations. Helen described the following:

> I cannot explain to the children what happens when we switch the light on and off more than simply to say that it is so. I don't have enough knowledge for that, so I do not know what the children learn from this. I cannot answer

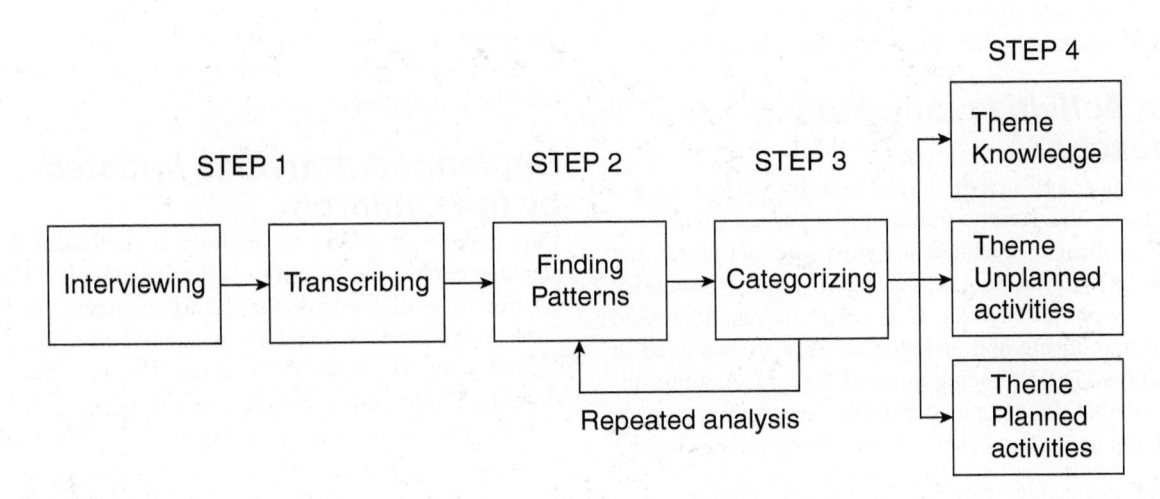

Figure 1 Process of analysis.

their questions about *why*. But I do highlight that it is technology even if I can't explain *why*.

The preschool teachers pinpointed that to create a learning situation, the teacher needs the knowledge and ability to explain and discuss different processes of how everyday technology works. They all experienced a lack of this ability, for instance, when Helen described not being able to explain what happens to make the light turns on and off when one presses a button on the wall or when Sarah described what happens when one opens and closes the tap. The awareness of trouble with handling the *why* question is an issue they considered to be a problem in children's learning of technology. For children to gain an understanding of what technology is and how it can be used to explain how things work, it is important to discuss the *why* issue.

In the preschool curriculum, technology is emphasized as one of the most significant pedagogical areas. All of the preschool teachers were aware of that but expressed frustration over their limited knowledge and the fact that they could not live up to expectations. Anne described this as follows:

> The curriculum states that one should distinguish technology in everyday life and explore how simple technology works. If we don't understand what technology is, how do we get children to understand what it is?

Although the preschool curriculum has been strengthened and the teacher's mission has expanded, the preschool teachers found it difficult, and hence challenging, because they do not have sufficient knowledge of technology. If they cannot explain, or even have knowledge of, how a simple technology works, they cannot challenge children and help them understand how it works. This lack of knowledge in dealing with the *why* issue will impact how they act toward the children in technology-related activities that are either planned by them or unplanned and initiated by the children in their free play.

Planned Activities Initiated by the Teacher

Planned activities are activities planned by the preschool teacher. However, the preschool teachers described such activities as being unusual. Planned activities are activities that include teaching materials that provide step-by-step instructions on how to carry out the activity. Issues that may be addressed with the children during and after the activity are included in these instructions. Despite being unusual, the preschool teachers emphasized that these planned activities are the best way for children to learn about technology. Maria stated the following:

> It is important to have planned activities in technology because we challenge the children's learning process by preparing questions for them based on the teaching materials. It is the best way for the children's learning.

A crucial factor for choosing to work with technology in planned activities is the safeness of relying on teaching materials. As Maria highlighted, it provides opportunities to be involved in the activity, and that it is the best way of challenging the children in their learning. This is because the teaching materials often have detailed instructions and describe what happens in every exercise. This enables the preschool teacher to answer the *why* questions.

The guidelines that these materials provide regarding, for example, prepared questions, enable the preschool teachers to handle the *why* issue. Emmy described the benefit of these materials:

> A good thing is that the teaching materials make us active and have prepared answers that we give the children, so they understand how things work. The materials not only give instructions on what to do but also explain what happens, so we can tell the children how to understand the phenomena. This is the key.

The preschool teachers pinpointed that the teaching materials create good conditions for working with technology in preschool. The key in planned activities is that the teaching materials enable the preschool teachers to take an active approach in working and interacting with the children. The materials provide facts to help the teachers address the *why* issue or, more specifically, to explain what and how different phenomena appear. Thus, it is the teacher who poses questions to the children, not vice versa, and above all, they have the answers to the questions and are able to answer the children's *why* questions. The preschool teachers' experience of the materials is that they enable them to exert control over the situation, especially because they feel prepared and confident to address the children's questions. They highly value this approach to working with technology when they see the learning opportunities that it provides.

Unplanned Activities Initiated by the Children

Unplanned activities in technology are activities that are initiated and carried out by children during free play. Opportunities for free play allow space for children's innate curiosity to discover, solve problems, and create an understanding of the world around them. The preschool teachers pinpointed that preschool should provide children with a safe environment that simultaneously challenges and encourages play and activities related to technology. Furthermore, children should be challenged to explore the world around them, and the activities should provide space for the children to execute their own plans, fantasies, and creativity in play and learning. The preschool teachers also emphasized that children are offered a variety of technical tools in the preschool environment. Elisa described the following:

> Our environments offer building blocks and Lego. We also offer hammers, nails, and pieces of wood collected outdoors that they can build with. But mostly they play with technical material that we have indoors.

Many of the preschool teachers' statements concerned, as Elisa expressed, materials that they connect to construction play and activities that take place indoors. They all expressed that children show curiosity about using technical materials and tools.

Building activities are based on children's natural curiosity and joy of discovery. The children initiate technical activities every day when they, by nature, use play, fantasy, and creativity, especially in construction play. For example, Jennifer described the following:

> It happens every day that children sit and build with blocks and construct houses and towers of various kinds. They are so creative and full of fantasy. Sometimes they have even drawn on paper an outline of what they want their building to look like. They sit and discuss different possibilities and solutions to build, for example, a tower, in the best way so that it will not collapse. I mean, that's very creative.

Jennifer described a common unplanned activity in technology initiated by children with a focus on building things. The children sometimes start the activity by drawing a sketch to clarify their thoughts and ideas and what the goal, or final product, is. Based on the sketch, they start to construct. The preschool teachers described how the children use their creativity and fantasy to develop technical solutions and show a natural interest in creating things. A cornerstone of technical skills is being able to express oneself using speech, models, or drawings. In this process, they develop and make comparisons of their own and other constructions, which increases their understanding of the technological possibilities. In working with their own constructions, they learn to detect similar technological solutions in their environment.

Unfortunately, the preschool teachers' limited knowledge of technology influences their actions toward the children in the activities that the children initiate. Sofia stated the following:

> The children get frustrated when it collapses and do not know how to place blocks to build as planned. They often ask us teachers why it collapses and how to build successfully. It often ends with us saying we don't know and that they should try again, and we walk away. We do not know how to explain to the children why it collapses or how to construct the building for it to stand. We don't have the technical knowledge to answer their question. It might sound silly, but it is like this. It often ends with the children becoming bored and switching activities.

The children show an interest in something and are stimulated and challenged through play, environment, materials, and other children. Unfortunately, the preschool teacher's actions do not encourage the children in their activities. Consequently, they do not stimulate the children's learning about technology. When the children's buildings collapse, they ask for support and help from the preschool teachers to get deeper knowledge to continue with the activity. Instead of giving support and encouragement by engaging in discussions with the children to find solutions, the teachers fail to stimulate the children's interest, curiosity, creativity, and motivation to go further. A possible approach is to encourage children to develop and make comparisons between their own and others' construction to increase their understanding of the technological possibilities. In working with their own constructions, they could also learn to detect similar technological solutions in their environment. The situation that Sofia described could be turned into an excellent learning moment; instead, her experience has been that the children stop and switch activities.

Discussion

The aim of this study was to investigate how preschool teachers' knowledge of, and approaches to, technology influence how they act in different learning activities with children. In line with prior research (e.g., Plowman et al., 2010; Siu & Lam, 2005; Smith, 2001), the results show that preschool teachers' knowledge of technology is limited. Moreover, the excerpts from our interviews with preschool teachers indicate how this limited knowledge influences the teachers' leadership behavior toward the children in technology-related activities. Our results provide insights for both planned activities initiated by teachers and unplanned activities initiated by children during free play. The results also show that the core of how the teachers' knowledge of technology influences their leadership behavior in these two types of activities is their ability to deal with children's *why* questions.

A compensatory approach is evident in the teachers' leadership behavior toward the children. It is visible in planned activities initiated by the teachers in which they rely on prepared teaching materials to compensate for their lack of knowledge of technology. These materials also provide tools for dealing with children's *why* questions, such as step-by-step instructions on how certain activities can be carried out and examples of issues to address with the children. Such compensation causes the teachers to prefer working with technology in planned activities, even if such activities are unusual. In unplanned activities initiated by the children during free play, the compensatory approach is replaced with an avoidance approach, evinced in the teachers' leadership behavior toward the children. It is visible, for example, when the preschool teachers are invited to participate in the activity because a child needs support or wants to discuss solutions to go further in the activity. In such an instance, the teacher cannot rely on any teaching materials and has neither the tools nor the knowledge to deal with the child's *why* questions. Instead of support with problem solving to motivate the children, the teachers walk away and avoid interaction while the children carry out these activities.

According to path–goal theory (House, 1971, 1996), preschool teachers' behavior strongly affects their ability to be supportive, motivating, and challenging. Our results show that the teachers' knowledge of technology is crucial because it influences their leadership behavior toward the children. Consequently, such a direction sets limitations for the children's outcomes, such as learning, and one can question how discovery, creativity, fantasy, and problem solving can be motivated in this case. Aligned with Senesi (1998), this implies that an enhanced understanding of technology affects how learning processes aimed at achieving certain goals can be pursued in activities related to technology. This also affects how children are being helped to develop knowledge of technology and technological skills within the preschool environment.

Despite the preschool teachers' experienced inability to challenge children's learning about technology, they are aware of the importance of the children receiving support from their teachers. Thus, to further children's thinking in finding possible solutions to problems, preschool teachers must understand what is required of leadership behavior and must consciously reflect on what is happening in the process. When children are challenged by the preschool teacher with open questions focused on the *why* issue, they get the opportunity to reflect on what is happening which can be compared with being encouraging and supportive (Stables, 1997). The preschool teachers highlighted that their view and knowledge of technology result in them influencing the children's learning negatively by their actions. This leadership behavior is a consequence of the teachers' self-expressed limited knowledge of technology, which further influences their inability to answer the children's *why* questions. Enabling learning requires that the preschool teacher to be aware of the goal of an activity. Therefore, they provide planned activities, in which they have control, that open up opportunities for learning in a more profound way than what takes place during unplanned activities.

According to previous research (e.g., Siraj-Blatchford, 2001; Siu & Lam, 2005), preschool teachers should offer children a chance to develop an understanding of the world around them at an early stage. Because young children have an innate curiosity to discover and solve problems, activities involving technology could be welcomed in the preschool environment. This would require that the preschool teachers capture such possibilities by gaining knowledge of how a preschool environment can be equipped to encourage and develop children's discovery of technology. We have identified that preschool teachers may be prone to compensatory and avoidance approaches. However, in line with Csikszentmihalyi (1990) and Dörnyei and Ushioda (2011), we argue that a problem-solving approach may be fruitful in preschool teachers' leadership behavior toward children and that such an approach can be valuable both in planned and unplanned activities. Such an approach will allow the teachers to pay attention to the technology, thereby making it visible to the children. In turn, this can create opportunities for the teachers to experience and handle situations that motivate learning.

Conclusion

The results highlight the importance of developing preschool teachers' knowledge and understanding of technology, which will also enable them to develop their ability to explain and clarify concepts and various technical phenomena. Moreover, such development will enable the preschool teachers to create learning environments for children in which technology becomes something natural. It will also help the preschool teachers become proficient, for example, in problem solving and asking reflective questions—thus enabling them to adopt a problem-solving approach. The development of possibilities for children's learning about technology will be affected in both planned activities initiated by teachers and, most importantly, in unplanned activities initiated by the children during free play.

For children's learning, interest, and motivation to be strengthened, it is not sufficient to equip the physical environment of the preschool in such a way that it encourages and develops children's interest in discovering technical phenomena. Preschool teachers need to take advantage of the unplanned experiences and capitalize on teachable moments when any opportunities for instruction present themselves by chance, for example, by reflecting on problem solving with the children. Preschool teachers should exploit children's natural curiosity for learning and their problem-solving approach. In this way, the teachers can support the children in discerning what technology is in everyday situations instead of making technology invisible.

References

Can-Yaşar, M., İnal, G., Uyanık, Ö., & Kandır, A. (2012). Using technology in pre-school education. *US-China Education Review*, *4*, 375–383. Retrieved from http://www.davidpublisher.org/Public/uploads/Contribute/5530c55ecd8d1.pdf

Corbin, J., & Strauss, A. (2015). *Basics of qualitative research: Techniques and procedures for developing grounded theory* (4th ed.). Thousand Oaks, CA: Sage.

Csikszentmihalyi, M. (1990). Literacy and intrinsic motivation. *Daedalus, 119*(2), 115–140.

Denzin, N. K., & Lincoln, Y. S. (Eds.). (2000). *Handbook of qualitative research* (2nd ed.). Thousand Oaks, CA: Sage.

Dörnyei, Z., & Ushioda, E. (2011). *Teaching and researching motivation* (2nd ed.). Harlow, England: Longman.

Eisenhardt, K. M. (1989). Building theories from case study research. *Academy of Management Review, 14*(4), 532–550. doi:10.2307/258557

Fairclough, N. (1992). *Discourse and social change*. Cambridge, England: Polity Press.

Gibbert, M., Ruigrok, W., & Wicki, B. (2008). What passes as a rigorous case study? *Strategic Management Journal, 29*(13), 1465–1474. doi:10.1002/smj.722

House, R. J. (1971). A path goal theory of leader effectiveness. *Administrative Science Quarterly, 16*(3), 321–338. doi:10.2307/2391905

House, R. J. (1996). Path-goal theory of leadership: Lessons, legacy, and reformulated theory. *Leadership Quarterly, 7*(3), 323–352. doi:10.1016/S1048-9843(96)90024-7

Mawson, B. (2010). Children's developing understanding of technology. *International Journal of Technology and Design Education, 20*(1), 1–13. doi:10.1007/s10798-008-9062-8

Mawson, W. B. (2011). Emergent technological literacy: What do children bring to school? *International Journal of Technology and Design Education, 23*(2), 443–453. doi:10.1007/s10798-011-9188-y

Miles, M. B., & Huberman, A. M. (1994). *Qualitative data analysis: An expanded sourcebook* (2nd ed.). Thousand Oaks, CA: Sage.

Mezias, S. J., & Scarselletta, M. (1994). Resolving financial reporting problems: An institutional analysis of the process. *Administrative Science Quarterly, 39*(4), 654–678. doi:10.2307/2393775

Milne, L., & Edwards, R. (2013). Young children's view of the technology process: An exploratory study. *International Journal of Technology and Design Education, 23*(1), 11–21. doi:10.1007/s10798-011-9169-1

Mumby, D. K., & Clair, R. P. (1997). Organizational discourse. In T. A. van Dijk (Ed.), *Discourse as social interaction* (pp. 181–205). Thousand Oaks, CA: Sage.

Öqvist, A., & Malmström, M. (2016). Teachers' leadership: A maker or a breaker of students' educational motivation. *School Leadership & Management, 36*(4), 365–380. doi:10.1080/13632434.2016.1247039

Parker-Rees, R. (1997). Learning from play: Design and technology, imagination and playful thinking. In *IDATER 1997 Conference* (pp. 20–25), Loughborough, England: Loughborough University. Retrieved from https://dspace.lboro.ac.uk/2134/1458

Plowman, L, Stephen, C., & McPake, J. (2010). Supporting young children's learning with technology at home and in preschool. *Research Papers in Education, 25*(1), 93–113. doi:10.1080/02671520802584061

Rohaan, E. J., Taconis, R., & Joechems, W. M. G. (2010). Reviewing the relations between teachers' knowledge and pupils' attitude in the field of primary technology education. *International Journal of Design and Technology Education, 20*(1), 15–26. doi:10.1007/s10798-008-9055-7

Senesi, P.-H. (1998). Technological knowledge, concepts and attitudes in nursery school. In *IDATER 1998 Conference* (pp. 27–31). Loughborough, England: Loughborough University. Retrieved from https://dspace.lboro.ac.uk/2134/1436

Silverman, D. (2013). *Doing qualitative research* (4th ed.). Thousand Oaks, CA: Sage.

Siraj-Blatchford, J. (2001, July–August). *Emergent science and technology in the early years*. Paper presented at the XXIII World Congress of OMEP, Santiago, Chile. Retrieved from http://www.327matters.org/Docs/omepabs.pdf

Siraj-Blatchford, J., & MacLeod-Brudenell, I. (1999). *Supporting science, design and technology in the early years*. Buckingham, England: Open University Press.

Siu, K. W. M., & Lam, M. S. (2005). Early childhood technology education: A sociocultural perspective. *Early Childhood Education Journal, 32*(6), 353–358. doi:10.1007/s10643-005-0003-9

Skolverket [Swedish National Agency for Education]. (2016). *Läroplan för förskolan Lpfö 98:* Reviderad 2010 [Curriculum for the Preschool Lpfö 98: Revised 2016]. Stockholm, Sweden: Author.

Skolinspektionen [Swedish Schools Inspectorate]. (2012). *Förskola, före skola-lärande och bärande: Kvalitetsgranskningsrapport om förskolans arbete med det förstärkta pedagogiska uppdraget* [Preschool, before school-learning and carrying: Quality review report on preschool work with the reinforced pedagogical assignment]. Stockholm, Sweden: Author. Retrieved from https://www.skolinspektionen.se/globalassets/0-si/01-inspektion/kvalitetsgranskning/forskola-2011/kvalgr-forskolan2-samf.pdf

Smith, M. W. (2001). Children's experiences in preschool. In D. K. Dickinson & P. O. Tabors (Eds.), *Beginning literacy with language: Young children learning at home and school* (pp. 149–174). Baltimore, MD: Brookes.

Stables, K. (1997). Critical issues to consider when introducing technology education into the curriculum of young learners. *Journal of Technology Education, 8*(2), 50–66. doi:10.21061/jte.v8i2.a.4

Turja, L., Endepohls-Ulpe, M., & Chatoney, M. (2009). A conceptual framework for developing the curriculum and delivery of technology education in early childhood. *International Journal of Technology and Design Education, 19*(4), 353–365. doi:10.1007/s10798-009-9093-9

Tu, T. (2006). Preschool science environment: What is available in a preschool classroom? *Early Childhood Education Journal, 33*(4), 245–251. doi:10.1007/s10643-005-0049-8

Williams, R. (2002). *Retooling: A historian confronts technological change*. Cambridge, MA: The MIT Press.

Yin, R. K. (2003). *Case study research: Design and methods* (3rd ed.). Thousand Oaks, CA: Sage.

Yukl, G. A. (2013). *Leadership in organizations* (8. ed., Global ed.). Boston: Pearson.

Critical Thinking

1. How can teachers mitigate the causes of their lack of confidence in using technology?
2. How can they be supported in the classroom in their implementation of technology?

Internet References

6 Hands-On Center Ideas for Using Technology in Pre-K and Kindergarten
https://www.weareteachers.com/6-hands-on-center-ideas-for-using-technology-in-pre-k-and-kindergarten/

Preschool STEM Activities
https://thestemlaboratory.com/preschool-stem-activities/

Using Technology Appropriately in the Preschool Classroom
https://www.childcareexchange.com/using-technology-appropriately-in-the-preschool-classroom/using-technology-appropriately-in-the-preschool-classroom-page-2/

ANNA ÖQVIST is an assistant professor in the Department of Arts, Communication and Education at Luleå University of Technology in Sweden.

PER HÖGSTRÖM is an assistant professor in the Department of Arts, Communication and Education at Luleå University of Technology in Sweden.

Öqvist, Anna.Högström, Per. "Don't Ask Me Why: Preschool Teachers' Knowledge in Technology as a Determinant of Leadership Behavior." Journal of Technology Education, v29 n2 p4–19 Spr 2018. Used by permission of Council of Technology Teacher Education and the International Technology and Engineering Educators Association.

Article

Prepared by: Sheron Fraser-Burgess, *Ball State University*

The U.S. Is Falling Way Behind in STEM But Kentucky's Powering the Comeback

GARRIS LANDON STROUD

Learning Outcomes

After reading this article, you will be able to:

- Place United States relative to global standards of science education/STEM education.
- Describe the steps that Kentucky has taken to be competitive in STEM.

Maybe you're already aware, but the United States isn't exactly globally competitive in science education. As of 2015, we ranked 24th out of 71 countries included in a major international study. If you're only concerned with beating out countries like Kazakhstan and Albania, then I've got great news. If you want the U.S. to lead the world in science, a lot needs to change.

Compared to the real heavyweights like Singapore, Finland and Hong Kong, the United States lags far behind in science achievement, and that's bad news for our students. We can do better than that, and we should.

A nation's performance in science, technology, engineering and mathematics (often just called STEM) is an indicator of its potential for innovation, so it's really important that our schools are getting it right when it comes to promoting science literacy and technology competency.

Fortunately, we're making steps to promote higher achievement in STEM, and the leader of the cause is none other than the Bluegrass state.

Making Schools More Accountable for Science

Kentucky is revamping its entire accountability system, but the biggest impact is likely to be felt in science classrooms. This spring marks the first time in several years that science will once again be an assessed subject, which means that students in grades 4, 7 and 11 will take a comprehensive test toward the end of year to measure their proficiency in science.

They Provide Meaningful Feedback to Teachers and Administrators About the Quality of Science Teaching That's Going On

This science test is based on the newest science standards and was developed by Kentucky science teachers themselves but consists of more thorough questions and a deeper exploration of science concepts than past tests. Kentucky is also building in opportunities for science teachers to implement their own means of testing, in the form of things called through-course tasks, which are teacher-selected assessments or projects that complement whatever content was being taught anyway. The difference is that they provide meaningful feedback to teachers and administrators about the quality of science teaching that's going on. Together, all this means that Kentucky will hold students to high expectations of success in scientific literacy—exactly what we want.

Bringing Computer Science to Another Level

Kentucky has also been pushing for more opportunities in computer science and digital literacy. In a recent interview, Education Commissioner Stephen Pruitt spoke openly about the need for these programs.

"The United States currently has more than 494,000 unfilled computing jobs, but only 43,000 computer science graduates to fill those jobs," Pruitt said. "By creating more opportunities for computer science learning, we will reach, keep and engage more students in learning, create a pool of more qualified people to fill existing job openings and stimulate suppressed economic regions of our state by developing a high-tech, skilled workforce."

Kentucky is fulfilling its goals by implementing computer science classes at every level in some districts—elementary, middle and high school. The goal is to add standards for computer science so that students from across the Commonwealth can graduate and feel competent in their computer skills, whether that leads them to further education or a high-paying job.

Working Together

None of these efforts to promote STEM in Kentucky would be successful without meaningful collaboration. Fortunately, the commonwealth is building relationships and putting our money where our mouth is to make STEM better.

We have amazing support from businesses, organizations and statewide initiatives that all share a common goal: giving Kentucky students access to modern, meaningful STEM learning experiences.

For starters, organizations like AdvanceKentucky are teaming up with the Department of Education to train additional computer science teachers, add Advanced Placement (AP) computer science courses for high school students and provide professional development opportunities statewide.

One company, Alltech, sponsors annual science competitions for K-12 school students which it uses to help recruit young talent for potential research jobs later on. AllTech is also known for donating science labs to local Kentucky teachers, but that's not all.

After building the labs, they also donate a cool $35,000 so that the teachers can stock them.

That kind of collaboration happens when there's buy-in from everyone involved, and our students' success in STEM is something we should all rally behind. We've got a long road ahead to get where we want to be, but fortunately we may have found our leader in the Bluegrass State.

Critical Thinking

1. Why have the implemented changes been linked with expediting computer literacy and STEM education?
2. What does it mean to name local corporations in Kentucky as stakeholders in this quest?

Internet References

Current State of STEM Education in the US: What Needs to Be Done
https://mandlabs.com/blog/current-state-of-stem-education-in-us-what-needs-to-be-done/

Science, Technology, Engineering, and Math
https://www.ed.gov/stem

STEM Education Data
https://nsf.gov/nsb/sei/edTool/

GARRIS LANDON STROUD is a teacher in Greenville, KY, and was recently named a 2017–2018 Kentucky State Teacher Fellow. He blogs at KentuckySchoolTalk.org.

Stroud, Garris Landon. "The US Is Falling Way Behind in STEM But Kentucky's Powering the Comeback." https://educationpost.org/the-us-is-falling-way-behind-in-stem-but-kentuckys-powering-the-comeback/. Used by permission of the author.